PSYCHOANALYTIC EXPLORATIONS OF TECHNIQUE

Discourse on the Theory of Therapy

PSYCHOANALYTIC EXPLORATIONS OF TECHNIQUE

Discourse on the Theory of Therapy

EDITED BY

HAROLD P. BLUM, M.D.

INTERNATIONAL UNIVERSITIES PRESS, INC.

New York

Second Printing, 1980

Library of Congress Cataloging in Publication Data

Main entry under title:

Psychoanalytic explorations of technique.
   Includes index.
   1.   Psychoanalysis—Addresses, essays, lectures.
I.   Blum, Harold P.
RC504.P78   616.8'917   79-22349
ISBN 0-8236-5053-7

Manufactured in the United States of America

CONTENTS

INTRODUCTION

This volume, reflecting the most current thinking on psychoanalytic theory and technique, includes a wide variety of viewpoints on an equally wide variety of subjects.

As an applied scientific method, clinical psychoanalysis is not a rigid, invariant, or absolutely precise procedure. It is an applied science—not without its artistic qualities—and a mode of psychological investigation. The psychoanalytic process allows for flexibility and innovation. It is not, however, either eclectic or pragmatic, nor is it a psychotherapy constructed and altered to fit a particular syndrome or treatment situation. Whereas clinical psychoanalysis is a specific, well-defined process, it is continually being refined. As the contents of this book demonstrate, certain ambiguous areas still require further investigation.

Essential for developing and validating our theory and for refining the psychoanalytic process is the correlation of clinical data and theoretical inferences. The psychoanalytic process itself derives from the clinical application of psychoanalytic principles; psychoanalytic technique in turn rests upon and is inseparable from the theory of technique.

Our technique has often lagged behind theory, but it has also responded to and stimulated theoretical discourse. Technical modifications may be adapted to special situations, but when they are used consistently these modifications usually go hand in hand with an altered theoretical position. Such alterations and modifications require periodic exploration and evaluation, both of which they receive in the present volume.

Some of our current controversies echo discussions that have taken place in the past, even if they employ different terminology. Others differ from their antecedents, although

their roots lie in the past. Contemporary concerns are, ex-
pectedly, often a blend of the old and the new, a blend in
which the old, the revised, and the new are not necessarily
distinguished.

　　These concerns involve questions of the analytic attitude,
regressive and progressive forces in the psychoanalytic situation, and noninterpretative therapeutic components of the
psychoanalytic process. They include such questions as the
importance of the analyst, not only as the infantile object of
transference, but as a mature new object and as a real person.
What is the relation of the classical analytic attitude to such
proposals as the need for a diatrophic attitude and the communication of a therapeutic intent? What is the importance
of the empathy of the analyst beyond its significance for
proper understanding and interpretation? Does empathy have
a therapeutic value in its own right and a role in mobilizing
the patient's developmental potential? Is ego development in
the analytic process still viewed primarily and essentially as
the result of the analysis of intrapsychic conflict? Does greater
knowledge of ego development and object relations permit the
analysis of structural problems which may have preceded
intrapsychic conflict and which do not originally involve
intrapsychic conflict even though they may be later inter-
twined with conflict and defense? Can arrests and deviations
of development be overcome? To what degree are ego deficits
analyzable and reversible, and how does the recognition of
ego deficits and deviations influence psychoanalytic technique? In a widened scope of psychoanalysis, do we invoke
different techniques for different conditions, such as in so-
called borderline cases and narcissistic personality disorders?
Do not departures from psychoanalytic technique inevitably
risk distortion of the transference and of the psychoanalytic
process? How does a wider understanding of preoedipal development and disorder lead to refinements in interpretation and
reconstruction?

　　An understanding of development and structure formation is also pertinent to current considerations of the patient's capacity and desire to cooperate and to collaborate in the analytic process. The patient's goals of gratification and rapid relief contrast with long-range analytic goals such as insight and ego growth. How is a therapeutic or working alliance developed, and does the alliance significantly contribute to the attainment of analytic goals? Does not the concept of an analytic alliance or pact enlarge the understanding of the psychoanalytic process beyond the analysis of transference and resistance?

In addition to the regressive trends mobilized by psychoanalysis, there is more emphasis now on progressive forces in the analytic situation, on the mobilization of developmental tendencies toward ego mastery, and on the patient's increasing share of the analytic work. Analytic work is concentrated in the here and now of the transference, but without genetic interpretation and reconstruction the transference, as the repeated past, is not differentiated from the present reality. Is not an understanding of childhood sources of adult neurosis and the infantile determinants of unconscious intrapsychic conflict essential to what is meant by psychoanalytic insight fostering structural change?

No collection of papers could possibly encompass the entire range of technical questions, problems, and discussions; we have tried to make it representative.

Our selection opens with a group of papers devoted to the central psychoanalytic pursuit of insight in child and adult analysis; it continues with considerations of the nature of therapeutic action, transference, interpretation, the analytic alliances, object relations theory and technique, with separation-individuation theory and its clinical application. These original papers conclude with a survey and critical essay surveying recently published books on psychoanalytic technique; they are followed by three classical papers on technique, papers of a prior generation of analytic thought which illuminate contemporary discussions of the psychoanalytic process. The first of these defines parameters in relation to an ideal model of technique. Another deals with problems in management of the transference. The book appropriately closes with a paper on countertransference, a subject of essential importance to any discussion of the theory of therapy.

This book is an expanded version of a supplementary issue of the *Journal of the American Psychoanalytic Association*. The reader will therefore understand that reference listings containing the words *This Journal* refer to articles that originally appeared in the *Journal of the American Psychoanalytic Association*.

In conclusion, I would like to express my thanks to Mrs. Natalie Altman for her devoted assistance in preparing this book for publication.

Harold P. Blum, M.D.

PSYCHOANALYTIC EXPLORATIONS
OF TECHNIQUE

Discourse on the Theory of Therapy

THE ROLE OF INSIGHT IN PSYCHOANALYSIS AND PSYCHOTHERAPY —INTRODUCTION

ANNA FREUD, C.B.E., L.L.D., Sc.D., M.D. (HON.)

I N INTRODUCING THIS DISCUSSION I have a sense of inadequacy, since, during my whole working life as an analyst, I have never made the quality of "insight" my special subject of study. When working with adults, I shared the common opinion that the patient's acknowledgment of his psychic disorder and the desire to cure it are indispensable preconditions for his treatment. I also shared with my colleagues the common experience that, at least so far as the neuroses and the character disturbances are concerned, analysis tends to fail where such insight is missing and where entry into analytic therapy is due not to the patient's attitude in this respect but to familial or to social pressure.

When it came to children, I merely classed their lack of insight with the absence of the numerous other characteristics which, for the analyst, distinguish the immature from the mature patient and make child analysis such a hazardous and difficult undertaking. I refer in this respect to the child's inability or unwillingness to embark on free association; to the difference in his transference reactions; to his unreliable treatment alliance; to his diminished sincerity and frustration tolerance; to the preponderance of motor action over verbal expression; etc.

Introduction to the Anna Freud-Hampstead Center Symposium held by the Michigan Psychoanalytic Society, November 11, 1978.

In fact, it needed a Symposium such as today's to make me isolate the capacity for insight from this larger series and accord it special status for investigation into its role.

I assume Mrs. Kennedy's permission when I extract from her forthcoming paper (1979) the statement that, from the child patient under five and, indeed, through much of the latency period, we have no reason to expect either a rational or an objective appraisal of internal conditions, since the prerequisites for such insight are not yet developed within the structure. Obviously, then, child analysis has to proceed without them, a not unfamiliar situation, since in its technique we deal generally with substitutes for the tools of adult analysis. The questions which arise in this particular instance are merely whether there are any valid substitutes for the missing insight; how the replacements are made; how far an individual not cognizant of his own pathology can be induced to wish for its removal; can be made to join in the effort to correct it; how, in short, the whole difficulty caused by the lack of this particular quality can be circumvented.

Such questions are more easily answered in the physical field. Here, too, the young child who suffers from an illness is quite oblivious of its cause, is incapable of rational understanding for it, and even replaces the absent reality appraisal with the most fantastic misconceptions. Nevertheless, he is amenable to nursing or medical care under the condition that he feels pain. The child cooperates with doctor, nurse, or mother so long as their actions serve the immediate relief of pain. His cooperation ceases abruptly as soon as the therapeutic measure is a long-term one and is experienced by him as more painful in the present than the pathological condition to which it is applied.

Transferred to the mental sphere, this raises some corresponding expectations. Pain caused by the mental disorder may prove the substitute we are looking for as the basis for the child patient's treatment alliance with his analyst. However, we are right to ask to what extent this is the case.

Much of the symptomatology of the very young causes distress and upset to the responsible adults while being taken for granted by the child himself. This is true for the psychologically based early sleep disturbances, the disorders of food intake and elimination, the arrests, delays, inhibitions, and defects of motor, intellectual, emotional, and moral development. Understandably enough, under these conditions, insight into the disturbance, wish for its removal, alliance with the therapist were always demanded from the parents rather than from the child.

However, the nearer to the truly neurotic pattern, as in the anxiety states and the obsessional involvements, the more acute the distress felt by the child himself and, accordingly, the greater the chances of his accepting help. Examples of this are truly numerous. Children may plead to "have the devil taken out who urges them to commit acts" of which they themselves disapprove. They may complain about "the nonsensical actions which something forces them to undertake." They may beg for reassurance that they are "not naughty," "will not die in the night," and so forth. Such pronouncements when made during diagnosis are usually understood as signs of insight and raise hopes for the child's readiness to embark on psychoanalytic treatment. In fact, they are untrustworthy as heralds of therapeutic cooperation. What they reveal is not a realization of internal conflict or of the power of frightening fantasy which blots out reality. The child gives evidence of his panic and upset at finding himself at the mercy of alien powers or of feeling attacked by a nagging, critical authority which he does not recognize as his own emerging superego.

Once the child has entered treatment, it soon becomes obvious how far the analytic method of dealing with psychic pain by following it back to its origins runs counter to the child's own natural inclinations. Quite different from the total helplessness vis-à-vis physical suffering, his whole organism is geared toward dealing with mental pain. The developing defense mechanisms of the ego have as their sole aim the reduction or total abolition of anxiety, unpleasure, and upset. Thus, the child's automatic reaction to danger in the outside world is flight; in the inner world, avoidance, i.e., phobic retreat; or denial with consequent counterphobic attitudes. Anxiety arising from drive activity is countered first by externalization, with increasing structuralization by blotting out the drives' mental representatives, i.e., by repression; the remaining worries to be removed by reaction formations. And so forth.

These mechanisms need to prove ineffective before the child turns to external help at all. Moreover, when he does, he merely clamors for support to strengthen them, certainly not for their abolition. To replace them by uncompromising confrontation with the root of the trouble itself, as analysis does, increases the very distress the child is eager to avoid. So far as his automatic response is concerned, the remedy is indeed no improvement of the trouble.

Different from adult analysands, whose resistances are lodged either in the id or the ego or the transference, with children, the bulk of their resistance, or at worst their total unwillingness to be analyzed thus stems from their ego's age-adequate preference for clinging to its own methods for safeguarding or reinstating well-being and for their inclination to reject all others. Analytic insight belongs to the latter category, and it taxes the therapist's technical skill and ingenuity to lead his patients toward accepting it. Finally, as outlined in Mrs. Kennedy's developmental paper, the child's advancing age and maturity help to unfold a capacity which gradually narrows the gap between the classical psychoanalytic method and the technical modifications forced on the child analyst.

REFERENCES

Kennedy, H. (1979), The role of insight in child analysis: A developmental viewpoint. *This Journal*, 27 (Suppl.):9-28.

20 Maresfield Gardens
London NW3 5SX, England

THE ROLE OF INSIGHT IN CHILD ANALYSIS: A DEVELOPMENTAL VIEWPOINT

HANSI KENNEDY

SOME TIME AGO I CONCLUDED a short paper on "Problems in Reconstruction in Child Analysis" (1971) by suggesting that our interpretive interventions are aimed at enabling the child to resolve conflicts impeding his development, rather than at giving the child insights into what happened to him in the past. My argument emphasized the fact that young children usually forget whatever insights they acquire during their analysis, even though their developmental progress is satisfactory. Since that time it has been increasingly clear to me that I omitted to explore the kind of insights children acquire during analysis and their capacities for doing so during different developmental stages.

This realization provided the motivation for starting, some eighteen months ago, a small study group[1] whose purpose was to closely scrutinize the role of insight in child analysis. Our findings form the basis of this paper, and I gratefully acknowledge my indebtedness to all the participants on whose contributions and clinical material I have freely drawn. Nevertheless, the views expressed are my own and are not necessarily shared by other members of the group.

The initial question presenting itself concerned the

Presented at the Anna Freud-Hampstead Center Symposium held by the Michigan Psychoanalytic Society, November 11, 1978.

[1] The members at various times were: Maurice Apprey, Pauline Cohen, Audrey Gavshon, Ann Hurry, Hansi Kennedy (Chairman), Dr. Ehud Koch, Laurie Levinson, Stephanie Smith, Helge Staby, Robin Turner, Catherine Weinmann, Marie Zaphiriou.

9

meaning of the concept of insight. While some children are described in clinical discussion as having "good insight," it was not at all clear whether this referred to children who were in touch with their own feelings, were especially aware of their problems, or even had insight into their own unconscious motivations. Nor was it clear at what stage in treatment this "good insight" manifested itself. Was it present initially at the time of referral, or did it develop during or at the termination of treatment? Furthermore, did "good insight" correlate with analyzability (as one might expect) and, conversely, did "lack of insight" tend to lead to negative treatment results?

Throughout the development of psychoanalysis, "conscious awareness" and "self-understanding" have, *inter alia*, been considered important as "curative factors."[2] In the extensive literature exploring how, when, and under what conditions therapeutic changes occur, few papers deal specifically with the role of insight in psychoanalytic therapy, though exceptions include articles by Kris (1956), Meyerson (1965), Richfield (1954), and Hatcher (1973). These papers share the following points of view. First, "awareness of one's feelings," "self-knowledge," and "insight" are related phenomena which play an important part in the therapeutic process, but are of course also in evidence in people who are not undergoing analysis. Second, self-observation is a prerequisite for the acquisition of insight, but does not necessarily lead to it. Self-observation can be utilized for gaining gratification; it can be at the service of a critical superego; it can be used defensively; or, for that matter, it can even signify a pathological split in the ego. Hatcher (1973), for example, points out that self-observation is not necessarily connected with *conscious awareness* as it occurs in dreams. Third, insight can be purely "intellectual"—an early recognition by Freud (1913) when he spoke of patients "knowing and not knowing." In later papers, this kind of

---

[2] For an excellent historical review of Freud's views, see Bush (1978).

intellectual insight is often contrasted with emotional insight. Richfield (1954) suggests a connection between these and the two types of knowledge described by Bertrand Russell as knowledge by description and knowledge by acquaintance. The latter involved experiential contact with the subject. The importance of "experiential insight," as contrasted with intellectual understanding, has often been stressed, particularly by those authors who believe that reliving in the transference is the one crucial element leading to psychic change (Strachey, 1934).

Kris (1956) defined insight as *a process* which makes use of the ego function of self-observation in both "experiential" and "reflective" form. The former provides material for understanding, the latter the active effort to understand. Miller et al. (1965) distinguish four forms of self-observation: consciousness of self, as in early infantile self-awareness; cognition of self; critical self-evaluation, and integrative self-observation as an autonomous ego function. This list serves as a useful starting point for a developmental scrutiny of insight. Let us start by examining the concept of "infantile self-awareness."

We must assume that, in the infant, whatever penetrates the stimulus barrier provides "experiential material." But what kind of "experiential awareness" can we assume in someone entirely under the impact of primary-process functioning? Such experiences can only have the most tenuous associations, and, initially, experiential awareness can only amount to transitory feeling-states. Because of the pleasure-seeking quality of the drives, the most primitive differentiation of experiences probably occurs around those associated with pleasure.

Gradually some ego functions will evolve due to the continued *interaction between* drives and the impingement of the external world, and on the basis of the constitutional and maturational aspects of ego development. This will enable the infant to build, little by little, rudimentary representations of his experiences and, on the basis of this further differentiation between them, to begin to establish body boundaries and to distinguish between inside and outside, the "me" and the "not me."

We may now speak of infantile experiential awareness if this means that some integration can occur of experiences that are intrapsychically, though not yet objectively, meaningful. It is important to keep in mind that these first differentiations are probably made on a purely subjective basis; that is, that pleasurable experiences are assigned to the "me" and unpleasurable ones to the "not me" (Freud, 1915; Sandler and Rosenblatt, 1962). But can we see this as a primitive form of self-observation?

The infant will by now have some capacity to differentiate between feelings, but will have minimal ability to contain and control them. Instinctual wishes seek satisfaction, and the infant has little capacity to delay their gratification, whatever the demands of reality. Some scanning of experiential content arising from instinctual wishes, perceptions, and especially the feeling states to which they give rise, will now occur, and this function may well be an antecedent of the "inner" eye that is needed for self-observation. Because of the infant's limited capacity to tolerate painful feeling states, the inner eye will need to become increasingly more selective in its perceptions— painful experiential awareness has to be denied or externalized, that is, intrapsychically shifted from the self- to the object representation, however rudimentary these will be.

In so far as the child has established trust in the object, he will increasingly expect the object to provide satisfaction and to remove painful feelings. The location of "bad feelings" in, and the expectation of good feelings from, the "outside" is quite in keeping with the young child's mode of functioning. Contradictory contents, feelings, and wishes can exist side by side, for there is very little causality, very little notion of time, very little reality appraisal, and very little reality testing.

The development described extends through the preverbal phase. With the gradual acquisition of language, cognitive development is significantly accelerated. Word representations create new possibilities for integration of experiences (Yorke, 1965). Verbalization is also an important tool in learning to contain and control feelings and actions (Katan, 1961).

With this degree of structuralization in the mental apparatus, the child can begin to make some limited sense of his experiences. This is the earliest stage at which we would consider accepting children for analytic treatment. Whatever rudimentary capacity for self-observation the child has now acquired will be in the service of maintaining his current states of well-being rather than subserving an active effort to understand himself. Even when self- and object representations are more consolidated and he has the capacity to sustain a special relationship to his love objects, the full achievement of object constancy—which requires recognition of the object's own needs and feelings—is likely to be beyond his capacities. Until the age of six or seven years the child is cognitively egocentric and his understanding of others is limited to subjective experiences (Rees, 1978).

According to Kris (1956), insight depends on the "integrated, sequential operation of several ego functions." Because control over affective discharge is needed, affects must be accessible, must not be overwhelming, and must not be acted out. Tolerance of painful affects is necessary, as well as the capacity for controlled ego regression. According to Hatcher (1973), detached, objective self-observation must have an "intrapsychic focus" and the ego's integrative function must "bring insight into useful contexts." *Quite obviously the use an adult patient is expected to make of his "experiential insight" is quite beyond the capacities of an under-five or a latency child.*

Let me try to illustrate these points with clinical examples. Young children express their wishes, feelings, and fantasies freely; and while this makes the analyst's task of understanding the material easier, the child's inadequate defenses, his tendency to enact, and his cognitive immaturity make analytic work more difficult. Our youngest patients are constantly threatened and often overwhelmed by their feelings and wishes because they lack adequate controls. Child analysts know only too well that they are liable to be hit and hugged or kicked and kissed, often within a few moments. Contradictory wishes and feelings can still exist side by side. Under the immediate impact of strong feelings the young child will be quite unable to reflect; and he will often need to be controlled. The analyst's constant endeavor to put the child's wishes and feelings into words aims at channeling action into thought and verbal expression.

Carol, only two years, nine months when she began treatment, was referred because of her unremitting jealousy of her eighteen-months-younger sister, whom she openly attacked at every opportunity. In her very first session she crawled and talked baby language. She readily agreed with her therapist's view that she wished to be a baby. She followed this by talking about her sister, who was "a nuisance, always taking away my things and disturbing me." On many subsequent occasions Carol played at being a baby with great enjoyment, commenting gleefully: "Look at me, I am a baby," thereby inviting the therapist to become the admiring and approving mother. This wish continued to be similarly enacted at home, although her mother disapproved of such behavior. Carol was looking for ways of gratifying her wishes and not for understanding. Like most young children, she often protested when her therapist discontinued participation in play to offer explanations. She imperiously demanded that the therapist "stop talking and play" or "stop talking and cry" when the latter tried to step out of the role assigned her in a fantasy enactment and made interpretations. These protests continued throughout her treatment.

Carol's wish to be a baby was not conflictual. To avoid conflict over anger with her mother and to avoid painful feelings of rejection, her ego complied with her regressive wishes. But this readiness for regression also created technical difficulties in the analysis. She often took verbalization of her barely defended regressive wishes as license to regress; and this, too, is typical of young children. For example, Carol messed with pools of water, which she repeatedly and deliberately made on the floor. When the therapist commented that she must be reminded of her former wishes to play with her urine puddles, Carol at once wanted to urinate on the floor. Quite apart from any pleasure gain that might have been achieved in this way, she probably lacked adequate orientation in time to make an appropriate appraisal of what were past and what were current wishes.

The acquisition of insight is further impeded by the child's inability to tolerate painful feelings and the almost universal readiness to "externalize" everything painful and conflictual. At the beginning of treatment, Carol attributed everything that made her feel bad to her baby sister. Later, she came to refer to her so-called symptoms as "hurts." Externalizations such as these continue well into latency and beyond.

Carol's precocious ego development and unusual verbal capacity frequently enabled her to report on events that had occurred at home or nursery school and even to put her fantasies into words. Early in her analysis she confided: "I get cross with the baby and shove her down the hole, and she comes out again, and I get cross." On other occasions she got excited when attacking a doll in the treatment room and suggested the analyst should join her in "flushing the baby down the lavatory." Once, after ten months of treatment, she listed the "hurts" she wanted to get rid of as "monsters, bugs, things that make me sad and naughty." Then she cheerfully suggested, "Let's throw all the hurts out of the window," and proceeded to enact this with much satisfaction.

This acknowledgment of "things" that made her anxious and unhappy demonstrates a capacity for self-observation of

both an "experiential" and a "reflective" kind. Her wish to
get rid of these "things" could even form a basis for
establishing a rudimentary treatment alliance. However, her
understanding of the treatment process was limited by her
"cognitive style," in which early patterns of externalizing
unwanted experiences went hand in hand with the impingement of pleasurable anal-aggressive fantasies. Carol was only
capable of finding *concrete solutions* in keeping with her
conceptual and intellectual functioning.

A similar example is taken from the treatment of a four-
year-old little girl. Rosmarie was very deprived and excessively demanding when she was brought to the Clinic because
of her mother's alarm at the child's request to suck at her
breast. Indeed, there was a good deal of oral fantasy content.
In this connection, it is of interest that she attempted to rid
herself of her fear of monsters by suggesting that they be
locked into a cupboard in the treatment room "so they will
starve and be dead."

The child analysts' interventions repeatedly introduce a
sequence of cause and effect and suggest the need to look for
motivation. To some extent the child will try to identify with
the analyst's reasoning at his higher level. Carol's therapist
had explained that talking might help to get rid of the
"hurts." In a subsequent session Carol remarked impatiently:
"We are talking now—why don't they go away?" Once,
when she had a bad knee during a holiday, she told her
mother that her therapist would make it better.

None of this implies an objective understanding of the
treatment process or of the role of the therapist. It is simply
in keeping with the child's perception of the adult as
possessor of magical powers. This, too, impedes work as a
joint endeavor between patient and analyst in an attempt to
reach insightful understanding. The very young child assumes
that the adult is all-knowing and all-powerful and therefore
sees failure to meet his needs and wishes as deliberate refusal
to help. This will mobilize anger and hostility. With the

gradual internalization of a self-critical attitude (the precursors of superego development) the child will feel increasingly
threatened by the omniscient therapist who may at any
moment retaliate and punish him. Repercussions of this
affect the relationship with the analyst even in children of
latency age. If the child's conceptual ability is still tied to
magical thinking, this will influence his understanding of the
treatment process. For example, Nancy, age six, said of her
therapist; "If he was really clever he would do magic."

Young children see the world in terms of their own
wishes and feelings and are tied to their current experiences.
They understand other people mainly from a subjective point
of view, which also precludes the possibility of gaining
"objective" insight. Even after a great deal of working
through of many aspects of his castration anxiety, a four-
year-old boy could not conceive that his therapist did not
want a penis. He generalized his own intense concerns with
phallic pride and oedipal rivalry. At the end of his analysis he
brought his therapist a present of a box "so that you can
catch a snake to put in it."

Transference interpretations are particularly difficult for
young children to comprehend. The oedipal child usually has
intense transference involvements with the analyst. This is
not only because the one-to-one contact in the analytic
situation lends itself to oedipal fantasy enactments or because
such fantasies are less conflictual in displacement, but also
because there is an affective overspill. The child's ego is
simply not strong enough to sustain itself adequately in the
face of id pressures. The child cannot easily contain the
intensity of his feelings. He finds it hard to distinguish reality
from fantasy and to recognize the "unreality" of transference
feelings. His sense of the continuum of past, present, and
future is still relatively undeveloped and contributes to this
difficulty. Real insight of how the past affects current
experience will be extremely rare in the under-five.

Although psychological development proceeds with

forward and backward moves, entry into latency marks the attainment of significant emotional, social, and cognitive development. How does this affect the latency child's capacity and wish for insight? Self-observation, now strongly under the influence of superego strictures and high self-ideals, exposes the latency child to the experience of further inner conflicts from which he wants to escape. His newly acquired controls over his wishes and feelings strongly resist regression, and he now has a greater and more effective range of defenses available. Still battle-scarred from oedipal disappointments, he tries increasingly to turn away from adults and toward peer relationships, and away from conflictual situations. There is fresh impetus for his interests and curiosity to turn toward the external world. He will endeavor to externalize defensively his internalized conflicts and to look for environmental solutions in preference to internal changes (A. Freud, 1965). All this will strongly work against introspection and sustained and active participation in analytic work, in spite of the new cognitive capacities for insight which should now be available. Secondary-process functioning is much more firmly established. The latency child can use thought and language as efficient tools for dealing with experiential content. His reality testing, time sense, and verbal/conceptual memory organization and reasoning are well established. In other words, the latency child has the capacity for insight, but will fight strongly against it.

Latency children who readily acknowledge and verbalize their problems and wish for help at the beginning of treatment are often referred to as "insightful," but this can be misleading. In talking openly about their symptoms and reasons for referral, they may simply reiterate what they have learned from others or manifest their overcompliance by saying what they feel is expected of them. Other children, who may possibly have a greater awareness of difficulties and a more pressing wish for help, may be unable to verbalize because they feel too anxious, too ashamed, or too guilty.

This can lead to the conscious withholding of material or even the deliberate distortion of the truth for a considerable time. Rachel, for example, was seven when she was referred for treatment after she had developed a "touching" symptom which strongly suggested links with masturbation conflicts. At the beginning of treatment she completely denied awareness of the symptom or any worries about masturbation; and, indeed, the symptom completely disappeared for several months. When her masturbation conflicts eventually emerged in analysis, she seemed relieved and spontaneously admitted that she had not told the truth in the initial interviews. She confessed that she had deliberately stopped herself from touching the knuckle of her left hand whenever she felt the temptation to do so because she had felt too ashamed.

Children's responses to interpretations may be misleading as indicators of insightful understanding. Interpretations may be rejected or ignored, yet lead to changes in the analytic material without any indication of whether such changes occurred in response to fresh understanding or to a defensive strategy. An overready acceptance of interpretations may show the child's need for compliance rather than indicate real understanding. Pseudo-insights are used defensively to gain approval and are frequently also utilized to gain gratification; for example: "I know I want things because I am jealous of the baby, but let me have a new toy just today and then we can talk." The search for gratification and intolerance of pain remains operative, too, in latency children, and with some analytic patients it reaches such a pitch that they cannot bear to hear the therapist speak. They run out of the treatment room, cover their ears, or make silence a condition of attendance. To her therapist's suggestion that a current separation might be especially painful because it reminded her of past losses, Nancy, age six, responded with a worried, "Don't talk about it—I might remember." Her remark indicated that considerable analytic progress had been made in Nancy's treatment, inasmuch as, for many weeks, she had insisted that the therapist only read stories to her and had literally tried to shout him down whenever he tried to speak to her directly. This may be an extreme example of "counterinsight," but we found only one latency child among the cases we examined who could be said to have actively and consistently participated in the analytic work throughout his treatment. At first, this child, David, explained that he wanted "to help the analyst to understand his feelings better," but later he evidently wanted to gain better understanding of his difficulties, which he recognized as inner problems.

David was eight years, nine months at referral. He already showed at the Diagnostic Interview that he had an awareness of his difficulties, a capacity for self-observation, an ability to reflect, and unusual verbal facility. His ability to use metaphors poignantly was evident when he described himself in the first treatment session as "feeling shipwrecked and in need of help." Much later in treatment he described the analytic process as "taking the fizz out of the bottle," which he explained by observing that one had to let feelings out slowly so that they didn't explode when "bottled up." More indicative of his wish for insight was his continued attempt to work out the reasons for his actions, feelings, and thoughts. Early in the treatment David spontaneously reported a dream—many children do—but when his therapist remarked that dreams sometimes helped in understanding hidden reasons, he made efforts to remember his dreams and to bring associations. He often reported on changes he perceived in the relative pressures from conflictual forces and showed how he was integrating insights gained from interpretations by bringing them back in different contexts. Of course, even in this analysis there were long periods of resistance. When he was overwhelmed by intense transference feelings, he could not use any of these capacities.

It is not uncommon for latency children to identify with

the therapist's analyzing function, but then to apply it only in relation to others. Michael, age nine, told his mother to stop shouting because she frightened him and because it would make her feel bad afterward. This was his way of searching for external solutions; if his mother could change, he would not have to. Child patients also often start to interpret their own behavior or conflicts by attributing the understanding to the analyst. A child may say: "You will say I am doing this to punish myself." This is also a way of "disowning" insight or, at best, an indication of lack of conviction—knowing without believing. Although these examples suggest some degree of budding insights, they show even more clearly how the inner eye is attempting to look in a different direction.

In contrast, adolescents become very introspective and spend much time thinking about themselves. In the effort to establish their identity, they repeatedly compare themselves with others, wish to be different from their parents, and need to prove their independence. They feel confused and overwhelmed by the intensity of their wishes, feelings, and conflicts, and desperately attempt to use their intellect to find solutions. Michael, for example, age fourteen, said: "Germs and genes are really similar. Genes decide what character you have and germs decide what illnesses you have. Like my father, I am passive until someone pushes me all the way. I am very observant, but I can be very ignorant like my mother when I do not want to understand something. I must have got my nervousness from my mother. It is my nervousness that I want to change." Adolescents with obsessional defenses are especially prone to ruminate and intellectualize about themselves, while those with inhibitions and low self-esteem often have difficulties in communicating their self-reflections. Lisa, fifteen, showed awareness of feelings and ability to reflect, but at the beginning of treatment she communicated in a "telegraphic" style which pointed to conflicts over talking about herself. Later she only reverted to this after frequent and long silences, which were very painful for her. At such times she also stared at a rug in the treatment room as though to avoid looking at her therapist. The suggestion was eventually made that the use of the couch might facilitate talking. Lisa rejected this outright and said that she needed to watch the analyst's facial expressions for clues. As she gradually became more actively involved in the analytic work, she tried to explain the continuing periods of prolonged silence as "feeling empty" or "blanking out." Eventually, in the 34th week of treatment, she said: "I know I am silent, but before I will be able to use the couch—I feel there is an in-between step. I must be able to ask myself, when I am silent, what am I feeling? Not just I feel empty, but why am I empty, and that will take a long time yet."

The adolescent, certainly the younger adolescent, has a capacity to comprehend what is involved in the analytic work, is introspective, and seeks better self-knowledge, but he cannot permit himself to relinquish ego control, even temporarily, and to lose himself in his transferences and associations. This fear of passive surrender will clearly have different genetic roots in different individuals, but at this developmental level generally relates to the adolescent's terror of the intensity of id pressures and the emotional turmoil of his inner world.

Adolescents can establish a good treatment alliance, but their conflicts over dependency often interfere. Malcolm, seventeen, read Freud so that he could be self-sufficient and analyze himself. Defensive reasons were not far to seek. Transference revival of oedipal longings were ushered in with an attack on Freud's paper on Little Hans and followed by a weekend when he experienced "a flash of insight." He reported that he had suddenly become aware that his transference longings, intensely experienced in the present during the weekend break, were revivals of childhood feelings and that his response to reading Freud's paper was a defensive intellectualization.

Quite a number of our older adolescents use the couch and are prepared to try to free associate. Richard, age sixteen, referred himself in fear that he might mess up his school-leaving exams. He also felt depressed and extremely isolated. From the beginning of analysis he showed a good propensity for forming a treatment alliance. He reacted to initial clarifications by expansion of relevant material, he continued working between sessions, and he frequently made links with material that had previously emerged. He came to his sessions when he did not want to, recognizing that to stay away would be his loss. The analytic material centered primarily on the urgent problem of suicidal wishes, defenses against aggression, and the wish for and fear of closeness. But he remained cut off from his past and very much involved with current difficulties. When work on oedipal problems began, it was initially guilt-provoking rather than guilt-relieving, and, for the first time, genuine resistance set in. After much working through of oedipal material, he began to allow himself much more "freely floating thought" both within the session and by himself. He also began to remember dreams and to bring memories of his childhood. His main interest and concern, however, remained with his current difficulties and with the future, rather than with the reconstruction of the past.

Let me sum up briefly what has emerged from this attempt to construct a developmental line for the capacity for insight: from the infant's transitory awareness of pleasurable and painful feeling states to the adult's detached and objective self-observation with an intrapsychic focus which, together with the ego's integrative functions, bring insight into useful psychic contexts. And let me, then, try to answer some of the questions posed at the beginning.

Under-fives have a limited capacity for the kind of self-observation that leads to awareness of wishes, feelings, and, quite often, to some awareness of their difficulties. It is not easy to mobilize this into a treatment alliance because of the divergent aims of the child and the analyst; the former seeks gratification, the latter understanding. Although the child's capacity to reflect will be accelerated and his self-knowledge widened as a result of the analytic work, the young child lacks the necessary cognitive skills to gain "objective" insight.

The impetus of *latency development* turns curiosity and interest toward the external world. Although the cognitive capacities for insight are more readily available, the latency child's participation in the analytic work will fluctuate. He will resist introspection and insight into inner conflicts and will look for environmental solutions and external changes.

Adolescents are introspective, think about themselves, and use their intellectual capacities to gain fuller understanding; and they have the potential for gaining objective insight into unconscious motivation and conflict solutions. But they are less interested than adults in piecing together their past because their current difficulties and apprehensions about the future absorb them so completely.

We can see that the thrust of developmental and maturational forces, which promote progressive development will, all along, determine and influence the child's greater involvement with his *present and immediate* concerns than with *his past*. This must be an important reason why, generally, we do not aim, in child analysis, to reconstruct for the child a true and "objective" picture of his past, but focus on dissecting his adaptations to the pressures he feels operate on him now. This focus, of course, includes tracing past experiences which determined particular modes of his present functioning, but this will serve mainly to provide a conceptual framework whereby he can understand his present difficulties better. We have to keep in mind that, for the *under-fives*, past and present are often merged, not just because of the restricted time span between past and present, but, more important, because of the forward and backward movement of development, the relative ease of regression, the lack of adequate orientation in time—which alone can place experiences in sequence—and the lack of a reality-orientated conceptual memory organization. In fact, the young child lacks an adequate concept of the past. The *latency child* has acquired a concept of *the* past but emotionally turns away from *his* past. He is involved with his current life and looks for here-and-now solutions to his problems. Even transference feelings, as I mentioned before, are difficult for him to recognize as stemming from the past. In the *preadolescent*, the past is often so vividly revived in the present that the distinction becomes blurred once more; whereas the *adolescent* is so concerned and overwhelmed by the intensity of current feelings and conflictual wishes that there is no real chance of cathecting the past.

We see the child's difficulties and symptoms as current maladaptations which prevent his taking the next step in development, and our precise treatment aim is to enable him to take this step. What level of insightful understanding is needed for this to occur?

The analytic situation provides opportunities for the child to relive current as well as regressively reactivated past experiences in a new way. On the most primitive level the interaction between child and analyst represents the situation of the infant whose mother can contain, meet, and anticipate her child's needs. When the child analyst understands the child's symbolic play but responds to it in an indirect way (either through play or verbalization), the child will feel understood, although he will not gain conscious awareness of what he is expressing. His feeling understood may represent his past infantile experience of his mother's responding appropriately, with her more sophisticated understanding, to his needs. Much of this "understanding" the child has to take on trust—mother understood what he needed before he could.

Kris (1956) speaks of id aspects of insight or "infantile prototypes," which, he suggests, are more often an oral interchange than an anal one. I want to suggest that the infantile prototype of experiencing the analyst as an expressor of insights relates to the kind of interchange where mother's responses to the child's needs were adequate and led to his feeling safe and understood. I would call this, not an "*oral interchange,*" but an "*oral-phase*"*experience.* The revival of such experiences in the analytic situation, albeit on a higher level of organization, may make it possible for the child to feel supported and safe enough to become increasingly able to tolerate his painful feelings, a prerequisite of analytic work.

Our work with children is aimed at fostering self-awareness and self-knowledge. With under-fives this usually goes hand in hand with the developmental process itself. The analytic work fosters the child's ability to contain and verbalize wishes and feelings, and to reflect. Indeed, the way in which parents have helped the child deal with his feelings during his early development may have influenced his capacity for self-awareness and insight. "I know you are angry, but hitting the baby hurts him" may enhance his self-knowledge more than a command "not to be naughty." It also introduces a sequence of cause and effect and the notion of looking for motivation. It is certainly a technique we use widely in our therapeutic work with under-fives.

The analyst's interventions organize and articulate what the child is experiencing. Whenever the analyst interprets and expresses "his insights" in terms that the child is capable of understanding, some new integration will take place. However, as I have tried to show, children are not actively motivated to seek insight, and very often even defend against its acquisition. The need to be compliant, the wish to please the therapist and to get approval, will help reinforce a wish for understanding, and this wish will ultimately contribute to the treatment outcome.

However successful the outcome of treatment may be in terms of making new adaptations and progressive moves, children do not usually fully internalize the analyzing function, nor do they acquire a full dynamic and genetic understanding of their unconscious conflicts. The insights gained usually permit a better grasp of current conflict situations and lead to new ways of meeting them; but such insights will not necessarily help the child deal with conflicts at later developmental stages. As part of the infantile amnesia, the prelatency child will usually repress much of the "analytic insights" gained during treatment, and older children often cannot recall much of what transpired in their analysis. We must assume that their "analytic understanding" becomes absorbed into the general experiential matrix. This, perhaps, is what happened to Little Hans who, when interviewed years later, had no apparent recollection of his famous and apparently successful childhood therapeutic experience.

Summary

I have traced a developmental line for the capacity for insight. The conclusions reached are based on psychoanalytic material gathered from treatment cases at the Hampstead Clinic over the past 25 years. I have elaborated on the relevance these conclusions have to techniques employed in the analysis of children.

REFERENCES

Bush, M. (1978), Preliminary consideration for a psychoanalytic theory of insight: Historical perspective. *Internat. Rev. Psycho-Anal.*, 5:1-13.

Freud, A. (1965), *Normality and Pathology in Childhood. Writings*, 6. New York: International Universities Press.

Freud, S. (1913), On beginning the treatment (Further recommendations on the technique of psycho-analysis, 1). *Standard Edition*, 12:147-158.

―――― (1915), Instincts and their vicissitudes. *Standard Edition*, 14:134-136.

Hatcher, R. (1973), Insight and self-observation. *This Journal*, 21:377-398.

Katan, A. (1961), Some thoughts about the role of verbalization in early childhood. *The Psychoanalytic Study of the Child*, 16:184-188. New York: International Universities Press.

Kennedy, H. (1971), Problems in reconstruction in child analysis. *The Psychoanalytic Study of the Child*, 26:386-402. New York: Quadrangle.

Kris, E. (1956), On some vicissitudes of insight in psychoanalysis. In: *Selected Papers*. New Haven: Yale University Press, 1975, pp. 252-271.

Meyerson, P. (1965), Modes of insight. *This Journal*, 13:771-792.

Miller, A., Isaacs, K., & Haggard, E. (1965), On the nature of the observing function of the ego. *Brit. J. Med. Psychol.*, 38:161-169.

Rees, K. (1978), The child's understanding of his past. *The Psychoanalytic Study of the Child*, 33:237-259. New Haven: Yale University Press.

Richfield, J. (1954), An analysis of the concept of insight. *Psychoanal. Quart.* 23:390-408.

Sandler, J. & Rosenblatt, B. (1962), The concept of the representational world. *The Psychoanalytic Study of the Child*, 17:128-145. New York: International Universities Press.

Strachey, J. (1934), The nature of the therapeutic action of psychoanalysis. Reprinted in: *Internat. J. Psycho-Anal.* (1969), 15:127-159.

Yorke, C. (1965), Some metapsychological aspects of interpretation. *Brit. J. Med. Psychol.*, 38:27-42.

21 Maresfield Gardens
London NW3 5SX, England

THE ROLE OF INSIGHT
IN PSYCHOANALYSIS

Peter B. Neubauer, M.D.

ALTHOUGH IT IS GENERALLY AGREED that the development of insight is fundamental to the therapeutic effect of psychoanalysis, it has not been determined exactly how insight is effective. Nunberg's (1937, p. 161) statement still holds: ". . . any attempt at forming a theory of therapy is bound to prove incomplete and may even involve a number of contradictions." I hope to raise questions here that may help toward eventually establishing an integrated theory of insight.

No fully satisfactory analytic definition of insight exists. Webster (1965) defines it psychiatrically as "recognition of one's own illness." Concepts of analytic insight have changed as psychoanalytic theory has changed. In terms of topographical theory, during insight, unconscious thoughts and feelings become conscious or preconscious as repression is lifted. With the development of the structural approach, insight was seen to involve the integration into the ego of aspects of the id. Freud's "Where id was, there ego shall be" (1933, p.80) defined the task of analysis. Essentially, insight during psychoanalysis comprises the expansion of the ego by self-observation, memory recovery, cognitive participation, and reconstruction in the context of affective reliving.

It is not certain whether and under what circumstances insight produces a therapeutic effect. Some think it an instrument by which an analytic result is achieved, while others maintain that insight is the result of—a by-product of—an analytic process that is therapeutic in itself. Actually, the attainment of insight does not guarantee therapeutic

Presented at the Anna Freud-Hampstead Center Symposium held by the Michigan Psychoanalytic Society, November 11, 1978.

improvement. There are many patients whose knowledge of themselves has markedly increased without consequent conflict resolution. Indeed, at times we observe therapeutic results without a significant increase in self-understanding. We must define those characteristics of self-knowledge which indeed constitute insight and further the therapeutic process. The relative paucity of papers on the subject of insight indicates that we take its role for granted and have not bothered to explore fully the relation of insight and clinical improvement.

It is generally understood that analytic insight contains both cognitive and affective components which are intimately interwoven. Valenstein (1962) asserts that "[I]n psycho-analysis, the element of emotion, as it bears upon a proportionate and properly tuned integrated degree of emotional reliving, would seem to be of fundamental significance to the final development of insight" (p. 322). He assumes that affective knowledge merges into conation. Thus he reiterates that "[e]xtended self-knowledge combining both affective, conative, and intellectual components, amounts to the mutative or dynamic insight" (p. 323). He expects that the therapeutic task integrates affects and thoughts and that this will lead to a new *Erlebnis* as a result of a balance between the two. Valenstein agrees with Richfield (1954) who proposed the existence of two forms of cognition, the "ostensive" and the "descriptive." Ostensive insights incorporate "the actual conscious experience of their referents. They are obtained through the direct cognitive relations involved in the acquisition of knowledge by acquaintance-ship" (p. 405). Descriptive insights "provide the patient with truths about himself by making use of his capacity to comprehend the words employed in any interpretation" (pp. 404-405). These two forms may refer to insight as an experience and insight as a therapeutic function.

Cognitive insight is only effective when coordinated with affective experiences. Affectless intellectual insight is not therapeutic. And emotional reliving by itself does not necessarily lead to insights into affective experiences, wishes, feelings, and anxieties. The defensive use of isolation may separate aspects of insight and prevent full and integrated insight. Hartmann (1939) wrote: "Defenses (typically) not only keep thoughts, images, and instinctual drives out of consciousness, but also prevent their assimilation by means of thinking. . . . Interpretations not only help to regain the buried material, but must also establish correct causal relations, that is, the causes, range of influence, and effectiveness of these experiences in relation to other elements" (p. 63). Insight depends upon the assimilation of unconscious tendencies under the aegis of the synthetic function of the ego. In addition, as Noy (1978) stresses, the reality principle asserts its influence on the ego's organization.

Freud believed that interpretation of defense and of content and construction of the past in relation to the present are central therapeutic measures. Through them the analyst facilitates insight. While implementation of free association tends to suspend ego controls, reality testing, and defensive maneuvers, interpretation and construction strengthen ego mastery and foster tolerance of the irrational, painful affects and thoughts that the neurosis and the transference contain.

In the "Outline," Freud (1940) pointed out that the analyst serves the patient as an authority, as a substitute for his parents, as a teacher, and as an educator. He stressed the functions of analysts bringing the mental processes of the patient's ego to a normal level, transforming what was unconscious and repressed into preconscious material and thus returning it once more to the possession of the ego. Nevertheless, despite such transformations, psychoanalysis may have a limited therapeutic effect. Freud suggested that excessive quantities of libidinal and aggressive energies may interfere with appropriate ego functioning in such cases. Furthermore, he recognized that reconstruction does not always lead to a substantial flood of new memories and recognition; nor is it always necessary to propose the correct reconstruction to instigate progress in the analytic work.

So far, we have discussed the topographic and structural considerations and the link between thoughts and affects. We have seen that the synthetic function of the ego is essential to the development of insight, a fact that has influenced a number of authors who have furthered our understanding of insight. Nunberg (1937) asserted that ". . . the term unconscious is not limited to meaning that ideas or emotions have vanished from consciousness; it may merely mean that the connections between elements which previously belonged together have been severed and that the elements remain isolated in the mind. Not only may the affects be separated from the ideas, but also the ideas themselves may be divided into their component parts . . ." (p. 161). These assumptions led Nunberg to a new proposition. The return of the repressed with its shift of the defenses and the economic transformation in the course of an analysis will not be sufficient to give to the ego the possession over id contents; the ego must exercise its tendency toward connecting, uniting, and blending—namely, its synthetic function. It is clear from Nunberg's description of the synthetic function (1931) that a libidinal aim has been transformed into an ego activity.

As the individual develops, we can observe two interrelated components: an ever increasing differentiation and specification of functions, and the continuing process in which new organizations form. Emerging functions bring about coordinations which lead to intra- and interstructural alliances. Insight depends upon those synthetic activities of the ego which bind together various isolated parts into a new ego organization.

It is here that Kris (1956) made an important contribution. Viewing Nunberg's (1931) synthetic function as closely tied to libidinal influences, he examined the economic components of insight. He distinguished between various forms of insight in terms of the amount of neutralized energy invested, i.e., the degree of freedom from drive influence.

The synthetic function of the ego binds and connects and permits assimilation into the ego. However, it remains under the influence of libidinal strivings and, hence, may lead to resistances and new symptom formation. The synthetic function must be differentiated from what Hartmann (1939) calls the *organizing function* of the ego, which uses neutralized energy. Kris (1956) employs the term *integrating function* of the ego, a term which connotes a more autonomous range of ego functions than the concept of synthesis. The organizing function assists in the establishment of ego autonomy.

Insight, then, may be close to drive expression or free from it. During analysis one may be able to follow the various forms of insight, determine when it is close to or free from drive expression and the economic factors that determine the degree of drive dependence. These factors may have particular relevance for the understanding of insight in child and adolescent analysis and the fate of insight after analysis.

Kris (1956) continually refers to the "function of insight" and not to insight as an experience or as an end product. He thus avoids considering whether insight is the result of the synthetic or integrative function or a necessary step toward it. This approach allows us to follow insight during the process of analysis. Any interpretation or any reconstruction offered to the patient is only a step which leads to a new interpretation and refinements in reconstruction. With each formulation, the analyst attempts to make connections—to "link" present and past wishes, defenses, and fears—and to offer, so to speak, the ego examples of integrative thinking. At the same time, Kris is careful to warn that it is not possible to guide patients in their synthesis, it is only possible, by analytic work, to prepare them for it.

In other words, insight is continuously changing during analysis. It may be close to drive expression or part of autonomous functions; it will link some components at one time and others at other times until integration occurs. It can be the product of interpretation that alters the defensive structure, or it can be the means by which the ego asserts its control. During an analysis, insight fluctuates topographically and structurally. But at the end of treatment we expect a new structural stability.

It is striking that after analysis insight may not be maintained, particularly if we mean by it the memories of conscious retention of events, ideas, and affects which entered awareness during the course of the analysis. It is not what has been recovered that is retained, but rather new structure and function. A new *Gestalt* is established, a reorganized ego structure. Normal repression may occur concomitant with processes of integration and lead to forgetting of the conscious insights even though there is a new personality organization.

Today, when object relations theory and technique are given special consideration, the interaction of therapist and patient can be studied in reference to insight. There are those who stress the role of the analyst as a primary object, i.e., pretransference features, rather than insight. They usually emphasize the role of the analyst in assisting the patient to differentiate self from object, and the shift from primary narcissism to object cathexis. Some are more cautious and suggest that the unconscious communications between the patient and the analyst on these relatively primitive levels of experience "co-exist with the more advanced levels of mental functions and organization of mental content, and continue to exert their influence throughout life" (Loewald, 1979).

Those who emphasize the re-experiencing of early needs and wishes in the analytic relationship often assign a secondary role to interpretation, reconstruction, and insight. They rely upon object relations and identification with the therapist rather than transference interpretation. Sometimes the analyst will keep noninterpretive interventions within the bounds of psychoanalytic technique, but at other times these types of interventions appear to be beyond psychoanalysis proper and may interfere with the development of an analytic process. One has to differentiate technique that aims at the development of insight from technique that has other aims. In the latter, insight may appear as a by-product. The psychoanalytic process seems to best allow us to follow the intricacies of the patient's experiences, feelings, and ideational contents.

Years ago Augusta Alpert (1959) employed a "corrective object relation" treatment for prelatency children. A special teacher-therapist was assigned to the child to establish a close relationship or, better, to permit the child to form a close contact with her. This treatment's aim was to correct deficient development. The children would soon regress to earliest point of fixation and then use the therapist as a good primary object. The interaction was one of appropriate stimulation and of affective empathic participation. There was no transference in the usual sense, for transference depends upon the capacity to differentiate the primary from the new object. Nor did the teacher-therapist offer the child interpretation. It was through the corrective relationship that the child was able to achieve a developmental progression previously lacking. These children progressed enough to have internalized conflicts, which were taken up later on when they were assigned for psychoanalytic treatment. "Corrective object relations" did not aim at insight, but corrective experiences, not at reliving, but at living, not at reconstruction but at regression followed by progression.

The reader will recognize in this type of child therapy features that have been suggested by some as new methods of adult analytic treatment.

Some of these corrective features may occur in any analysis, but the therapist's attitude and approach to these aspects makes the difference between psychotherapy and analysis. If the therapist intentionally offers himself as a model and teaches the patient how to control his drives or modulate his affects, he will preclude analysis and insight. Insight is a special feature of the psychoanalytic process.

Many of the same formulations regarding the patient's achieving insight apply to the analyst as he helps his patient. For instance, the analyst must connect affect and thought, as Valenstein (1962) shows the patient does. The analyst must utilize his own integrative-ego capacity to determine the pattern of the patient's associations, to formulate his dynamics. The analyst must, to paraphrase Kris's formulation, be able to regress under the auspices of the therapeutic work to his earliest psychic experiences and at the same time maintain a neutralized or even autonomous ego function. Through such transitory regression, the analyst is able to empathize with his patient. Indeed, the empathic interactions between analyst and analysand are necessary for the analyst's formulating and timing his verbal interventions properly, thus facilitating the patient's insight in the "good" analytic hour.

A few remarks about insight in child analysis are in order. If we define insight as the capacity to maintain cognitive awareness of formulations based upon new ideas about himself and his surroundings, then the child will not give much evidence of such a process. As Anna Freud (1965) states, the child lacks introspection and consequently has less insight into the nature of his neurotic difficulties than does an adult.

The relative lack of introspection involves a general ego attitude characteristic of childhood and adhered to by the child as an effective deterrent against mental pain. We can assume that, due to the closeness to drive influences, insight in children may occur but not attain the degree of autonomy or integrative power we observe in adult analysis.

Nevertheless, a child often is capable of an uncanny awareness and "knowing" even when he is not able to express it verbally in an articulate form. The child's closeness to drive influences does not exclude the ability to carry out synthesizing functions in various stages of his development. We can see the child's search for insight when we study the "theories" he forms in response to his experience. His own explanatory ideas at times are maintained over many years. His curiosity and need to arrive at causative connections allow us to study those mental processes, which seem to be forerunners of true autonomous insight. These capacities are used in child analysis. The child's interest in observing himself and others, his primitive theory-building, and his willingness to explore wrong assumptions and evaluate reality are mobilized during analytic treatment.

Piaget's (1973) work will help to clarify the child's methods of achieving insight. When the latency-age child is asked to reproduce a design he had previously been shown, he will do so by his recall of the operation involved and not by a clear memory of the image of that design. The memory of *how* it was done leads to the achievement. Similarly, insight may at a certain stage relate more to the recovery of memories of actions than a clear reproduction of the visual memory of the event. It reminds us of the child's tendency to act rather than to remember.

It is interesting to compare psychological findings derived from tests and those of child analysis. Piaget's controlled studies of mental functions clarify cognitive aspects of memory, while clinical observations allow us to perceive the affective component and resistances that codetermine memory and forgetting. In screen memories, for instance, affects and defenses determine which elements are recalled.

Because children possess a lower level of cognition than adults, their reactions to interpretations and reconstructions differ. Piaget's finding that increased cognitive development enhances the capacity to reconstruct earlier experiences more realistically confirms our analytic findings. If we offer a child a reconstruction and he confirms it, we must nevertheless ascertain his cognitive level and evaluate his response. He may not have experienced the reconstruction as an inner truth or with a feeling that he has been understood. The fact that an adult, by contrast, is more likely to develop a feeling of conviction about the reconstruction constitutes a marked difference between child and adult analysis.

Cognitive studies also reveal limitations in the child's sense of time, which may hamper the analytic process. During analysis the patient ordinarily regresses so that he confuses past and present, while, as a result of an adaptive splitting of the ego, he differentiates the two. The child may be unable to maintain the differentiation sufficiently to appreciate a reconstruction or understand the transference. Transference interpretations and reconstructions depend upon our ability to differentiate and then compare past and present without confusing them. The child, however, seems to measure time according to events.

Nunberg referred to the sense of time in the treatment of adults. As the past becomes reactivated in the transference situation, as the blending of the past with the present occurs in the object relationship, the ego is unable to maintain time differentiation; the sense of time is interrupted. Testing of reality also becomes disturbed. As the analysis proceeds, however, the adult's cognitive capacity allows him to recognize the temporal confusions. We have to study each stage of development and observe those conditions within each organizational level which permit synthesis and integration correlated to cognitive development.

I have followed in a sketchy way the history of insight in psychoanalytic therapy. A number of questions remain unanswered. Is the insight gained during analysis by reconstruction, by re-experiencing in the transference, and by interpretation, by the slow building of connections between psychic elements, the past and the present, different from the intuitive insight of artists and poets or the insight of the normal man in everyday life? Is the difference related to the degree of neutralization or the degree of autonomy which analysis strives for? Do the synthetic and integrative functions occur silently, even unconsciously? Can such functions be an expression of insight or lead to insight even when they are unconscious? Can insight be unconscious? Is insight necessary to secure therapeutic success? Is it the highest form of mastery which will secure permanency or at least stability of new structures and function?

Does our clinical experience teach us that those patients who have achieved a stable and organized insight are those who have been cured? Or do we observe that insight may shift from one area to another, may surface and then disappear again? Do we observe that at the end of the analysis changes have occurred without being reflected by a stable "knowledge" of the sum of the experiences? The issue here is cognition and its relationship to awareness or consciousness.

Inasmuch as insight refers to cognitive as well as affective mental activities, child analysis has to address itself to the phases of cognitive organization. Investigations by Piaget and others can be of great assistance as we coordinate knowledge of these ego activities with our theory of therapy. We can follow the line of development from egocentric to reality-assessing thought processes and relate them to the role of insight. The question arises whether these cognitive schemata take place silently or to what degree they reach organization in the conscious sphere. One has to differentiate the process of emerging function from the contents of awareness. This brings into focus the role of self-observation as one of the major components of insight. Another requirement of insight is the ability to distinguish object- and self-representations in the context of stable organization of time and space. These different components of insight are all significant to the understanding of the role of insight in psychoanalysis.

Summary

I have described some of the vicissitudes of acquiring insight in both child and adult analysis, giving particular attention to the part played by the ego's synthetic, organizing, or integrating function.

REFERENCES

Alpert, A. (1959), Reversibility of pathological fixations associated with maternal deprivation in infancy. *The Psychoanalytic Study of the Child*, 14:169-185. New York: International Universities Press.

Freud, A. (1965), *Normality and Pathology in Childhood: Assessments of Development. Writings*, 6. New York: International Universities Press.

Freud, S. (1933), New introductory lectures on psycho-analysis. *Standard Edition*, 22:5-182.

_____ (1937), Constructions in analysis. *Standard Edition*, 23:257-269.

_____ (1940), An outline of psycho-analysis. *Standard Edition*, 23:144-207.

Hartmann, H. (1939), *Ego Psychology and the Problem of Adaptation*. New York: International Universities Press, 1958.

Kris, E. (1956), On some vicissitudes of insight in psychoanalysis. In: *Selected Papers*. New Haven: Yale University Press, 1975, pp. 252-271.

Loewald, H. (1979), Reflections on the psychoanalytic process and its therapeutic potential. *The Psychoanalytic Study of the Child*, 34, in press.

Noy, P. (1978), Insight and creativity. *This Journal*, 26:717-748.

Nunberg, H. (1931), The synthetic function of the ego. *Internat. J. Psycho-Anal.*, 12:123-140.

_____ (1937), The theory of the therapeutic results of psycho-analysis. *Internat. J. Pyscho-Anal.*, 18:161-169.

Piaget, J. (1973), *Memory and Intelligence*. New York: Basic Books.

Richfield, J. (1954), An analysis of the concept of insight. *Psychoanal. Quart.*, 23:390-408.

Valenstein, A. (1962), The psychoanalytic situation: Affects, emotional reliving, and insight in the psycho-analytic process. *Internat. J. Psycho-Anal.* 43:315-327.

Webster's Third New International Dictionary (1965), Springfield, Mass.: G & C. Merriam Co.

33 East 70th Street
New York, New York 10021

THE CURATIVE AND CREATIVE ASPECTS OF INSIGHT

HAROLD P. BLUM, M.D.

M Y FOCUS HERE is upon the vital importance of insight for psychoanalytic therapy, theory, and technique. In affirming the curative and creative roles of insight, I am not subscribing to its idealization or assigning to it magical qualities. In analysis, insight is the one element that is never in excess and yet is never complete. I shall maintain that insight propels the psychoanalytic process forward and is a condition, catalyst, and consequence of the psychoanalytic process. There is a circular interaction between the development of insight and productive analytic work leading to structural change.

Obtaining insights, of course, is not confined to psychoanalytic situations. Artists and poets, more in contact with the unconscious, probed and provided insights into the human mind that preceded and probably facilitated psychoanalytic discoveries. If such insights did not necessarily have therapeutic effects, creative persons such as Sophocles and Shakespeare achieved extraordinary understanding of normal fantasy, psychic conflict, and character disorder that continue to inspire psychoanalytic study.

Despite the punitive expulsion from paradise for gaining forbidden knowledge, the quest for insight has always paralleled the "bliss of ignorance." The hero of the oedipal myth moves and wavers between insight and blindness. Oedipus seeks the truth while asserting innocence of his guilt and ignorance of his identity. Analogous to the analytic process, the oedipal myth depicts the struggle between insight and resistance to insight. Oedipus attempts to evade and avoid the very clues and evidence for which he searches, and

Presented at the Anna Freud-Hampstead Center Symposium held by the Michigan Psychoanalytic Society, November 11, 1978.

resistance is relinquished with the incontrovertible evidence that brings coherence and conviction.

Allied to the poetic and Biblical maxims, "This above all: to thine own self be true," and "the truth shall make you free," Freud (1937, p.148) asserted: " . . . the analytic relationship is based on a love of truth. . . . " He had also stated (1933, p. 156), "I have told you that psycho-analysis began as a method of treatment; but I did not want to commend it to your interest as a method of treatment but on account of the truths it contains, on account of the information it gives us about what concerns human beings most of all—their own nature—and on account of the connections it discloses between the most different of their activities. As a method of treatment it is one among many, though, to be sure, *primus inter pares*. If it was without therapeutic value it would not have been discovered, as it was, in connection with sick people and would not have gone on developing. . . . " These comments are closely related to Freud's (1933, p. 80) definition of the analytic goal, " . . . to strengthen the ego . . . to widen its field of perception and enlarge its organization. . . . Where id was, there ego shall be."

Insight may also be achieved in psychotherapy, but is more limited, circumscribed, and superficial, often confined to current derivatives of unconscious conflict in one sector of the personality. In supportive or suppressive psychotherapy, as opposed to expressive or uncovering psychotherapy, the therapist may deliberately eschew insight as a goal. In psychotherapy, resistance may be selectively analyzed or reinforced. In some respects, the role of insight might be conceptualized as on a continuum in psychoanalysis and analytic therapy, but there are critical contrasts between the two forms of therapy which involve the concept of psychoanalytic insight. Psychoanalytic insight reaches and resolves unconscious conflict and is, by far, more pervasive, influential, and enduring than in nonanalytic therapy. Even in analytic psychotherapy, attaining some insight is far more likely to have enduring benefit than purely supportive treatment (Kernberg, 1972).

The limitations of psychotherapeutic goals and methods leaves significant transference and resistance unanalyzed, and rapid benefits frequently derive from forms of "transference cure" and positive changes in symptoms or defense. Psychotherapy depends heavily upon other therapeutic elements that are peripheral to insight in psychoanalysis. Abreaction and verbalizaᴛ. n and the analyst's clarifications and confrontations are attuned to the preconscious, but are preparatory and corollary to analytic interpretation (Bibring, 1954). Interpretation leading to insight is the specific and most powerful agent of the psychoanalytic curative process.

The type of insight into preconscious problems achieved from clarification and education is not comparable to analytic insight. Solutions to preconscious problems are ancillary to interpretation of unconscious conflict and its pathogenesis. In analysis, systematic interpretation deals with renewed resistance and is followed by working through, continued analytic work, and continued application and extension of insight. Assimilation of insight is usually gradual, piecemeal, and tenuous until the patient "makes it his own." Analytic insight is confirmed and recreated in the wealth of interlacing, convergent analytic data. The limits of the analytic method, of course, the depth to which interpretation and reconstruction can reach, the lack of personality change despite apparent insight are salient and significant problems for other lines of inquiry.

The psychoanalytic process represents an altogether unique form of investigation and treatment. The process is classically defined in terms of transference and resistance and their vicissitudes and interpretation. Correct interpretation and reconstruction depends upon and conveys insight, so that insight may be stated to be a *sine qua non* of psychoanalysis. Indeed, the psychoanalytic process can be differentiated from psychotherapies because it is a definable process requiring free association and interpretation and leads to insight. An analytic process depends upon correct analytic technique. In psychoanalysis, an opening phase is followed by the development of the transference neurosis, interpretation and working through of remobilized unconscious conflicts, resolution, if not dissolution, of the transference neurosis, and analytic termination with its own phase characteristics.

The analyst's insight, often enriched and advanced by creative patients, should be distinguished from the patient's insight. The analyst must have insight into the patient's defenses, conflicts, and character. The analyst's insight is neither symmetrical nor synchronous with that of the patient, and both precedes and permits proper interpretation and reconstruction. Analytic insight is necessary for the conduct of clinical analysis and resolution of countertransference. The analyst's surpassing insight and special knowledge may be of great preventive value, e.g., regarding parenting and child guidance. Optimally, the insight should emerge from and be part of the analytic process without resort to direct educational measures or advisory parameters. Analysis aims to minimize noninsightful influences and maximize the development of insight. It is not always easy to disentangle the effect of analytic insight from other therapeutic influences, or what appears to be the failure of insight to be effective from other problems of the analytic process, analyzability, and technique. Incomplete, unaccepted, and pseudo insight are everyday problems of analytic work, and countertransference may impede or not heed the patient's insight. The analyst may tactlessly misuse insight for narcissistic or sadistic purposes, disrupting treatment (Bird, 1957).

The analytic process proceeds with the patient's achieving increasing insight into the unconscious pathogenic childhood conflicts and their later derivatives and effects. Kris (1956), in his most illuminating discussion of vicissitudes of insight, referred to its use and abuse, to its gradual acquisition and assimilation, its loss and reappearance. Noting that apparent insight could be subverted for purposes of defense or infantile gratification, he described id aspects and infantile prototypes of insight, e.g., in oral incorporation and tactile grasp. That insight may represent a fecal gift or phallus, magic power, penetration, impregnation, etc. is now common knowledge. Kris pointed particularly to the proliferation of intellectualization as pseudo insight. Some "good hours" are then too good to be true.

Analytic advance proceeds from effective analytic work and increasing ego dominance. The "good hour" has been "prepared" for unconsciously by the preceding analytic work and culminates in new autonomous insight. The neutralized insight that is achieved is ego-integrated into the personality largely out of awareness and contributes to the autonomy of other ego functions. The therapeutic alliance and reality ego are strengthened, and the dynamic processes that lead to insight are beneficially effected by insight in circular processes. Insight, for example, overcomes barriers to curiosity, stimulates inquiry, and facilitates introspection and self-observation which may, in turn, widen insight (Hatcher, 1973). Changes in defense, memory, integration, and other ego functions result from and contribute to insight.

Different levels and availability of insight may be followed and contrasted before, during, and after analysis. For example, insight into a patient's character and symptoms will illuminate and connect genetic, dynamic, structural, and adaptive considerations of the case.

Kris (1956, p. 270) further remarked, "Without other dynamic changes insight would not come about but without insight and the ego's achievement which lead to insight, therapy itself remains limited and does not retain the character of psychoanalysis." Loewenstein (1956) virtually echoed these remarks. He pointed out that the ability to distinguish between the transferred past and present reality of experience was a function of insight and crucial to the therapeutic effects of psychoanalysis. He regarded enlarging insight as "decisive for the outcome of psychoanalytic work."

Though there is no classical paradigm of technique to which all analysts subscribe, the goal of analysis remains insight, achieved largely through interpretation. In Eissler's (1953) model, any technical deviation from insight via interpretation was a complicating parameter. Technical parameters have often involved attitudes toward transference.

One of the challenges to the psychoanalytic theory of therapy that has periodically resurfaced in different guises was proposed by Alexander (Alexander, French, et al., 1946). The crux of his therapy was not insight, but a corrective emotional experience. According to Alexander, the transference neurosis could become a regressive evasion, and the analyst should play a benevolent role, antithetical to the threatening role assigned to him in the patient's transference fantasy.

Even today, considerable numbers of psychotherapists regard the analytic situation as too regressively satisfying or as too depriving and too remote from the present and from reality. Various alterations of the psychoanalytic method and conversions to forms of psychotherapy are thus rationalized and justified in terms of transference avoidance, gratification, or manipulation. Unanalyzed transference may be utilized for magical reassurance, suggestion, direction, supportive care, etc.

Psychoanalytic technique has evolved in coordination with psychoanalytic theory. New perspectives have been both enlightening and confusing, and bear on the relative importance of insight in clinical psychoanalysis. The nontransference relationship and the most mature and primitive layers of transference have been carefully dissected (Stone, 1967; Greenson, 1967; Loewald, 1978). The analyst was also encountered as a real, new, and consistently mature object, a model for identification. Such identifications were related to the patients' taking over analytic aims, functions, and goals (Sterba, 1934) and to ego and superego develop-ment. Mature selective identifications are synergistic with insight, and the role of insight has to be considered with internalization and integrative processes. Many factors in analysis contribute to insight and personality growth, but are subordinate to insight. Insight is complemented by the analyst's usually silent auxiliary ego functions, but insight has priority and independently affects the analytic process and positive analytic development. Analytic "cure" is primarily effected through insight and not through empathy, acceptance, tolerance, etc. Serious questions arise, to which I shall later return, concerning the structural development necessary to achieve, use, and retain insight. How much analytic ego growth might occur preceding, permitting, and perhaps by-passing the effects of insight? Can the analytic method really stimulate ego growth without benefit of insight and conflict resolution? Are there technical additions or modifications that could promote ego growth without compromising and distorting the psychoanalytic process? There are also parallel questions concerning the value and validity of verbal insight into the early preverbal phase and its special problems (Blum, 1977; Loewald, 1978).

In general, there is more contemporary emphasis upon developmental tendencies mobilized by analysis than upon regression and repetition compulsion. The ego attempts to be active where it was passive or helpless (Freud, 1926), and this point of view has long been part of analytic theory. Ego synthesis, the domination of the primary process by the secondary process, the striving toward active ego mastery of trauma (Freud, 1926), the urge to complete development (Bibring, 1937; A. Freud, 1965, p. 28) support the effects of insight and blend with insight in personality reorganization and structural change.

Because of various needs, the patient may select from the array of therapeutic elements offered by psychoanalysis those less or not connected with insight. Elements of authority and suggestion, for example, are unintended yet unavoidable. What the patient selects and utilizes in the psychoanalytic situation will further the analyst's insight into the patient's ego strengths and psychopathology, just as parameters selected by or forced upon the analyst should be concordant with understanding of the patient's structural fragility or deficit (Eissler, 1953; A. Freud, 1965, p. 229).

Freud's final views of the analyst's multiple functions ranged beyond interpretation and insight, and envisioned the developmental and technical issues so relevant to contemporary controversy on the widened scope of analyzability and the analysis of ego distortions and deficits. Freud (1940, p. 181) asserted: "We serve the patient in various functions, as an authority and a substitute for his parents, as a teacher and educator; and we have done the best for him if, as analysts, we raise the mental processes in his ego to a normal level, transform what has become unconscious and repressed into preconscious material and thus return it once more to the possession of his ego."

His discussion also included caution against abuse of the opportunity for "after education" afforded by the parental transference and "new superego." He wrote: "In all his attempts at improving and educating the patient the analyst should respect his individuality. The amount of influence which he may legitimately allow himself will be determined by the degree of developmental inhibition present in the patient. Some neurotics have remained so infantile that in analysis too they can only be treated as children" (p. 175). These remarks are important considerations in child analysis, with infantile characters, borderline types, and cases of developmental arrest and deviation, but they remain pertinent to the general theory of therapy, i.e., the analytic process.

Surprisingly, and rather paradoxically, the origins and evolution of the psychoanalytic concept of insight have been relatively obscure. Zilboorg's (1952) statement remains a challenge for contemporary psychoanalytic thought: "Among the unclarities which are of utmost clinical importance and which cause utmost confusion is the term insight. It came from nowhere, so to speak. No one knows who employed it first, and in what sense" (p. 2). These reflections are related to perennial questions about the nature of insight, what it is, how it develops, why it works, etc.

The usual attribution (Sandler et al., 1973) ascribes insight to a term borrowed from psychiatry. Patients who do not recognize their own mental dysfunction or abnormality lack "insight," as in children and some cases of adult psychosis or alcoholism. Disturbance might be recognized, but only minimally, and even ascribed to external causes rather than internal difficulty. This type of insight (or its lack) is only superficially related to analytic insight which is much closer to the dictionary definition. Webster defines insight as penetrating and understanding the inner nature of things, a definition in accord with Freud's own use of the term. Freud's reference to creative insight has been overlooked in tracing the origins of the concept.

However, in Freud's Preface to the third English edition of "The Interpretation of Dreams" he made the following observation (1900, p. xxxii): "[This work] contains, even according to my present-day judgement, the most valuable of all the discoveries it has been my good fortune to make. Insight such as this falls to one's lot but once in a lifetime." It is clear that Freud was talking here about insight in its widest sense; the general meaning of insight into the nature of human mental processes, normal development and pathogenesis, as well as specific insight into a person's conflicts, character, temperament, and values, etc. Freud's insight was a special quality of his genius and capacity for ego mastery (the relationship between Freud's insight and his self-analysis will be discussed later in this paper). Theoretical and clinical insight are closely connected, though the present discussion is oriented toward insight in the analytic process where it gains life.

Psychoanalytic insight is different from but probably related to the type of insight associated with the solution to problems and to creative struggles. If we knew more, we might be able to categorize different forms of insight.

In a broad sense, resistance refers to resistance to insight. Psychoanalytic insight specifically follows the overcoming of resistance through interpretation. In turn, insight may overcome or elicit resistance. The correct interpretation of resistance results in the patient's coming to grips with the origin and genetic-developmental history of the resistance, the functions it serves, the nature of the danger situation that is being warded off, and the secondary gains derived from the associated infantile fixations and regressive adaptations, and the external rewards obtained from inhibitions and symptoms.

The patient becomes acquainted in an entirely new way with the unconscious danger situation as it presents itself in the analytic situation and as it is worked through with the help of analytic interpretation. Working through leads to the assimilation of insight and the progressive resolution of resistance to insight, leading to change (Greenson, 1967, p. 42). Danger is mastered by a mature ego rather than the weak infantile ego of the past. The history of the patient's reactions to danger, with its attendant anxiety and guilt, and the achievement of full conscious awareness of defensive maneuvers and forbidden unconscious impulses are intrinsic to the concept of psychoanalytic insight. Irrational evaluations and patterns of reaction are modified and mastered with development of insight. This can happen outside of psychoanalysis, but under those circumstances is, as I indicated earlier, likely to be sporadic and incomplete. Freud (1926, p. 153) stated: "The ego may occasionally manage to break down the barriers of repression which it has itself put up and to recover its influence over the instinctual impulse and direct the course of a new impulse in accordance with the changed danger-situation. But in point of fact, the ego very seldom succeeds in doing this: it cannot undo its repressions. It is possible that the way the struggle will go depends upon quantitative relations." We can add, with Freud as an example, that it also depends upon special ego endowment and qualities.

Insight is intrinsic to "seeing oneself" and gaining self-knowledge. It is immediate in the here and now of the transference, but it applies to the patient's entire life, and knowledge of the human condition. The transference is the principal but not the only locus of interpretation and source of insight. During intense resistance and a faltering therapeutic alliance, a correct interpretation may do wonders for continued analytic work. Insight may appear as a bolt from the blue, a gift of the gods, but is more likely to endure and enlarge with analysis of previous and subsequent resistance. The patient cooperates and participates in the analytic work, identifying with the search for insight and sometimes arriving at insights before the analyst. Beyond the relief of symptoms and inhibitions, insight becomes an ego aim and ego ideal, a motivation for further analysis. In theory and therapy, psychoanalysis is never without a goal — the goal of insight. Insight, the agency and goal of the analytic process, ideally becomes the patient's goal (Wallerstein, 1965) as well as the need and value of the analyst. Analytic insight extends to the widest understanding of the treatment process, relationship, and situation.

Making the unconscious conscious in a language that communicates the understanding achieved between analyst and patient contributes greatly to insight. But insight does more than make conscious; it establishes causes, meanings, and connections. The concept of insight changed with structural theory and ego psychology. Remembering and recalling, the lifting of infantile amnesia, had to be understood not as specific, isolated, often traumatic memories but against a whole psychological background and organization (Kanzer and Blum, 1967). Autobiography and life experience are reinterpreted (Kris, 1956), relived, and newly revised in analysis.

The patient's insights in analysis will have been brought into full consciousness and verbalized. However, the search for insight and the spread of insight also proceeds in silence and may recede from awareness. Past insight may be regressively lost or may become an intrinsic part of the ego reorganization and growth facilitated by the new insightful integration. The relationship of insight to consciousness and to verbalization or imagery needs further inquiry, including study of insight formation outside of awareness. Insight is not confined to verbal expression and may be communicated in other forms, as in play or art. The intuitive insight of creative artists and analysts are often preconscious, probably with unconscious determinants and contributions (Noy, 1972). Poetic insight, for example, may never achieve conscious reflective awareness. (I shall shortly give an example of Freud's extraordinary insight.) The acquisition and development of insight utilizes unconscious and preconscious ego functions, but "analytic insight" at least is crystallized and organized in its conscious creation.

Insight leads to reintegration by the rational ego. This is not a pale pseudointellectual, cognitive development, but is always associated with enrichment of the inner life (Pressman, 1969; Valenstein, 1962). The patient can then better recognize, express, and regulate emotions and mood states. Various grades of insight, such as intellectual, affective, dynamic, volitional, or neutral versus emotional, experiential versus descriptive (Reid and Finesinger, 1952; Richfield, 1954), are components of a holistic concept. Insight may be described as a complex, integrative, ego attribute (Zilboorg, 1952). Consideration of a number of interacting ego functions are necessary to describe the type of insight that leads to a sense of conviction and ultimately to structural change. Past and present, thought and feeling, cause and effect are reintegrated. The development of rational understanding, signal affect, and emotional sensitivity in relating unconscious conflict to various derivatives and experiences in the transference and in life is an essential ingredient of what we understand by insight (Kubie, 1950; Myerson, 1960). Insights are often disturbing if not painful. The greater equanimity and emotional equilibrium that comes with insight is associated with an appreciation of life's inevitable disappointments and renunciations. Ego assimilation of insight leads to control of impulses and action and capacity for adaptive action and appropriate behavior (Valenstein, 1962).

Insight brings with it intrapsychic and adaptive change. The obsessive patient's sadism is understood in a variety of contexts, particularly as it was manifested in the analytic transference and associated with reaction formation, undoing, and expiation. The isolated anger has been connected to the hostility and sadistic, spiteful attitudes. The unending doubting and counting have been related to the counting of money, possessions, and persons; the counting of one's love objects to insure their existence, and the inability to end the counting without ending their existence and the patient's own security. The origins of the counting will have been explored, and the sublimations of the conflicts and symptoms associated with the obsessive counting will have been recounted, revised, and extended in many directions in the course of the analysis. The patient will have a new appreciation of himself and his family and will not be driven by obsessive thought and attempts to undo his sadistic wishes.

I should like to give a vignette of the emergence of insight in the analytic situation in a setting of considerable transference tension and turbulence. The patient is a highly educated male businessman, proud of his family and his socioeconomic success but disturbed by his continuing difficulties in relation to his wife and children. He has often commented about varying degrees of irritability and bickering and associated to a scene at the dinner table in which there was considerable regressive behavior by the children, characterized by giggling, being ill-mannered, and not listening to their parents. When his daughter reached across the table to grab some favorite food he automatically slapped her hand. He knows that sometimes he is excessively provoked and ill-tempered.

There are things that are difficult to tell me. He would like to present a more admirable picture of himself to himself and to me. He sadly thinks of his parents shopping very carefully for food, watching every penny, and walking distances for opportunities for small sales and savings. He is ashamed to think of incidents where he has been dishonest and, in fact, a cheat. In order to earn extra money when he was a teenager, he had worked as a waiter. Soon becoming proficient, he was given the opportunity to collect the tips of the other waiters, and then began a dishonest scheme. He pocketed some of the tips that belonged to the others. He remembers a particular customer who wanted his bill reduced and indicated as much with an ingenious minimum of words and facial expression. A rapid collusive understanding developed in which the patient reduced the bill in order to gain a larger tip. He went on to describe how mortified and humiliated he was at an early experience when he was caught as a child stealing a chocolate bar.

I pointed out to him that he was describing incidents in which he had been greedily grabbing what didn't belong to him, and that he had started the session by describing the scene at the table in which he had slapped his daughter for grabbing food. The patient himself then recognized that his daughter had been punished for his own guilty deeds, that he had scapegoated her for a conflict externalized onto her which relieved him of blame. At the dinner table and in the scene at the restaurant table, he had wanted some extra food and a large tip. He identified with the customer's entitlement in wanting a lower bill, and then made the connection to the anticipation of receiving the bill from the analyst (his waiter) that session. He had not consciously thought about it or been aware of the anticipation of the bill either at home or, up to that point, in the session. But he wanted a tip of more time and, unconsciously, a "doctored" bill.

Many dynamics and genetics are suggested in this little vignette. The patient (and analyst) dealt with extraanalytic material before the transference fully emerged in the session, and he was able to integrate his conflicts both in the analytic situation and as they were in effect externalized and lived out in the family situation. The guilty culprit who unconsciously wishes to cheat the analyst and receive a doctored bill becomes the punitive parent who mistreats his "mischievous" child.

The analytic work and integrated efforts continued after the session and into the next hour. He realized upon leaving that he had not mentioned his reactions to his clients and partners. He refuses requests of clients to falsify records and bills, but he had forgotten a current temptation. Charged with responsibility for depositing the firm's receipts, he had fantasied, indeed, he had been momentarily tempted to take some of the money for himself. The past scene of taking his co-waiters' tips was very much alive, and he became more aware of tendencies to repeat in different forms and disguise. He could be generous with family and friends, but he began to recognize that he was also engaged in acts of undoing and restitution. Analytic insight developing in the analytic situation was being extended in many different areas and directions.

Insight promotes structural change and then reflects that change. I do not think that the reverse sequence of structural change causing insight is reliable, and would not assign insight a secondary role in the analytic process. The personality reorganization and ego development that occur in analysis require insight. As a "developmental process," analysis has prerequisites of a capacity to participate in an analytic process, secondary process, and sufficient pre-existing development to provide for controlled regression, signal anxiety, differentiation of fantasy and reality and of past and present, thought and action, the development of self and object constancy, language, self-observation, and self-criticism are clearly required. It is probably true that some patients become analyzable in the process of analysis, but such difficult patients probably have hidden ego strengths, can eventually attain and retain insight, and primarily recover from regression rather than major developmental arrest and defect. Children who never reached object constancy were unable to establish firm enduring treatment alliances with their analysts (A. Freud, 1965, p. 41), and I believe that this applies with rare exceptions to adult patients as well. The achievement of self- and object constancy is conditional upon cognitive and affective development, ego discrimination, and synthesis, and is necessary for further ego development. In assessing the limits of clinical insight, we have to consider the developmental level and stability of these basic ego functions in addition to the defenses. Kris (1956, p. 270) stated: ". . . the complexity of the ego functions which participate in the process of gaining and using insight may well account for the wide variations of the impact of insight on individual cases."

The nature of insight itself undergoes development. Insight into unconscious conflicts and processes is not an expectable part of normal development, and much of analytic insight into, e.g., a patient's cannibalistic impulses or incestuous passions, were never conscious in childhood. Structural development in childhood proceeds with "normal" repression, with adaptive as well as pathogenic uses of defense. The normal, adaptive formation of the superego represents a new level of structure and integration, which occurs without insight into the unconscious origins, content, and function of the superego. Analytic insight into structure formation does not mean that structural malformations or arrest are necessarily analyzable or reversible.

How much development is necessary for the most limited insight? The child must have negotiated separation-individuation (Mahler et al., 1975) and have some advanced structuralization and critical ego functions, as previously noted. Contrasting the problems that preoedipal trends introduce into the transference relationship, A. Freud (1965, p. 40) referred to "the beneficial elements contributed by the appearance in the transference of object constancy and the attitudes belonging to the positive and negative oedipus complex with the coordinated ego achievements of self-observation, insight, and secondary process functioning." That the limits of insight depend upon developmental achievements is also related to the emphasis upon the resumption of development at the termination of child analysis (A. Freud, 1970; Van Dam et al., 1975). The insight of children and of infantile adults is developmentally restricted. Comparisons of reconstructions in adult and child analysis should provide valuable information on insight and development and, in turn, should facilitate increasingly accurate reconstructive insight. Studies of insight in children at different developmental levels and of adults with developmental deficits and deviations will delimit those patients who can optimally or minimally use insight, and those who might benefit from preparatory psychotherapy and then analysis.

The breadth and depth of insight varies with the phase of analysis, the resolution of the transference, and the patient's ego development and resources. It is well to add here that the types of insight that are communicated to patients today are by no means identical with what was analytically interpreted in the pioneer days of psychoanalysis (Blum, 1976, 1977). The difference in the range, type, and depth of our interpretations can by no means be entirely attributed to changes in the patient population. (Our technique influences the analytic data obtained, which in turn is the source of theory. Proper technique is molded to theory, so that theory cannot be divorced or discarded from analytic work.)

Our insights into the roots of the personality are much greater today, and we have benefited from the contributions of ego psychology, structural theory, and developmental knowledge. We know more and convey greater insight in longer analyses than in the pioneer days. Greater knowledge of the preoedipal period and its influence on the Oedipus complex and later personality is exemplified in the recent concepts of developmental lines (A. Freud, 1965) and separation-individuation (Mahler et al., 1975).

Similarly, our understanding of later phases of life—for example, latency, adolescence, and young adulthood with the stresses and developmental challenges of parenthood—are also available for a more complete interpretation. The infantile neurosis is the core of the transference neurosis, but we know much more about its complex web of origins (Rangell, 1975), about its antecedents and developmental transformation, and the powerful influence for better and worse of the earlier and later phases of life. Traumatic experience and pathogenic reality situations are better understood, especially in terms of strain patterns rather than isolated single shocks.

What about the fate of insight after psychoanalysis? The maintenance and even expansion of insight post-termination is in need of study in follow-up research and reanalysis. Having learned to free associate, observe, and interpret by the end of analysis, few patients are able to sustain independently the type of ongoing analytic process that Freud (1937, p. 249) described as the appropriate result of training analysis: ". . . we reckon on the stimuli that he has received in his own analysis not ceasing when it ends and on the processes of remodelling the ego continuing spontaneously in the analysed subject and making use of all subsequent experiences in the newly-acquired sense. This does in fact happen, and in so far as it happens, makes the analysed subject qualified to be an analyst himself. . . ."

Reflecting upon the wide variations of the impact of insight in individuals, Kris (1956, p. 270) observed:

> With some individuals the result of analysis seems to be connected with a lasting awareness of their own problems, a higher degree of ability to view themselves; with others this is not so—and yet the two groups of patients cannot be distinguished according to the range of therapeutic effects. This possibly finds a parallel in the study of what patients retain in memory of the course of analysis, a problem frequently accessible in repeated analyses. It is well known that the variations are extraordinarily wide. It seems that insight with some individuals remains only a transient experience, one to be obliterated again in the course of life by one of the defenses they are wont to use. And it is not my impression that these individuals are more predisposed to future illness than others. This might well remind us how much remains unknown about the conditions under which the ego does its silent work.

Myerson (1960, 1965) discussed similar problems and described different modes of insight with different ego reactions and depth. Full postanalytic insight into intra-psychic conflict represented an internalization of the analytic process.

Insight may have self-propelling and compelling effects, as Freud noted. Following the principle of multiple function, it tends to catalyze further insight with creative stimulation of comprehension, connection, and new levels of integration. This, of course, does not occur in any straight line, and as indicated previously, new insights are often followed by renewed resistance and regressive retreat. Interpretation must be repeated and insights tested and contested. Insight in one area may be exploited for resistance to insight in another area. A patient may understand his phallic-urethral strivings but not his narcissistic need for unlimited power and prestige. In predisposed patients, insights may trigger negative therapeutic reactions or may be victoriously attained only after the rival analyst has been vanquished.

Without overlooking the possible subversion or loss of insight, the impact and influence of insight may be quite silent yet very significant for personality development and ego dominance. Freud (1927, p. 53) referred to the broad civilizing influence of insight in humans driven by instinct and irrational illusions when he stated, "The voice of the intellect is a soft one, but it does not rest till it has gained a hearing. Finally, after a countless succession of rebuffs, it succeeds. This is one of the few points on which one may be optimistic about the future of mankind. . . ."

Insight is related to the mastery of conflict and regression, but also to creative solutions and to the creation of new organization and structure. There is a creative dimension to insight and its achievement and consequences (Noy, 1978). Analysis diminishes the compulsion to repeat and liberates integrative functions. The reorganization of the personality on new levels of development is clearly more than a recovery of lost memories and past relationships. Causes and connections are established which never existed in the same way with cognitive and affective changes. Insight surpasses the recapture of lost connections, resources, and abilities, and proceeds to the creation of new meaning, modes of understanding, and new adaptive possibilities and opportunities. The reciprocal insight, imagination, and integration of analyst and patient has an artistic, aesthetic quality. Referring to the correspondence between creativity and the insight of the analytic patient, Anna Freud (1957, p. 491) stated, "What we wish him to achieve is the creation of new attitudes and relationships on the basis of the newly created powers of insight into his inner world."

We know very little about the creative genius responsible

for the discovery of psychoanalysis and the seemingly spontaneous insights that characterized his self-analysis and his applications of analytic thought. The burgeoning of Freud's insight has been ascribed to his self-analysis and was in many respects an essential product of his self-analysis. His systematic self-analysis usually is said to differentiate Freud's preanalytic period and the emergence of psychoanalysis; and his earliest analytic investigations foreshadowed his later conceptualizations.

But where did his self-analytic ability come from? It was not the result of a protracted analytic process, but the creation of the analytic method simultaneous with insights into himself and others. In some ways this occurred preceding deliberate self-analysis. The creative leaps of the imagination were often "quantum leaps," in which insight spontaneously emerged as well as appearing after long preparation and the culmination of inner struggle, experiment, and study. The interweaving of primary-process regression, interpretive self-observation, and secondary-process integration became for Freud a creative process of insight and discovery. The analytic process deliberately fosters both regression and reintegration, and new insights have creative elements and novel configurations. It follows that insight is in many respects related to creativity, and promotes rather than impairs creative discovery and expression. Insight and creativity are complementary, and it is not insight but the absence or deficit of insight that threatens ego flexibility and creativity. All patients, and creative personalities in particular, stand to benefit from stimulation and enhancement of creativity in clinical psychoanalysis with expanding insight. Freud's self-analytic discoveries exemplify how naïve is the notion that psychoanalysis endangers creativity.

Freud, with his uncanny capacity to learn from his experimental efforts, his trials and errors, soon found the roots of hypnosis in unconscious predispositions. Of hypnosis, Freud (1917, p. 462) declared, "We psycho-analysts may claim to be its legitimate heirs and we do not forget how much encouragement and theoretical clarification we owe to it." Relevant to problems of parenthood and creativity, I should like to call attention to a virtually unknown gem of the Freudian literature. It is in the prepsychoanalytic publications and is called, "A Case of Successful Treatment by Hypnotism" (Freud, 1893). We can observe the father of psychoanalysis arriving at the most extraordinary insights into the psychology of motherhood before his own self-analysis and long before he had turned particular attention to the study of mothering and the mother-child relationship (Blum, 1978).

The paper was published at the same time as Breuer and Freud's (1893) "Preliminary Communication," and recounts the daring therapeutic intervention of a young Viennese physician. Here is Freud on a house call, confronting an acute emotional crisis. It was the case of a mother with postpartum depression who was unable to feed her newborn baby. Freud's account is precious and timeless, and significant for the history of psychoanalysis. Clinical observation and theoretical construct followed one upon the other. His remarks on the constitutional predisposition are still the open question he pondered.

The patient was a young woman between twenty and 30 years of age with whom he had been acquainted since childhood. She had an apparently happy marriage and had intended to nurse her first child. Freud (1893, pp. 118-120) describes what happened on that occasion: "The delivery was not more difficult than is usual with a primiparous mother. . . . There was a poor flow of milk, pains were brought on when the baby was put to the breast, the mother lost appetite and showed an alarming unwillingness to take nourishment, her nights were agitated and sleepless. At last, after a fortnight, in order to avoid any further risk to the mother and infant, the attempt was abandoned as a failure and the child was transferred to a wet-nurse. Thereupon all the mother's troubles immediately cleared up." This was, of course, in a society and culture in which there were no sterile formulas and milk substitutes. So, without a wet-nurse, a mother's refusal to feed her newborn was tantamount to infanticidal threat.

Freud was called in three years later when a second baby was born, but " . . . the mother's attempts at feeding the child herself seemed even less successful and to provoke even more distressing symptoms than the first time. She vomited all her food, became agitated when it was brought to her bedside and was completely unable to sleep. She became so much depressed at her incapacity that her two family doctors— . . . Dr. Breuer and Dr. Lut—would not hear of any prolonged attempt being made on this occasion."

A final therapeutic effort was to be made. When Freud was called in, he found the patient on the evening of the fourth day lying in bed, " . . . furious at her inability to feed the baby—an inability which increased at every attempt but against which she struggled with all her strength. In order to avoid the vomiting, she had taken no nourishment the whole day. . . . Far from being welcomed as a saviour in the hour of need, I was obviously being received with a bad grace and I could not count on the patient having much confidence in me." Undaunted, Freud promptly hypnotized his patient and reported the following hypnotic suggestion: "Have no fear! You will make an excellent nurse and the baby will thrive. Your stomach is perfectly quiet, your appetite is excellent, you are looking forward to your next meal, etc." He then tells us that the patient slept peacefully, took nourishment herself, "and fed the baby irreproachably." However, later the next day her vomiting returned. "It was impossible to put the child to her breast. . . ." Freud now acted with "greater energy," and induced a second hypnosis, reporting the following extraordinary intervention: "I told the patient that five minutes after my departure she would break out against her family with some acrimony: what had happened to her dinner? did they mean to let her starve? how could she feed the baby if she had nothing to eat herself? and so on." When he returned on the third evening, the patient refused further treatment, saying she had an excellent appetite, plenty of milk for the baby, and had no difficulty in feeding her child. Freud further stated, "I had many opportunities of satisfying myself in a friendly way that (mother and child) were both doing well. I found it hard to understand, however, as well as annoying, that no reference was ever made to my remarkable achievement." (Did Freud also wish to be fed?)

A year later when a third child was born, the patient succumbed to the same postpartum depression and responded again to the same hypnotic psychotherapy. Freud then proceeded to a discussion of the case, which included the observation that the mother behaved as though it was her will not to feed the child on any account. Although the mother wanted to carry out her intentions to nurture the child, she was unaware of the "counter-will," the forerunner of the formulation of unconscious intrapsychic conflict. The case, as Freud described, " . . . is a typical one and throws light upon a large number of other cases in which breast-feeding or some similar function is prevented by neurotic influences" (1893, p. 123).

Here we see Freud's genius at work—his immediate empathy and insight in a classic case of crisis intervention. I do not believe that we can find a better example of the intuitive appiication of psychoanalytic insight to a psychological crisis situation than Freud's second intervention. This intervention is by no means hypnotic suggestion. In fact, it is a break with the entire tradition of hypnotic suggestion and may be stated to represent an extraordinary early psychoanalytic interpretation. Hypnotic magic has been replaced by psychoanalytic insight. It is as if Freud recognized that hypnotic suggestion and pure wishful denial only increased the resistance and tendency to regression. Disappointed with hypnotic suggestion, he gave the patient an awareness of her inner conflict. She was offered the opportunity to deal with it in an entirely new way and permission to recognize and express her inner feelings and attitudes. Her inner conflicts were objectionable not only to her but to her entire family and probably to the family doctors.

Freud's interpretation conveyed his awareness of both her wish to feed the baby in accordance with her mature conscious personality inclinations and her unconscious infantile wishes to be fed. He recognized and accepted her anger and indirectly interpreted her oral aggression and regression. In authorizing her to awaken "crying" to be fed, comforted, and cared for, he implicitly identified her envious identification with her infant, her dependent longings, and her rage over her own unsatisfied infantile hunger. Unlike the first hypnotic intervention, and unlike all preceding hypnotic and psychotherapeutic interventions, Freud told the patient, who was in an agitated depression, that she would wake up angry. How did he know that a depressed patient was angry at not being fed? He realized that the patient needed to express the anger in conjunction with her depressive conflicts. He appeared to recognize the presence of universal oral fantasies at the very root of postpartum depression. His seemingly spontaneous understanding of the core conflicts in the situation and his innovative interpretation defy explanation. The case report represents a confluence of Freud's burgeoning insight into the development of the origins of depression and into a very important dimension of female psychology. In addition to the dynamic appreciation of conflict and symptom formation, the genetic principle emerged. The helpless dependence and orality of her newborn have revived the mother's own infantile wishes. Her own needs for nurturance are reactivated under the demands of nurturant motherhood. This mother could accept neither her own infantile demands nor those of her infant. Her (unconscious) rage at her own infant and at her mother, represented by the family, who should feed her was turned on herself. In pursuing and conveying a more insightful understanding of the patient's postpartum problems, Freud again broke with Breuer (the family doctor) who was reluctant to proceed in this direction.

As a lucid example of brief psychotherapy using psychoanalytic insight, Freud's intervention could be a paradigm for similar application of psychoanalytic knowledge. Psychoanalytic psychotherapy applies psychoanalytic understanding in very helpful ways to a wide scope of disturbances and can be geared toward insight or auxiliary ego support. Observations and inferences derived from the psychoanalytic psychotherapy of psychotics, borderlines, etc. have also provided valuable theoretical insights.

Even in brief psychotherapy, a little insight may go a long way. The flicker of illumination in the dark may lead to light at the end of the tunnel. The tenuous insight may be assimilated in a working through in life. In my opinion, psychoanalysis will continue to be the source of scientific psychological treatment, guiding psychotherapy with its unique insights. While differing in process, technique, and goals, psychoanalysis is the foundation of derivative psychotherapy in providing psychoanalytic understanding of both the psychopathology and the psychotherapy.

Summary

Insight is a *sine qua non* of the psychoanalytic process and is a condition, catalyst, and consequence of the psychoanalytic process. Analytic insight is defined and differentiated from other types of self-knowledge and awareness and from pseudo insight; there are different levels and underlying processes in the development of insight. The importance of insight is delineated in theory and therapy, in analyst and patient, and in psychoanalysis and psychotherapy. Psychoanalysis aims to minimize noninsightful influences and to maximize insight leading to structural change. Psychoanalysis is not without a goal, but has the inexorable goal of expanded insight. Clinical limitations to gaining and retaining insight are recognized. Stress is placed on the acquisition and creation of insight and its relation to ego development, analytic progress, and adaptive mastery. Insight and creativity are complementary, and insight has creative and novel configurations. Although it is organized and consolidated in conscious verbalization, insight may proceed outside awareness. An unnoticed case of Freud's provides an example of creative insight. The achievement of insight effects and reflects structural change. Clinical psychoanalysis maximizes insight and minimizes other therapeutic influences.

REFERENCES

Alexander, F., French, T., et al. (1946), *Psychoanalytic Therapy: Principles and Applications*. New York: Ronald Press.

Bibring, E. (1937), On the theory of the results of psycho-analysis. *Internat. J. Psycho-Anal.*, 18:170-189.

_____ (1954), Psychoanalysis and the dynamic psychotherapies. *This Journal*, 2:745-770.

Bird, B. (1957), The curse of insight. *Bull. Phila. Assn. Psychoanal.*, 7:101-104.

Blum, H. (1976), The changing use of dreams in psychoanalytic practice: Dreams and free association. *Internat. J. Psycho-Anal.*, 57:315-324.

_____ (1977), The prototype of preoedipal reconstruction. *This Journal*, 25:757-785.

_____ (1978), Reconstruction in a case of postpartum depression. *The Psychoanalytic Study of the Child*, 33:335-362. New Haven: Yale University Press.

Breuer, J. & Freud, S. (1893-1895), Studies on hysteria. *Standard Edition*, 2.

Eissler, K. (1953), The effect of the structure of the ego on psychoanalytic technique. *This Journal*, 1:104-143.

Freud, A. (1957), Foreword to Marion Milner's *On Not Being Able to Paint*. *Writings*, 5:488-492. New York: International Universities Press, 1969.

_____ (1965), *Normality and Pathology in Childhood*. *Writings*, 6. New York: International Universities Press, 1966.

_____ (1970), Problems of termination in child analysis. *Writings*, 7:3-21. New York: International Universities Press, 1971.

Freud, S. (1893), A case of successful treatment of hypnotism. *Standard Edition*, 1:116-128.

_____ (1900), The interpretation of dreams. *Standard Edition* 4.

———— (1917), Introductory lectures on psycho-analysis, lecture 28. *Standard Edition*, 16; 448-463.

———— (1926), Inhibitions, symptoms and anxiety. *Standard Edition*, 20:77-175.

———— (1927), The future of an illusion. *Standard Edition*, 21:3-56.

———— (1933), New introductory lectures on psycho-analysis. *Standard Edition*, 22:3-182.

———— (1937), Analysis terminable and interminable. *Standard Edition*, 23:211-253.

———— (1940), An outline of psycho-analysis. *Standard Edition*, 23:141-207.

Greenson, R. (1967), *The Technique and Practice of Psychoanalysis*. New York: International Universities Press.

Hatcher, R. (1973), Insight and self-observation. *This Journal*, 21:377-398.

Kanzer, M. & Blum, H. (1967), Classical psychoanalysis since 1939. In: *Psychoanalytic Techniques*, ed. B. Wolman. New York: Basic Books, pp. 93-146.

Kernberg, O. et al. (1972), Psychotherapy and psychoanalysis. Final report of the psychotherapy research project of the Menninger Foundation. *Bull. Mennin. Clinic*, 36, 1 & 2.

Kris, E. (1956), On some vicissitudes of insight in psychoanalysis. In: *Selected Papers*. New Haven: Yale University Press, pp.252-271.

Kubie, L. (1950), *Practical and Theoretical Aspects of Psychoanalysis*. New York: International Universities Press.

Loewald, H. (in press), The waning of the Oedipus complex. *This Journal*, 27.

Loewenstein, R. (1956), Some remarks on the role of speech in psycho-analytic technique. *Internal. J. Psycho-Anal.*, 37:460-468.

Mahler, M, Pine, F., & Bergman, A. (1975), *The Psychological Birth of the Human Infant*. New York: Basic Books.

Myerson, P. (1960), Awareness and stress: Post psycho-analytic utilization of insight. *Internat. J. Psycho-Anal.*, 41:147-156.

———— (1965), Modes of insight. *This Journal*, 13:771-792.

Noy, P. (1978), Insight and creativity. *This Journal*, 26:717-748.

Pressman, M. (1969), The cognitive function of the ego in psycho-analysis. II, Repression, incognizance, and insight formation. *Internat. J. Psycho-Anal.*, 50:345-351.

Rangell, L. (1975), Psychoanalysis and the process of change: An essay on the past, present, and future. *Internat. J. Psycho-Anal.*, 32:167-177.

Reid, J. & Finesinger, J. (1952), The role of insight in psychotherapy. *Amer. J. Psychiat.*, 108:726-734.

Richfield, J. (1954), An analysis of the concept of insight. *Psychoanal. Quart.*, 23:390-408.

Sandler, J., Holder, A., Dare, C. (1973), *The Patient and the Analyst*. New York: International Universities Press.

Sterba, R. (1934), The fate of the ego in analytic therapy. *Internat. J. Psycho-Anal.*, 15:117-126.

Stone, L. (1961), *The Psychoanalytic Situation*. New York: International Universities Press.

Valenstein, A. (1962), The psychoanalytic situation: Affects, emotional reliving, and insight in the psychoanalytic process. *Internat. J. Psycho-Anal.*, 43:315-324.

Van Dam, H. Heinicke, C.M., & Shane M., (1975), On termination of child analysis. *The Psychoanalytic Study of the Child*, 30:443-474. New Haven: Yale University Press.

Wallerstein, R. (1965), The goals of psychoanalysis: A survey of analytic viewpoints. *This Journal*, 13:748-770.
Zilboorg, G. (1952), The emotional problem and the therapeutic role of insight. *Psychoanal. Quart.*, 21:1-24.

23 The Hemlocks
Roslyn Estates, New York 11576

COMMENTS ON THE THERAPEUTIC ACTION OF PSYCHOANALYSIS

EDWARD JOSEPH, M.D.

You will recall Freud's famous definition of psychoanalysis: a form of therapy, a theory of human behavior, and a method of research; let us remember that clinical work forms the basis of the two latter portions of the definition. All psychoanalysts, regardless of their area of interest, undertake the psychoanalytic treatment of patients, and it is in the clinical situation that they either undertake their research or evolve their theory. Within the psychoanalytic situation consisting of a patient and a psychoanalyst are aspects that are encountered everywhere, regardless of who undertakes the psychoanalysis.

An important clinical issue, one that cannot be overestimated, is the nature of the therapeutic effect that psychoanalysis exerts. This issue has bedeviled the field from the beginning. Closely allied to it is the fact that the interests of the patient and the interests of the psychoanalyst may not necessarily coincide.

A patient comes to a psychoanalyst for help with his problems, as manifested by anxiety, symptoms, difficulties in living or in human relationships, or because somebody in his environment insists that he is disturbing. Most patients are not seeking understanding of themselves as a primary goal, and would be content to ignore their inner mental life—its sources, evolution, development and content—if only they

President of the International Psycho-Analytic Association and Professor of Psychiatry, Mount Sinai School of Medicine.

could feel better. The patient's goal is therapeutic gain through the psychoanalytic procedure. To the psychoanalyst, exploring, understanding, linking past and present memories, fantasies, affects, and defenses, and, in so doing, tracing out certain aspects of development, are all important approaches, with the therapeutic gain a side benefit which, while important, is not as significant as the greater freedom of mental functioning a patient may gain. To the psychoanalyst the disappearance of symptoms is not as important as to the patient, for the analyst has a more distant goal of therapeutic gain than the patient. And an immediate symptomatic relief that might be available is often put aside by the analyst in favor of the longer range goal of greater freedom and control of mental life. For these reasons the interests of the patient and of the psychoanalyst may not coincide and may sometimes seem to be in conflict.

Given that patients come for therapeutic gain and that psychoanalysis is undertaken for that reason, an important question is whether there is a therapeutic benefit in psychoanalytic procedures. If the answer is in the affirmative, then important consequences ensue for psychoanalysis and its role in therapies of the future, to say nothing of its effect on training future psychoanalysts. It then becomes possible to ask how such benefits come about and how they can be understood. If the answer is in the negative, then this also has important consequences for the future, and it could be asked why the procedure has no therapeutic benefit.

In fact, there are many who feel that psychoanalysis as a therapeutic tool is a questionable one. At one end of the spectrum are those (such as Eysenck) who feel that psychoanalysis has no therapeutic effect at all, even in the so-called classical cases of neurosis. These opponents of psychoanalysis in effect claim that psychoanalytic undertakings have not benefited anyone, that so-called symptomatic improvement or therapeutic gain would have happened in a variety of other ways, and that appropriate "scientific" studies of a controlled nature have not been made in order to demonstrate the efficacy of psychoanalysis as a therapeutic tool. Because this has not been done, they say, and because there are no carefully gathered statistics, they question the therapeutic efficacy of psychoanalysis and correspondingly question any of the findings or conclusions derived from a psychoanalytic approach. They say, in effect, that unless psychoanalysis is an effective therapy it is not a valid theory of human behavior or an effective research tool.

At the other end of the spectrum are those who feel that psychoanalysis is the treatment of choice for all neurotic and even psychotic conditions, limited only by considerations of the time and money it requires and the availability of psychoanalysts. Between the two extremes lies a range that extends from those who feel that psychoanalysis is the treatment of choice for the so-called classical neuroses (hysteria, phobias, obsessive-compulsive neurosis) and that only with modification of the standard technique can it be applied to other disorders (Eissler, 1965). A more moderate position states that psychoanalysis as a treatment of choice is appropriate for patients ranging from the classical neuroses to borderline to narcissistic disorders (Stone, 1954; Kohut, 1971; Kernberg, 1968). The application of psychoanalysis to a "widening scope" of patients has been accompanied by the implication that it is an effective approach to utilize in this range of disorders.

Another approach to the therapeutic effectiveness of psychoanalysis is to state that therapy is not the goal of psychoanalysis. Rather, it is a procedure designed to explore mental life in depth and to extend the range of understanding of mental processes. Anyone undertaking psychoanalysis should understand that goal and, to the extent that it is achieved, has gained from the experience regardless of any therapeutic benefit. Those who so argue also feel that psychoanalysis is a hermeneutic or social science (Ricoeur, 1977; Lesche, 1973) rather than a natural science (Modell,

1978). If it be hermeneutic, then it need be and can be applied only to a very few, and those few psychoanalyses undertaken are for the advancement of theory formation and for research purposes. It if be a natural science, then many more individuals may be psychoanalyzed with a therapeutic goal in mind, and advances of a research or theoretical nature will be added benefits.

While statistical and other outcome studies have not been adequately carried out with regard to psychoanalysis for a variety of reasons, there remains the clinical impression held by many that therapeutic gains are achieved by the procedure (Stone, 1975). These gains are of sufficient magnitude to warrant its continued use for therapeutic reasons. Therefore, one is warranted in recommending the procedure as treatment.

The implications for training are self-evident in that, if psychoanalysis should be utilized only for aims of research and theory formation, then few psychoanalysts would be needed and these few would have to be carefully selected, carefully educated, and carefully utilized. On the other hand, following the assumption of the therapeutic value of psychoanalysis, the teaching of psychoanalysis as a technique is in the best medical and scientific tradition, as well as being for the ultimate benefit of people. This is the course taken by psychoanalytic societies and institutes around the world, so there are an ever increasing number of psychoanalysts entering the field and ultimate membership in the International Psycho-Analytic Association.

Be that as it may, around the world, both the patient and the psychoanalyst assume that the treatment will be of some therapeutic benefit to the patient. The psychoanalyst may have arrived at this conclusion by virtue of his own clinical experience or by virtue of the experience of others whom he respects. Either way, he undertakes a psychoanalysis with the assumption that there will be a therapeutic gain to the patient.

A psychoanalyst undertaking a properly conducted psychoanalysis proceeds with certain assumptions, regardless of the theoretical framework within which he operates. The basic assumption is that much of the mental life of a patient, as of anyone, is unconscious. The analyst anticipates there will be resistances encountered when his procedure attempts to make the unconscious mental content conscious to the patient. Again, regardless of his theoretical frame of reference, he assumes that transference manifestations will appear at some time in varying forms and in varying degrees. He is prepared to look for these and to respond, within his frame of reference, appropriately to them. Since he assumes that the therapeutic benefits of psychoanalysis will come through exploring the mental life of the patient from its earliest periods up to the present time, he will employ a method of free association as a means of obtaining access to that mental life. He is fully prepared for difficulties in achieving the goal of free association, but he is ready to utilize various approaches that will enhance the free-association method. One of the techniques utilized everywhere is that of verbal interpretation of the patient's communications.

The analyst assumes that part of his role in the psychoanalytic situation is to hear, receive, and understand the communications transmitted to him both verbally and nonverbally by the patient. Based upon that hearing and understanding, the analyst will then utilize his interpretive approach to gain further access to the inner life of the patient, to further the utilization of the free-association method and make it still more free, and, at the same time, to give meaning and added understanding to various elements of the patient's communications. Finally, part of the more or less general approach utilized everywhere to facilitate the procedure will include arrangements about frequency of sessions (usually four to five times a week, although occasionally only three), fees, use of the couch, and application of the rule of "abstinence" by the analyst.

The essential features of the psychoanalytic situation are designed to facilitate the psychoanalytic undertaking, which has as its goal a variety of outcomes. To the patient, the outcome is the therapeutic benefit in terms of symptomatic relief, while to the analyst the outcome may include, depending upon his point of view and frame of reference, the working through of inner conflicts (either intersystemic or intrasystemic) derived from earlier levels of development and manifesting themselves in the current life of the patient. To some analysts, these conflicts may arise primarily from an oedipal level of development and be focused there, regardless of what other factors may enter into them. To other analysts, the conflicts are inevitably preoedipal and derived from earlier levels of infantile development. To some analysts, the conflicts may be based upon fantasies derived from the very earliest periods of life and represent inevitable developmental stages within the first six to nine months of life, which cannot be adequately worked through without the assistance of psychoanalysis and a psychoanalyst.

To many analysts, the patient's inner life might be dominated by failures of development, and the goal of psychoanalysis is therefore to remove blocks and barriers that precluded the normal unfolding of developmental stages. To some, the goal of psychoanalysis is to correct either vicissitudes of aggressive or libidinal instinctual maladjustments or vicissitudes of the earlier relationships with objects and a failure of object-seeking aims. Finally, the impingement of reality (external reality in particular), the nature of the early care-taking objects, or other reality-oriented experiences will also play a role and must be worked through in the course of a successful psychoanalysis. Thus, the theoretical framework utilized by the analyst will determine the goals and aims of the psychoanalytic undertaking, although it will not in any way change the outward form and the various procedures utilized in the course of a psychoanalysis.

The question then arises how each of these various goals

might be obtained if the procedures utilized are the same and if the ultimate aim of a psychoanalysis is achieved. The only variable in the procedures just described is in the content of the interpretations and interventions of the analyst as derived from the patient's communications. It would therefore seem that either the content of the psychoanalytic intervention is important in determining the nature of the ultimate outcome, whatever outcome might be aimed at, or that one or more of the more invariant procedures played a role in the outcome achieved. For the purposes of discussion, these have been separated out more than actually occurs in practice. In fact, the frame of reference utilized by the psychoanalyst determines the nature of the interventions he uses, their timing, their form, and their content in the course of the process of understanding the patient. For example, the therapeutic technique utilized by an ego psychologist would tend to involve interpretation of aspects of the transference relatively well into an analysis after much work had been done on defensive structures and other content. On the other hand, to a Kleinian (see Segal, 1977), interpretations of transference aspects occur very early in analysis, even in the first sessions. Again, to utilize the same contrast, a Kleinian might well interpret relatively early what an ego psychologist would interpret very late in the course of an analysis.

There are relatively invariant dimensions of the psychoanalytic situation, regardless of frame of reference. The invariant aspects of the psychoanalytic procedure include the assumption of unconscious mental activity, earlier developmental or maturational difficulties, the attempt to achieve free associations as a technical procedure, and the development of the transference of whatever nature that may become. From the analyst's side, it is the analytic interventions that are the invariant factor, that is, that such interventions are even made. This is not to suggest that the therapeutic gains achieved by psychoanalysis are merely transference gains (in the pejorative sense), but rather the fact that such gains can be made suggests that therapeutic gains come about through the fact of working with some portion of the unconscious mental life of a patient.

Freud (1937), speaking of a complete exploration of unconscious mental life, pointed out that analysis is a never-ending undertaking, that the tremendous realm of unconscious life is never exhausted. One might say, corollary to this, that the therapeutic benefits of a variety of theoretical and technical approaches rests on the fact that each of these deals with some portion of an individual's unconscious life, although no one analysis deals with all aspects. Alteration of any one portion of the inner world leads to a readjustment of the relationships between other unconscious portions of the mind, a process that goes on silently. In line with this thought is the well-known phenomenon reported by many psychoanalysts that patients will report the disappearance of problems or difficulties that have never been analyzed during the course of an analysis.

Analogous to this concept that no psychoanalysis is ever complete, that each analysis deals only with some portion of a patient's unconscious mental life, is the fact that psychoanalysis has no completely unified theory bringing together all of the findings and various theoretical implications arising from them. There is no one truth in psychoanalysis; there are a multitude of truths behind which, no doubt, lie still more complex phenomena that are yet to be uncovered. Whether at some time in the future there will be a unifying overall theory of psychoanalysis is open to question. At any rate, it does not exist at the present time, and adherents of each school of thought within the analytic field need to know each other's concepts and technical approach. Psychoanalytic theory is always derived from and tested in clinical investigation. Moreover, psychoanalytic theory has to be internally consistent as well as consistent with clinical data. Psychoanalysis enables therapeutic gains to be achieved through the illumination of various aspects of the recesses of unconscious mental life, which in a circular process contributes to psychoanalytic knowledge.

Summary

Together with some of the problems inherent in psychoanalysis as a therapy, I have described what the various schools of psychoanalysis hold in common—the basic assumptions, if you will, underlying any properly conducted psychoanalysis.

REFERENCES

Eissler, K. (1965), *Medical Orthodoxy and the Future of Psychoanalysis.* New York: International Universities Press.

Freud, S. (1937), Analysis terminable and interminable. *Standard Edition*, 23:216-253.

Kernberg, O. F. (1968), The treatment of patients with borderline personality organization. *Internat. J. Psycho-Anal.*, 49:600-619.

Kohut, H. (1971), *The Analysis of the Self.* New York: International Universities Press.

Lesche, C. (1973), On the metascience of psychoanalysis. *The Human Context*, 5:268-284.

Modell, A. (1978), The nature of psychoanalytic knowledge. *This Journal*, 26:641-658.

Ricoeur, P. (1977), The question of proof in Freud's psychoanalytic writings. *This Journal*, 25:835-871.

Segal, H. (1977), Psychoanalytic dialogue: Kleinian theory today. *This Journal*, 25:363-370.

Stone, L. (1954), The widening scope of indications for psychoanalysis. *This Journal*, 2:567-594.

—— (1975), Some problems and potentialities of present-day psychoanalysis. *Psychoanal. Quart.*, 44:331-370.

Mount Sinai School of Medicine
1 East 100th Street
New York, New York 10029

CONTEMPORARY ISSUES IN THE THEORY OF THERAPY

LEO RANGELL, M.D.

I N 1954 A CLUSTER OF PAPERS APPEARED in this journal attempting to define the essence of psychoanalysis. The thrust of those contributions was to delineate psychoanalysis from its more diffuse derivative, dynamic psychotherapy, which was then burgeoning in the United States. The historical background for this strong emergent interest stemmed from the inroads made by psychoanalysis in permeating American psychiatry at that time. One result of that success was a need to establish the borders of the more circumscribed discipline to prevent its being engulfed and rendered invisible by the larger, more eclectic science.

It is fitting that this subject, so central to our scientific and therapeutic method, serve as a background for the coming exchange occasioned by the first scientific Congress of the International Psycho-Analytical Association to be held on the American shore. Recent decades have seen a steady and increasing exchange of views between American[1] psychoanalysts and the rest of the psychoanalytic world. Our views of psychoanalysis as a process and treatment in 1979 as compared with those of 1954 will be set forth against a background of changing historical times.

The ground behind the figure today, in contrast to the picture a quarter of a century ago, is not one of expansion and engulfment but of shrinkage and separation. The psychiatric and general intellectual surround today is more questioning than embracing, and presents what Anna Freud

---

[1] Hereafter, when I say "American" I will mean "North American." South America has always been closer in psychoanalytic training and history to the English and other European psychoanalytic centers.

(1969) has described as "difficulties in the path of psycho-analysis." The obstacles are internal as well as external; they derive not only from the mood of the times and the attitudes and expectations in the minds of individuals but from changes within psychoanalysis itself, changes that affect the basic nature of the analytic process. While some of these changes result in increased clarity and precision, others produce a blurring from within.

The viewpoint from which I will describe my views today derives from a sustained interest in the subject and a continual personal exposure to the changing issues involved on the American as well as the international scene (Green, 1975; Rangell, 1975; Shengold and McLaughlin, 1976; Weinshel, 1976).[2]

Psychoanalytic controversies have recently centered around the clinical handling of anxiety by Freudians and Kleinians (Joseph, 1978; Rangell, 1978), the works of Kohut (1971, 1977), and Kernberg (1975), what Wallerstein (1978) has termed "the great metapsychology debate," around the works of George Klein (1973), Holt (1973, 1976), Gill (1973, 1976), and others, and the global revision of psychoanalytic theory suggested by Schafer (1976) with his "action language" of psychoanalysis.

Among the subjects I have chosen, three are areas of dispute, and several others are points to which I wish to add something either new or, in my opinion, not sufficiently emphasized.

The Process

The analyst still establishes the analytic atmosphere and a therapeutic alliance with the rational ego of the patient.

---

[2] These statements are schematic and not to be taken literally. There is of course no uniform or homogeneous American, English, or European view, and this is becoming increasingly the case since the lively interpenetration of influences taking place between continents.

(Every aspect of the subject at once introduces areas of disagreement and differences of concept. I will not, however, choose each one of them for enlargement.) By interpreting transference and resistances he aims to proceed from the surface to the depth. The treatment of a phobia, I suggest, can be taken as a model for the treatment of all neurosis. In a paper (1952) on the treatment of a classical phobia (the patient was an adult male with a phobia for dolls), I described the phobic object as the hub of a wheel. From the hub, numerous spokes radiate outward, each representing an origin, a motive, a cause, or a historical determinant feeding into the doll hub. The various spokes also have irregular interconnecting links joining the various parts together into a network. In his "Studies on Hysteria" (Breuer and Freud, 1893-1895), Freud employed a similar analogy of a wheel to describe psychoanalytic treatment. Regarding the pathogenic material as stratified in layers of different resistance potential, with the pathogenic nucleus at the core, he stated, "The analyst should himself undertake the opening of the inner strata and the advancement in the radial direction, while the patient should take care of the peripheral extension."

As models to demonstrate confluence of etiology and treatment, these descriptions still hold. But to the individual patient these are now, as they were in 1895, only models. While the concept of stratification is illuminating, both microscopically in an hour and macroscopically in a life, movement and insight are always irregular, are never linear, unidirectional, or even regularly circular, but always a network, a skein, an unpredictable puzzle. It is much as Freud (1913) compared analysis to chess; only the opening and closing moves could be taught and planned; everything in between is idiosyncratic.

But while the analysis gyrates in all orbits and planes, through the ebb and flow of regressions and progressions, periods of disease and plateaus of health, the movement of the treatment during the regressive half of the psychoanalytic procedure relentlessly reverses the developmental path of the neurosis to ultimately reach at least the shadows if not the substance of "the infantile neurosis." In the analysis, the latter is traced in both directions—genetically and historically back to its origins, and progressively through its developmental stages to its intermediate and present forms and effects.

Transference Versus Reconstruction

The transference neurosis is the path to the goal, the means by which the origins of the patient's neurosis become manifest. Here enters the first of the major controversies I wish to go into in some depth. Coming late to Freud and only after a struggle (1905, 1912), transference quickly came to be widely appreciated and to occupy a central position in the conduct of analysis. What I wish to point out, however, as an empirical observation—which because it is so contrary to a modern current may cause some surprise—is that this too, regardless of its appropriate and indispensable place, can be and in fact has been overdone. The analysis of transference over a period of some years, and prominently today, is often allowed to obscure all other important and necessary elements of the analytic process. A good thing has become hypertrophied and a source of complications.

The initiator of this train of thinking was Strachey (1934) who pointed to the interpretation of the here and now in the transference as the chief "mutative" event of analysis. Leaning and building upon this statement, schools as well as individuals throughout the analytic world have ever since adopted it in theory or even more widely in practice. To hear a case so described is to listen to a continuous transference interchange and to interpretations repeatedly and exclusively of transference. Transference is so directly applied to every statement emanating from the patient that often there is no build-up of a consolidated "transference neurosis" but an unending procession of transference phenomena.

Along with an increasing knowledge of the intricacies of transference and an ability to detect its manifestations where it would otherwise remain elusive has come the error of the transference being thought of not as the means but the end. Past history, intrapsychic thought, and historical material— "content" as it is called—are considered secondary and deflective of the real analysis, i.e., the analysis of the ongoing transference interplay. All else of the patient's past follows automatically, if necessary at all. "Conflicts of the remote past," wrote Strachey, remain "concerned with dead circumstances and mummified personalities." When a patient in analysis looks back "at what he once felt with his parents," writes Heimann (1956), he does so "coolly and intellectually." The analysis drains the patient's energy away from his past to the person of the analyst, where only what is "immediate" (Heimann, 1956), "at the point of urgency" (Strachey, 1934), or "happening now" (Heimann, 1956) carries conviction and therapeutic effect. Similar opinions are too numerous to attempt to annotate.

Emanating from Europe, mostly England, the centrality of transference has not been limited to the Kleinian or the British object relations school; it is being expressed increasingly strongly in the United States and squarely within the classical and structural mold as well. In a moving paper, sensitive in its subtle clinical evocations of transference, Bird (1972) carries transference to the highest and even exalted levels. Considering the first few pages Freud ever wrote on transference—the postscript to the Dora case (1905)—"among the most important of all Freud's writings," Bird goes on to state that transference "may well be the basis of all human relationships," "one of the mind's main agencies for giving birth to new ideas," and "involved in all the ego's differentiating, integrative, and creative capacities." In his subsequent writings on transference, Bird feels, which were related to his own developmental struggles, Freud was alternately brilliant and powerful, on the one hand, but retracting and perplexingly disappointing, on the other.

Gray (1973), exploring the ego's capacity to perceive intrapsychic events, emphasizes, not without balance and perspective, that concern with external reality allows the patient to detract from the immediacy of the analytic involvement. Transference-influenced thinking and behavior occurs, Gray points out, from the moment of the patient's decision to enter analysis. The most recent to express the use of transference as an overriding principle in the theory of technique is Gill (Panel, 1978; see also Gill, 1979). Based largely on his clinical and experimental research, Gill states that Fenichel neglects transference in favor of defense analysis. Taking issue with Fenichel's rules, "resistance before content" and "surface before depth," Gill considers priority at all times to lie with transference over defense.

One result of the strong move in this direction is that the transference neurosis becomes the neurosis, that antecedents and genetic roots are not only out of reach but more and more become unnecessary. Gill makes the point more explicitly than others. "The issue is in fact that of the general model of the analytic process. Is the analysis of the transference auxiliary to the analysis of the neurosis, or does the transference become the current representation of the neurosis so that its analysis becomes the equivalent of the analysis of the neurosis? My position is that the latter model is the better one."

These proposals provide an interesting follow-up to comparative views expressed by Gill and myself in 1954. In a definition of psychoanalysis I offered then (1954), I felt the need to include the resolution of both the transference and the infantile neurosis as the goal of analysis. This made for a more cumbersome definition than the one given by Gill (1954) at that time, that interpretation and resolution of the regressive transference neurosis was the essence of psychoanalytic technique. While I confess that I have always admired the greater succinctness and elegance of Gill's shorter definition, the recent discussion clarified the difference. I did not appreciate what existed then, and am relieved that I sacrificed brevity at that time for what I felt to be indispensable elements.

No small change has gradually taken place in the central rationale of psychoanalysis. To some of the authors quoted, to others perhaps less so, the genetic view has become superfluous. Out of sight or gone is the traditional view of reconstruction, of Freud's (1914) "remembering" what has been forgotten and repressed—not "repeating" or "working through," both of which can theoretically be achieved in the transference alone. It is true that for Freud the illness "is brought, piece by piece, within the field and range of operation of the treatment," but he says in the same sentence, "we have to do our therapeutic work on it, which consists in a large measure in tracing it back to the past" (p.152). More and more has this been lost. Everything outside of the actual analytic hour becomes secondary and a resistance, memories included. This is opposite to the trend of earlier years when neo-Freudians wished to externalize the face of analysis as much as possible to the social surround. The present direction is the reverse, more classical than the classical, to the extent that the external world that is eliminated includes the patient's internal as well as external past.[3]

In contrary vein, if I view what I actually do with

---

[3] In this discussion I have not gone into conflicting definitions and variants of transference, which are relevant to but would not alter the problem of this general orientation. These would include, besides the transference from past to present, displacement from the analyst to other figures, the reverse transference of Fenichel (1941a); the rational transference, also described by Fenichel, akin to and part of the therapeutic alliance; the mature transference, the primal, primitive, or basic transferences variously described by Stone (1961), Greenacre (1954), E. Bibring (1954); the basic trust of Erikson (1950); or all of these differentiated from the real or nontransference relationship described by Greenson (1972) and Greenson and Wexler (1969).

patients as an empirical observation, I spend a significant portion of my analytic time looking from transference, beyond and through it, to round out the roots from which it springs—not always or often with major reconstructions, but frequently and routinely with mini-connections. Since transference is by definition the past and the present, its revelation is not complete unless both surfaces have been exposed. And to those analysts who feel that insight flows automatically from the transference to the past, I would say that in my experience such diffusion of insight is by no means automatic but continues to require analytic work. Bird, quoting Freud, speaks of the danger that analysis, by attention to dreams, symptoms, and history, will become an "explanatory art." Clearly an opposite trend, of feeling without explanation, is equally prominent and equally incomplete. I would aim rather for "an explanatory experience" that includes both. (Nothing can take the place of actual case presentations to demonstrate the principles here being compared. For a clinical discussion that comes close to providing this see the dialogue on anxiety reported by Gaddini and Kuchenbuch [1978].)

Two final empirical observations: one is that I have found it overwhelmingly the case that a sense of conviction is not achieved from analysis of transference alone, as is claimed, without linkage to its roots. Such experiences occur frequently in life with repetition not therapy. A second is that overemphasis of transference can not only block the completion of further necessary work but can actually be harmful. The "adhesiveness of the libido" described by Freud (1937) often stems not from an unanalyzed libidinal need for attachment on the part of the patient, but from a relentlessly faulty technique which leads in the same direction, on the part of the analyst. Patients may go along with such an example of what Fenichel (1941a) calls "a monomania" of the analyst and use such transference interpretations for defensive purposes. Patients treated with excessive, even compulsive concentration on transference can emerge looking and feeling analyzed but with a pathetic and clonelike quality of dependence. They cling to their analysts, can become devotees, even benefactors of analysis, but with a shallow defensiveness through which the opposite can break through. The same end result can come from too little as too much interpretation of transference. And countertransference can lead equally in either direction. Nunberg (1926) long ago noted this complication and its relation to failures in analysis, citing a patient who failed "because the desire to get well gave place altogether to the transference."

The magnitude of the divergence we have been discussing is such that what is striking is how little open debate it has engendered in the literature (differences are no longer clearly geographic but now overlap in all areas). In a rare but strong paper criticizing "transference interpretations only," Leites (1977), quoting Anna Freud, Stone, Greenacre, Loewenstein, Brenner, and others in agreement with his view, notes how tentative and equivocal these and other authors are in espousing interpretations of content as well, as though this has somehow become a forbidden or deflecting activity in analysis. A scholarly review of the literature is included, which indicates a strange inhibition in this regard. Although Anna Freud (1969) regards the "unique role given to transference . . . [as] one of the points of controversy in the analytic world," Leites observes how little this "controversy" has been aired either in her writings or in those of others. Freud (1912) can be and is quoted on both sides of this controversy: it is on the field of transference "that the victory must be won," but it is also the phenomena of transference that "do us the inestimable service" of leading to the forgotten past. Fenichel (1941a) midway in the history of psychoanalysis took a straightforward position: transference and extratransference analysis both go on and are necessary. Menninger and Holzman (1973) are also more explicit than others: regarding resistance, transference, and content, "All three are necessary at different times."

It is not a question of transference versus reconstruction but of transference only versus transference and the original neurosis. Transference, the central armature of the therapeutic process, is not the sole activity of the analytic clinician. Past and present are continually reciprocal, transference facilitating recall of the past, and the past illuminating the current in the transference.

While analysts of diverse persuasion have been quoted as uniting on the centrality of transference, the contents of their interpretations, i.e., the intrapsychic contents to which their interventions lead, vary widely with their theoretical orientations. The Kleinians generally present interpretations beyond data and below defenses, memories, or preconscious readiness. Object relations analysts starting equally from transference stress dyadic experiences of separation-individuation, with an emphasis which appears exclusive on subject-object relations, projective, introjective, and retrojective mechanisms. Analysts backed by ego- and structural theory who also give priority to transference phenomena generally impart interpretations of intrapsychic conflict in principle connected with associative data. While the interventions may seem forced or to block other important elements, they are characteristically closer to rational thought processes and under the aegis of applying secondary- to primary-process mentation. Structural concepts can of course also become reified and irrational. And interpretations made without regard to defense, as described in the preferred formulation of Gill, may at times also be unavailable to secondary-process judgment.

Oedipal—Preoedipal

To continue the process: What is the patient's past neurosis, "the infantile neurosis" to which analysis leads (this is predicated on the view I have been presenting that the transference neurosis is the path and the means to that end)? Here is the logical area from which to compare methods of treatment, considering how much technique is bound to views of etiology. From the beginnings of psychoanalysis separate schools have arisen over divergent theories of the oedipal and preoedipal years, the relative roles of castration and separation, sexual conflicts versus problems of self-differentiation, the early-mother relation versus later triangular conflicts of the oedipal period.

The hope is always to base treatment on more accurate knowledge. The "widened scope" of 1954, which extended analysis to pregenital pathology, was felt to require sharpening of the border between psychoanalysis and psychotherapy. The Kleinians, going beyond this to the first year of life, were more secure in extending the analytic method to this earliest period with confidence in the validity and efficacy of their connections. Recent developments in the seventies on narcissism and borderlines move upward again to the separation-individuation phase, with a new look at early self-object relations, but also with new theoretical proposals and orientations.

Apropos of the subject of narcissism and borderlines, in addition to the wide interest in the role of transference in these cases, there is an equal interest in primitive stages and their reconstruction. Kohut (1971, 1977), one of the two most widely followed in this area, does deal strongly with the transference in his method of treatment, emphasizing his particular theories and method of handling narcissistic transference as central to the achieving of his therapeutic results. Reconstructions, however, of the earliest developmental phases of the "self" are also copiously included in his clinical case histories. Kernberg (1975), the other major contributor in this field, generally balances transference and reconstruction, using both energetically and with obvious reciprocal enhancement.

Reconstruction has always been to the oedipal and preoedipal period. Whether this latest era of research into narcissistic states has (a) reached a new source of origins hitherto inaccessible to analysis, (b) sharpened the instrument with which to make contact with such a period, or (c) added new and significant changes to psychoanalytic theory, as is claimed, are all open to question. We are now at a point which inevitably follows the period of excitement which takes place when scientific work is subject to the excesses of group psychology.

The cases reported during this surge of activity are, in my opinion, not a different stratum of patients upon whom analytic treatment was now being applied than cases treated by others before or since. Some original "classic" cases of Freud would be "borderline" by today's terms. Kohut's cases of alienation and narcissistic concerns have the same psychopathology as the foregrounds or backgrounds of neurotic cases which I and other analysts have had in analysis for many years. Kernberg's selection of problems around splitting, of fusion of self and object and the failure to differentiate, of good and bad kept apart in self- and object representations, of unresolved conflicts over aggression, of a failure of fusion of aggression and libido, occur commonly but again over the entire spectrum of pathology. Changing styles and increased complexity do not make for the diagnosis of borderline. Narcissism is like anxiety, ubiquitous and with infinite variations. In general, these are the patients of the "widened scope" (Stone, 1954) of the fifties, or even earlier, Reich's (1933-1934) character cases brought up to today's social style. Because we know more does not mean that the patients are more disturbed.

The helpful observations that have been made apply to all cases, not just this segment. In fact, rather than seeing these cases initiating new methods to be applied to others, the reverse has been true—accepted procedures have been seen to apply to these cases as well. That transference idealization, for example, should not necessarily be analyzed, as Kohut accentuates in the treatment of these patients, is true at times in all cases and for other transference mechanisms as well, as I pointed out in the discussion of transference above. Interpretations of this as of other unconscious elements depend on the status of anxiety with regard to impulse and defense. Other aspects of Kohut's suggestions, which amount to complicity with the patient's distortions, are open to question equally in the cases he is speaking about as in all others. Similarly, what is valid about splitting or the vicissitudes of self- and object representations, which Kernberg contributes, applies to all patients, not specifically to the "more disturbed." Kernberg, for his part, has made more use of standard analysis in many of these cases than he has of the reverse, extending special parameters in the opposite direction.

An interesting comparison can be seen between the two major contributors to this field from the standpoint of their developing basic theories. While Kohut's ideas were first presented (1971) as within existing psychoanalytic theory, his new "psychology of the self" (1977) is considered to replace structural and metapsychologic theory. We seem to be witnessing a current version of Erikson's (1956) "ego identity" of a few decades ago, which many thought of as underplaying the unconscious; more is lost in explanatory power than gained by these replacements in basic theory.

In the case of Kernberg's contributions, the opposite trend seems to be in process. While first presenting his theoretical orientations as new explanations of ambivalence, conflict, and symptom formation, his direction has since gradually moved toward and into the mainstream of psychoanalytic theory. Kernberg's subsequent more detailed descriptions of the vicissitudes of self- and object representations have become more and more confluent with the formulations of Jacobson (1964), with the theories of Mahler (Mahler and Furer, 1968; Mahler et al., 1975), Hartmann

(1950), and Rapaport (1959) before him, and with techniques and parameters recommended by Stone (1961), Loewenstein (1958), and others. His recommendations for psychoanalytic treatment for patients with severe psychopathology who qualify for it similarly correspond with basic analytic procedures. Kernberg (1979) states that there is no borderline patient without oedipal conflicts, albeit distorted by pre-existing ones, which is confluent with what has always been thought.

I would stress and have us benefit from continuities as much as separations. Fixations and regressions have always connected earlier with later pathology, making for a continuum of understanding between them. The recent work referred to has stressed the extension of psychoanalysis into borderline and narcissistic phenomena, just as developmental and etiological studies have carried our understanding in the reverse direction. Complementary to these clinical findings, a spurt in experimental research and direct observations on the separation-individuation phase has also linked the two early levels of development from which differences of approach have stemmed. Mahler (Mahler and Furer, 1968; Mahler et al., 1975) has recently done for separation-individuation and its subphases what Freud and others had accomplished over years about libidinal and ego phases culminating at the oedipal-phallic level. Roiphe (1968) and Galenson and Roiphe (1974; Roiphe and Galenson, 1972) have further linked oedipal and preoedipal stages by demonstrating what clinicians had always suspected and felt, the ubiquitous preludes to genital conflicts in the second year of life bridging between oral and phallic levels in both sexes. Older contributions which link early and later levels, not sufficiently appreciated in terms of today's interests, are Lewin's (1933) paper on the body as phallus and Fenichel's (1936) subsequent work on the girl as phallus. Both show how self and phallus can have an intrapsychic link and be used as interchangeable symbols one for the other, a thought which should find a place in Kohut's theory of the self.

The question comes up of how applicable infant and child observations are to the clinical situation. Although the value of child analysis to the analysis of adults has also been questioned (Brenner, in Weinshel, 1976), many analysts of both children and adults attest to the mutuality between their work and how knowledge derived from each can be of aid to the other. While care should be taken not to impose theory on clinic, and many interpretative "leaps" to earliest phenomena are beyond data or credibility, Greenacre (1975), Blum (1974, 1977), and the clinical-theoretical writings of many others have shown how far reconstruction can be accomplished with reliable methodology, rationality, and conviction.

To return to technique: the analyst roams. I have described how he moves between transference and nontransference, between phenomena stemming from early and later stages of development. Conflicts in all patients present derivatives of all levels, oedipal in borderlines, and separation-individuation, including rapprochement, (Mahler et al., 1975) throughout life. With his free-floating attention, the analyst oversees the patient's associations to past and present, the transference and external figures, the unconscious and reality, dreams, symptoms, memories, and fantasies, the trivial and everyday. Any fixation point is to be avoided and overcome. It is like a needle on an instrument panel which, when it gets stuck, needs to be tapped so that it may move freely again over the field.

Any repetitive pattern can be a defense, an alerting signal for the analyst to step in. Fenichel (1941a) has pointed out the fallacy and rigidity of the analyst's excessive passivity. In a description still applicable today, he differentiates necessary activity on the part of the analyst from the manipulative role-playing advocated by Ferenczi and Rank (1923) and developed into a more global and systematic theory in later years by Alexander (Alexander, French et al., 1946). Bibring (1954) made explicit the therapeutic maneuvers and types of activity engaged in by the analyst as compared to the psychotherapist.

Emphasis of one aspect at the expense of another, dreams over waking life, sexual conflicts over issues of security, infantile over later problems, can stem from an attitude of the analyst as well as from the patient. Resistances and defenses without what is defended against, even genetic reconstructions without reconstruction upward, may reflect, besides countertransference, an analyst's theoretical orientation or even his immersion in a research of the moment and does not speak for his even interest in the life of the patient.

This attention to the totality of the associative range goes with the view of analysis as a general psychology, another controversial point. Starting with an interest in the patient's conflicts, the analyst does not turn his attention away from the conflict-free to which these lead. Periods of crisis and solution each have their days. In a patient now an adult, analysis of his past and present should not fail to illuminate the nodal period of his coming into maturity, the psychological soil from which he made his crucial choices of occupation, marriage, where he chose to settle and live his life, in relation to parents and early figures. The pursuit of conflict, as the analysis of a dream, leads to a periphery in life's activities which becomes open-ended and indefinite, as Freud (1900) describes every dream as leading from the known to the unknown, to "a nexus of obscurity" into which it fades. A recurring theme in different forms is the ubiquitous anxiety sequence which is analyzed wherever it appears and can be understood.

Cognitive-Affective Duality

How does the analyst acquire his knowledge and convey back to the patient the data he accumulates? Here is an area of cognitive-affective duality at the heart of the psychoanalytic method. Fenichel (1941a) points to the Scylla and Charybdis between knowing and feeling, intellectually formulating an understanding of the case and empathically reverberating to the patient's affective experiences. Directed at that time to Reik's (1933) distrust of theory, that having a "blueprint" will only constrict the patient, the same dilemma exists today and is international in scope. Comparable to Reik's fear in the thirties, is Bion's (1970) psychological-philosophic stance against the analyst's being burdened by knowledge, memory, or understanding, all of which, Bion feels, conspire against fact and truth. Though this stance is in essence inconsistent with an analytic alliance and analytic work, it elicits agreement from various segments of the analytic world.

The truth is that both are necessary and neither is contradictory to nor exclusive of the other. The humanist and scientist are combined in the analyst. So are common sense and being natural contained in his stance, as described and demonstrated repeatedly by Fenichel in examples of his technique. This has also been emphasized recently by Lipton (1977) who pointed to Freud's "natural" attitudes in his clinical work with his early patients. Isakower (1957) is especially remembered by his supervisees for imparting to them a sense of how they were to fuse primary- and secondary-process receptors into their "analyzing instruments."

Empathy, however, not only necessary but indispensable, is not to be confused with countertransference. Here, another area of debate and unclarity exists. Occurring universally, is countertransference a means or a complication of treatment? Without going into this subject further here, I believe and have expressed myself elsewhere toward the latter view. Countertransference, never absent to some degree, should be understood as much as possible, the part attributable to the patient's behavior (as an afferent stimulus to the analyst) utilized in the analysis, and the part emanating from the analyst's unconscious controlled and eliminated from interfering wherever it can be.

All of the problem areas discussed so far can be subsumed under a more inclusive conflict, an anti-intellect, antirationality, antiscience, wave, part of an oscillation between the same two poles ever present in the larger culture. To some extent such a sentiment (a combination of affect and ideation) contains the rational within it, opposing intellectuality as a defense, a repressive measure in itself, as when Loewald (1978) points to "the madness of unbridled rationality." In part, however, it speaks directly for the irrational, on the basis that secondary process is incompatible with the creative in man, a fallacy which used to be commonly pointed out about the neurotic artist who approaches the analyst with the same question in mind.

This duality, present also in psychiatry and the wider humanistic sciences, has shown itself in psychoanalysis from the beginning and perhaps always will. From Freud-Jung through Ferenczi-Rank-Reik versus Fenichel-Hartmann-Rapaport, to the later Fenichel-Alexander splits in the United States, the current Kleinian-Freudian, the transference-reconstruction, oedipal-preoedipal, object relations versus intrapsychic-metapsychologic, and even, to some extent, to the "two theories versus one," all represent the questioning of the rational, scientific, left-hemispheric, "truth"-seeking side of analysis considered as a threat, not a help, to the affective, right-hemispheric, creative life. Rationality in all of these conflicts is said to "dehumanize" the patient. I have made the point that this assumption is unfounded in each duality I have taken up.

To study the patient's double-sided (or better, tripartite) psychic life, the analyst uses both the cognitive and affective sides of his analytic instrument. All four surfaces, two from each participant, mesh and interact in the psychoanalytic process. The material from both is then subordinated, to be sure, to rational understanding which psychoanalysis cannot disown as its central guide. "The subject-matter not the method of analysis is irrational," says Fenichel (1941a). Alexander's "corrective emotional experience" is a valid component of the treatment process and should not be denied or disengaged from, as it has been by classical analysts generally and by some of the writers discussed here, in espousing their respective points of view (Kohut, 1971; Gill, 1978). Emotional experiences that are corrective and therapeutic are part of all analytic procedures. But the affective is incomplete without being fused with the rational, which Alexander downplays and others minimize from other directions as well. We do not analyze a dream with a dream. Blum (1979) cogently speaks of the "creative insight" we impart. The insightful or partially insightful creativity is then left to the patient's ego integration. Kohut (1977), in his concluding statement, subordinates insight to experience both in the classical, structural-conflict neuroses and in disorders of the self, and offers a different perspective on the role of truth as a supraordinate value in the treatment process. In the final analysis, each analyst, and every patient, ultimately, too, must decide the right combination for himself.

At the Core of Change

This leads to the other side of the therapeutic coin, from the activities of the analyst to the role of the patient. Having spoken so far about the analyst's role, what does the patient do with what he experiences and is told? What takes place in the patient to proceed and make progress, even ultimately to the end and a cure? What cures?

To this phase of the analytic process, not to be minimized in the attention it is due, I wish to offer, not attempts at clarification or choices between alternatives, but what I hope is a contribution to the literature on this subject. A factor I wish to emphasize which is not sufficiently explicit is that an active role on the part of the patient is necessary and must be continuously enlisted.

Let me introduce the subject clinically by a short exchange with a patient. For a period of time a patient's response to every interpretation or achievement of a piece of insight was "So what?" or "So what happens now?" or "So what am I supposed to do?" and such. The question (or group of questions) was one I soon came to feel as a genuine and understandable seeking of information. What was the purpose of what we were doing, he was asking, what was he to know, and what was he supposed to do? "You ask 'So what?'," I told him one day, "and not 'So why?'" In this interpretation, for that is what it was, I pointed to the absence of psychological curiosity about the roots of each newly exposed piece of irrational behavior. Each piece of insight as it was arrived at by analytic work contained both an explanation and a new fact to be explained. "You are anxious because you thought your mother would leave you." "You thought your mother would leave you because you had bad wishes toward her." "You had bad wishes toward her because. . . ." The progression was toward crucial oedipal days of his life, which were being reached by increments, in typical analytic zigzag paths, with stops and starts.

The patient was asking "So what?" at steps along the way partly from impatience to have his behavior improve more rapidly, and partly to block the progression to more painful insights. He was not being reprimanded, but being given an idea, the absorption of which was in fact necessary for his continuing role in the treatment. Nor was he being ordered to think along these lines. The patient received the idea (not after one but several times) as an interesting and, as it turned out, useful interpretation, which was crucial for his continuing to partake in the analysis. Yes, why didn't he automatically care more about "Why?" Every patient in analysis needs precisely that motivation for progress and for the effects of the analysis to take place. Only after a series of "whys" have struck a kind of bottom for at least that sequence—there are many such series, and eventually they converge or at least interrelate; here are the hub or many hubs and spokes of the wheel again—can the patient come to at least some intermediate platform upon which he can say, "Aha, so that is why," and at times, "So that is what I can do about it." If, instead, the patient asks again, "So what?" this is where the analyst acts, in free-floating as in attached (phobic) anxiety. "So now you can face the cause and do what you choose to do," he says, i.e., as with the patient who can now approach the phobic object if he chooses. I will later elaborate on this crucial point of choice after taking up a few other sections of this subject.

First, to return to the question: what causes change and—where it occurs—cure? What comes from the analyst and what is necessary from the patient? Much has been written, many discussions held, and many answers given; most are about the first question, few about the second. No one has ever felt that the answers were sufficient. The questions and some of the answers still necessary to give have to do with what I consider the core of the process of change.

Freud left some timeless aphorisms: "To make the unconscious conscious" in the old but still useful topographic sense; "Where id was there ego shall be," in more modern structural terms; to "remove the resistances," added Fenichel (1941a) in a dynamic formula. Loewald (1978) recently adds the reverse: "Where ego is there id shall come into being again to renew the life of the ego and of reason." Reason and rationality can also become irrational, Loewald emphasizes; the id has been too much relegated to oblivion by traditional theory and methods; instincts, affects, primitivity must have their place as well. Here is a rapprochement with the "feeling" half of the analytic world; only a combination of affect and cognition constitutes the means and ends of analytic cure.

Intellectual and emotional insight together, to be

effective, by undoing unconscious structuralized conflicts release psychic energy for the pursuit of healthier activities and more appropriate channels for discharge. Along the way toward achieving this is a constant series of microidentifications (Kohut's "transmuting internalizations") with the analyzing function of the analyst, which enables analysis to take place, first partially and experimentally, then with more familiarity and sureness, and finally, with an autonomy which one hopes will continue with self-analysis afterward. This process is not "introjection of the analyst," which is still believed and advocated by individuals and even schools. The latter, when it occurs, needs to be analyzed, just as idealization of the analyst needs to be, although carefully timed and of course with defenses considered. Failure in this respect leads to similar not uncommon outcomes which I took up under other unresolved issues of transference, of patients who adhere to the analyst or psychoanalysis—the object symbiosed to changes, not symbiosis—after which, when these wear down, other objects and groups come along to whom they cling. This is currently an important sociocultural factor to be aware of; analysis should help to resolve not foster it.

I would like to take this opportunity to briefly include several special considerations in determining treatment outcome which I have long thought about and which I feel have been neglected.

A Matter of Quantity

The first is a quantitative factor, which I feel needs to be added in establishing goals, assessing progress, acknowledging limitations, and understanding cases which begin to look like "negative therapeutic reactions." The well-known factors considered to explain the latter: the unconscious sense of guilt, need for punishment, even a basic masochistic nature (Freud, 1920) are not, in my opinion, all or sometimes even basic in explaining the recalcitrance of certain patients. What I have in mind is a quantitative factor in the relationship between the subject being analyzed (I do not mean the patient but the mental condition for which he comes) and the analytic method being used. Psychic trauma, I have pointed out (1973), is not a circumscribed and time-limited event even when it does happen in dramatic and isolated form. Traumatic events and even chronic traumatic *conditions* acquire their accumulated weight not during the actual times, acute or chronic, in which they originally take place, but by a much more significant factor of psychic life.

Traumatic experiences are repeated in memory and unconscious fantasy countless, even infinite, numbers of times. In a patient now an adult they have lasted his lifetime; this is common experience. Comparable to the long-release capsules administered to patients instead of the tablet or capsule which acts for a limited time, psychic traumata, after the initial events, are broken up into small chronic-release doses in an effort to overcome their traumatic effects. Microscopic and spread out, these result in the "strain trauma," which also occurs from ongoing traumatic conditions (Kris, 1956; Sandler, 1967; Solnit and Kris, 1967), in which the stimulus barrier is not rent but bent. This is what Fenichel (1945) means by his statement that there is traumatic neurosis behind every psychoneurosis.

Unconscious fantasies revolving around traumata which themselves consist of impulse-defense compromise formations interspersed with traumatic memories, together serve the same purpose as traumatic dreams, i.e., attempts to solve and work through the original traumata. Repetition compulsion can be due not only to pressure of instincts but to habitual attempts by the ego to master such events. It is against the chronic strain that results and not the limited times of the original occurrences that the analytic experience is pitted. It can be an uneven battle. Besides helping to explain frenetic conditions in human relationships, this is why I stated in the same paper (1973) that analyzing the unconscious is at times like shining a flashlight into the Grand Canyon.

Signal Anxiety

A second factor crucial in this narrative of the course of a psychoanalytic therapy is the history and changes in signal anxiety. Considering how its central role is acknowledged both in neurosogenesis and as the motive for treatment, it is surprising how little attention is paid to the vicissitudes of signal anxiety as an indicator of progress and of the end result. While wide insights expand the possibilities of life as a result of analysis, the final result upon which I wish to comment (not chronologically but in terms of effects on causality) is a two-step process which is a *sine qua non* at the core of treatment. Here, to again use the metaphor I started with, is the hub of the therapeutic wheel.

What takes place as a direct result of analysis is an intrapsychic change during the "microdynamic" sequence (Rangell, 1963a, 1963b, 1969a), which is a routine part of thought. Intrapsychic trial actions, which still go on routinely, result now less in signals of danger, the latter being more limited to realistic fear. The result is a wider choice for the ego of what it can safely do. What the patient, with his newly expanded ego possibilities, unconsciously chooses to do next is then his own. Anxiety or the lack of it is what occurs automatically (Schur, 1953, 1958; Rangell, 1955, 1968). The rest is the patient's active even if unconscious choice.

The Role of the Patient

This leads into my final point, the second of the two-step process at the final core of therapy. With less signal anxiety the patient has more choice. The next necessary move after every such happening is his. A last link necessary in the therapeutic chain without which change cannot occur has, in my opinion, remained virtually unspoken in the theory of therapy. Yet its failure to take place can vitiate the entire work.

Broadly speaking, the following sequence takes place. The patient brings material. The analyst gives explanations.[4] Anxiety does or does not diminish automatically as a result. What happens after that is for the patient to actively do. I am not speaking of an overt, conscious, or motor act, but of an active rather than passive process in the unconscious. If anxiety is less, the patient's choices are more but, in any case, the choices are his. Precedents for such a stance have been laid down throughout the analysis by the analyst's having left all decisions to him in the past.

The nature of the activity to which I am referring is what I have described (1969b, 1971) as the unconscious roots of the decision-making process, the ego's "actions" in routine life following the results of "trial actions" in the unconscious. After the testing for anxiety, it is the subsequent process that opens the "sluices"—a term borrowed from Rapaport—to behavior, from affects to action to symptoms or the gamut of idiosyncratic and ad hoc responses characteristic of any individual person.

It was a similar thought of an active process that induced Schafer (1976) to adopt his "action language" of psycho-analysis, with which he then wished to replace metapsychologic and structural theory. G. Klein (1973) similarly preferred the whole "person" to the ego as the executive

---

[4] Explanations of transference and past origins. I am summarizing globally here. While the discussions have led from both of these mainly to objects in the past and present, I have omitted the more purely intrapsychic analysis of unconscious fantasies and their accompanying affects. Also not taken up are the analysis of specific affects, the relative roles of anxiety and depression (Brenner, 1975), the destratification of affects in the clinical situation, and the role of anxiety behind other affects of unpleasure, the last two of which were elaborated in the Congress in Jerusalem (Rangell, 1978).

agent. And Kohut (1977) feels that his new "psychology of the self" is now able to include choice, intention, and action into theory, where he could not comfortably fit these in before. I feel that these phenomena had already been included in a coherent explanation some years before within the existing metapsychologic and structural view.

In contrast, however, the literature on technique characteristically assumes an opposite stream of effects predominantly automatic in occurrence. From Freud and the pioneers through to the later texts on technique, what are usually emphasized as the peak events are the liberation of the ego by the solution of conflict, after which changes spontaneously occur. Energy is liberated, new channels found, all more or less in a passive patient. I cannot do justice to individual texts for lack of space, but am describing a general view on these points by the reading and practicing analytic public. Occasionally, more accurate phrases are used, such as that analysis "makes possible" or offers patients "a possibility of working out a viable, non-neurotic, solution" (Waelder, 1960). Mostly, such ideas are obscured by a more universal concept of a series of events which just "happen" spontaneously. Their occasional appearance, however, attests to the fact that in practice one generally "knows" better.[5]

Acknowledged or not, empirically, this is a point at which the patient may choose to call a halt. Many refractory cases considered "negative therapeutic reactions" for any of the conventional mechanisms mentioned above actually only

---

[5] The trial action is active, the anxiety automatic, the subsequent path a result of an active process again. I cannot elaborate here on the subject of activity-passivity-automaticity except to say that, besides anxiety and affects as automatic phenomena—which can, however, be "tamed" and brought under partial control (Fenichel, 1941b; Jacobson, 1953)—structural change, for example, can also fall under this same category of automatic development. I will also not, however, go into the difficult subject of structural change which has been made even more ambiguous by concepts related to it introduced in the literature on narcissism and borderlines.

"choose" to change less than the analyst may think desirable. A variety of further dynamic situations are now possible.

One is that the choices, even with neurotic anxiety sharply diminished, may still not be as free as the analyst thinks or the patient would like. Strictured and constrained even after the liberation from conflict, internal as well as external forces may still hem him in. Reality factors and paranosic gains from without can be matched by internal limitations which mitigate equally against the expansion of life. The patient may not be capable of sublimatory activity or possess the wisdom, humor, talent, or creativity which Kohut asserts can be liberated with a change in the self. Limited ego capacities, narrowness if not deficiencies, a paucity of learned information or of developed channels of discharge, excessive passivity, or a low level of instinctual strengths, libidinal or aggressive, may determine the continuation of life patterns long present without a strong motivation or ability making for a possibility of significant change. Growth and development, moreover, capacities for which can be built in, also cannot be expected to progress more energetically after conflicts have been removed than was characteristic of the individual before the conflicts began. Loewald (1978) stresses the moral function of analysis as the patient owning up to his past to direct his present and future. Is this not the integrative function of the ego in the broadest sense, to acquire hegemony over one's history, the id, superego, and through the values incorporated in the latter, one's social surround?

Summary

I have drawn comparisons of psychoanalysis as a process and as a treatment between 1954 and 1979. I have selected for discussion controversies centering on the subjects of transference versus reconstruction, oedipal versus preoedipal, and the cognitive-affective duality. Also considered were the quantitative factors in the negative therapeutic reaction, the fate of signal anxiety, and the role of the patient in the process of cure.

REFERENCES

Alexander, F., French, T. M., et al. (1946), *Psychoanalytic Therapy: Principles and Application.* New York: Ronald Press.

Bibring, E. (1954), Psychoanalysis and the dynamic psychotherapies. *This Journal,* 2:745-770.

Bion, W. R. (1970), *Attention and Interpretation: A Scientific Approach to Insight in Psychoanalysis and Groups.* New York: Basic Books.

Bird, B. (1972), Notes on transference: Universal phenomenon and hardest part of analysis. *This Journal,* 20:267-301.

Blum, H. P. (1974), The borderline childhood of the Wolf Man. *This Journal,* 22:721-742.

———— (1977), The prototype of preoedipal reconstruction. *This Journal,* 25:757-785.

———— (1979), The curative and creative aspects of insight. *This Journal,* 27 (Suppl.):41-69.

Brenner, C. (1975), Affects and psychic conflict. *Psychoanal. Quart.,* 44:5-28.

Breuer, J. & Freud, S. (1893-1895), Studies on hysteria. *Standard Edition,* 2.

Erikson, E. H. (1950), *Childhood and Society.* New York: Norton.

———— (1956), The problem of ego identity. *This Journal,* 4:56-121.

Fenichel, O. (1936), The symbolic equation: Girl=phallus. In: *Collected Papers,* 2nd series. New York: Norton, 1954, pp. 3-18.

———— (1941a), *Problems of Psychoanalytic Technique.* New York: The Psychoanalytic Quarterly, Inc.

———— (1941b), The ego and the affects. In: *Collected Papers,* 2nd series. New York: Norton, 1954, pp. 215-227.

———— (1945), *The Psychoanalytic Theory of Neurosis.* New York: Norton.

Ferenczi, S. & Rank, O. (1923), *The Development of Psychoanalysis.* New York: Dover, 1956.

Freud, A. (1969), Difficulties in the path of psychoanalysis: A confrontation of past with present viewpoints. *Writings,* 7:124-156. New York: International Universities Press, 1971.

Freud, S. (1900), The interpretation of dreams. *Standard Edition,* 4 & 5.

———— (1905), Fragment of an analysis of a case of hysteria. *Standard Edition,* 7:3-122.

———— (1912), The dynamics of transference. *Standard Edition,* 12:99-108.

———— (1913), On beginning the treatment. *Standard Edition,* 12:121-144.

———— (1914), Remembering, repeating and working-through. *Standard Edition,* 12:145-156.

———— (1920), Beyond the pleasure principle. *Standard Edition,* 18:1-64.

———— (1937), Analysis terminable and interminable. *Standard Edition,* 23:209-253.

Gaddini, E. & Kuchenbuch, A. (1978), Dialogue on "Different types of anxiety and their handling in the psychoanalytic situation." *Internat. J. Psycho-Anal.*, 59:237-243.

Galenson, E. & Roiphe, H. (1974), The emergence of genital awareness during the second year of life. In: *Sex Differences and Behavior*, ed. R. C. Friedman, R. M. Richart, & R. L. Van der Wiele. New York: Wiley, pp. 223-231.

Gill, M. M. (1954), Psychoanalysis and exploratory psychotherapy. *This Journal*, 2:771-797.

—— (1973), Introduction to George Klein's "Two Theories or One?" *Bull. Menninger Clinic*, 37:99-101.

—— (1976), Metapsychology is not psychology. In: *Psychology Versus Metapsychology: Psychoanalytic Essays in Memory of George S. Klein*, ed. M. M. Gill & P. S. Holzman. *Psychol. Issues*, Monogr. 36. New York: International Universities Press, pp. 71-105.

—— (1978), The transference in Fenichel's *Problems of Psychoanalytic Technique*. Panel on Psychoanalytic Classics Revisited. American Psychoanalytic Association, New York City, December.

—— (1979), The analysis of the transference. *This Journal*, 27 (Suppl.):263-288.

Gray, P. (1973), Psychoanalytic technique and the ego's capacity for viewing intrapsychic activity. *This Journal*, 21:474-494.

Green, A. (1975), The analyst, symbolization and absence in the analytic setting (on changes in analytic practice and analytic experience). *Internat. J. Psycho-Anal.*, 56:1-22.

Greenacre, P. (1954), The role of transference: Practical considerations in relation to psychoanalytic therapy. In: *Emotional Growth*. New York: International Universities Press, 1971, pp. 627-640.

—— (1975), On reconstruction. *This Journal*, 23:693-712.

Greenson, R. R. (1972), Beyond transference and interpretation. In: *Explorations in Psychoanalysis*. New York: International Universities Press, 1978, pp. 441-450.

—— & Wexler, M. (1969), The nontransference relationship in the psychoanalytic situation. In: *Explorations in Psychoanalysis*. New York: International Universities Press, 1978, pp. 359-386.

Hartmann, H. (1950), Comments on the psychoanalytic theory of the ego. In: *Essays on Ego Psychology*. New York: International Universities Press, 1964, pp. 113-141.

Heimann, P. (1956), Dynamics of transferences. *Internat. J. Psycho-Anal.*, 37:303-310.

Holt, R. R. (1973), The crisis of metapsychology. Address to the American Academy of Psychoanalysis. Unpublished.

—— (1976), Drive or wish? A reconsideration of the psychoanalytic theory of motivation. In: *Psychology versus Metapsychology: Psychoanalytic Essays in Memory of George S. Klein*, ed. M. M. Gill & P. S. Holzman. *Psychol. Issues*, Monogr. 36. New York: International Universities Press, pp. 158-197.

Isakower, O. (1957), Problems of supervision. Report to the Curriculum Committee of the New York Psychoanalytic Institute. Unpublished.

Jacobson, E. (1953), The affects and their pleasure-unpleasure qualities in relation to the psychic discharge processes. In: *Drives, Affects, Behavior*, ed. R. M. Loewenstein. New York: International Universities Press, pp. 38-66.

_____ (1964), *The Self and the Object World.* New York: International Universities Press.

Joseph, B. (1978), Different types of anxiety and their handling in the analytic situation. *Internat. J. Psycho-Anal.,* 59:223-228.

Kernberg, O. F. (1975), *Borderline Conditions and Pathological Narcissism.* New York: Aronson.

_____ (1979), Some implications of object relations theory for psychoanalytic technique. *This Journal,* 27 (Suppl.):207-240.

Klein, G. S. (1973), Two theories or one? *Bull. Menninger Clinic,* 37:102-132.

Kohut, H. (1971), *The Analysis of the Self.* New York: International Universities Press.

_____ (1977), *The Restoration of the Self.* New York: International Universities Press.

Kris, E. (1956), The recovery of childhood memories in psychoanalysis. In: *Selected Papers.* New Haven: Yale University Press, 1975, pp. 301-340.

Leites, N. (1977), Transference interpretations only? *Internat. J. Psycho-Anal.,* 58:275-287.

Lewin, B. D. (1933), The body as phallus. In: *Selected Writings.* New York: The Psychoanalytic Quarterly, Inc., 1973, pp. 28-47.

Lipton, S. D. (1977), The advantages of Freud's technique as shown in his analysis of the Rat Man. *Internat. J. Psycho-Anal.,* 58:255-273.

Loewald, H. W. (1978), *Psychoanalysis and the History of the Individual.* New Haven: Yale University Press.

Loewenstein, R. M. (1958), Remarks on some variations in psychoanalytic technique. *Internat. J. Psycho-Anal.,* 39:202-210.

Mahler, M. S. & Furer, M. (1968), *On Human Symbiosis and the Vicissitudes of Individuation: Infantile Psychosis.* New York: International Universities Press.

_____ Pine, F., & Bergman, A. (1975), *The Psychological Birth of the Human Infant: Symbiosis and Individuation.* New York: Basic Books.

Menninger, K. A. & Holzman, P. S. (1973), *Theory of Psychoanalytic Technique.* New York: Basic Books.

Nunberg, H. (1926), The will to recovery. In: *Practice and Theory of Psychoanalysis,* Vol. 1. New York: International Universities Press, 1948, pp. 75-88.

Panel (1978), Psychoanalytic Classics Revisited. The American Psychoanalytic Association, December.

Rangell, L. (1952), The analysis of a doll phobia. *Internat. J. Psycho-Anal.,* 33:43-53.

_____ (1954), Similarities and differences between psychoanalysis and dynamic psychotherapy. *This Journal,* 2:734-744.

_____ (1955), On the psychoanalytic theory of anxiety: A statement of a unitary theory. *This Journal,* 3:389-414.

_____ (1963a), The scope of intrapsychic conflict: Microscopic and macroscopic considerations. *The Psychoanalytic Study of the Child,* 18:75-102. New York: International Universities Press.

_____ (1963b), Structural problems in intrapsychic conflict. *The Psychoanalytic Study of the Child,* 18:103-138. New York: International Universities Press.

_____ (1968), A further attempt to resolve the "problem of anxiety." *This Journal,* 16:371-404.

_____ (1969a), The intrapsychic process and its analysis: A recent line of thought and its current implications. *Internat. J. Psycho-Anal.*, 50:65-77.

_____ (1969b), Choice-conflict and the decision-making function of the ego: A psychoanalytic contribution to decision theory. *Internat. J. Psycho-Anal.*, 50:599-602.

_____ (1971), The decision-making process: A contribution from psychoanalysis. *The Psychoanalytic Study of the Child*, 26:425-452. New York: Quadrangle.

_____ (1973), On the cacophony of human relations. *Psychoanal. Quart.*, 42: 325-348.

_____ (1975), Psychoanalysis and the process of change: An essay on the past, present and future. *Internat. J. Psycho-Anal.*, 56:87-97.

_____ (1978), On understanding and treating anxiety and its derivatives. *Internat. J. Psycho-Anal.*, 59:229-236.

Rapaport, D. (1959), *The Structure of Psychoanalytic Theory. Psychol. Issues*, Monogr. 6. New York: International Universities Press, 1960.

Reich, W. (1933-1934), *Character Analysis*. New York: Touchstone Books, 1974.

Reik, T. (1933), New ways in psychoanalytic technique. *Internat. J. Psycho-Anal.*, 14:321-334.

Roiphe, H. (1968), On an early genital phase: With an addendum on genesis. *The Psychoanalytic Study of the Child*, 23:348-365. New York: International Universities Press.

_____ & Galenson, E. (1972), Early genital activity and the castration complex. *Psychoanal. Quart.*, 41:334-347.

Sandler, J. (1967), Trauma, strain and development. In: *Psychic Trauma*, ed. S. S. Furst. New York: Basic Books, pp. 154-174.

Schafer, R. (1976), *A New Language for Psychoanalysis*. New Haven: Yale University Press.

Schur, M. (1953), The ego in anxiety. In: *Drives, Affects, Behavior*, ed. R. M. Loewenstein. New York: International Universities Press, pp. 67-103.

_____ (1958), The ego and the id in anxiety. *The Psychoanalytic Study of the Child*, 13:190-220. New York: International Universities Press.

Shengold, L. & McLaughlin, J. T. (1976), Report on Plenary session on "Changes in psychoanalytic practice and experience: Theoretical, technical and social implications." *Internat. J. Psycho-Anal.*, 57:261-274.

Solnit, A. J. & Kris, M. (1967), Trauma and infantile experiences: A longitudinal perspective. In: *Psychic Trauma*, ed. S. S. Furst. New York: Basic Books, pp. 175-220.

Strachey, J. (1934), The nature of the therapeutic action of psychoanalysis. Reprinted in: *Internat. J. Psycho-Anal.* (1969), 50:275-292.

Stone, L. (1954), The widening scope of indications for psychoanalysis. *This Journal*, 2:567-594.

_____ (1961), *The Psychoanalytic Situation*. New York: International Universities Press.

Waelder, R. (1960), *Basic Theory of Psychoanalysis*. New York: International Universities Press.

Wallerstein, R. (1978), Psychoanalysis and academe. Paper presented at "Bridges, Psychoanalytic Essays in Honor of Leo Rangèll, M.D.," San Diego, California, September 24.

Weinshel, E. M. (1976), Concluding comments on the Congress topic. *Internat. J. Psycho-Anal.*, 57:451-460.

456 North Carmelina Avenue
Los Angeles, California 90049

THE CONCEPT OF
"CLASSICAL"   Arthur F. Valenstein, M.D.
PSYCHOANALYSIS

T HIS PAPER REFLECTS A LONG-STANDING INTEREST in comparative
studies of various psychotherapies and different approaches to clinical psychoanalysis. Perhaps it is timely, in
this era of the broadly extended scope of psychoanalysis, to
consider once again the nature of therapeutic psychoanalysis
as such; that is, in the narrower or special sense which is
implied when one speaks of "classical psychoanalysis."

When I suggest that reconsideration is indicated at this
time I do so advisedly. For example, one of the panels which
was on the scientific program of the American Psychoanalytic
Association in December 1977 was titled, "The Nature of the
Therapeutic Action of Psychoanalysis."[1] Is this so different
from the main symposium on "The Curative Factors in
Psycho-Analysis," held at the 22nd Congress of the
International Psycho-Analytical Association in Edinburgh in
1961? Twenty-five years earlier the archetypical scientific
meeting on this subject took place, the Marienbad Symposium, in 1936, on "The Theory of the Therapeutic Results of
Psycho-Analysis." Are such reappearances of essentially the
same topic indicative of a principle of redundancy which, for
whatever reason, pervades psychoanalysis and its scientific
life? Or is there a specific reason for the periodic recurrence,
perhaps at twenty-year intervals, more or less, of this
particular thematic inquiry on psychoanalytic scientific and

An earlier version of this paper was presented to the Baltimore-District of
Columbia Society for Psychoanalysis on November 19, 1977, and to the Cleveland
Psychoanalytic Society on January 20, 1978.
[1] It was followed in May, 1978, by a reciprocal panel on "The Nature of the
Therapeutic Action of Psychoanalytic Psychotherapy."

113

educational programs? Possibly there is a need to define and redefine the unique characteristics of psychoanalysis as a theoretically "curative" treatment in itself, in response to successive waves of psychotherapies which claim to be, or are actually, innovative. Many of them take as their rationale one or another feature of the psychoanalytic theory of the mind and of human behavior and, in this regard, some principle or agent particular to psychoanalytic technique as we have known it.

If we are to foresee with any clarity where psychoanalysis as a method of treatment is going, or even might best go, then we had better know where we are now, and from where we have come. By no means is it implied that we should indenture ourselves into a ritualistic observance of what has been, or inure ourselves against change, as if the past were gospel and our only source of professional security (see Stone, 1975). However, we might at least expect that significant modifications in the set and therapeutic intent and technique of clinical psychoanalysis be explicitly and reasonably set forward, and that they be subject to comparative appraisal with respect to conventional technique. Otherwise, we might very well lose what we have; lose the essential rationalism and realism of the analytic instrument and procedure, which in my experience is the very centrum of the classical psychoanalytic tradition.

Just what is meant by "classical analysis?" Is it simply a euphemism to indicate a technical continuity with analysis as it was elaborated and practiced by Freud and his immediate followers—i.e., "Freudian" psychoanalysis? Or does it imply more than historical kinship?

Is the notion that there is a definable, a succinctly describable therapeutic technique that we might call classical psychoanalysis something of a mythic belief? It has been said that *every* analysis, even of the so-called "good" or "normal neurotic," depends upon the assumption of a *normal* ego, with which we might make a working or therapeutic alliance. The paradox is, just as Freud pointed out (1937, p. 235), that "a normal ego of this sort is, like normality in general, an ideal fiction. . . . Every normal person, in fact, is only normal on the average. His ego approximates to that of the psychotic in some part or other and to a greater or lesser extent; and the degree of its remoteness from one end of the series and of its proximity to the other will furnish us with a provisional measure of what we have so indefinitely termed 'an alteration of the ego'." But has not Freud also given us a way out of our dilemma, in the very relativism which is implicit in his construct of a continuum from the ideal so-called normal to its exactly reciprocal negative-ideal of the utterly abnormal? Perhaps we can find some tangibility for our quest of a classical model for psychoanalysis if we attend more particularly to the extremes of the continuum rather than to the more ambiguous qualitative and quantitative middle sector. Perhaps it is in this diagnostic zone that we are properly guarded as to the applicability of the "standard" analytic method, and well aware that analytic technique may have to be modified to some extent in the interest of achieving therapeutic results.

To take the question now from the other side, the assumption that there is a describable psychoanalytic technique we term classical suggests that there are "unclass-ical analyses" or "deviate analysis," that is to say, analyses that have been so *modified* in technique, or in the theory of its practice, that they are no longer "classical." Do we not mean that such therapies have irretrievably departed in definitive ways from that describable standard which over time has acquired the typification known as classical? In the opinion of some analysts, including myself, such treatments probably belong more appropriately into the larger and more variegated group of psychoanalytic psychotherapies.

So, commonly, classicism is understood to signify ri-gidity. I should like to emphasize, though, that psychoanalysis as such, that is to say, classical analysis, contrary to a general and often pejorative misconception, is not necessarily rigid or clinically "precious." As a matter of fact, in an article written over fifteen years ago (1962) I stated: "The effectiveness of the classical or standard psychoanalytic method, as it has developed and endured for sixty years, is due to it being in itself (to paraphrase Hartmann) much more preadapted to the average expectable clinical situation than may usually be realized. That is to say, it is applicable to a considerable range of clinical situations, unless it is prejudiced by irreversible or unanalyzable deviations in technique or innovations which make it no longer psycho-analytical in the classical sense" (p. 319).

In searching back through the literature for a satisfactory definition, I found only a rather extended and limitedly useful one by Greenson (1958). However, I did encounter in the various discussions certain common elements which circumscribe or define the concept from within in terms of its ingredients and its essential core in practice. I noted, furthermore, that as part of a panel discussion, "Variations in Classical Psycho-Analytical Technique," read before the 20th Congress of the International Psycho-Analytical Association in Paris in 1957, Loewenstein (1958) sidestepped defining classical psychoanalytic technique and its delimitation from related therapeutic procedures. He said, "I shall refrain from this because I do not know any fool-proof definition of classical psychoanalysis. It would evidently have to be based on the importance we ascribe to the analytic way of dealing with resistance, transference, transference neurosis, and working through" (p. 202).

On the same panel Eissler (1958) stated: "One of the most challenging problems we face is to locate the borderlines, the points where the application of certain tools or combinations of tools, justified as they may be in view of the patient's personality structure, become incompatible with the requirements of classical technique" (p. 222).

With respect to defining classical psychoanalysis, Eissler (pp. 222-223) suggested:

> The science of interpretation is the bulk and main chapter of the classical psychoanalytic technique. Whether we interpret from the surface down or in the opposite direction, it is either correct or incorrect classical technique but not a variation of that technique. That term [variation] should be reserved exclusively for the introduction of tools that lie outside interpretation . . . . classical technique is . . . one in which interpretation remains the exclusive or leading or prevailing tool. . . . In my estimation what determines whether or not a psycho-analytic technique is classical depends on what vehicle carries the interpretation to its *locus operandi* in order to effect a change in the patient's personality structure. In the cathartic treatment it was hypnosis, later it was suggestion and its equivalents. It was a real triumph of Freud's ingenuity that he developed a technique in which the therapeutic agent and vehicle were of the same kind and interpretation became in principle the exclusive tool.

We might consider this the most classic of classic definitions, but then, appreciating what prevails in the actual clinical situation, wherein other principles and therapeutic agents are participatory in the analytic process, we might turn to Edward Bibring (1954) who wrote a noteworthy paper on "Psychoanalysis and the Dynamic Psychotherapies." In it, he laid the essential groundwork of conceptual formulation and terminological definition which should stand us in good stead during this time of debate which polarizes the so-called outmoded orthodoxy of classical psychoanalysis in contrast to the so-called new, more enlightened, flexible, object-oriented psychoanalysis of today, in which the *real* relationship to the analyst as a *real* person in his own right is considered to be pivotal. Bibring pointed out that insight, whether through clarification or interpretation, is by no means the only principle made use of in psychoanalysis, much less psychotherapy; although psychoanalysis proper is predominantly and ultimately dependent upon interpretation as the main therapeutic principle (the keystone to the arch) which brings about insight as the essential therapeutic agent for change. However, in his discussion he also specified the principle of manipulation as one of the basic therapeutic principles, i.e., "the employment of various emotional systems existing in the patient for the purpose of achieving therapeutic change either in the technical sense of promoting the treatment, or in the curative sense, for manipulative measures too can be employed in a technical as well as a curative way" (pp. 750-751). The latter clearly is what is involved in interpersonally promoted experiential effects leading to transference "cures."

In concluding, Bibring (p. 768) pointed to the shift in emphasis "from insight through interpretation to experiential manipulation."[2] In calling attention to the common trend, at that time, to adapt the method of psychoanalysis to the treatment of special conditions, Bibring was by no means devaluating or deploring transference manipulation for the treatment of conditions outside the reasonable domain of psychoanalysis proper. Rather, he was establishing that there might be a legitimate adaptation of psychoanalysis for the elaboration of a whole range of dynamic psychotherapies extending from those close to psychoanalysis, which aim at insight predominantly through interpretive methods, to those which perhaps necessarily depend upon interpersonal experiential methods for those conditions, including borderlines, more or less—and I would think there are more rather than less—for whom interpretation and insight is only limitedly effective.

It might be interesting at this point to reflect briefly on

---

[2] Note how immediately relevant this is now, 25 years after it was written.

the definition of classicism in general, because it might help us to understand why it is so difficult to give an exact and succinct definition for "classical" psychoanalysis. The notion of what is classic is drawn from history and from archeology; it concerns that period in history, for example, the time of the Greeks or the Romans, embodying a cultural moment in which artistic and social form was established in very specific and authoritative ways. It became known as "classic," probably only later on, as departures from classic form or traditionalism, whether artistic or in patterns of living, were introduced from outside. In *Webster's Third New International Dictionary* (1965), one of the definitions of "classical" is: "regarded as of first historical significance," also, "used of a coherent and authoritative theory, method, or body of ideas commonly after new developments or general change of view have made it generally less authoritative." A further definition is "of any form or system felt to be the authentic, authoritative, or time-tested one in comparison with later modified or more radical forms deriving from it."

From this it can be seen that the quality of classicism, or a certain traditionalism, of a certain standard, is not simply a matter of definition; it is something that grows historically with usage and the passage of time. The interesting point about psychoanalysis is that so-called orthodoxy, a term to which I am antipathetic, suggests ritualism, rigidity, and adherence to absolute *rules*. The term classic, or standard, on the other hand, indicates a describably traditional usual, the existence and application of particularized criteria within relativistic limits. It does leave room for variation in the sense of flexibility within, however, certain general and specific limits. As I see it, one does have to count upon certain attributes for analysis, just as Eissler specified in 1953 when he underscored the necessity of a *reasonably* intact or standard ego. Reasonably, in this context, means a potential for introspection and yet a capacity to evaluate the yield. One must count upon the patient's ability to make an object tie and yet to permit facultative regression in the service of the analysis; for some capability of reaching one's affects and yet the ability to cognitively appreciate and meaningfully understand what comes forward when emotional conflicts from the past are reactivated in the present and brought into consciousness through the transference. The analytic situation also depends upon the analyst to be paramountly a person who is trustworthy unless proven otherwise. For an analysis to be viable, there must be a certain mutuality, what Freud (1937) called a mutual "love of truth"; some ability to share in the unraveling of a historical puzzle which might then have as a most important by-product the freeing of one from misadventures and misconceptions out of the past. I share very much Bibring's point of view toward analysis as such, in contradistinction to its close relatives, namely, well-designed psychoanalytic psychotherapies. But, as I see it, even though many ingredients, including transference effects, play their part, the ultimate therapeutic agent in psychoanalysis is *interpretation* which leads then to insight. And by interpretation I mean "appropriate verbal interventions of an explanatory nature which in timing, form, and specificity seem correct in the context of the analytic data as they have been evolving" (Valenstein, 1973)

The term insight suggests the literal "seeing into"—or the achieved recognition of—the knowing to a larger extent cognitively and by experience, as it were, of the nature of one's mental functioning and behavior. This particularly relates to the past and present, to the reality of what was past and what is present, of what is fact and what is fantasy. Psychoanalysis, which seeks to cure through insight, makes use of ego functions, of the capacity to live in reality, of the tension-management function of the ego, through which tension or instinctual discharge is optimally achieved, i.e., in conformance with the reality principle. Thus, cure through insight depends upon integrative trends and the potentiality of the pleasure ego to become at the same time also a reality ego. In that respect, Strachey's (1934) concept of the "mutative" interpretation is relevant. An interpretation is correct, i.e., effective, by reason of its timing and content when it coincides with the immediate incipient awareness of the transference experience and events of a given moment or phase; or, reciprocally, under particular circumstances is imminently germane to complementary extratransference events and experience, which also are practically within awareness. Such interpretations dynamically connect with, or can be brought to vitally conjoin with the past and paradigm sources of the transference in *statu nascendi* preconsciously. Concomitantly they are analogous to appropriate vectors (dynamically sound, well engineered), which serve the aim of reality; of what is real in contrast to what is fantasy; administered in optimal (manageable) "doses" (Strachey, 1934, pp. 283-284). They constitute integrable increments of insight, with integration being the outcome of a sufficient "working through."

It is important to bring a theory of cure through insight—through ideation—into congruence with the concept of learning through the concrete—through experience. This can be so if it is recalled that thought, i.e., ideation, is token or experimental action. Through the transference there occurs a certain kind of experience, with the action being predominantly expressed as verbalized thought, yet affect-laden, as close as possible to the *Erlebnis* (Wittels, 1947). This should be sufficiently *action* in essence and effect to bring about change through ego modification and restructuralization (see Valenstein, 1962, p. 323 for a discussion of insight and the action system).

Strachey's views had a pivotal effect upon the theory of psychoanalytic technique and continue to exert a major influence upon current technical practice. He emphasized that the really mutative, in other words, vitalistically influential interpretation, could be *only* a transference interpretation. Thus, in effect, he underscored the essential (and possibly exclusive) importance of the transference experience in the here and now. Although Strachey in this paper and again at Marienbad (1937) attributed to the transference interpretation a crucial role in the therapeutic action of psychoanalysis, he did not exclude the genetic point of view. But the genetic implications of transference interpretation, not to mention the working through of insight from the present to the past, to the paradigm infantile or childhood events and fantasies from which the transference had evolved, received very little if any attention. Nor was the reciprocity between transference and extratransference phenomenology and interpretation, which should be considered more fully but which goes beyond the scope of this paper, mentioned at all. It could have been Strachey's inclination—and I think it no doubt became the position of many who have followed from him—that it may be relatively superfluous to search out the genetic antecedents, and that the transference interpretation in the here and now might be the *sine qua non* for the "cure" and sufficient in itself. A good many analysts seem to have taken from his paper implicitly the plausibility that everything should be in the transference, that everything should be viewed as occurring in the here and now, and that psychoanalytic technique should take that direction. The consequence, in my opinion, is the watering down of the significance of the genetic point of view so far as interpretation and insight is concerned.

Lampl-de Groot (1976) cautioned that

> Some analysts consider the analytic treatment process to be exclusively a development of a transference neurosis and its resolution by interpretations. I disagree with these authors. I even consider this definition to be dangerous. In my view the transference is a tool; albeit a very mighty one, but not an aim in itself. Viewing it as an aim may invite the analyst to focus only on the transference and to draw every communication of the

patient into the transference. This tempts the analyst to overestimate the special meaning he has for the patient. Pleasant as this may be for the analyst, it may stimulate his hidden grandiosity and prevent the countertransference from becoming conscious. In this case it often becomes the obstacle to the course the analysis should run.

Similarly Grete Bibring (1954) suggested that there was an occupational hazard to which psychoanalysts are exposed. She said that if, finally, everything positive that the patient might say about the analyst were considered reality, and everything negative, transference, then it would appear that the analyst had succumbed to the "analytic disease."

Apropos of all this I found it quite fascinating to reread a section of Fenichel's retrospectively prophetic statement in his 1941 monograph (pp. 99-100). To quote him:

> We began our discussions with a description of the eternal Scylla and Charybdis of analytic technique—too much talking versus too much feeling. In the early days of psychoanalysis the topological formula to the effect that in analysis 'the unconscious is made conscious' held sway. This formula was better known than the dynamic one, as yet not understood, that analysis must 'abolish resistances'. At that time, therefore, the greater danger was the Scylla of too much talking or intellectualization: the analyst guessed at complexes, named them and depended upon that for the cure. . . . Ferenczi's and Rank's book [1923] represented a reaction against this situation. They emphasized again and again that analysis is not an intellectual but an affective process, a 'process of libido flow' in which emotional experiences are relived in the transference and previously hidden material thus revived for the ego's disposal. The authors certainly went too far to the other extreme. In their emphasis on experiencing they became admirers of

abreaction, of acting out, and thus working through was the loser. When we re-read the book today [1941] we get the impression that in the history of psychoanalysis Scylla periods and Charybdis periods alternated and that it must have been very difficult to pass evenly between the opposite dangers.

One additional point regarding the concept of classicism and analysis: as you might see by now, it is by no means a static concept although it has a certain conservatism in it historically with regard to change from what is a relatively established standard technique. However, if one thinks of the technique of analysis before 1936-1937, before Anna Freud's *The Ego and the Mechanisms of Defense* (1936) as that time when analysis was predominantly "id" analysis—it was still, nonetheless, a classic procedure, depending upon transference and the analysis of resistance to a full understanding of the transference neurosis. Then one might consider that a second phase gradually developed thereafter, a second phase wherein the classic procedure became, shall we say, neoclassic? After Anna Freud's book, the technique of analysis shifted in that it became not only "id" analysis but also "ego" analysis, which approached unconscious content through the analysis of the defenses. Furthermore, the analysis of the defenses in themselves yielded genetic data about character formation, and the particular complex ways in which character structure develops, about how individualistic traits undergo variations and change, and then become more or less fixed with the passage of time.

So there would be really these two phases, both of them encompassed by the concept and within the rubric of classic Freudian analysis. In other words, from 1937 on, ego analysis became very much a part of classical procedure. But it also depended upon interpretation as the main therapeutic agent. This is an example of growth consistent with and within the classical model.

To take up matters from a somewhat different but related direction within the present historical period, I shall briefly consider some aspects of several of the various psychoanalytic movements or even schools that are presently in favor, among them the object relations psychological approach to human development and behavior for which there is such enthusiasm, especially in some quarters. This is consequent to the broadened scope of the practice of the psychoanalyst and his or her attempt to apply psychoanalytic concepts and principles of treatment to conditions that are inaccessible to the standard psychoanalytic method. To a certain extent though, more so in some quarters than others, the intention, perhaps inadvertent, is to change analysis technically so as to make patients analyzable who heretofore would have been considered unanalyzable. I have in mind the marked interest in the narcissistic personality disorders and the borderline states.

Going back to the literature of about 25 years ago, I am impressed by how much of it is exceedingly relevant to psychoanalytic and psychotherapeutic practice today. Under the impact of the changes in technique that were proposed and practiced in the late forties and early fifties there were a number of articles published in a single issue of this *Journal* (1954, pp. 565-797) which are for the most part germane to the current state of affairs. If integrated, they would take us quite a way toward a comprehensive theory of psychotherapy, as well as the special theory of psychoanalysis as a highly systematized treatment method embodying a theory of "cure."

The first set of papers in 1954 by Leo Stone and Edith Jacobson, with a discussion by Anna Freud, was addressed to "The Widening Scope of Indications for Psychoanalysis." The second set derived from an earlier panel (1952) which had taken as its topic "The Traditional Psychoanalytic Technique and its Variations." The third set derived from another panel of the American Psychoanalytic Association

(1953) concerned with "Psychoanalysis and Dynamic Psychotherapy—Similarities and Differences." A careful reading of that issue of the *Journal* will show how much old wine has been put into new bottles.

Related to this part of my discussion are two quotes, the first from Gill (1954) who, discussing terminology, wrote, "The word 'psychotherapy' is used in two main senses, first as a broad term to include all types of therapy by psychological means, under which psychoanalysis is included, and second in a narrow sense to designate methods of psychological therapy which are not psychoanalysis, even if they are grounded in the theory of psychoanalysis. The latter restricted sense is the one generally employed if it is not further specified, and it is the one we are using here" (p. 772). Rangell (1954) defined psychoanalysis proper as follows: "Psychoanalysis is a method of therapy *whereby* conditions are brought about favorable for the development of a transference neurosis, in which the past is restored in the present, *in order that*, through a systematic interpretive attack on the resistances which oppose it, there occurs a resolution of that neurosis (transference *and* infantile) *to the end* of bringing about structural changes in the mental apparatus of the patient to make the latter capable of optimum adaptation to life" (pp. 739-740).

From early on in the history of psychoanalysis, a distinction was made between the so-called transference neuroses and the narcissistic neuroses. This distinction grew out of the clinical experience that the analyst could count upon a basic trust and therapeutic rapport, later termed the therapeutic alliance or working alliance, for some patients who by reason of it were able to establish a meaningful transference neurosis and to use free association and the interpretive interventions of the analyst to successfully analyze and resolve it. But then there were other patients who seemed incapable of doing so, patients who either stringently defended themselves against significant and enduring object ties, including an attachment to the analyst, or who were able either to acknowledge or else disavow objects only insofar as they either replicated or else failed to exactingly fulfill the patients' egocentric perceptions and expectations. Such patients fell within the group of more or less unanalyzable, even through not necessarily untreatable, narcissistic personality disorders. And for the patient considered to be borderline, the issue also was one of basic trust, compounded, however, by an excess and volatility of emotion and/or peremptory action in association with a predilection for psychotic transference responses.

The attempt to treat such conditions led to active therapeutic procedures and interventions considerably beyond or outside of interpretation. The rationale was that the ameliorative or, should I say, the curative therapeutic effect necessarily occurred within the context of a transactional transference-countertransference (in the broad sense) field of patient and therapist, and in the form of what was appropriately termed by Alexander (Alexander, French, et al., 1946) the corrective emotional experience, actively facilitated by manipulation of the transference. The causative factor of the genetic paradigm in the infantile (childhood) neurosis and repetition thereafter was acknowledged but apparently considered relatively unimportant, even though a literal cognitive insight might be implicit and possibly made explicit. Just as one learns through experiencing in growing up, so was it proposed, in effect, that one might learn again, but now differently, through the therapeutic corrective experience in the context and content of the transference.

This modification of procedure, namely, the introduction of an active "manipulative" principle in the form of psychotherapeutic and psychoanalytic innovations somewhat akin to role-playing, is readily traceable to the proposals some 57 years ago by Ferenczi and Rank (1923) of an active technique. Theoretically it connects with the current view of the earliest preverbal development originating pivotally in the emergence experientially of a consistent sense of self and of objects out of the undifferentiated self-object representation of the mother-child symbiotic phase. Kohut (1971, 1977) postulates an independent development of narcissism from the beginning, unfolding sequentially in its own right, in relation to self and objects, in association with the vicissitudes of libido and aggression, but not necessarily as a variation or expression of either. It starts with investment in the nuclear *self-object* (representation) and progresses toward the narcissistic investment in the emergent self. To put it another way conceptually, the sequence would seem to proceed from an original (primary) narcissism of the undifferentiated *self-object* matrix to a later (secondary) phase of narcissistic regard for the self—parallel to but not necessarily reciprocal with libidinal investment in and regard for objects. Presumably an uneven or defective ego develops due to excessive stimulation, or dissonance in the mother-child complementarity, or psychological trauma during this very early vulnerable period, probably a matter of unempathic parenting or parental deprivation, etc.

As I understand it, Kohut might specify the outcome as a deficit in a normal narcissistic investment of the self. Technically, it apparently follows that a narcissistically impoverished self-representation should be structurally modifiable through recapitulating the developmental failure in the context of an experientially corrective mirror transference. Kohut (1971) formulated that in the narcissistic personality disorders, the corrective handling and interpretations, i.e., the experiential aspects of the transference, which he terms "transmuting internalizations," will have structure-building effects in their own right. Arrested development, the outcome of which was damage to the self, in terms of a psychology of the self, responds to the analyst's receptiveness to deficiencies in the ego in terms of a psychoanalytic ego psychology. Presumably, as a "Restoration of the Self" (1977) takes place, the patient might even move to the oedipal level.

Gitelson (1952, p. 208) implied that the oedipal phase was the beginning of normality, at least to the extent that its centrality excluded (and he quoted here from Fenichel [1931, p. 181]) "Those cases of extreme malformations of character which resemble a lifelong psychosis and in which . . . the subject's object relations were destroyed root and branch at an earlier period, or because such relations never existed at all." Kohut mentions neither Gitelson's formulation nor Fenichel's earlier contribution, nor does he relate his approach to the "corrective emotional experience" introduced by Alexander and French (1946). Were the question posed, possibly Kohut might minimize or refute their historical relevance to his predilections for diagnosis and technique. It does seem, however, that he has gone a route similar to Alexander's. If this appraisal of Kohut's theory and practice of analysis is correct, the primary intention of analysis becomes the undoing and/or completion of faulty development through what in essence would seem to be a corrective emotional experience in the setting of a full-fledged interpersonalization of the transference. The heretofore familiar and useful clinical concept of unconscious intrapsychic conflict, both in the inter- and intrasystemic sense, would hardly seem to pertain. And presumably the theory of psychoanalytic technique as being primarily an articulate interpretive procedure which ultimately depends upon rational explanatory means of resolving psychic conflict, formerly unconscious but now made conscious, predominantly but not solely through the transference neurosis, would no longer be of cardinal importance.

Kohut is ambiguous in his discussion of the role of interpretation in the treatment of narcissistic personality disorders. He explicitly discounts the value of insight for structure building, whether in the analysis of narcissistic characters or of "patients suffering from structural neuroses," and states, "It is not the interpretation that cures the patient" (1977, pp. 30-31). Yet, in his technique in actual practice, it appears that he does make use of interpretation, as if narcissistic patients should be and are accessible to cogent explanatory interventions, much as in the usual psychoanalytic situation. In my experience, though, it is dubious whether paramountly narcissistic individuals are substantially responsive to the specific *content* of emotionally informed, secondary-process interventions. Within the context of a narcissistic transference situation, interpretations probably serve transference aims, perhaps by communicating empathic resonance and thereby reinforcing the corrective impact of the literalized transference experience.

I know that Kohut and his group originally indicated that their analytic approach for "The Restoration of the Self" was specific for the treatment of narcissistic character disorders for which analysis in the standard form is ineffective. Possibly they practice a more traditional conflict analysis for more "ordinary", or usual neurotics with a cohesive sense of self (an intact, more or less normal ego). The only trouble is that there is reason to doubt that this distinction is really applied when it comes to current practice and teaching. What is more, are "transference cures" achieved predominantly through corrective emotional experience "analytic cures" per se? Or is it more heuristic to place them within the broader rubric of analytically oriented psychotherapies?

To mention another contemporary American analyst who has gained a considerable audience and following with respect to the treatment of narcissistic neuroses and borderline conditions, Kernberg attributes defective ego structure to a failure to integrate split introjects during early development. As he put it recently (1976), "The strategical aim in working through the transference is to resolve those primitive dissociations of the self and internalized objects and thus to transform primitive transferences into higher level or integrated transference reactions, more realistic and more related to real childhood experiences" (p. 800).

Kernberg is more circumspect in suggesting that

"psychoanalysis and psychotherapy should be most carefully differentiated." He is also more restrained than some in indicating (1976) that most borderline patients respond best to a modified psychoanalytic procedure or psychoanalytic psychotherapy, but he nonetheless does emphasize that some may indeed be treated by a nonmodified (*classical?*) psychoanalytic procedure. A careful reading of his various publications (1968, 1975, 1976) suggests that Kernberg expects more from interpretation in its ostensive content and the power of its explanatory meaning than I believe can actually occur in the psychoanalytic psychotherapy of borderlines, especially in its prolonged initial phase.

Borderline individuals are for the most part erratically prone to archaically intense and labile transference reactions. In my experience, such patients simply cannot tolerate, much less have a basic confidence and consistent trust in, the kind of "therapeutic technical neutrality" and equidistance with respect to conflict that are basic to the materialization and maintenance of a standard or classical analytic situation. For patients with preconflict ego distortions (i.e., self-object aberrations), the very nature of the transference, which is archaic and actualized, precludes therapeutic neutrality. The patient's ego is simply too idiosyncratic or fragile to make or maintain a consistent and reliable object tie to the therapist. The therapist, then, must necessarily provide that kind of auxiliary-ego support which small children count upon from their parents.

My impression is that most patients who are borderline, like those who are severely narcissistic, are also relatively inaccessible to interpretation and to the insight that correct interpretation intends, during at least a prolonged earlier phase of their treatment. The treatment of such conditions during a lengthy preanalytic phase has to be paramountly experiential and developmentally reparative insofar as possible. As I wrote in an·earlier paper (1973), "Since the major disturbance in self and object relations constitutes an early

developmental defect in ego structure, psychoanalytic interpretations [i.e., articulate explanations at a predominantly
cognitive-conative level of communication], which after all
cannot really reach the primary process preverbal-earliest
verbal level of development, are nonmutative and relatively
ineffective [in their content]" (p. 390). If they are to mean
anything, they have to resonate with the immediate
essentially transactional experiential elements in the therapeutic situation.

Nonetheless, there is therapeutic value indeed in
reasonable and plausible interpretive activity, but such
interpretations are inexact (Glover, 1931), in effect, intellectually appealing and persuasively correct though they may
be. They operate at a level of implicit or explicit reconstruction of external and intrapsychic events and impressions
which cannot be expected to be discretely rememberable at a
secondary-process level. They may, however, fill out the pre-
science of affective states and predilections which quite
probably are all that remain from very early preverbal
primary-process self- and object oriented experience. However, by their very relevance to that early experience, such
communications convey an empathic resonance which
actualizes the supportive and even nutritive and corrective
potential of the interpersonalized transference situation.

To turn back to the broader issue of psychoanalysis at
this present time, by coincidence—or is it just coincidence?—
the trend in the theory and practice of analysis toward the
external and *real* world of objects, and the analyst as a *real*
person, has surfaced at a time when there has been a
considerable disillusionment with science and rationalism;
inclusive of that humanistic hybrid science, psychoanalysis,
as it is or has been. To some extent the priority heretofore
given to rational considerations and the reality principle, has
been displaced by what amounts to "cures through love" and
a resurgent interest in faith, mysticism, etc. If humanistically
enlightened understanding, i.e., the search for "truth" was

the ideal of the late nineteenth century, then learning through living free and changing through direct encounter and involvement and catharsis has become the current trend. Clearly this has meaning for a shift in favor or fashion as to what should be the relative balance in therapy between cognitive aspects, affective involvement, and action. Fenichel's bipolar hazards of Scylla and Charybdis are still with us; only that the tilt now is very distinctly toward affect and experientialism rather than interpretation (in the discrete secondary-process, articulate sense) and insight. The enthusiasm for cure embraces the notion of an intensified and interpersonalized transference mutualization, reminiscent of "transactional" changes as curative factors proposed by various schools which emphasize interpersonal relations.

This leads me to close this brief reflective essay with a final quote, this time from Glover (1955)

> And here, I think, we may end on a note of reassurance. It is foolish to pretend that psycho-analysis is a panacea for human ills. It is foolish to pretend that it is not, like all other psycho-therapies, a fallible instrument. But that is no reason why it should not be applied in difficult or even incurable cases. Provided the technique has been carried out to the best of the analyst's ability, the failures so frequently experienced, though by no means so frequently recorded, are honourable failures. They may lead ultimately to a strengthening of the therapeutic instrument. There is no need for analysts to gloss over their failure or to pretend that many modifications of technique intended to cover failure are not transference therapies; there is no need for them to be jealous either of the sometimes striking results obtained through rapport therapy or of the occasional cures spontaneously effected by patients themselves; and there is no need either to feel inferior or to ape superiority in the presence of their psychiatric

colleagues; psycho-analysis, whatever its limitations, and these are numerous enough, can well afford to stand on its own feet [p. 258].

It is certainly in order to continue our psychoanalytic research into the nature and reasons for success or failure of the various psychotherapies, analytic or otherwise, which are in the professional and public domain at this time. Psychotherapies in which experiential manipulation of the transference is pivotal can be efficacious for both the transference neurosis and the historically termed narcissistic neuroses, namely, the more severe disturbances, inclusive of the narcissistic character disorders and borderline states, not to mention the frank psychoses, for which they are the treatment of choice, at least during an initial period if not longer. In conclusion, though, I favor the elaboration of a substantive distinction between a widened and more scientifically sophisticated scope of psychoanalytic psychotherapy in contradistinction to a broadening out and qualitative shift in the concept and practice of therapeutic psychoanalysis, as such.

Summary

In this essay, the term classical psychoanalysis is discussed historically and conceptually. What characterizes classical analysis and distinguishes it from current innovative trends in the practice of psychoanalysis is reviewed from a comparative standpoint. The impact of the widened scope of conditions the psychoanalyst currently includes in his therapeutic work is considered, with special attention to the distinction between psychoanalysis per se in the classical sense and psychoanalytic psychotherapy.

REFERENCES

Alexander, F., French, T. M., et al. (1946), *Psychoanalytic Therapy, Principles and Applications.* New York: Ronald Press.

Bibring, E. (1954), Psychoanalysis and the dynamic psychotherapies. *This Journal*, 2:745-770.

Bibring, G. L. (1954), The training analysis and its place in psycho-analytic training. *Internat. J. Psycho-Anal.*, 35:169-173.

Eissler, K. R. (1953), The effect of the structure of the ego on psychoanalytic technique. *This Journal*, 1:140-143.

—————— (1958), Remarks on some variations in psycho-analytical technique. *Internat. J. Psycho-Anal.*, 39:222-229.

Fenichel, O. (1931), The pregenital antecedents of the oedipus complex. *Collected Papers*, 1st series, New York: Norton, 1953, pp. 181-203.

—————— (1941), *Problems of Psychoanalytic Technique*. New York: The Psychoanalytic Quarterly, Inc.

Ferenczi, S. & Rank, O. (1923), *The Development of Psychoanalysis*. New York: Dover, 1956.

Freud, A. (1936), *The Ego and the Mechanisms of Defense*. New York: International Universities Press.

—————— (1954), The widening scope of indications for psychoanalysis: discussion. *Writings*, 4:356-376. New York: International Universities Press, 1968.

Freud, S. (1937), Analysis terminable and interminable. *Standard Edition*, 23:216-253.

Gill, M. (1954), Psychoanalysis and exploratory psychotherapy. *This Journal*, 2:771-797.

Gitelson, M. (1952), Re-evaluation of the role of the Oedipus complex. In: *Psychoanalysis: Science and Profession*. New York: International Universities Press, 1973, pp. 201-210.

Glover, E. (1931), The therapeutic effect of inexact interpretation: A contribution to the theory of suggestion. *Internat. J. Psycho-Anal.*, 12:397-412.

—————— (1955), *The Technique of Psychoanalysis*. New York: International Universities Press.

Greenson, R. R. (1958), Variations in classical psycho-analytic technique: an introduction. *Internat. J. Psycho-Anal.*, 39:200-201.

Kernberg, O. F. (1968), The therapy of patients with borderline personality organization. *Internat. J. Psycho-Anal.*, 49:600-619.

—————— (1975a), *Borderline Conditions and Pathological Narcissism*. New York: Aronson.

—————— (1976), Technical considerations in the treatment of borderline personality organization. *This Journal*, 24:795-829.

Kohut, H. (1971), *The Analysis of the Self*. New York: International Universities Press.

—————— (1977), *The Restoration of the Self*. New York: International Universities Press.

Lampl-de Groot, J. (1976), Personal experience with psychoanalytic technique and theory during the last half century. *The Psychoanalytic Study of the Child*, 31:283-296. New Haven: Yale University Press.

Loewenstein, R. (1958), Remarks on some variations in classical technique. *Internat. J. Psycho-Anal.*, 39:202-210.

Stone, L. (1975), Some problems and potentialities of present-day psychoanalysis. *Psychoanal. Quart.*, 44:331-370.

Strachey, J. (1934), The nature of the therapeutic action of psychoanalysis. Reprinted in: *Internat. J. Psycho-Anal.* (1969), 50:275-292.

———— (1937), Symposium on the theory of the therapeutic results of psycho-analysis. *Internat. J. Psycho-Anal.*, 18:139-145.

Valenstein, A. F. (1962), The psycho-analytic situation: Affects, emotional reliving, and insight in the psycho-analytic process. *Internat. J. Psycho-Anal.*, 43:315-324.

———— (1973), On attachment to painful feelings and the negative therapeutic reaction. *The Psychoanalytic Study of the Child*, 28:365-392. New Haven: Yale University Press.

Webster's Third New International Dictionary (1965), Springfield, Mass.: G. & C. Merriam Co.

Wittels, F. (1947), A neglected boundary of psychoanalysis. *Psychoanal. Quart.*, 18:44-59.

140A Foster Street
Cambridge, Mass. 02138

WORKING ALLIANCE, THERAPEUTIC ALLIANCE, AND TRANSFERENCE

CHARLES BRENNER, M.D.

I NTEREST IN THE THERAPEUTIC or working alliance dates from a paper by Zetzel (1956) on transference. The idea of an alliance between analyst and the reasonable part of the patient's ego had been referred to earlier by Bibring (1937), but it attracted little interest in discussions of psychoanalytic technique. Since Zetzel's paper and a later one by Greenson (1965), interest in the subject has been much more widespread. For example, Modell (1972, p. 263), in a review of Zetzel's collected papers, wrote that "much of what Zetzel described concerning the capacity for the development of the therapeutic alliance ... is noncontroversial." Similarly, Lampl-de Groot (1975, p. 668) wrote that "most authors" distinguish between transference and working alliance.

There are analysts, however, who question the validity of the distinction just referred to. Arlow and I (1966) raised questions concerning the theoretical assumption on which Zetzel based her idea of a therapeutic alliance, namely, that the analytic situation is necessarily a repetition of the relationship between mother and infant. More recently, Kanzer (1975) and Arlow (1975) each expressed reservations about the concepts of therapeutic and working alliance, emphasizing the technical difficulties to which they are likely to give rise. I share their misgivings (Brenner, 1976, p. 120) and join with them, if Lampl-de Groot is right, as members of an unconvinced minority. I believe that it is neither correct nor useful to distinguish between transference and therapeutic or working alliance. In order to support my opinion I shall, in this paper, review the meaning of therapeutic and working

137

alliance as I understand it, as well as the data on which the concepts were originally based. Because I believe there is a close relation between these concepts and the question of gratification vs. frustration of transference wishes in analysis, I shall spend some time discussing the latter topic as well.

Zetzel's concept of therapeutic alliance can be summarized as follows. According to her, when a patient enters analysis he "is asked to relinquish crucial inner defenses and controls against ego-alien impulses and fantasies previously motivated by signals of internal danger" (1966, p. 100). Still according to Zetzel, "The patient, however, will only be capable of tolerating the added stress roused by specific fantasies which emerge in his transference neurosis, if his basic needs and anxieties have been acknowledged in the opening stages of treatment" (1966, p. 100). Acknowledging a patient's basic needs and anxieties, said Zetzel, is what an analyst must do at the start of analysis in order to make possible what is analysis proper, namely, the interpretation of the patient's instinctual conflicts, especially as they become manifest in the transference neurosis. Therapeutic alliance, according to Zetzel, precedes analysis. It is different and distinct from the transference neurosis. It is essentially, in her view, a recapitulation of the very early relation between mother and infant. As an infant turns with expectant faith to its mother for help, so does a patient turn to his analyst. An analyst, therefore, must be like a good mother, with "intuitive adaptive responses" (1966, p. 97) to each patient's needs and anxieties. Thus, "the initial stage [of analysis] involves achievement of a special object relationship leading to a new ego identification" (1966, p. 92), i.e., an identification (= alliance) with the analyst. As already noted, this ego identification "is to be regarded as an essential prerequisite . . . to the analytic process itself" (1966, p. 99).

In her 1956 paper Zetzel gave no clinical illustrations. In the paper just quoted, she gave two illustrative clinical excerpts, one from an analysis she had supervised, the other, apparently, from an analysis she had conducted herself. This case material will be discussed below.

Greenson's concept of therapeutic alliance—he prefers the term working alliance—essentially corresponds with Zetzel's. His first extensive presentation was in 1965, though it was by no means his only one (see Greenson, 1966, 1967). Like Zetzel, Greenson (1965) separated working alliance from transference neurosis. The latter, he said, must be analyzed for analysis to be successful, while the former must be established for the latter to be analyzable. According to Greenson, a good working alliance is essential throughout an analysis. He believes it can be best established—or, perhaps, only established—if an analyst, in addition to showing by his day-to-day behavior a "consistent and unwavering pursuit of insight in dealing with any and all of the patient's material and behavior" (1965, p. 221) also creates a proper working atmosphere (1965, p. 223). In other words, according to Greenson, in addition to being analytic, which is crucial, an analyst must also be human. "Essentially the humanness of the analyst is expressed in his compassion, concern, and therapeutic intent toward his patient. . . . Humanness is also expressed in the attitude that the patient is to be respected as an individual. . . . Basically . . . humanness consists of understanding and insight conveyed in an atmosphere of serious work, straightforwardness, compassion, and restraint" (1965, pp. 223-224). Greenson included in his paper illustrative material from the analyses of four of his own patients. This material will be discussed below.

In trying to reach a decision about the validity of the concept of therapeutic alliance as something distinct from transference neurosis, one is faced first of all with the question of the basis on which to test it. It seems to me that a pragmatic test is likely to be the most useful. To marshal arguments for and against the concept of therapeutic alliance that rest on its compatibility or incompatibility with psychoanalytic theories of transference, or of conflict, or of the relative importance of oedipal and preoedipal factors in later mental functioning runs the risk of engaging in a logomachy—a mere war of words. If it were possible, the most useful test of the validity of the concept of therapeutic alliance would probably be via clinical conferences—perhaps a continuous case seminar—over an extended period. Since that is rarely feasible, one can at least examine the illustrative case material offered to support the validity of the concept in question. After all, both Zetzel and Greenson have said, in effect, that their clinical experience has convinced them that analysts must be more than merely analytical in their behavior with their patients. They must have "intuitive adaptive responses" (Zetzel); they must create the right "kind of atmosphere" (Greenson). What is the clinical material that illustrates the soundness of these claims?

Zetzel (1966, pp. 94-97) presented material from the beginning of an analysis she supervised. It was the candidate-analysts's first case. The patient was a 25-year-old "girl [who] suffered from serious inhibitions in respect to her heterosexual relationships." "In the initial interview, after careful consideration, the fee set had been somewhat higher than the patient anticipated. The patient had agreed that she could pay this moderate fee but had clearly felt disappointed." From the very start of her first hour the patient showed evidence that she was disappointed and angry at having to pay more than she had expected (or hoped) to. (1) "She . . . commented that analysis is a luxury." (2) She classified "herself as a receptive character." (3) "She . . . speculated about her mother. She was probably a hoarder. This was not fair to her mother who would be horrified." (4) " . . . she referred to some recent dealing with a printer in connection with some work he was to do for her employer. He agreed to do a job for $35; the patient asked her employer for $60 just to be sure. The printer then sent a bill for $120. In a very angry voice the patient said: 'I told him I didn't think much of his way of doing business. I'm glad I told him.' " In her report, Zetzel called attention to the patient's anger at her analyst as well as to indications, in this and other things she said during her first analytic hour, that an analyst might despise and laugh at "crackpots" like her.

The analyst himself made no comment about all of this to his patient. It was, after all, his very first analytic patient. "In subsequent hours during the first week of analysis, there was considerable additional material of a similar nature, with an increasing tendency to view the rather silent analyst as an unreal, omnipotent figure. The patient felt threatened by feelings of helplessness against which she defended herself through denial and some displacement. The candidate concerned, discussing the situation in his supervisory session, became aware of his rigidity and concern lest any activity on his part should be regarded as unanalytic in respect to this, his first analytic patient. He adopted, subsequently, a slightly more active and human attitude, indicating to the patient his recognition of her anxiety" (p. 96). This resulted, we are told, in an immediate improvement of the analytic situation. The patient became more comfortable, and her reality testing improved in the sense that she realized (and said) that her analyst was not a special Olympian figure, as she had imagined him to be, but an ordinary person like herself.

According to Zetzel, this vignette illustrates the bad effect of excessive rigidity on the part of an analyst and the good effect of a more relaxed and human attitude with a patient in whom the unfamiliar analytic situation stirred up basic anxieties that derived from her very early relationship with her mother, with "related changes in the perception of reality which, unchecked, might have hindered the development of a satisfactory analytic situation" (p. 97). When the analyst became more human, the patient became more secure in her relationship with him, with the result that "she could not only reintegrate previously achieved ego capacities but could also initiate the added ego maturation which would later become achieved through the analytic process" (p. 97).

The reader will note that we have not been told just what it was that the analyst did after the supervisory hour that he had not done before—information that seems to me too important to have been omitted. Some details concerning just what the analyst did and how the patient responded should help in deciding how instrumental the change in his attitude and activity really were.

Equally important, it would seem, is Zetzel's failure to pay any attention to the fact, which she recognized, that the patient was disappointed and angry about the fee she had to pay. It seems likely that the patient was not only disappointed and angry, but ashamed and frightened as well. At least she called herself greedy and fancied she was being laughed at. Should none of this have been interpreted to the patient? Was it best that nothing was said to her about being angry at her analyst and afraid to say so for fear of being laughed at and thought greedy? Zetzel did not even discuss the possibility of making such an interpretation. She did raise the possibility of making an immediate deep (i.e., genetically oriented) interpretation of the "type . . . described by Mrs. Klein and her followers" (pp. 95-96), and dismissed the idea as unwise. Such an interpretation, according to Zetzel, would have dealt with features of the patient's early relationship to her mother as demonstrated in transference to her analyst. In Zetzel's opinion it would have been premature to make such a reconstructive interpretation in the first hour. I agree with that opinion, but I am not persuaded that the patient's reaction to her fee was of so little importance as a determinant of her view of her analyst as an "unreal, omnipotent figure" and of the fact that for several days she "felt threatened by feelings of helplessness" (p. 96). Apparently something the analyst said or did after his first supervisory hour reassured her. Perhaps he smiled at her as he greeted or dismissed her. Whatever it was, it helped her to feel more positively toward him and relieved her distress. But would it not have been as effective symptomatically, and more useful analytically, to have dealt with the patient's initial difficulty by interpretation rather than by being more "human" and "relaxed"? What Zetzel recommended worked in the case she reported, but it is hardly a convincing illustration of her general thesis, I think.

One can see also how difficult it is to discuss the matter away from the clinical material, so to speak. The questions one wants answered about the analyst's actual behavior, for example, could be answered only in the setting of a seminar or a dialogue, and in such a setting, with discussion back and forth, one might also expect much more to emerge in the way of clinical material that would be pertinent to the task of deciding on the validity of Zetzel's generalizations about therapeutic alliance as distinct from transference in analysis.

Her second illustration is less useful for discussion than her first, for it contains no analytic material but merely a summary statement that the patient "had experienced unusual difficulty in accepting the passive components of the analytic situation. It had been hard for her to lie down, hard for her to free associate, and particularly hard to accept the slow, often mysterious nature of the analytic process. She wanted to be active, to work hard, and to make things happen. Though a positive therapeutic alliance had been established with ease, she was anxiously aware of her need to remain in control" (p. 102). All of this, according to Zetzel, was related to the patient's oedipal wishes and conflicts, which were abundantly demonstrated in the course of her analysis. This is neither new nor unusual, nor did Zetzel consider it to be so. Her point was that interpretation alone would not have been enough. What she called a dual approach is necessary, and she described it as follows. "In the initial stages of analysis it had been necessary to give due recognition to her fear of passivity and loss of control. As the analysis progressed, however, her anxiety diminished, not only through interpretation of the transference neurosis, but also through her increased capacity to tolerate passivity, frustration and delay. This, in turn, initiated a more mature positive ego identification with the analyst and qualitative changes in the analytic situation itself" (p. 103), which led to analytic progress. One is left without more information than that regarding what factors in the analytic situation other than interpretation increased her capacity to tolerate passivity, frustration, and delay.

Here again, therefore, one cannot judge from the printed record what data persuaded Zetzel that more than correct transference interpretations are necessary for analytic progress, that therapeutic alliance is distinct from transference neurosis, and that it is no less important to foster the alliance than to interpret the transference.

Greenson's (1965) illustrative case material was drawn from the analyses of four of his own patients. Three of the four had been in analysis previously, two with other analysts, one with Greenson himself. Each patient had been or seemed to be "unanalyzable or interminable" (p. 200). This was due to previously unrecognized difficulty in the working alliance (= therapeutic alliance) between patient and analyst.

The first patient was a middle-aged man who had had more than six years of analysis with a previous analyst. "Certain general conditions had improved, but his original analyst believed the patient needed additional analysis because he was still unable to marry and was very lonely" (p. 205). When he began analysis with Greenson, Greenson promptly recognized evidence of an extremely compliant attitude that was expressed by his behavior during the analytic sessions. The patient never took the initiative "about recognizing and working with his resistances." He waited for Greenson to point them out, but he always responded immediately when Greeson did intervene, since not to do so would have been a "sign of resistance," which the patient thought was bad (p. 205). In the course of Greenson's attempts to deal with his patient's resistance, which Greenson formulated as an inability to establish a satisfactory working alliance, it became clear that the patient's "striking passivity and compliance were . . . a form of ingratiation, covering up an inner emptiness, an insatiable infantile hunger, and a terrible rage" (p. 206). After six months Greenson concluded that he was attempting to analyze an unanalyzable patient and referred him to a colleague for psychotherapy.

Here again it is difficult to see what relevance the illustrative material has to the thesis that there is a working alliance that is distinguishable from the transference neurosis and that must be fostered by being tactful and human with analytic patients. Greenson himself made clear that this was a patient who was unanalyzable and who could accomplish nothing of value in analysis despite Greenson's strenuous efforts to enlist his cooperation in the analytic work. Greenson made equally clear his opinion that the first analyst's failure to recognize that, despite his compliance, the patient was unanalyzable had resulted in more than six years of therapy that was a mere "caricature of analysis" (p. 206). If this case material illustrates anything about the working alliance, it illustrates that serious transference resistances are not successfully resolved by being human and making efforts to enlist a patient's cooperation. It may well be that the patient was, as Greenson believed him to be, wholly unsuitable for analysis from the start and that interpretation of his emptiness, hunger, rage, and defensive compliance would have been no more successful than was Greenson's humanness in mitigating the patient's resistance to analysis; but, certainly, interpretation couldn't have been less success-ful than being human was. This illustration hardly serves to recommend the value of Greenson's (and Zetzel's) technical maneuvers.

The second patient was a woman who had been in analysis with Greenson for four years and returned for further analysis after an interval of six years. The second time, Greenson, older and more experienced, recognized more clearly than he had done during the patient's first period of analysis that her way of talking during sessions—her way of "associating"—must be analyzed if she was to work to capacity in analysis. Only by bending every effort to analyze her transference behavior—her "misuse" of the procedure of analysis (p. 208)—was Greenson able to ensure that his patient's second analysis was more fruitful than her first had been.

Interesting and convincing as is this clinical material in many respects, I do not see that it supports Greenson's thesis. It is always enjoyable to read—or listen to—clinical material. It is instructive and delightful to do so when it gives one a chance to observe a master like Greenson at work. But here again is case material that seems to illustrate something quite at odds with Greenson's generalizations about working alliance. It is material illustrating very well that, when a patient's ability to cooperate in the work of analysis is compromised, it is often a consequence or manifestation of transference and that it is dealt with best by correct understanding and consistent interpretation.

Greenson's third patient was a young man who had previously been in analysis with another (male) analyst for two and a half years. This analysis "had left him almost completely untouched" (p. 209). The patient consciously withheld embarrassing thoughts, refused to divulge "many conscious secrets" (p. 210), and was silent for long periods during many sessions.

Greenson attributed the patient's resistance during his first analysis to the analyst's behavior. It was for this reason, he believed, that the patient "had not been able to form a working alliance." In contrast to the patient's first analyst, Greenson was tactful and explained why he behaved as he did on some occasions. Instead of telling the patient "that it was customary not to smoke during sessions," as the first analyst had done, Greenson explained that what was important was to know "what feelings, ideas, and sensations were going on in him at the moment that he decided to light the cigarette . . . that it was preferable for such feelings and ideas to be expressed in words instead of actions" (p. 210), since in that way they could be understood. Greenson followed a similar course in a later hour when the patient asked if Greenson was married: "I then pointed out to him how, by not answering his question and by asking him instead to tell his fantasies about the answer, he revealed the cause of his curiosity. I told him I would not answer questions when I felt that more was to be gained by keeping silent and letting him associate to his own question. At this point the patient became somewhat tearful and . . . told me that in the beginning of his previous analysis he had asked many questions. His former analyst never answered nor did he explain why he was silent. He felt his analyst's silence as a degradation and humiliation and now realized that his own later silences were a retaliation for this imagined injustice" (p. 211).

Here, then, is some case material that illustrates the point about a working or therapeutic alliance that Greenson and Zetzel make. Being intuitive and tactfully human fosters a patient's ability to work analytically. Failing to be so interferes with the development of that ability and may make analysis impossible. But would it not be equally correct to say that the first analyst did not recognize that certain aspects of the analytic situation—his own lack of response to questions, his advice not to smoke, and his failure to offer explanations for his conduct—angered the patient and resolved him to get even in kind? And is this not transference? Not every patient gets angry at his analyst's behavior. Not every angry patient is unable to complain, nor is every one spitefully stubborn even at his own expense. Was it the first analyst's behavior that stalemated the first analysis, or was it, more importantly, the first analyst's failure to understand and interpret his patient's transference resistance?

I do not raise these objections to Greenson's (and, I suspect, Zetzel's) explanation because I am in favor of rudeness or aloofness on the part of an analyst toward his patients. I raise them because I am convinced that it is important to every analyst's technical proficiency to understand his patients as fully and as correctly as possible. To modify merely by one's behavior, as Greenson did, a transference reaction so intense that it stalemated analytic progress for two years, without even raising the question why the patient reacted as he did—to proceed as though it is natural (human?) to be angry with someone who tries to be helpful in a way that one doesn't understand the reasons for—seems to me to be of doubtful value in analysis. No two analysts behave exactly the same. Some explain why they discourage smoking and don't answer questions; some don't explain. Experience indicates that either course of behavior is compatible with technical proficiency. What is not compatible with it is failure to recognize a patient's anger if one doesn't explain, and consequent failure to bring it into the analysis. And it can, in some circumstances, be equally damaging to fail to recognize a patient's unexpressed reaction when one *does* explain. In my opinion, it is not being more or less "human" that is most important. What is most important, I believe, is to understand correctly the nature and origin of one's patients' transference reactions however one behaves.

Greenson's fourth patient was also a young man. After two years of analysis during which the patient was superficially cooperative but took nothing seriously, Greenson told the patient they were getting nowhere and suggested interrupting treatment. The patient expressed some disappointment, but obviously didn't take Greenson's suggestion for interruption of treatment any more seriously than he had taken whatever else Greenson had said during the previous two years. Instead, he went on talking as though nothing of consequence had been said. Greenson interrupted angrily to ask him what he thought he was doing. The patient responded that Greenson sounded annoyed with him, to which Greenson replied that he certainly was. This really shook the patient. He sat up and soon confessed that he often thought of Greenson laughing at him, being angry, and being sexually excited. It turned out that the patient's father had frequently taken the patient's temperature rectally when he was a boy. The patient then "proceeded to [tell] a host of homosexual and sadomasochistic fantasies. The persistent reasonableness [had been] a defense against these as well as a playful attempt to tease me into acting out with him" (p. 214). After this confrontation, analytic progress became possible. According to Greenson, this material is illustrative of a pseudo or false working alliance that had to be changed into a true working alliance before analysis could progress.

Once again, I believe, we have been presented with interesting and instructive clinical material that does not support or illustrate Greenson's main thesis: that working alliance is different from transference neurosis. This was a patient who for two years acted out in analysis his unconscious wish to provoke his analyst to attack him. Only when this was understood and analyzed could analytic progress be made. If the material illustrates anything, it illustrates that when a patient is so uncooperative and resistant as to cause the analysis to reach an impasse, correct understanding of unconscious transference wishes, and correct interpretation to the patient based on that under-standing, may resolve the seeming impasse and make cooperation and further progress possible.

In short, I am convinced by all the available evidence that the concepts of therapeutic alliance and working alliance that have been current in psychoanalytic literature since 1956 are neither valid nor useful. In analysis, resistances are best analyzed, not overcome by suggestion or by some corrective emotional experience. That is to say, their nature and origin are to be understood and, when understood, interpreted to the patient.

This is not to say that one can always analyze resistance

successfully. In the first place, it is not always possible to understand the nature and origin of resistance. And even when an analyst believes he does understand a resistance, at least to considerable degree, interpretation does not always lead to constructive change. Analysis is not a panacea, nor is it universally applicable. Sometimes a patient who seemed eminently suited for analysis before analysis began turns out not to be so when analysis has got under way. However, when a patient *is* in analysis, the better one understands his resistances and the more knowledgeably one is able to interpret their determinants to him, the better the chance that the patient can cooperate constructively. Whether at the beginning, in the midst, or in the final stages of analysis, timely, accurate interpretations that are based on correct understanding are far more useful in promoting a patient's ability to do his part than is any behavior, however well intentioned, humane, and intuitively compassionate, that is intended to make him feel less withdrawn, uncomfortable, or antagonistic. In analysis, it is best for the patient if one approaches *everything* analytically. It is as important to understand why a patient is closely "allied" with his analyst in the analytic work as it is to understand why there seems to be no "alliance" at all. As Friedman (1969) remarked, any idea that, apart from wanting help and gratification from his analyst, a "patient wishes to, or should wish to, engage in a process *per se* [i.e., wishes to engage in analysis for its own sake] is supported by neither analytic theory nor common-sense" (p. 152).

As we have seen, the practical importance of the concept of a therapeutic or working alliance between patient and analyst, according to Zetzel and Greenson, lies in the recommendation that if analysts are more relaxed, more human, more giving to their patients, the analytic process will profit thereby. Clearly, one of the problems involved in following their recommendation is the question of frustration vs. gratification of transference wishes. We all agree that abstinence (= frustration of wishes of instinctual origin) is a necessary part of the analytic situation. However, since *some* degree of gratification of *some* unconscious infantile wishes is inescapably part of every relationship with another person, including one's analyst, the questions that naturally arise are "How much frustration? How much gratification? When? and what kind(s)?"

The most thoughtful, penetrating, and thorough discussion of the whole problem of frustration vs. gratification of patients' wishes in analysis is to be found in Stone's *The Psychoanalytic Situation* (1961). Stone emphasized repeatedly something to which, I believe, neither Zetzel nor Greenson paid sufficient attention, namely, that one cannot make generalizations that cover every case. Whenever one must decide whether to gratify a patient's wishes, whether by answering a question or by giving information about oneself or by a schedule change or in any other way, the decision should rest on the analyst's understanding of that patient's conflicts, on his understanding of that patient's transference at that time and, thus, on the analyst's prediction, based on his best clinical judgment, of the likely effect on the course of the analysis of gratifying or frustrating the patient's wish(es) at that moment. In addition, Stone emphasized how difficult it often is to be sure that one *does* understand correctly and that one is making the correct decision.

Thus, Stone was both cautious and circumspect in his technical recommendations, which may be summarized as follows. Rules—e.g., the rule of abstinence—are recommendations with a purpose, not orders to be followed blindly and without exception. Stone believes that an analyst should be guided in his behavior by the recognition of what Stone insists is fundamental to the analytic situation, namely, that the patient is there for help and that he views his analyst as his doctor (by which Stone means therapist, not necessarily an M.D.) on whose professional commitment he can count (p. 42). Thus, "There are occasions when, for example, it is insufficient to interpret why a patient does not go for physical examination, or for contraceptive advice" (p. 32), times when his analyst should advise him or her to go. More than that, according to Stone, the psychoanalytic method as such "imposes certain severe restrictions" (p. 42) on analytic patients, and he deems it neither humane nor wise for an analyst to be unnecessarily frustrating: ". . . the intrinsic formal stringencies of the situation are sufficient to contraindicate superfluous deprivations in the analyst's personal attitude" (p. 22). Specifically, Stone can see more potential good than harm for analysis if a patient knows a few simple facts, not too intimate, about his analyst and his personal life.

I thoroughly agree with Stone's major emphases: that analysis is a form of therapy, that a patient should be able to count on his analyst's professional commitment to him as a "doctor," that the business of analysis is to analyze *that* case, that technical rules are not commandments, and that in every instance one should be guided by one's analytic understanding of the entire analytic situation. Moreover, the examples of analytic reserve that Stone cites with disapproval seem as unwarranted to me as they do to Stone. It seems to me, however, that what Stone recommends with respect to what wishes are permissibly and usefully gratified in analysis is likely not to be in the best interests of analytic progress. Nor do I agree that it is in the nature of things that patients will suffer from what Stone calls the severe restrictions of the analytic situation, and that analysts, as good doctors, should aim at keeping to an irreducible minimum the suffering they must impose on their patients by subjecting them to analysis. I have no doubt that it is as possible to pervert analysis as it is to pervert anything else and that an unconsciously cruel or sadistic analyst can misuse analysis to gratify his unconscious wishes under the guise of authoritarian analytic "correctness." I can believe, too, that patients who stay long in such a situation are all the things Stone says they are encouraged by their unconsciously sadistic analysts to be: passive, submissive, awestruck, worshipful and masochistic (p. 66). But to agree that a sadistic analyst and a masochistic patient can unconsciously pervert analysis is not to say that the analytic situation is a source of suffering to patients in and of itself.

I believe, in fact, that the truth is quite otherwise. Provided his analyst is competent (= adequately trained and himself sufficiently well analyzed), it is a patient's own illness that determines whether he experiences the analytic situation in and of itself as a source of pain, as essentially neutral, as a welcome anodyne, or as a positive source of pleasure. Every experienced analyst has had patients who felt analysis to be each of these at the start. Every patient has times during his analysis when he feels analysis to be each of them in turn. Whatever an analytic patient feels about the analytic situation, whether it be suffering, indifference, or gratification, is analytic material. It should, in principle, be treated like any other material: understood if possible and interpreted if appropriate. It is neither inhumane nor inhuman for an analyst to be guided by this principle in his attitude and behavior toward his patients.

If, for example, a patient suffers a catastrophe or a success in life, it is not the best for him and his analysis for his analyst to express sympathy or congratulations before "going on to analyze." It is true enough that it often does no harm for an analyst to be thus conventionally "human." Still, there are times when his being "human" under such circumstances can be harmful, and one cannot always know in advance when those times will be. As an example, for his analyst to express sympathy for a patient who has just lost a close relative may make it more difficult than it would otherwise be for the patient to express pleasure or spite or exhibitionistic satisfaction over the loss. As another example, it is difficult for me to imagine instructing an adult patient to have a physical examination or to go for contraceptive information. I can easily imagine saying to a patient that there must be a reason why he is neglecting his health and that I wonder what his thoughts are about it, or to another that there must be some reason why she is inviting or risking pregnancy and that I wonder what she thinks about it. Either such statement, however phrased, is perfectly in keeping with an analytic attitude on the part of an analyst. Either is quite as analytic, i.e., quite as appropriate to an analytic situation, as it would be to point out to a patient that he invariably tells his dreams at the end of an hour or that he is consistently late in paying his bill—to choose two everyday examples. I cannot imagine circumstances that would justify telling an analytic patient to get a physical examination or to be fitted for a diaphragm any more than I can imagine telling an analytic patient to please tell his dreams early in the hour and to be prompt in paying his bill.

As I have written elsewhere (1976), I believe that an analyst's human responsibility to his patients is to understand them as best he can and to convey to them what he understands for their benefit. An analyst's behavior and attitude are unique, to be sure, but they are none the less human and humane for being unique. When analysis is applicable and effective, it offers the best method that is now available for reducing neurotic suffering. For an analyst to be consistently analytic with his patients may hurt more at the moment than for him to be other than analytic, but it is not cruel. It is the best way we have of helping those who come to us for relief of pain not to continue to suffer in the future as they have in the past. When any doctor *cannot* cure, he is reduced to doing his best to relieve pain. "*Sine opio nulla medicina,*" was good medicine when nothing but palliatives were known. I believe it was in that sense that Freud (1912) compared psychoanalysis to surgery, namely, that both look to cure patients rather than merely to make them comfortable. When a doctor believes he can *cure* a patient, however, neither he nor his patient will be dissuaded from making the attempt because some suffering is unavoidably involved.

I cannot believe that any analyst who deserves the name thinks of analysis as something other than therapy. I am sure that every analyst feels a professional commitment to his patients of the sort that both Stone (1961) and Greenson (1967) have rightly emphasized. I agree, as well, that analysts should be alert to whatever difficulties a patient may have in cooperating in analysis, however covert and subtle those difficulties are. I do not believe, though, that therapeutic alliance or working alliance are useful concepts. I do not agree with Zetzel that an alliance is distinct from the remainder of a patient's transference nor with Greenson's less sweeping formula that working alliance and transference neurosis are to be distinguished from one another even though they are closely related. A patient's resistances in analysis are analytic material. Whatever may be their intensity and however they show themselves—in the transference or in some other way—they are best understood and dealt with when the analyst views them as analytical material and attempts to analyze them. These are conclusions I have reached pragmatically, though I believe them to be consonant with psychoanalytic theory as well. They are conclusions based on experience with my own analytic patients as well as with cases brought to me for consultation and supervision by colleagues, and on a careful, sympathetic study of the reasons advanced to support the usefulness or necessity of distinguishing between alliance and the rest of the transference by those colleagues, led by Zetzel and Greenson, who have argued for doing so. I believe that the distinction they propose is a specious one and that its consequences for analytic practice are, generally speaking, undesirable.

Summary

Examination of the clinical evidence offered by proponents for the concepts of therapeutic and working alliance leads the author to conclude that neither concept is justifiable. Both refer to aspects of the transference that neither deserve a special name nor require special treatment. The related topic of frustration/gratification as necessarily inherent in the analytic situation is also considered.

REFERENCES

Arlow, J. A. (1975), Discussion of Kanzer's paper. *Internat. J. Psychoanal. Psychother.*, 4:69-73.

―――― & Brenner, C. (1966), The psychoanalytic situation. In: *Psychoanalysis in the Americas*, ed. R. E. Litman. New York: International Universities Press, pp. 23-43; 133-138.

Bibring, E. (1937), Symposium on the theory of the therapeutic results of psycho-analysis. *Internat. J. Psycho-Anal.*, 18:170-189.

Brenner, C. (1976), *Psychoanalytic Technique and Psychic Conflict*. New York: International Universities Press.

Freud, S. (1912), Recommendations to physicians practising psychoanalysis. *Standard Edition*, 12:109-120.

Friedman, L. (1969), The therapeutic alliance. *Internat. J. Psycho-Anal.*, 50:139-153.

Greenson, R. R. (1965), The working alliance and the transference neurosis. In: *Explorations in Psychoanalysis*. New York: International Universities Press, 1978, pp. 199-224.

―――― (1966), Contribution to discussion of *The Psychoanalytic Situation*. In: *Psychoanalysis in the Americas*, ed. R. E. Litman. New York: International Universities Press, pp. 131-132.

―――― (1967), *The Technique and Practice of Psychoanalysis*. New York: International Universities Press.

Kanzer, M. (1975), The therapeutic and working alliances. *Internat. J. Psychoanal. Psychother.*, 4:48-68.

Lampl-de Groot, J. (1975), Vicissitudes of narcissism and problems of civilization. *The Psychoanalytic Study of the Child*, 30:663-681. New Haven: Yale University Press.

Modell, A. H. (1972), Review of *The Capacity for Emotional Growth* by E. R. Zetzel. *Psychoanal. Quart.*, 41:261-265.

Stone, L. (1961), *The Psychoanalytic Situation*. New York: International Universities Press.

Zetzel, E. R. (1956), Current concepts of transference. *Internat. J. Psycho-Anal.*, 37:369-378.

_____ (1966), The analytic situation. In: *Psychoanalysis in the Americas*, ed. R. E. Litman. New York: International Universities Press, pp. 86-106.

1040 Park Avenue
New York, New York 10028

THE CONCEPT OF THERAPEUTIC ALLIANCE: IMPLICATIONS FOR THE "WIDENING SCOPE"

Homer C. Curtis, M.D.

O VER THE PAST 25 YEARS there has been an increasing tendency in psychoanalysis to extend our sphere of interest beyond the patient's intrapsychic life to embrace all aspects of the therapeutic relationship, including the analyst's self-observations. Numerous trends of variable importance have contributed to this expansion, including ego psychology; developmental psychology; psychoanalytically oriented psychotherapy—especially of borderline and psychotic patients; studies of empathy and countertransference, the "analyzing instrument," the "corrective emotional experience," object relations theory, etc. A significant contribution to this trend has been the study of the collaborative aspects of the analytic relationship, as exemplified in the concepts of the "therapeutic alliance" (Zetzel, 1956a) and the "working alliance" (Greenson, 1965). In examining the theoretical and clinical implications of these latter concepts one can more clearly delineate some of the gains and insights as well as the problems and confusions typical of the general trend itself. Certainly, this extension has made more explicit many elements of the analytic process which had been treated pragmatically as "givens" to be taken for granted. At the same time, an overemphasis on one aspect of the total process

A revised version of a paper presented at the Annual Meeting of the American Psychoanalytic Association in Quebec, April, 1977.

159

has too often meant a shift of focus away from and the relative neglect of the nuclear analytic concepts of the unconscious, intrapsychic conflict, free association, and interpretation of transference and resistance. It is clear from some writings on the subject and from the often indiscriminate use of the terms therapeutic alliance and working alliance in some discussions of clinical material that the problem exists in this conceptual area.

Historical Background

The collaborative aspects of the relationship between patient and analyst have been recognized from the earliest stages of psychoanalysis. For example, in "Studies on Hysteria" (Breuer and Freud, 1893-1895) Freud states that "we make of the patient a collaborator." The focus on intrapsychic conflict and its derivatives, however, pre-empted the field, with the alliance between patient and analyst accorded the status of a background "given." Nevertheless, it occasionally emerged in Freud's writings in the form of "compliance enough to respect the necessary conditions of the analysis" (1914, p. 154); "the ego, which is our collaborator" (1916-1917, p. 437); "the analytic situation consists in our allying ourselves with the ego of the person under treatment. . . . The ego, if we are able to make such a pact with it, must be a normal one" (1937, p. 235); "The analytic physician and the patient's weakened ego, basing themselves on the real external world, have to band themselves into a party against the enemies, the instinctual demands of the id and the conscientious demands of the super-ego" (1940, p. 173).

Other authors have also made explicit the cooperative factors in the analytic relationship. Sterba wrote of the "ego alliance" and the "therapeutic split in the ego" (1934); Bibring (1937) stressed the importance of the "analytic atmosphere" as a therapeutic force.

While most of these references deal with the mature,

rational, and intellectual capacities of the patient to work with the analyst, the importance of other motives in producing a collaborative effort have also been stressed. Freud (1912) spoke of the "effective positive transference." And said that the patient must have a sufficiently firm emotional attachment to the physician so that he will not again take flight from his illness (1913). After stating "the primary motive force in the therapy is the patient's suffering and the wish to be cured that arises from it" and "In the course of the treatment yet another helpful factor is aroused. This is the patient's intellectual interest and understanding," he declares that these are not enough to withstand the resistances. More is required in the form of "the new sources of strength for which the patient is indebted to his analyst [which] are reducible to transference and instruction" (1913, p. 143). Much later (1940, p. 175) he again emphasized the contribution of transference as follows: "It alters the whole analytic situation; it pushes to one side the patient's rational aim of becoming healthy and free from his ailments. Instead of it there emerges the aim of pleasing the analyst and of winning his applause and love. It becomes the true motive force of the patient's collaboration; his weak ego becomes strong; under its influences he achieves things that would ordinarily be beyond his power."

We may thus delineate, on the one hand, the contribution of the patient's rational, mature capacities (including the wish to be relieved of suffering) and, on the other hand, the irrational transference needs. In addition to these, some writers suggest further conceptual refinements. Dickes (1975), in viewing the total therapeutic relationship, wishes to separate out from the mature, rational relationship what he calls the "real relationship." He describes this essentially as the affective and instinctual components (such as friendliness and sexual feelings) which, while not infantile in aim, he calls nonrational. The intent here seems to be to distinguish this aspect of the healthy, mature relationship from the more cognitive, rational elements which contribute so much to the capacity to work cooperatively in the analysis.

I believe this is an unnecessary and even artificial distinction and would prefer to consider these affective elements essential aspects of the overall interactions between two adults who can in a friendly, mutually respectful undertaking comprehend the special qualities, purposes, and functions of both participants. The mature quality of the aims of these motivations is the basis for distinguishing the real relationship from the transference. For example, a woman patient being analyzed by a relatively young and handsome candidate became aware early in the analysis of being sexually attracted to the analyst. With some embarrassment she was able to verbalize these feelings. It became clear that the analyst had the physical and psychological characteristics which had always attracted the patient and had indeed led to her choice of a husband. Beyond her embarrassment in revealing her sexual attraction there was no sense of conflict, anxiety, or guilt, and she felt quite able to observe, judge, and limit her feelings. This relative comfort and tolerance later changed as a sense of anxiety set in, accompanied by anxious dreams about men pursuing and seducing her and, for a time, more insistent fantasies of demanding a response from the analyst. This shift in the quality of the patient's subjective experience and material alerted the analyst to the invasion of the real relationship, including the patient's sexual feelings, by the developing transference neurosis. To disentangle the two sources and aims of her sexual urges occupied the analysis for a long time and became the focal point of the analysis. It was often a difficult task to get the patient to step back and examine her feelings, rationalized as they were by the attractiveness of the analyst. Looked at from the other side of the relationship, we must also recognize that for a male analyst to have sexual feelings toward a beautiful woman patient need not just be countertransference. While such responses always need to be carefully scrutinized and analyzed, it is likely that they will be a source of difficulty only in proportion to the amount of infantile motivation contributing to the reaction. Experiences of this sort have led to the saying, "analysis is an old man's game."

Dickes further suggests that the negative transference can also contribute to the attachment of the patient to the analyst, who becomes the object on whom the patient can vent his aggression without fear of retaliation. As with the sexual drive, aggression seeks an outlet, and such an opportunity for discharge acts to bind the patient to the treatment. Dickes stresses that too much aggression, especially in regressed form tends to disrupt the therapeutic situation. As has often been noted, the distinction between positive and negative forms of transference is clinically difficult, especially since aggression is most likely to be expressed in ambivalent transference forms such as sadomasochism with strong admixtures of sexual drive. It is thus of questionable conceptual value to make such a sharp separation of positive and negative, and it seems sufficient to recognize the power of the transference to facilitate the analytic work or to disrupt it depending on the specific form of the transference derivatives.

In a closely reasoned study, Friedman (1969) examines some of the problems and paradoxes in the concept of the therapeutic alliance as it has developed since Freud. He points out that while Freud spoke of the need for a "normal ego" in order for the patient to make a pact with the analyst, he felt that the major motivating force in the patient's collaboration was the libidinal (transference) attachment to the analyst. However, since the transference was also recognized as a major resistance to be removed by analysis, there is the paradox of aiming to remove the main source of the patient's motivation to share in the work of the analysis. By examining the contribution of a number of those who have written on the subject, Friedman demonstrates how each emphasizes one or the other side of the paradox and shows how each tries to resolve it. Sterba (1934), for example, stresses those elements of the ego focused on reality, the "observing ego," which is strengthened by analysis and reduction of transference. This raises the question of what then motivates the analysis. Sterba's only answer to this is to speak of identification with the analyst, which he acknowledges is encouraged by suggestion (an id element) and some positive transference, at least initially. Representing the other extreme of the paradox is Nunberg (1928, 1932) who says that the patient is motivated to work with the analyst primarily to achieve transference gratification, protection, and comfort, for which he is willing to give up repressions and recover memories. The threat of loss of the analyst's love and protection forces the patient to accept insight. Friedman characterizes this view as an indulgent, magical alliance with a fantasy analyst followed by desperate appeasement, a kind of bondage rather than alliance.

These are extreme views of each side of the paradox, with Sterba's approach seen as a rationalistic therapeutic alliance without a motor while Nunberg's is a libidinal, energetic alliance without a therapeutic orientation. Friedman sees Fenichel (1941) as a moderator of these two views, agreeing on Sterba's division of the ego into observing and experiencing parts, but also agreeing that the irrational motives (the transference) stressed by Nunberg must be relied on for long periods of time and eventually analyzed because they are infantile. Friedman sees this, however, as the same paradox in a different form, namely, that if the patient is satisfied, he has no incentive to change, and if he is not satisfied, he isn't willing to change.

In an attempt to find some striving in the patient which is harmonious with the analyst's aims, Friedman turns to Loewald's (1960) idea of the child's need to identify with one's growth potential as encouraged by the parent. This is viewed as providing hope, and structures reality in a promising fashion. Friedman elaborates on this view, seeing it as based on an anaclitic attitude with expectations of a diatrophic response from the analyst, especially in the first part of the analysis (a concept very similar to that of Zetzel [1966] which will be considered later, although, surprisingly, Friedman makes no mention of her work in his paper). Friedman stresses the value of hope, not just the irrational hope of transference gratification (Nunberg), but a more realistic hope which provides some correspondence with the analyst's aims. He quotes French (1958) who says that the ability to reopen poorly resolved issues is related to the periodic resurgence of hope for greater fulfillment. This appears to be closely related to a view of transference described by Freud (1914, p. 154) as "an intermediate region between illness and real life," as well as by Nunberg (1951, p. 5) who states that "Repetition compulsion points to the past, transference to actuality (reality), and thus, in a sense, to the future." Further, Bibring (1943) in his study of the repetition compulsion finds not only a conservative, reproductive aspect, but also a restitutive factor which assimilates disturbing tensions and tends to re-establish homeostasis.

In looking for other ways of resolving the dilemma Friedman describes, it might be helpful to reconsider several implied premises concerning the nature of transference and the motivations for the patient's collaboration with the analyst. First of all, transference is not composed solely of infantile id strivings, but also contains elements of ego defense and superego, all aspects of the organized unconscious fantasy, projections of which are manifest as transference phenomena. Secondly, the mature personality of the analytic patient does not consist only of ego defenses and reason. Instead of strictly separating id (too often conceived of as consisting only of *infantile* strivings) from the ego along macrostructural lines, we may conceive of structural organizations containing mature drives related to, executed, and facilitated by mature ego functions. Alongside the infantile drive-ego organizations that are the source of transference (which both motivates and resists analysis) these mature drive-ego constellations provide the adult object-related liking, respect, pleasure in mastery, as well as the intellectual and reasoning capacities, which are also sources of motivation to work with the analyst. This conception avoids the false dichotomy of the id-motor and the drive-free rationalistic ego and conforms to the clinical observations of a variety of motivations which provides the impelling force to analyze. This can be seen as an example of Waelder's (1936) principle of multiple function which states that all psychological phenomena manifest elements from all parts of the personality.

The Therapeutic Alliance

As has been described previously, the cooperative aspects of the analytic relationship have long been recognized and the words "pact," "alliance," "therapeutic split in the ego," and "collaboration" have been applied to this area of the relationship. However, it has been primarily since Zetzel spoke of the "therapeutic alliance" in 1956 that the term has attained a general currency and a significant place in discussions of the theory and technique of the analytic process. (Incidentally, in her paper, Zetzel [1956a] attributes the concept to Edward Bibring, referring to "his description of an alliance between the analyst and the healthy part of the patient's ego. . ." [p. 170].) In her paper, primarily devoted to a delineation of the difference between the Kleinian and classical views of transference, she takes as a point of departure the issue of regression in the formation of the transference neurosis. She points out that most analysts see this movement to earlier states of mental functioning as both indispensable in revealing unconscious fantasy, and a resistance in the sense of a blind attempt to live out conflicts rather than to comprehend and resolve them through verbal insight, genetic reduction and structural change. To accomplish this a therapeutic alliance dependent on stable mature ego functions of reality testing, object constancy, impulse control, tension tolerance, etc. is needed to contain and delimit the regression while analysis of the transference is taking place. Following Hartmann, she speaks of the development of these and other mature ego qualities out of primary and secondary autonomous ego sources and processes, to the point of relative stability and distance from their connections with infantile aims and conflicts. Without such resources and achievements, a suitable therapeutic alliance cannot be formed; examples of such cases would be borderline and psychotic patients. By contrast, Zetzel points out the Kleinian disregard for structural considerations and the emphasis on primitive fantasies dynamically active at all times in all behavior. In Kleinian theory, regression is considered desirable and not to be feared; and therapeutic alliance, to the extent that it is considered at all, is a by-product of deep and early transference interpretations, which are said to relieve the patient's anxiety and diminish resistance.

Thus, Zetzel stresses the importance of mature ego function as the basis for the therapeutic alliance, although she also speaks of "transference as therapeutic alliance" (presumably the "effective positive transference" of Freud) and identification with the analyst as a further element. The important point here is that this rather traditional view appears to have undergone significant change by the time her paper "The Analytic Situation" appeared in 1966. Here she stresses the analogy of the analytic situation and the early mother-child relationship, being influenced in the new direction by a number of authors who pointed to certain features of the analytic situation which seem to them to be a repetition of that fundamental relationship. Greenacre (1954), for example, refers to this early stage as the "matrix" of transference. Perhaps most influential was the concept advanced by Spitz (1956) that the analytic patient was like a "helpless infant" who required the "diatrophic" (maternal and supportive) response of the analyst, ideally applied carefully and selectively. Gitelson (1962) expanded on this "anaclitic dyad" model, advocating the explicit expression by the analyst of supportive feelings toward the patient. In his monograph, Stone (1961) wrote in a more temperate way of the value of a warm, humane therapeutic attitude toward the patient.

Building on these concepts, Zetzel advances the idea that the mature ego functions which serve as the basis of the therapeutic alliance could only be established if the early object relationship with the mother had been sufficiently satisfying so as to lead to "mastery of the depressive position" (Klein, 1948) and consolidation of "basic trust" (Erikson, 1950) and "expectant faith" (Freud, 1905). That Zetzel doubts the achievement of this state of maturity in most patients is evidenced by her assumption that, in the first part of analysis, all patients will experience some degree of "primitive objective anxiety," which is due to regression. This regression is seen as threatening the integration of the mature ego functions and identifications and must be responded to by the analyst's intuitive reactions of support in order to foster the therapeutic alliance. It is Zetzel's contention that this anxiety in the first phase of analysis is "real" or "objective" anxiety, that is, the anxiety experienced with disruption of ego organization such as is prototypically experienced as fear of loss of the object (separation anxiety in the strict sense). This anxiety, according to Zetzel, is not to be confused with anxiety attendant upon the threatened emergence of repressed conflictual material in the transference. She is thus postulating two different spheres of interaction and intervention. One, the sphere of the therapeutic alliance, consists of the "effective positive transference" and the mature ego functions associated with a capacity for object relations, which with all analytic patients are unstable enough that regression in the analysis threatens to disrupt the ego organization, leading to primitive objective anxiety; this requires active, supportive ("diatrophic") interventions by the analyst to provide an experience that fosters a special object relationship, new ego identifications, a better reintegration, and further growth of the basic ego qualities. The second sphere, that of the transference neurosis, consists of the derivatives of intrapsychic conflict projected onto the relationship with the analyst and accompanied by signal anxiety related to fear of loss of love or punishment; this requires interpretation of resistance and transference to provide insight, leading to working through, genetic reduction, and structural change. A further distinction is implied in the nature of the regression and the specific areas of the personality affected by the regression. If we follow Zetzel's conceptions, the regression she refers to as leading to "primitive objective anxiety" is potentially deeper and affects the ego capacities for reality testing, object relations, and tension tolerance. The regression in the sphere of the transference is more selective and limited, affecting primarily the defensive organization, allowing the expression of less disguised derivatives of repressed infantile drives. Not only does this distinction raise the question of whether the relatively autonomous sphere of the ego in neurotic patients is indeed so tenuously structured, it also seems to unduly splinter the neurotic personality structure that is relatively unified, apart from the specific area of conflict.

In developing this point of view, Zetzel finds support in a statement by Bibring (1937) where, in speaking of modifications in the superego during analysis, he states:

> In my opinion the analyst's attitude, and the analytic atmosphere which he creates, are fundamentally a reality-correction which adjusts the patient's anxieties about loss of love and punishment, the origin of which lies in childhood. Even if these anxieties later undergo

analytic resolution I still believe that the patient's
relationship to the analyst from which a sense of security
emanates is not only a pre-condition of the procedure
but also effects an immediate (apart from an analytical)
consolidation of his sense of security which he has not
successfully acquired or consolidated in childhood. Such
an immediate consolidation—which, in itself, lies outside
the field of analytic therapy—is, of course, only of
permanent value if it goes along with the coordinated
operation of analytic treatment [pp. 182-183].

While a decision on the validity and usefulness of
Zetzel's views does not depend on her interpretation of Bibring's statement, it may be helpful to examine this
interpretation, since it can sharpen the issues she raises.
Zetzel understands him to be speaking of primitive,
"objective" anxiety, that is, the anxiety associated with ego
disruption, the genetic basis of which is fear of the loss of the
object as in separation anxiety in the first years of life. In
fact, Bibring speaks, not of fear of the loss of the object or
fear of ego disruption, but of fear of loss of love and fear of
punishment, genetically later types of anxiety (Freud, 1926)
occurring after the establishment of object constancy, a
relatively cohesive sense of self, and verbal and symbolic
capacities. These latter two types of anxieties are encountered
as the crucial fears in the unconscious fantasies revealed in
the analyses of neurotic patients and expressed in the
transference neurosis. While they are capable of being
alleviated at least temporarily by noninterpretive, educative,
and suggestive techniques as advocated by Bibring to further
the analytic process, he says they may "later undergo
analytical resolution." Furthermore, the "consolidation" of
the patient's "sense of security" by these nonanalytic means
"is, of course, only of permanent value if it goes along with
the coordinated operation of analytic treatment." This clearly
emphasizes that Bibring considers the anxieties in the first

part of analysis to be derived from intrapsychic conflict and signal the beginning mobilization of transference fantasies about the analyst. Ultimately, these will be systematically interpreted, after the initial establishment of the "analytic atmosphere" or therapeutic alliance, in which the more acceptable, modulated "effective positive transference" combines forces with the patient's mature ego functions.

In advancing the hypothesis that all analytic patients experience primitive objective anxiety requiring diatrophic supportive interventions, Zetzel departs from the view expressed in her 1956a paper, which differentiates neurotic patients from borderline and psychotic patients whose "relative failure of ego development . . . precludes the development of a genuine therapeutic alliance" (p. 176). These sicker patients require preliminary psychotherapy utilizing "positive transference as a means of reinforcing, rather than analysing, the precarious defences" (p. 177). This earlier view stressing the relative stability and autonomy of the mature ego functions of the neurotic patient, as contrasted with the sicker patients, was opposed to the Kleinian neglect of structural considerations in the view that primitive fantasy pervades all behavior in all patients and that the stability of the ego at any given time is dependent on the state of the relations with external and internal objects. However, in her later paper (1966) Zetzel appears to move closer to the Kleinian position by postulating that even neurotic patients in analysis cannot maintain their mature ego functions on a sufficiently stable level to form a therapeutic alliance without the help of early nurturing, supportive interventions and a diatrophic relationship with the analyst. This implies an instability and relative lack of autonomy in the ego structures of reality testing, capacity to maintain self-object differentiation, impulse control, and tension tolerance, which are essential for a therapeutic alliance. From a clinical point of view, such a tenuous ego integration is at the mercy of real and fantasy object vicissitudes, and most analysts agree that patients of this type require supportive psychotherapy or analytic parameters (Eissler, 1953). While the "widening scope of psychoanalysis" has brought many such patients to the analyst, there is no question that there are also many patients whose ego functions and capacity for object relations permit them to comprehend and utilize a psychoanalytic situation without the need for supportive interventions which, while aimed at cementing a therapeutic alliance, are likely to provide regressive transference gratifications to the detriment of transference analysis.

As pointed out by Arlow and Brenner (1966), Zetzel's hypothesis that the psychoanalytic situation uniformly recreates the earliest mother-child relationship seems an unduly broad generalization based more on analogy than on clinical data in each case. While turning to another person for help may have some of its genetic roots in the mother-child relationship (as, for that matter, every human relationship may have), it does not follow that it is the only derivation of the capacity to trust and to cooperate with another person, given the many complicated object ties and experiences encountered in development. In addition, it does not follow that the contribution made to the therapeutic alliance from the early mother-child relationship consists of dynamically active motivations with the same primitive aims of merging or separating from the mother. In most neurotic patients, achievements of identification and individuation have resulted in relatively stable psychic configurations and structures with a change in aim. To assume that every later relationship contains the same aims and meanings as the prototypical one is what Hartmann (1939) calls a genetic fallacy. If, like Klein, Zetzel claims that all patients are struggling with dynamically active fantasies of the first years of life, her recommendation for immediate interpretive intervention to calm objective anxiety and supply nurturing support seems functionally close to the Kleinian view that early deep interpretations are necessary to relieve persecutory anxieties. While the verbal content of the two types of intervention may differ, they share the common therapeutic purpose of calming objective anxiety and promoting trust, which, if accomplished, is most likely due to the nonspecific elements of reassurance and interest.

These considerations suggest the possibility that, in this view of the primitive sources of the therapeutic alliance, Zetzel found a means of reconciling the Kleinian and classical orientations, a task which seems to have occupied much of her interest (Zetzel, 1956b). While being unable to accept some of the Kleinian ideas which strained logic, she found much of value and hoped to accomplish some integration of Klein's views within the mainstream of psychoanalysis. Her theory of the therapeutic alliance seems an implicit, although partial, fulfillment of this hope.

The Working Alliance

Compared to Zetzel's explication of her theory of the therapeutic alliance, the concept of the working alliance as advanced by Greenson (1965) is relatively limited and simple. Assigning priority to Zetzel in introducing the term therapeutic alliance to make explicit what had been recognized but insufficiently stressed, Greenson preferred the term "working alliance" because it emphasized the rational, intentional effort to work purposefully in the analytic situation. Although the two concepts overlap, with both containing rational and nonrational elements, Zetzel's focus is more on the nonrational, primitive sources of collaborative effort and Greenson's on the mature ego capacities to work rationally.

Greenson stresses the danger of overemphasizing the conflictual transference elements at the expense of recognizing and fostering the capacity of the patient to deal with reality, including the reality of the analytic situation and the humanness of the analyst. He deplores the too literal application of Freud's mirror metaphor, implying that some analysts deal only with transference and limit their interventions to interpretation. In so doing, the analyst minimizes the patient's realistic perceptions and motives, insisting on the primacy of unconscious fantasies as the true source of behavioral phenomena. Carried to an extreme, this could lead to abuses such as is illustrated in the perhaps apocryphal story told in various versions of the analyst who fell asleep during an analytic session. His snoring alerted the patient, who awoke him by calling his name, whereupon the analyst interpreted "You always wanted your mother's attention." Although this may well have been true, the first order of business was certainly to acknowledge the appropriateness of the patient's observation and to apologize for the lapse. Only then might the analyst expect to explore with the patient the transference dimension of the interaction.

It is of course a matter of analytic judgment whether an answer, explanation, or acknowledgment of a patient's question or observation about the analyst is in the best interests of the analytic process. Such a decision needs to take into account the patient's capacity to tolerate delay and uncertainty, the nature and extent of the issue in question, the empathic grasp of the patient's transference position, and the analyst's introspective awareness of his own motivation, including countertransference elements. Only then might the analyst be able to decide to pursue the transference meaning directly or to defer that temporarily to mend or support the therapeutic alliance, which will make analysis of the transference possible. It is common clinical experience that it is more likely to be the patients with more primitive psychopathology or neurotic patients in times of greater regression who require special interventions to shore up their capacity to work analytically. For example, a man who entered analysis for depression, vague feelings of anxiety, a sense of aimlessness, and inability to form close relationships experienced great discomfort on attempting to use the couch and free associate. Because of the diagnostic impression of impairment in his ability to distinguish reality, to tolerate anxiety, and to trust other people, I encouraged him to set his own pace in using the couch. The first interviews were conducted face to face in discussing his history. As he became more comfortable, he insisted on trying to lie on the couch. When this precipitated too much anxiety, he sat on the edge of the couch, alternately facing me and then looking away. During this time, I made it a point to speak freely and frequently in response to his recounting his history and current problems, stressing that his reactions, anxieties, etc., were understandable and similar to those of many other people. Within certain limits, I answered his questions, and, when I sensed he was not too anxious, I took the opportunity when he asked questions to suggest that we look first at some of his own answers and speculations. After this period of support and training he finally could use the couch, as long as we discussed factual, day-to-day experiences. In lieu of visual contact I provided him with verbal support, and when he became anxious at some noise I might have made, I would casually explain that I had shifted my position, or was making a note, etc. The effect of this gradual building up of a supportive, trusting relationship was to allow him to use some free association to which I could respond with clarifications and cautious dynamic interpretations. Some analytic work was able to be accomplished, but I was always aware of his need for support, for help in assessing reality, and for a model to identify with and to provide a better ego organization. Such clinical experiences demonstrate the way in which failure in development of crucial ego functions and distortions in personality organization necessitate changes in technical approach and impose limits on the analysis of coexisting intrapsychic conflict. Not only do drive-defense constellations contain primitive elements leading to intense and troublesome transference reactions, but the deficits in and impairments of those personality resources necessary for analytic collaboration may demand special interventions and "parameters" (Eissler, 1953) to achieve some greater cohesion prior to productive interpretive work.

Inasmuch as the fundamental goal in analysis is to promote psychological growth by means of conflict resolution and working through rather than providing a supportive, educational experience; by analyzing the infantile object relationship as revived in the transference rather than by building a mature object relationship; by removing interferences with reality functioning rather than by teaching the nature of reality, we must regard the therapeutic alliance as a necessary preliminary and ancillary process, a means to an end rather than an end in itself. The obvious danger in attempting to foster the patient's collaboration is the possibility that some aspects of the relationship may be labeled "realistic" and therefore not to be analyzed. This would be similar to taking a rationalization at face value, recognizing the realistic element, but stopping short of revealing the conflictual motivation which uses the rational aspect as a disguise, either primarily or after the fact. The problem may be clarified further by studying a clinical example offered by Greenson in a later paper (Greenson and Wexler, 1969). His patient, Kevin, in his fifth year of analysis responded to an interpretation with a criticism of the analyst, stating that he talked too much, exaggerated, and that his feelings would be hurt were these faults pointed out to him. The patient, while hesitant, still was able to state his criticisms clearly and directly and did not cover them by speaking in an angry manner, which he knew could be excused as "neurotic" and therefore not hurtful to the analyst. To inform the analyst of his observations was thus a realistic judgment and would be bound to hurt the analyst's feelings, which indeed was the case. The analyst told him his perceptions of these traits were accurate and, in so doing, felt that this was essential as a way of affirming the patient's capacity to judge reality and of supporting the working alliance. While stating that this acknowledgment was "unanalytic" inasmuch as it did not increase the patient's insight into his unconscious motivation, Greenson saw it as advancing the analysis.

Because Greenson does not give further details of the interactions preceding or following this episode, we are left with the perhaps erroneous impression that attending to the working alliance by acknowledging the accuracy of the patient's observations resulted in the neglect of the transference dimension. The patient's further associations are lacking, but several factors in the account call for consideration of transference meanings. For example, it might be questioned why the patient chose this particular time, after over four years of analysis, to verbalize his criticisms. Insofar as his criticism followed an interpretation, the nature of which is not revealed, an exploration of the patient's subjective response to the interpretation would quite possibly discover more than an objective perception of the analyst's shortcomings. It is common in analysis for a patient to react to an interpretation as if it were a criticism. This often permits the patient to avoid the pain, anxiety, and perhaps the truth of the interpretation by turning the tables on the analyst and offering critical "interpretations" to him. As a speculation, which needn't be factually true to illustrate the point, it is possible that the content of Greenson's interpretation was on the mark, but couched in unnecessarily florid and wordy terms. An understandable defensive reaction which would mitigate the narcissistic hurt as well as avoid the anxiety stirred up by the interpretation would be to shift the focus from the content of the interpretation to the form in which it was offered.

What I am stressing is the necessity of keeping open the possibility, or better, the likelihood of a transference element in even the most apparently realistic interaction between patient and analyst. Whereas it is true that a chimney is not only a phallic symbol but also a device to let smoke out of the house, the same double meaning of human behavior can be looked at from the opposite direction. The sometime overwillingness of analysts to expose their faults in order to demonstrate their humanness and acceptance of the patient as an equal may deflect the analytic effort from searching for knowledge of the inner life that can best be gained by analyzing. This tendency is reminiscent of an old joke in which a rental agent is showing an apartment to a prospective renter. When the latter complains of a bad odor in the apartment, the agent, in his eagerness to get the lease signed, replies, "Oh, that's just me. Ain't I a smelly son of a bitch!"

By its very nature, transference is an amalgam of past and present, infantile and adult, fantasy and reality, since it is formed by a projection of aspects of repressed fantasy onto objects in current reality. Viewed in terms of Waelder's principle of multiple function, a specific behavior occurs because it best fulfills the demands of all aspects of the personality and of reality. It is in the proportions of the motivational admixture that the significant clinical differences can be noted. Where the infantile elements predominate dynamically, we are dealing with transference, whereas when they are minimal the behavior reflects primarily the interests and functions of the mature personality organization. The latter sphere is the basis of the working alliance. Yet, especially in the regressive setting of the analytic situation, there will be shifting combinations of these motivations. It is the function of a transference interpretation to help the patient distinguish fantasy from reality, thus, paradigmatically, an interpretation includes attention to both aspects, as in the observation, "You are afraid of my disapproval now as you once were afraid of your father's disapproval." Making this delineation will be easier if the patient's reality testing enables him to see that the fear of disapproval does not derive from the analyst's actual behavior or attitude. Depending on the patient's working alliance based on his mature ego functions, the analyst must at the same time be alert for evidences of transference intrusions, which may in subtle ways find expression under cover of the alliance. In addition, the analyst must be willing to search his inner life for evidences of countertransference which not only cause blind spots but influence his analytic stance, thus making it more difficult for the patient to detect the transference contaminations of his perceptions of the analyst.

As an example of such a clinical problem, let me give a short excerpt from the case of a very intelligent college professor who entered analysis because of marital difficulties which were an expression of a more general problem in his relationships with women. He brought a considerable knowledge of psychoanalysis into analysis with him and had a fine capacity to introspectively capture subtle meanings in his free associations, which he often related to literary references, especially Greek mythology. He was a fascinating person to work with, and the analysis went along swimmingly as we developed our own analytic language and shorthand, seeming able to grasp each other's meaning very rapidly and intuitively. Considerable progress was made for many months until a time came when the material seemed rather repetitive and without clear direction, although our manner of working together seemed unchanged. The nature of the resistance was soon evident when, with some chagrin, I saw the answer in a dream reported by the patient with pleasure and fascination. In the dream he was reading poetry with an older man who was blind. The affect in the dream was a mixture of pleasurable closeness, with a touch of good-natured jousting. Of course, the blind poet represented me, not only an allusion to my first name but also to my blindness in not seeing that, in our enjoyment and satisfaction in working so well together and in sharing the same dedication and interest in psychoanalysis and literature, especially Greek mythology, I had unwittingly joined him in a mutual acting out of an unconscious homosexual fantasy, cast in platonic form in the dream. The humorous teasing quality in the dream referred to his fooling me, pulling my leg, and, most telling, "poking fun at me," which, when "Homer" was associatively connected to "homo," allowed me to interpret the defensive transformation of his dangerous homosexual feelings for me into the more acceptable intellectual communion. I pointed out to him that, in our mutual pleasure in working so well together, we had not realized that this had provided the framework for expression of his submerged erotic feelings toward me, which, from other material, was related genetically to experiences with an older brother. I chose not to burden him with the other results of the self-analysis of my countertransference, which, dynamically, had to do with phallic narcissistic intellectual pleasures and, genetically, was derived from a close attachment to a younger brother. In taking this approach, I was agreeing with those who recommend a limited acknowledgment of a slip or of the analyst's contribution to a transference-countertransference collusion without including those deeper motivations, revealed by self-analysis, which might confuse the patient and invite further transference gratifications and resistances. Here, again, the joke of the smelly real estate agent might be pertinent as an answer to those who advocate revealing to the patient some of the analyst's deeper countertransference motivations in the name of sharing and fostering the alliance.

Discussion

The work of Zetzel, Greenson, and others has served to bring to our attention an aspect of the analytic relationship which has long been taken for granted as a necessary foundation on which to base the analysis of intrapsychic conflict. By making this aspect explicit and worthy of study they are following the basic principle of trying to comprehend all aspects of the mind having some bearing on the psychoanalytic process. Certain of their theoretical and technical suggestions raise issues which challenge us to re-examine traditional views of the focus and scope of analysis. In so doing we are following the example set by Freud whose periodic reappraisals of theoretical and technical matters are well known. Certainly we can agree that sharpening our awareness of all psychological processes in our patients and in ourselves allows us to utilize those forces leading to collaboration in a more fruitful way even though there will be different ways of conceptualizing and justifying our views.

There is general agreement that the concept of therapeutic alliance covers all those motivations contributing to the collaborative efforts of analyst and patient in promoting the analytic process. There is thus a wide range of contributing elements of differing dynamic, genetic, and structural nature, such as the wish for relief and cure, the hope for more efficient and gratifying psychic functioning, intellectual interest, as well as the wish for love, approval, magical powers, and other nonrational motives. Diverse transference elements such as sadism may at times bind the patient to the analysis, but the main contribution from the nonrational sphere is the libidinally based feeling of dependence and the need to win approval. Whereas the latter are important and often crucial, the consistent and most reliable source of the cooperation between patient and analyst lies in the mature, realistic aspects of the analytic relationship, which depend on the ego functions of reality testing, capacity for self-object differentiation, tolerance for tension, and delay of gratification, etc. These mature ego functions may temporarily be impaired by intense transference neurotic forces, but they must be of sufficient stability to re-establish their dominance if analytic resolution is to occur.

It is this latter part of the alliance spectrum that Greenson, to stress the capacity to work purposefully, has termed the working alliance. The working alliance is thus a subsidiary concept and properly should not be juxtaposed to the therapeutic alliance as a co-equal concept. It may be conceptually clearer and simpler to avoid using the two terms interchangeably, as even Zetzel and Greenson have at times done, by the expedient of dropping the term working alliance and, instead, speaking of the mature, rational elements of the therapeutic alliance.[1]

Perhaps as a carry-over from the implicit pragmatic, "taken for granted" approach to analytic collaboration, a significant bias can be discerned in most writings on the subject, a bias that focuses mainly on the qualities in the patient which influence the alliance. Relatively less is said about the contribution of the analyst. Yet, if we speak of an alliance, we must consider what each partner brings to it. It has been noted, especially in studies of countertransference, that the principle of relative anonymity of the analyst too often spreads inappropriately from its proper and important place in the clinical setting into our study of the psychology of the analyst, as if he were a purified "analyzing instrument," if not a mirror. Yet, we are aware of the importance of recognizing our imaginative responses to the patient's material, based on the resonance of our unconscious processes with those of the patient. Such responses, to be useful, must be examined and processed by logical, cognitive capacities, enhanced by our training and experience. To be able to use our empathy and to recognize and analyze our countertransference for the ultimate benefit of the analytic process in the patient is the goal set for us by Fliess (1942), Isakower (in Malcove, 1975), and Kohut (1959) among others. The balanced views of such authors are in contrast to the theories of Racker (1968), Baranger and Baranger (1966), and others who, following Kleinian ideas of projective identification, assert that the analyst's felt response to the

---

[1] It has been suggested that the term "analytic alliance" might be preferable, since it not only covers the range of collaborative motivations but also implies the primacy of the analytic process rather than the therapeutic effect (personal communication, Edward H. Knight).

patient correctly reflects what the patient is experiencing. This simplistic view fails to allow for the complexities of the analytic interaction, the nature of countertransference blind spots, and depreciates the role of logical, cognitive processes.

Among the qualities and characteristics the analyst contributes to the setting up of an optimal analytic situation are, first of all, his competence and experience, which give coherence and direction to his free empathic responses. These capacities of the analyst, which the patient deserves, in turn deserve and elicit the patient's realistic trust and cooperation, and combine with the analyst's physicianly dedication and respect for the patient's individuality and goals to match the patient's mature object-related capacities. It is this mutually respectful and adult partnership that forms the solid and reliable nucleus of the therapeutic alliance. This not only allows a safe "regression in the service of the ego" (Kris) to form transference derivatives, but accounts for the accommodations which patient and analyst can make to each other's differences in cultural background, life experiences, character traits, etc. With this "reliable core," the analyst's personal character and analyzing "style" become less crucial and the patient needs less overt demonstration of "warmth" and support, being able to comprehend, for example, why the analyst prefers to allow free associations to produce interpretable material rather than influence the material through supportive and educative measures. Such an atmosphere of serious purpose and dedication by no means excludes evidences of humanitarian concern, respect, and compassion, but can avoid extremes of role-playing "warmth" or ritualized remoteness.

The capacity for empathy may appear to be a "gift," and indeed there may be some as yet unidentifiable constitutional *Anlage* for this important quality. It is more probable, however, that it represents the outcome of successful struggle with painful experiences leading to mastery and freer access to deeper levels of experience as compared to the less fortunate outcome where relative peace is purchased by repression and constricting character defenses. Empathy, as a trial identification which allows a reversible, shared, affective experience, should be differentiated from countertransference, although the boundaries may sometimes be indistinct. The latter, defined in its narrower sense as a transference response in the analyst, shares with the patient's transference the infantile aims and defenses that lead to confusion rather than insight. It is the capacity to detect and utilize these responses through self-analysis that permits the analyst to turn them to the patient's benefit.

The view expressed by Zetzel, which advocates fostering the alliance, especially in the beginning, by supportive and nurturing interventions must be subjected to clinical evaluation. It is the experience of many analysts that the need for such actively supporting measures is in inverse proportion to the strength and stability of the patient's mature ego capacities previously mentioned. In neurotically structured psychopathology, these mature capacities ensure an awareness of the purposes and nature of the analytic work, as well as limiting and containing transference regression, which is, in such patients, less primitive and more firmly object related. Such a patient accommodates to the analytic process, maintaining an "as if" objectivity in the face of transference experience without a need for nurturing support. Providing an atmosphere of respect, tolerance, and understanding while helping the patient expand his self-knowledge are the best guarantees of a therapeutic alliance. Especially in the first part of an analysis, the interventions by the analyst in the form of clarification (Bibring, 1954) not only facilitate the formation of transference but provide a sense of increased self-awareness and mastery as well as a basis for identification with the analyst's analyzing function. This obviates the need for gratuitous support likely to be experienced as gratification of dependent transference needs.

It is in the psychoanalytic psychotherapy of sicker patients that, following the model of child analysis, the ego insufficiencies require the analyst to undertake extra measures to supplement the immature or deformed ego's capacities. The provision of supportive nurturing words and attitudes not only makes possible some degree of insight, but offers a new object relationship for identification and structure formation and modification. In each case it becomes the task of diagnosis and continued empathic evaluation to determine the patient's therapeutic capacities and needs.

From this examination of the therapeutic alliance, we can detect some of the significant factors in the trend toward greater interest and attention to areas outside the sphere of intrapsychic conflict. In response to the need to help sicker patients by applying psychoanalytic principles, as well as the desire to explore all facets of the human personality, analysts and analytically informed workers have concerned themselves with clinical conditions long considered unsuitable for psychoanalysis. And, building on Freud's shift to the structural point of view, the ego's defensive and adaptive functions have been increasingly studied and applied in a variety of ways, in addition to the clinical situation. This expansion of the range of psychic processes under clinical, developmental, and research scrutiny has quite understandably led to controversy and a need for careful evaluation of the consequences. Although there is general agreement on the usefulness and validity of the application of psychoanalytic knowledge to inform some related fields of interest, it is in those clinical areas closest to psychoanalysis in its traditional form that confusion, both clinical and theoretical, has arisen. The most important aspect of this confusion centers in the area of the ego and the way in which differences in its organization affect the conceptualization and implementation of the therapeutic approach. Thus, we have seen the development of interest in special theories and therapies emphasizing object relations, countertransference, narcis-

sism, behavior, group and family interactions, and many
others.

As described previously, with borderline and psychotic
patients the deformities and deficits of ego organization shift
the primary focus of therapy away from structural conflict
toward measures aimed at repairing or building structure.
Even with neurotic patients it is often clear that not all of the
significant psychopathology is limited to the area of
intrapsychic conflict, and that such factors as developmental
arrest, structural deficits, deficiencies in self-representation
exist alongside symptoms and neurotic character defenses.
Such a clinical situation taxes the analyst's ability to
distinguish between fixed structural distortions, on the one
hand, and those character defenses which are still dynamically
linked to structural conflict, on the other. Even though such
character attitudes and behavior seem turned toward external
reality and play a part in current object relations, if they
express neurotic fantasy drives and defenses that are still
active, they may be regressively drawn into the transference
neurosis and subjected to analysis. What might appear to be
a schizoid isolation may actually be a defensive ego attitude
to avoid the anxiety aroused by intimacy, neurotically
misconceived as taboo. The latter requires analytic interpretation and conflict resolution rather than provision of a "new
object" and a real object relationship to belatedly build up
ego structure and capacities.

Examining the therapeutic alliance as conceptualized by
Zetzel (1966) and Greenson and Wexler (1969, 1970), we are
presented with two rationales and purposes of significant
difference. On the one hand, the therapeutic alliance is to be
fostered as a necessary preliminary and adjunct so that
analysis of conflict can take place. On the other hand, the
alliance and the measures to support it are seen as
therapeutic in their own right, providing a new and better
object relationship which will build new identifications and
reintegrate the ego through this nurturing experience. Hence,

for some analysts being a "new object" for the patient becomes a primary therapeutic task, equal with and sometimes superseding the analysis of conflict. While commonly recognized as a necessary modification of the classical model in some cases of child analysis and analytically oriented psychotherapy, it is this concept which is the center of controversy about the therapeutic alliance and, more generally, about theories and therapies included in the "widening scope of psychoanalysis."

Because it is clear that the real relationship does play a significant part in the total analytic process, it is important to define its place in such a way that it does not pre-empt the central role traditionally assigned to the analytic resolution of intrapsychic conflict by interpretation of transference and resistance. Ferenczi (1909, p. 55) quotes Freud as having said, "We may treat a neurotic in any way we like, he always treats himself with transferences." Thus, a patient may be relieved of symptoms as a result of transference and inexact interpretations (Glover, 1931). It is the task of the analyst to interpret those transferences and resistances with the collaboration of the patient whose reality-oriented capacities are strengthened by an identification with the analyst's analyzing function. This highly selective identification ideally is firmly established by the end of analysis and is an integrating force in the patient's ability to carry on his self-analysis. During analysis this will be accompanied by numerous other grosser and more personal identifications with the analyst's mannerisms, dress, values, and views (real or imagined), etc., which are apt to serve defensive functions and are therefore to be subjected to analysis.

In addition to the therapeutic alliance and the related identification with the analyzing function, the real relationship plays a role in the working-through process. After freeing up the resistances and structured conflict, the old drive-discharge patterns are amenable to change and growth, with experience, as in the normal process of development.

The analyst will naturally be chosen as a potential "new object" whether he agrees or not. While his human interest and respect will respond to the patient's new capacities, his dedication to the therapeutic goal of analyzing will limit these responses to those which will not restrict the patient either in his exploration for further transference meanings or in his search for new objects outside the analysis where the potential for growth and satisfaction is much greater. Rather than interacting with the patient in ways that might be appropriate for the normal social situation, the analyst must continue to help the patient understand the transitions he is going through by offering appropriate developmental constructions (Kanzer, 1975). To offer direct supportive or diatrophic interventions at such times runs the risk of binding the patient to the analyst in a dependent manner rather than freeing him to move in an independent, maturing direction.

Zetzel (1966) makes a distinction between the closed system of intrapsychic conflict and transference neurosis and the open system of the real relationship and therapeutic alliance. The former is to be approached by free association and interpretation, whereas the latter is said to require supportive measures similar to those of a good parent to foster development and reintegration. In actual clinical fact, free association covers both areas since it is the means whereby not only intrapsychic fantasy and transference material are expressed, but also the meanings and motives of the real relationship. The fundamental rule rests upon the integrity, honesty, and purpose of the real relationship and alliance while conveying content from both spheres. Furthermore, the transference itself is a bridge between the two systems, since what had been internal, ego-alien, autoplastic, and apparently nonpersonal becomes externalized and transformed into an interpersonal relationship, albeit with infantile aims, intermingled with the more mature aims of the real relationship. It is on the basis of such observations that Freud (1914, p. 154) said, "The transference thus creates an intermediate region between illness and real life through which the transition from one to the other is made." And Nunberg (1951, p. 5) said, "In so far . . . as in transference the wishes and drives are directed towards the objects of the external world . . . transference is independent of the repetition compulsion. Repetition compulsion points to the past, transference to actuality (reality), and thus, in a sense, to the future." Thus, while transference strives to reproduce past conflictual relationships, in reaching for new objects as surrogates there is also a striving for mastery of the painful aspects of the past and for solutions in the present.

Summary

As a result of studies in ego and developmental psychology, psychoanalytically oriented psychotherapy, empathy, countertransference, and object relations, the sphere of interest in psychoanalysis has been extended beyond the patient's intrapsychic life to embrace all aspects of the therapeutic relationship. A significant contribution to this trend has been a study of the collaborative aspects of the analytic relationship as exemplified in the concepts of therapeutic alliance and working alliance. A historical survey of writings on this subject serves as a background for a critical examination of the theoretical and clinical implications of these concepts. These studies have provided a useful conceptual basis for the understanding of many "given" aspects of the analytic relationship, delineating those personality attributes which make collaboration in the analytic work possible. This in turn has been helpful in making appropriate applications of psychoanalytic principles in the therapy of a broader range of clinical conditions. It is suggested that, along with the gains achieved by making explicit the rational and irrational elements of the collaborative aspect of analysis, there is also the danger of a shift of focus away from the nuclear analytic concepts of unconscious intrapsychic conflict, free association, and interpretation of transference and resistance. This danger lies especially in the tendency to see the therapeutic alliance as an end in itself—to provide a new and corrective object relationship—rather than a means to the end of analyzing resistance and transference.

REFERENCES

Arlow, J. & Brenner, C. (1966), The psychoanalytic situation. In: *Psychoanalysis in the Americas*, ed. R.E. Litman. New York: International Universities Press, pp. 23-43; 133-138.

Baranger, M. & Baranger, W. (1966), Insight in the analytic situation. In: *Psychoanalysis in the Americas*, ed. R.E. Litman. New York: International Universities Press, pp. 56-72.

Bibring, E. (1937), Therapeutic results of psychoanalysis. *Internat. J. Psycho-Anal.*, 18:170-189.

⸻ (1943), The conception of the repetition compulsion. *Psychoanal. Quart.*, 12:486-519.

⸻ (1954), Psychoanalysis and the dynamic psychotherapies. *This Journal*, 2:745-770.

Breuer, J. & Freud, S. (1893-95), Studies on Hysteria. *Standard Edition*, 2:1-309.

Dickes, R. (1975), Technical considerations of the therapeutic and working alliances. *Internat. J. Psychoanal. Psychother.*, 4:1-47.

Eissler, K. (1953), The effect of the structure of the ego on psychoanalytic technique. *This Journal*, 1:104-143.

Erikson, E. (1950), *Childhood and Society*. New York: Norton.

Fenichel, O. (1941), *Problems of Psychoanalytic Technique*. New York: Psychoanalytic Quarterly, Inc.

Ferenczi, S. (1909), Introjection and transference. In: *Contributions to Psycho-Analysis*. New York: Basic Books, 1950, pp. 35-93.

Fliess, R. (1942), The metapsychology of the analyst. *Psychoanal. Quart.*, 11:211-227.

French, T. (1958), *The Integration of Behavior*, vol. 3. Chicago: University of Chicago Press.

Freud, S. (1905), Jokes and their relation to the unconscious. *Standard Edition*, 8:3-249.

⸻ (1912), The dynamics of transference. *Standard Edition*, 12:97-108.

⸻ (1913), On beginning the treatment. *Standard Edition*, 12:121-144.

⸻ (1914), Remembering, repeating and working through. *Standard Edition*, 12:145-156.

⸻ (1916-1917), Introductory lectures on psychoanalysis. *Standard Edition*, 16:431-447.

⸻ (1926), Inhibitions, symptoms, and anxiety. *Standard Edition*, 10:87-174.

———— (1937), Analysis terminable and interminable. *Standard Edition*, 23:211-253.

———— (1940), An outline of psychoanalysis. *Standard Edition*, 23:144-207.

Friedman, L. (1969), The therapeutic alliance. *Internat. J. Psycho-Anal.*, 50:139-153.

Gitelson, M. (1962), On the curative factors in the first phase in analysis. In: *Psychoanalysis: Science and Profession*. New York: International Universities Press, 1973, pp. 311-341.

Glover, E. (1931), The therapeutic effect of inexact interpretation. *Internat. J. Psycho-Anal.*, 12:397-411.

Greenacre, P. (1954), The role of transference. In: *Emotional Growth*. New York: International Universities Press, 1971, pp. 627-640.

Greenson, R. R. (1965), The working alliance and the transference neurosis. In: *Explorations in Psychoanalysis*. New York: International Universities Press, 1978, pp. 199-264.

———— & Wexler, M. (1969), The non-transference relationship in the psychoanalytic situation. In: *Explorations in Psychoanalysis*. New York: International Universities Press, 1978, pp. 359-386.

———— (1970), Discussion: The non-transference relationship in the psychoanalytic situation. *Internat. J. Psycho-Anal.*, 51:143-150.

Hartmann, H. (1939), *Ego Psychology and the Problem of Adaptation*. New York: International Universities Press, 1958.

Kanzer, M. (1975), The therapeutic and working alliances. *Internat. J. Psychoanal. Psychother.*, 4:48-68.

Klein, M. (1948), *Contributions to Psycho-Analysis, 1921-1945*. London: Hogarth Press.

Kohut, H. (1959), Introspection, empathy and psychoanalysis. In: *The Search for the Self*. New York: International Universities Press, 1978, pp. 205-232.

Loewald, H. (1960), On the therapeutic action of psychoanalysis. *Internat. J. Psycho-Anal.*, 41:16-33.

Malcove, L. (1975), The analytic situation: Toward a view of the supervisory experience. *J. Phil. Assn. Psychoanal.*, 2:1-14.

Nunberg, H. (1928), Problems of therapy. In: *Practice and Theory of Psychoanalysis*. New York: International Universities Press, 1961.

———— (1932), *Principles of Psychoanalysis*. New York: International Universities Press, 1955.

———— (1951), Transference and reality. *Internat. J. Psycho-Anal.*, 32:1-9.

Racker, H. (1968), *Transference and Countertransference*. New York: International Universities Press.

Spitz, R. (1956), Transference: The analytic setting and its prototype. *Internat. J. Psycho-Anal.*, 37:380-385.

Sterba, R. (1934), The fate of the ego in analytic therapy. *Internat. J. Psycho-Anal.*, 15:117-125.

Stone, L. (1961), *The Psychoanalytic Situation*. New York: International Universities Press.

Waelder, R. (1936), The principle of multiple function: Observations on overdetermination. In: *Psychoanalysis: Observation, Theory, Application*. New York: International Universities Press, 1976, pp. 68-83.

Zetzel, E. (1956a), The concept of transference. In: *The Capacity for Emotional Growth*. New York: International Universities Press, 1970, pp. 168-181.

———— (1956b), Concept and content in psychoanalytic theory. In: *The Capacity for Emotional Growth*. New York: International Universities Press, 1970, pp. 115-138.

———— (1966), The analytic situation. In: *Psychoanalysis in the Americas*, ed. R.E. Litman. New York: International Universities Press, pp. 86-106.

111 North 49th Street
Philadelphia, Pa. 19139

THE GENESIS OF INTERPRETATION

Jacob A. Arlow, M.D.

T HE PRINCIPLES OF PSYCHOANALYTIC TECHNIQUE are derived from and reflect the psychoanalytic theory of the neuroses. Essentially, psychoanalysis is a psychology of conflict. Kris (1950) said that psychoanalysis is human nature seen from the standpoint of conflict. The basic setting of psychoanalytic treatment and investigation, the psychoanalytic situation, is structured in terms of the fundamental principles of psychic determinism, dynamic interplay of forces in conflict, and topographic considerations that indicate the influences of forces outside the consciousness. No matter how differently analysts may conceptualize the observations they make within the psychoanalytic situation, practically all agree that the psychoanalytic situation is the specific, essential, and irreplaceable method of treatment and investigation. The genetic viewpoint in psychoanalysis is empirically founded. It derives from repeated psychoanalytic observations demonstrating that the conflicts underlying neurotic symptoms have their origin in the instinctual wishes of early childhood. These unconscious conflicts cluster around organized unconscious fantasies whose derivative manifestations intrude upon conscious mental functioning not only as symptoms and dreams but also in the form of parapraxes, conscious fantasies, etc. (Arlow, 1969).

Fundamentally, the function of the psychoanalytic situation is to further several important technical goals. Foremost among these is to ensure that what emerges into the patient's consciousness is as far as possible endogenously determined, i.e., that the thoughts, fantasies, feelings, etc., that the patient perceives represent derivatives of the persistent pressure of his unconscious conflicts. The analyst

193

as participant-observer is in a position to study the interplay between impulse and defense, between moral pressures and aspirations, together with considerations of the realistic consequences of action (Arlow and Brenner, 1966). In effect, the analyst may be viewed as presiding over an operational field, observing and eventually influencing a dynamically unstable equilibrium.

The patient is supposed to follow the fundamental rule, that is, he is expected to report without criticism whatever occurs to consciousness. Whenever the analyst makes any interpretation or observation, he interrupts the patient in his reportorial enterprise. An intervention by the analyst has the effect of disturbing the dynamic equilibrium between impulse and defense. How the analyst intervenes at any particular moment in the therapeutic interaction depends upon how he assesses the nature of the dynamic equilibrium at the particular time. In a whimsical way, growing out of his interest in dream psychology, Lewin (1955) attempted to elucidate this aspect of the therapeutic situation in terms of the parallel between the therapeutic situation and sleep and dreaming. After all, psychoanalysis, he observed, developed out of a form of artificially induced sleep, hypnosis. The patient on the couch, associating freely and reporting derivatives of unconscious, instinctual impulses, may be likened to the person asleep in bed and dreaming. So long as the unconscious wishes behind the dreams are sufficiently disguised and distorted, the person will continue to sleep and dream. However, should these derivatives become manifestly threatening, causing anxiety, the individual's sleep will be disturbed and he will awaken in order to discontinue dreaming. The effect of the analyst's intervention may be elucidated in the light of the interplay of forces described in connection with sleep and dreaming. An interpretation directed toward the defensive maneuvers of the ego has the effect of saying to the patient, "Don't be so vigilant. Don't be so wakeful. Let yourself sleep and dream and produce derivatives of unconscious wishes." On the other hand, an interpretation directed toward revealing an id impulse is tantamount to saying to the patient, "Wake up. Observe the implications of what you have just been thinking or dreaming."

The analyst's interventions and interpretations, accordingly, have the effect of bringing about a split in the patient's functioning on the couch. Although he has been assigned the task of being a relatively passive reporter, telling indiscriminately whatever comes into his mind, the patient from time to time is interrupted in this operation by the analyst, who now directs him to be a more active observer and interpreter of his own productions. In a sense, he is being invited to imitate the way the analyst operates, a process which facilitates at least a partial identification with the analyst, i.e., with his role as observer and interpreter. Sterba (1934) has described some of the vicissitudes of this split in the ego in the course of analysis. Identification with the analyst in the course of analyzing has been emphasized by many as representing one of the most important factors in the therapeutic effect of psychoanalysis. Perhaps the most specific expression of this viewpoint was made by Strachey (1934). The most significant observation to be emphasized at this point is the shifting role of the patient. At first his role seems to be a passive one. He merely reports his perceptions of what has become conscious. As a result of the analyst's interventions, however, his role becomes an active one. He observes and reflects upon the nature, the sequence, the connection, and possible meaning of what he has been reporting. As we shall see later, a corresponding split and shifting *modus operandi* takes place in the analyst.

How one comes to understand the unconscious thoughts of another person, the patient, is a problem that has intrigued analysts from the very beginning. Freud (1915, p. 159) at first was quite reassuring. He stated, "Every beginner in psycho-analysis probably feels alarmed at first at the difficulties in store for him when he comes to interpret the patient's associations and to deal with the reproduction of the repressed. When the time comes, however, he soon learns to look upon these difficulties as insignificant, and instead becomes convinced that the only real serious difficulties he has to meet lie in the management of the transference." Certain passages from Freud's writings on technique would make it seem that the process of understanding unconscious mental processes is practically automatic. It operates on an unconscius level and casts the analyst in a passive-receptive role vis-à-vis the patient's productions. Freud said (1912, pp. 115-116):

> Just as the patient must relate everything that his self-observation can detect, aɪ.d keep back all the logical and affective objections that seek to induce him to make a selection from among them, so the doctor must put himself in a position to make use of everything he is told for the purposes of interpretation and of recognizing the concealed unconscious material without substituting a censorship of his own for the selection that the patient has forgone. To put it in a formula: he must turn his own unconscious like a receptive organ towards the transmitting unconscious of the patient. He must adjust himself to the patient as a telephone receiver is adjusted to the transmitting microphone. Just as the receiver converts back into sound waves the electric oscillations in the telephone lines which were set up by sound waves, so the doctor's unconscious is able, from the derivatives of the unconscious which are communicated to him, to reconstruct that unconscious, which has determined the patient's free associations.

Once again it should be noted that the analyst adopts the same passive-receptive, uncritical attitude toward the patient's productions that the patient has been encouraged to adopt in relation to the thoughts, perceptions, fantasies, feelings, etc. that occur to him.

Freud thus focused on the inner experience of the analyst as the guidepost to the proper understanding of the patient's mental life. The reassurances he offered to allay the alarm of the beginner in psychoanalysis, however, seem to have fallen a bit short of their intended goal. How to interpret the meaning of the analyst's inner experience has been and remains a subject of considerable controversy. As with the actual telephone in real life, the message being transmitted is frequently garbled, muddled, and indistinct. At different times in the history of psychoanalysis, the inner perceptions of the analyst have been understood in different ways by different observers. Isakower (1963) advanced an almost concretistic view of the process in his concept of "the analyzing instrument." According to Isakower, if the analyst had been properly analyzed himself, the correct interpretation would appear automatically in the analyst's mind in the form of a free association. Although it would seem that Isakower tried to give spatial dimension and material structure to "the analyzing instrument," as far as one can determine from his limited writing on the subject, his concept of the analyzing instrument was identical with Freud's original concept of the system *Ucs*. Through the process of intuition, the correct interpretation rose into consciousness very much as a derivative of an unconscious instinctual impulse would make its appearance in the mind of the patient.

The controversy over the phenomenon of countertransference is a long-standing and continuing one. How to define countertransference and what it signifies technically, insofar as understanding the patient's mental life is concerned, are still subjects of active debate. The issues in this controversy have perhaps been best summarized by Annie Reich (1951, 1960, 1966). She defines countertransference as the effects of the analyst's own unconscious needs and conflicts on his understanding or technique. In true countertransference, the patient represents for the analyst an object of the past onto whom the analyst's past feelings and wishes may be projected, just as in the patient's transference situation, where past wishes and feelings are projected onto the analyst. The provoking factors for such reactions may be something in the patient's personality or material or something in the analytic situation as such. This is the sense in which I understand the concept. There are those, however, who equate countertransference with the analyst's total response to the patient, using the term to include all conscious reactions, responses, and feelings toward the patient. In his lectures on technique, Loewenstein (1957) emphasized the need to differentiate true countertransference reactions from certain feelings and responses to the patient that the analyst should note and study as expressions of what is happening currently in the analysis. For example, if the analyst finds himself responding to the patient with feelings of sexual excitement, anger, depression, frustration, impotence, and confusion, he must always raise in his own mind the possibility that these feelings are what the patient consciously or unconsciously intended for him to experience. This approach stands in strong contradiction to the views of those who emphasize projective identification as a major factor in the therapeutic interaction, a view that has strong support among many of the followers of Melanie Klein, especially in South America. For them, what the analyst experiences inwardly constitutes a direct reflection and, therefore, an appropriate reading of the patient's conscious and/or unconscious wishes (Baranger and Baranger, 1966).

In recent years we have all been witness to a surge of interest in pregenital and developmental conflicts. This interest has been stimulated by the writings of the British school in the past, as well as by the more recent concern with borderline patients and narcissistic personalities. Emphasizing mechanisms of introjection and projection, some members of the British school reason that the analyst becomes identical with the patient's infantile objects, and, accordingly, analysis of any countertransference reaction reveals the infantile history. Thus, if the analyst feels anger toward the patient, this indicates that the infantile object was angry with the patient. Similarly, the analyst may assume that his own anger of necessity accurately reflects the patient's own anger or provocation. The analysis of the countertransference thus brings to light the development of the transference. A technical consequence of this approach is that transference and countertransference come to replace recall of the past, and even its reconstruction, as necessary steps in the evolution of the analysis (Reich, 1960). Some of these concepts come close to the misapplication of the concept of mirroring to problems of adult analysis. This concept of mirroring, borrowed from careful observations of the early mother-child interaction, assumes an extension of the early mutual identification, often erroneously mislabeled mutual empathy, into the adult analytic situation. Accordingly, some analysts regard failures to make correct interpretations as always indicative of some countertransference distortion (Langs, 1978). Further, the analyst's countertransference distortion is again simplistically used to analyze the patient's transference, which creates confusion about transference manifestations and associations produced by the patient. Transference tends to lose its significance as a repetition of the infantile past, and transference distortions are regarded as interactional to the real qualities and countertransference of the analyst.

In the same spirit, some analysts regard the reaction of hostile withdrawal on the part of narcissistic patients as proof of some failure of empathy on the part of the analyst (Kohut, 1971). The specific type of lack of empathy, they claim, can be traced to definite turning points in the analyst's own narcissistic evolution.

A truly adequate consideration of the various views concerning the analyst's response to the patient's material

and what it signifies would require a volume in itself. What
I propose, instead, is to consider in some detail the nature of
the analyst's experience during the process of analyzing and
to consider some of the steps by which he arrives at and
confirms his interpretations. As indicated earlier, quite like
the patient, the analyst undergoes a shift in roles during his
work. He suspends critical judgment and listens passively
and indiscriminately to what the patient is reporting. What
comes into his consciousness is what the patient is saying. At
that moment he has identified with the patient. After a while,
however, he departs from his passive-receptive role. The
change is not brought about by the intervention of another
person, as in the case of the analysand; it is brought about by
the analyst's awareness, through the process of introspection,
of some mental process within himself that has intruded into
his consciousness. The thought that first appears in the
analyst's mind rarely comes in the form of a well-formulated,
logically consistent, theoretically articulated interpretation.
More often what the analyst experiences takes the shape of
some random thought, the memory of a patient with a similar
problem, a line of poetry, the words of a song, some joke he
heard, some witty comment of his own, perhaps a paper he
read the night before, or a presentation at the local society
meeting some weeks back. The range of initial impressions
or, more correctly, the analyst's associations to his patient's
material, is practically infinite, and it may or may not seem
to pertain directly to what the patient has been saying. Either
immediately or shortly thereafter, a connection can be and is
made between what the analyst has been thinking and feeling
and what the patient has been saying. It is at that point that
the analyst's inner experience is transformed into an
interpretation. Sometimes the process occurs with a penetrating suddenness and spontaneity that suggests magical
insight. This is especially true when the patient's next
productions correspond exactly to what the analyst had been
thinking but had not yet said.

A number of things have to be noted in this chain of events. First, the analyst had made an identification with the patient, but, with the intrusion of the "extraneous" thought into his mind, he has ceased being the passive recipient of the patient's productions and has taken on the role of observer-interpreter. Second, and perhaps most important, is that the analyst's free association, even when it seems random and remote from the theme of the patient's thoughts, represents his inner commentary and beginning perception of the patient's unconscious thought processes. An exception to this is, of course, the situation of extreme countertransference reaction. Third, the analyst's free association represents a form of inner communication to himself, a first step in the awareness of the insight which he is about to apprehend. Fourth, what the analyst has perceived through introspection is the end result of a process of intuition. Intuition consists of being able to organize silently, effortlessly, and outside of the scope of consciousness the myriad of observations, impressions, facts, experiences, in a word, all that we have learned from the patient into a meaningful pattern without any sense of the intermediate steps involved. When we examine closely the full range of communication between analyst and analysand, such phenomena no longer suggest anything supernatural. The patient uses several modes of communication with the therapist. He expresses himself verbally and nonverbally. Mode of behavior, facial expressions, body posture, different gestures, all transmit meaning which augments, elaborates, or sometimes even contradicts what the patient articulates verbally. The timbre of the voice, the rate of speech, the metaphoric expressions, and the configuration of the material transmit meaning beyond that contained in verbal speech alone. All of these are perceived sometimes subliminally and are elaborated and conceptualized unconsciously, i.e., intuitively. There is something intensely aesthetic and creative about this mode of functioning. Scientific discoveries and artistic innovations of enormous complexity are known to have originated in precisely the same way. (The similarities between psychoanalysis and the aesthetic process have been discussed by Freud, 1908; Sachs, 1942; Beres, 1957; and Beres and Arlow, 1974.)

In addition to introspection and intuition there is a third process closely related to the way the analyst comes to understand the patient. This is the process of empathy. Empathy facilitates intuition, in fact makes intuition possible. It consists of a transitory or trial identification (Fliess, 1942) with the patient, followed by withdrawal and objective evaluation of the experience of identification. As described above, this takes place innumerable times in the course of the analyst's listening to the patient's productions. He is constantly changing his role from that of a passive recipient in identification with the patient to an active observer and interpreter of his experience, and thereby the patient's. The patient's productions impinge upon the analyst's mind in a manner corresponding to the way in which current realities, past experience, and transference determine which derivatives of the persistent unconscious fantasies will emerge into the patient's consciousness. The process may be compared to the relationship between current reality, i.e., the day residue, and the production of dreams. The shared intimacy of the psychoanalytic situation, the knowledge of secrets confided and desires exposed, intensifies the trend toward mutual identification in the analytic setting and, in the end, serves to stimulate in the mind of the analyst unconscious fantasies either identical with or corresponding to those decisive in the patient's conflicts and development. Analyst and analysand thus become a group of two sharing an unconscious fantasy in common, a feature which Sachs (1942) points out is distinctive for artistic creation.

The insight that comes from introspection, intuition, and empathy constitutes only the first part of the interpretive work. This is the subjective or aesthetic phase of the analyst's response. As intriguing and dramatic as it may be, it has to give way to a second phase of the interpretive process, one that is based on cognition and the exercise of reason. In order to validate his intuitive understanding of what the patient has been saying, the analyst must now turn to the data of the analytic situation. He must put his insight to the test of objective criteria in conformity with the data at hand. Most of the time the intuitive work has been so efficient that the sense of conviction is immediate, gratifying, and accompanied instantly by recollection of the supporting evidence from the patient's productions.

In general there are certain criteria that transform what would seem to be random associations or disconnected thoughts into supportable hypotheses that can be entertained with conviction and buttressed by fact. Only a stark listing of these criteria is possible here. Most important is the context in which the specific material appears. Contiguity usually suggests dynamic relevance. The configuration of the material, the form and sequence in which the associations appear, represent substantive and interpretable connections. Other criteria are to be seen in the repetition and the convergence of certain themes within the organized body of associations. The repetition of similarities or opposites is always striking and suggestive. Material in context appearing in related sequence, multiple representations of the same theme, repetition in similarity, and a convergence of the data into one comprehensible hypothesis constitute the specific methodological approach in psychoanalysis used to validate insights obtained in an immediate, intuitive fashion in the analytic interchange. In actual practice, the aesthetic and cognitive components of the interpretive work proceed side by side. They do, however, have different relevance at various junctures in the analytic experience and are determined not only by the flow of the material but by the nature of both the analyst's and the patient's characterological defenses and communicative styles.

What I have tried to demonstrate is the complexity of

the analyst's inner reaction to his patient's material. Much work remains to be done delineating the finer details of the analyst's subjective experience while listening to his patient. There are only a few articles in the literature that examine this problem in significant detail. As the analyst grows in experience, he recognizes that in the wide range of his inner reactions, he is becoming aware of clues pointing to the unconscious meaning of the patient's communications. No matter how distant the content of his thoughts may seem to be from the patient's preoccupations, he nevertheless appreciates them as clues or signals pointing to the unconscious meaning of the patient's communications. In organizing and conceptualizing his insights, the analyst must depend upon more than immediate, intuitive apprehension. In the long run, satisfactory interpretation and reconstruction must be buttressed and sustained by cognitively assembled and rationally disciplined data. Otherwise, the temptation is great to fit observations into the Procrustean mold of one's currently favored hypothesis or psychoanalytic model. Unfortunately, in science as in art, there are no short cuts.

Summary

Opinions regarding the significance of the analyst's response to his patient's productions differ. This response is only one of many steps by which the analyst understands his patient's productions. In this paper, I have suggested a rationale for the process of the origin of insight. There is a split in the analyst's functioning, corresponding to what takes place in the patient. Through a transitory identification with the patient—empathy—the process of intuition is facilitated. The analyst conceptualizes the clinical data outside of consciousness. The end product is the analyst's inner response, made conscious to him through introspection. The analyst's response is a form of inner communication. It has to be made consonant with the patient's material according to disciplined, cognitive criteria before being formulated into an interpretation.

REFERENCES

Arlow, J. A. (1969), Unconscious fantasy and disturbances of conscious experience. *Psychoanal. Quart.*, 38:1-27.

────── & Brenner, C. (1966), The psychoanalytic situation. In: *Psychoanalysis in the Americas*, ed. R. E. Litman. New York: International Universities Press, pp. 23-43.

Baranger, M. & Baranger W. (1966), Insight in the analytic situation. In: *Psychoanalysis in the Americas*, ed. R. E. Litman. New York: International Universities Press, pp. 56-72.

Beres, D. (1957), Communication in psychoanalysis and in the creative process: A parallel. *This Journal*, 5:408-423.

────── & Arlow, J. A. (1974), Fantasy and identification in empathy. *Psychoanal. Quart.*, 43:26-50.

Fliess, R. (1942), The metapsychology of the analyst. *Psychoanal. Quart.*, 11:211-227.

Freud, S. (1908), Creative writers and day-dreaming. *Standard Edition*, 9:141-153.

────── (1912), Recommendations to physicians practising psycho-analysis. *Standard Edition*, 12:111-120.

────── (1915), Observations on transference love. *Standard Edition*, 12:159-171.

Isakower, O. (1963), In: Minutes of the Faculty Meeting of the New York Psychoanalytic Institute, November 20.

Kohut, H. (1971), *The Analysis of the Self*. New York: International Universities Press.

Kris, E. (1950), On preconscious mental processes. *Psychoanal. Quart.*, 19:540-560.

Langs, R. (1978), *The Listening Process*. New York: Aronson.

Lewin, B. D. (1955), Dream psychology and the analytic situation. In: *Selected Writings*. New York: The Psychoanalytic Quarterly, Inc., 1973, pp. 264-290.

Loewenstein, R. M. (1957), Some thoughts on interpretation in the theory and practice of psychoanalysis. *The Psychoanalytic Study of the Child*, 12:127-150. New York: International Universities Press.

Reich, A. (1951), On countertransference. In: *Psychoanalytic Contributions*. New York: International Universities Press, 1973, pp. 136-154.

────── (1960), Further remarks on countertransference. In: *Psychoanalytic Contributions*. New York: International Universities Press, 1973, pp. 271-287.

────── (1966), Empathy and countertransference. In: *Psychoanalytic Contributions*. New York: International Universities Press, 1973, pp. 344-360.

Sachs, H. (1942), *The Creative Unconscious. Studies in the Psychoanalysis of Art*. Cambridge, Mass.: Sci-Art Publishers.

Sterba, R. (1934), The fate of the ego in analytic therapy. *Internat. J. Psycho-Anal.*, 15:117-126.

Strachey, J. (1934), The nature of the therapeutic action of psychoanalysis. Reprinted in: *Internat. J. Psycho-Anal.* (1969), 50:275-292.

120 West 59th Street
New York, New York 10019

SOME IMPLICATIONS OF OBJECT RELATIONS THEORY FOR PSYCHOANALYTIC TECHNIQUE

Otto F. Kernberg, M.D.

BECAUSE THE TERM OBJECT RELATIONS THEORY has been used by different authors in varying contexts and within a wide spectrum of approaches to psychoanalytic theory and technique, I think it may be helpful to start out with my own brief definition.

As I have stated elsewhere (1976a), I conceive of psychoanalytic object relations theory as a special approach or focus within psychoanalysis that examines metapsychological and clinical issues in terms of the vicissitudes of internalized object relations. Object relations theory considers the psychic apparatus as originating in the earliest stage of a process of internalization of object relations. This process covers, roughly speaking, the first three years of life—and results in the formation of substructures of the psychic apparatus that will gradually differentiate. The stages of development of internalized object relations—that is, the stages of infantile autism, symbiosis, separation-individuation, and of object constancy—reflect the vicissitudes of these

Medical Director, The New York Hospital-Cornell Medical Center, Westchester Division; Professor of Psychiatry, Cornell University Medical College; Training and Supervising Analyst, Columbia University Center for Psychoanalytic Training and Research.

Presented at a Panel on "Implications of Psychoanalytic Object Relations Theory for Psychoanalytic Technique," at the Fall Meeting of the American Psychoanalytic Association, New York, December, 1978.

earliest substructures of the psychic apparatus. Discrete units of self-representation, object representation, and an affect disposition linking them are the basic object-relations-derived substructures that gradually evolve into more complex substructures (such as real-self and ideal-self, and real-object and ideal-object representations). Eventually, they will become integrated as intrapsychic structures in the ego, superego, and id.

Underlying this conception is an assumption common to Jacobson (1964, 1971); Mahler (Mahler and Furer, 1968; Mahler et al., 1975); and myself, namely, that the earliest internalization processes have dyadic features, that is, a self-object polarity—even when self- and object representations are not yet differentiated; by the same token, all subsequent developmental steps also imply the presence of dyadic internalizations, that is, internalization of an object not only as object representation but as an interaction of the self with the object, so that units of self- and object representations (and the affect dispositions—the clinical manifestations of a drive derivative—linking them) are the basic building blocks for later internalized object and self-representations and, still later on, of the overall tripartite structure (ego, superego, and id).

Object relations theory, as defined, based upon Jacobson's, Mahler's, and my own work, is in contrast to the British school of psychoanalysis in that it integrates contemporary ego-psychological approaches with structural development, avoids telescoping intrapsychic development into the first year of life, assumes a more complex and gradual development of both ego and superego than the British school, and considers the relationships between early development, intrapsychic genetics, and structure formation as complex, indirect, and not immediately available in the early stages of psychoanalytic exploration. Hence, the object relations approach I have outlined is closer to Fairbairn (1952, 1963), Balint (1965, 1968), and Winnicott (1958,

1965), than to Melanie Klein (1940, 1945, 1946, 1957) and Bion (1967). However, the neglect of instinctual development in Fairbairn is sharply contrary to my approach.

In contrast to what might be considered an object-relations approach of Sullivan (1953) and his followers, object relations theory as outlined here has to do not only with interpersonal object relations, but is predominantly a metapsychological approach—an attempt to account for normal and pathological development in terms of the structures comprising the psychic apparatus. Finally, my definition is compatible with the developmental thinking of Erikson (1956, 1959, 1963), although not with his emphasis on adolescence as opposed to earlier stages of identity formation. It is also related to Lichtenstein's (1977) and Loewald's (1978) recent formulations.

Psychoanalytic object relations theory as defined is an integral part of contemporary ego psychology. It is not an additional metapsychological viewpoint nor does it conflict with the structural, developmental-genetic, dynamic, economic, and adaptive viewpoints; rather, it represents a refinement of the structural viewpoint that links structure more closely with developmental, genetic, and dynamic aspects of mental functioning; further, it occupies an intermediary realm between psychoanalytic metapsychology, on the one hand, and direct clinical formulations in the psychoanalytic situation, on the other.

Technical Implications of Object Relations Theory

An object relations focus is not geared exclusively to the understanding and treatment of patients with severe regression in the transference; it has applications for the standard psychoanalytic technique, many of which have long been integrated into that technique.

Within an object relations framework, unconscious intrapsychic conflicts always involve self- and object representations, or rather, conflicts between certain units of self- and object representations under the impact of a determined drive derivative (clinically, a certain affect disposition) and other, contradictory or opposing, units of self- and object representations and their respective affect dispositions reflecting the defensive structure. Unconscious intrapsychic conflicts are never simple conflicts between impulse and defense; rather, the drive derivative finds expression through a certain primitive object relation (a certain unit of self- and object representation); and the defense, too, is reflected by a certain internalized object relation. The conflict is between these intrapsychic structures. Thus, all character defenses really reflect the activation of a defensive constellation of self- and object representations directed against an opposite and dreaded, repressed self- and object constellation. For example, in obsessive, characterological submissiveness, a chronically submissive self-image in relating to a powerful and protective parental image may defend the patient against the repressed, violently rebellious self relating to a sadistic and castrating parental image. Thus, clinically, both character defense and repressed impulse involve mutually opposed internal object relations.

While, therefore, the consolidation of the overall intrapsychic structures (ego, superego, and id) results in an integration of internalized object relations that obscures the constituent units within the overall structures, in the course of psychoanalysis one observes the gradual redissolution of pathogenic superego and ego structures, and, in this context, the activation and clarification of the constituent internalized object relations in the transference. In this regard, Glover's (1955) classical formulation of the transference as reflecting an impulse and an identification may easily be translated into the transference as always reflecting an object relation under the impact of a certain drive derivative.

In other words, the unconscious intrapsychic conflicts reflected in neurotic symptoms and pathological character traits are always dynamically structured, that is, they reflect a relatively permanent intrapsychic organization consisting of opposite, contradictory, or conflictual internalized object relations. At severe levels of psychopathology where psychoanalysis is usually contraindicated (certain types of severe character pathology and borderline conditions) dissociative mechanisms stabilize such dynamic structures within an ego-id matrix and permit the contradictory aspects of these conflicts to remain—at least partially—in consciousness.

On the other hand, with patients presenting less severe character pathology and psychoneurosis, the dynamically structured intrapsychic conflicts are truly unconscious, and are predominantly intersystemic conflicts involving ego, superego, and id and their advanced, high-level or "neurotic" defense mechanisms. Here, in the course of the psychoanalytic process, the development of a regressive transference neurosis will gradually activate in the transference the constituent units of internalized object relations that form part of ego and superego structures, and of the repressed units of internalized object relations that have become part of the id. At first, rather global expressions of ego and superego functions make their appearance, such as generalized guilt feelings about unacceptable impulses, or broadly rationalized ego-syntonic character traits. Eventually, however, the transference is expressed more and more directly by means of a certain object relation which is used defensively against an opposing one reflecting the repressed drive derivatives. In the case of both defense- and impulse-determined object relations, the patient may re-enact the self-representation of that unit while projecting the object representation onto the analyst, or, at other times, project his self-representation onto the analyst while identifying with the object representation of the unit.

The fact that in the ordinary psychoanalytic case these transitory identifications emerge in the context of a well-integrated tripartite structure and a consolidated ego identity, with integration of both the patient's self-concept and his concepts of significant others—including the psychoanalyst—permits the patient to maintain a certain distance from, or perspective on, this momentary activation of a certain distortion of self- and object representation without losing, at least potentially, the capacity for reality testing in the transference. This permits the analyst to deal with the regressive transference neurosis from a position of technical neutrality, by interpretive means; and it permits the patient to deal with interpretations introspectively, searching for further self-understanding in the light of the analyst's interpretive comments. In spite of temporary weakening of reality testing during affect storms and transference acting out, this quality of the psychoanalytic process is one of its outstanding, specific features.

The analyst, while empathizing by means of a transitory or trial identification with the patient's experience of himself and his object representations, also explores empathically the object relation that is currently predominant in the interactional or nonverbal aspects of the transference, and, in this context, the nature of the self- or object representation that the patient is projecting onto him. The analyst's subjective experience, at that point, may include either a transitory identification with the patient's self-experience—as is the case in concordant identification—or with the patient's currently dissociated or projected self- or object representation—as is the case in complementary identification (where the analyst, rather than identifying with the patient's self or ego, identifies with his object representation or the superego in global terms (Racker, 1968).

Throughout this process, the analyst first transforms his empathic understanding into intuitive formulations; he later ventures into a more restrictive formulation that incorporates a general understanding in the light of all available information (Beres and Arlow, 1974). The empathy with, the intuitive understanding, and the integrative formulation of the patient's affect states during this process clarifies the nature of the drive derivative activated and defended against in the object relation predominating in the transference.

It needs to be stressed that what I have just outlined is a focus, from an object relations standpoint, upon the theory of psychoanalytic technique that permits us to maintain this same theory for varying technical approaches. This theory of technique takes into consideration the structural characteristics, defensive operations, object relations, and transference developments of patients who are fixated at or have regressed to a structural organization that antedates the integration of the intrapsychic structures, as well as of patients whose tripartite structure has been consolidated, that is, the standard psychoanalytic case that we have examined in detail. I am suggesting that this focus upon the theory of psychoanalytic technique for the entire spectrum of patients for which a psychoanalytic approach may be considered the treatment of choice facilitates the application of a nonmodified psychoanalytic technique to some patients with severe psychopathology, clarifies certain modifications of the standard psychoanalytic technique for cases where psychoanalysis is contraindicated for individual reasons, and, most importantly, implies a reconfirmation of standard psychoanalytic technique for the well-organized patient with solid integration of the tripartite structure. I shall now attempt to illustrate this approach by means of a clinical vignette from a standard psychoanalytic treatment.

Clinical Example

The patient, a mid-western professional in the field of the behavioral sciences, in his late forties, came for treatment because of chronic marital conflicts, severe work inhibition—particularly in the creative aspect of his research functions—and occasional sexual impotence with his wife. He was potent with prostitutes and, at the time of the episode to be described, in the second year of his psychoanalysis, sadistic sexual behavior with prostitutes had become a major form of acting out. The patient's father had been a prominent politician who the patient both feared and depreciated. His mother was a rather submissive, but complaining and guilt-evoking woman who seemed totally controlled by the powerful father and escaped from his demands and dissatis-factions by means of chronic hypochondriacal complaints.

We had already explored the patient's submissive behavior toward his wife, his chronic fear of displeasing her, and the revengeful enactment of sadistic behavior against other women as a displaced expression of his hatred toward her. On a deeper level, his sexual relations with prostitutes represented a dissociated identification with his sadistic father with whom he did not dare identify out of profound oedipal guilt. This latter material was only barely emerging in the psychoanalytic situation.

For several months, it had become apparent that the patient was presenting me with his "shameful" and self-defeating submission to his wife, implicitly blaming me for not helping him to become more assertive in his relation with her. For example, because of strict regulations that he felt she imposed upon him (regarding her hours of going to bed, turning out the lights, and her requests for silence in the home that interfered with his research work), his work inhibitions were allegedly further increased for which he implicitly blamed me. He also contrasted my efforts to help him gain understanding without giving him advice with the more active encouragement and sympathy he had obtained, he said, from his previous therapist. In fact, it gradually emerged that he had seduced his previous therapist into giving him advice on how to handle his wife, and eventually "proved" that therapist to be totally impotent in really influencing his marital difficulties.

The patient was also constantly examining my interpre-tations in the light of what he had learned in his professional training about psychoanalysis. He often reacted to my interpretations with an amused, ironical expression, implying that I could do better than that, or that I was not in my best form in giving that interpretation, or that I should pay more attention to him than to my theories, etc. The "spoiling" and devaluation of my interpretations, his efforts to "learn" what I had to teach him and to use it in his work without really absorbing my comments, gave the sessions a strong quality of narcissistic resistance. However, he showed a capacity for differentiating in depth his concepts both of himself and of the significant people in his life, which reconfirmed for me that he was not a narcissistic personality proper. My overall hypothesis at the time was that the patient was attempting to maintain me at a devalued, impotent level in order to avoid developing a frightening image of me as a brutal, overpowering father.

For several sessions preceding the one to be described, I had experienced a sense of impotence, an incapacity to know how I could convey to him an understanding that would be useful to him. This insecurity on my part was matched by the patient's shift from a previous attitude of ironic superiority (which he had in the past attributed to other men he experienced as rivals in his work) to a complaining, nagging protest over not getting any better, the uselessness of this treatment, the enormous sacrifices he had to make, and the lack of any "original contribution" on my part to what he knew about himself.

When, one day, I felt myself in a role similar to the role he described himself in vis-à-vis his nagging wife, I verbalized my sense that he was repeating in this session his relation with his wife with inverted roles. The patient now became tense and remembered that I had pointed out to him in the past that he had been attracted by masculine features in his wife. He said he felt I was accusing him of identifying with his wife and implicitly telling him that he was a homosexual.

His associations then shifted to his wife's rage with him

because once, when he attempted to have anal intercourse with her, she had felt brutally attacked and now, years later, still accused him of having behaved sadistically toward her. He then thought of prostitutes he had engaged to participate masochistically in sexual games in which he "playfully" acted like a sadist and had fantasies about giving such prostitutes enemas. He next remembered his mother and father jointly holding him while giving him enemas in his childhood.

Throughout these associations, I sensed an increasing fearfulness in him, and when I pointed this out to him, he remembered that I had blown my nose forcefully in the previous session, and that this seemed something "brutally uninhibited" to him. He then thought that I wouldn't take all that abuse from his wife if I were married to her, and also imagined me standing up to his boss very effectively, in fact, intimidating him, in contrast to the patient's always trying to play the nice boy. At this moment, I also experienced a sudden sense of intellectual clarity and power, quite in contrast to the helpless insecurity that I had experienced earlier. I felt that I now represented his powerful and brutal father, forcing him into homosexual submission, and that he was engaged in a pathetic effort to identify with me in his sadistic role with prostitutes, while leaving—in his fantasy—his wife and his work to me.

I proceeded to interpret the patient's image of me as a powerful man, strong, ruthless, and brutal with women—as he had perceived his father—and I raised the question whether his fear of my branding him as a homosexual might reflect his fear of his masculinity's being destroyed if he dared to compete with me, as father, in his behavior toward his wife and toward his boss. I later added that his intense search for sadomasochistic relations with prostitutes in recent weeks might serve the purpose of reassuring him against his fear of me and his temptation to submit to me (father). After some silence, the patient now said that it was very painful to think that because of his neurotic behavior he had lost valuable opportunities for advancement in his research work. He added, almost with a shudder, that he had never before thought that the reason why he had no child with his wife was because he had never dared to stand up to her unrealistic excuses for not wanting to have a child, and now it was probably too late.

It was now my turn to be shocked; although I had all along had the evidence that his not having had a child reflected the neurotic character of his marriage, I had never before been able to formulate this hypothesis—his not daring to have a child out of oedipal guilt and fear—precisely in my mind: presumably, I think, because of the intensity of his denial, and his secondary rationalizations of this problem in earlier stages of his analysis. My emotional reaction now became one of concern and strong positive feeling for the patient: I felt that, almost unwittingly, I had helped him to gain an understanding of a painful reality which indeed—given his present circumstances—most probably reflected a missed opportunity. I said it must be very painful for him to review the past joint decision with his wife not to have a child in light of this new understanding, and the patient acknowledged his sense of being understood by me. There followed a long silence, in which I experienced a strong current of empathy for him.

In short, I believe I have illustrated a relatively rapid shift in my empathy from, first, that with a projected self-representation of the patient (the helpless little boy masochistically submitting to a nagging mother) while the patient identified with the object representations of mother-wife; then, my empathy with his powerful and "brutal" father while the patient became his fearful and insecure self; and finally, my empathy with the patient's central self-experience. The first two identifications enacted in the transference were clearly of the complementary type, the last one concordant.

From a broader perspective, the patient was expressing in the transference his characterological defenses of superiority and irony against directly experiencing fear of and submission to a powerful, castrating father image. He then experienced this fear more directly, and also became more aware of the related masochistic submission to his wife, of his not daring to compete with father.

I have (1976a, Chap. 6; 1976b) elsewhere spelled out modifications of the standard psychoanalytic technique for patients with borderline personality organization; I shall now spell out some applications of this reformulation from the standpoint of object relations theory for the standard psychoanalytic case. It must be stressed that, with this reformulation of aspects of the theory of psychoanalytic technique, basic psychoanalytic technique itself does not change, but, in addition to expanding its boundaries, is enriched in daily practice. What follows is not an exhaustive list of applications; rather, it refers to frequent clinical situations for which the aforementioned ego psychological theory of object relations and the related theory of technique seem to me particularly useful.

Some Applications to Clinical Interventions

The Nature of the Conflicts to Be Interpreted

The earlier the development, fixation, or regression of psychopathology, the more seriously it affects, not only the development of ego and superego structures (which is reflected in the treatment in a premature activation of the constituent internalized object relations that ordinarily are integrated within more global ego and superego functions in early stages of a psychoanalysis), but also the capacity for entering a normal oedipal situation. Under these conditions, preoedipal conflicts, particularly a predominance of conflicts around preoedipal aggression, infiltrate all object relations.

In addition to reinforcing and fixating primitive defensive operations centering around splitting, excessive aggression also contaminates the later object relations characteristic of the Oedipus complex.

This creates characteristic distortions in the oedipal constellation, reflected in the following frequent findings: Excessive splitting of the preoedipal maternal image may be complicated later on by a defensive devaluation, fear, and hatred of the oedipal mother and an unstable idealization of the oedipal father that easily breaks down and is replaced by further splitting of father's image. This reinforces oedipal rivalry in men and penis envy in women, excessive fear and guilt over sexuality in both sexes, and the search for desexualized and idealized relationships, which influence the development of very early forms of homosexuality in both sexes. A predominance of sadistic and masochistic components in genital strivings are other consequences of this situation. Under these circumstances, the differentiation of parental images along sexual lines, typical for triangular oedipal relationships, may be complicated by splitting mechanisms, which make one sex good and the other bad, or by pathological fusion of the respectively idealized or threatening aspects of both sexes, so that unrealistic combined father/mother images develop: the "phallic mother" is only one example of these developments.

I am stressing that consequences of severe preoedipal conflicts include pathological development of oedipal conflicts but not an absence of them. I believe that the controversy regarding the predominance of oedipal versus preoedipal conflicts in regressive conditions, or when early ego distortion or lack of development of the definite tripartite intrapsychic structure exists, really obscures some of the significant issues. Not even in nonanalyzable borderline conditions or in cases with severe pathology of object relations, such as the narcissistic personality, have I ever been able to find a patient without evidence of crucial oedipal pathology: the question is not presence or absence of oedipal conflicts, but the degree to which preoedipal features have distorted the oedipal constellation and have left important imprints on character formation (Blum, 1977). It is only at advanced stages of resolution of severe psychopathologies stemming from the preoedipal period that one may indeed find a "clearing up" of the condensed oedipal-preoedipal transference. In this clearing up, early dyadic relationships with the preoedipal mother are reactivated in relatively undistorted ways, and conflicts between the search for closeness and even merger and the need for autonomy (or even differentiation) appear relatively directly in the transference. In contrast, in the advanced stages of psychoanalytic treatment of narcissistic personalities, when the pathological grandiose self has been systematically analyzed, the full-fledged oedipal conflicts typically predominate—with varying degrees of preoedipal condensation—as the core underlying conflicts.

*Varying Relationships Between Transference, Genetic
History, and Early Development*

Oedipal conflicts condensed with pathological preoedipal object relations contribute to creating fantastic transference developments. The predominance of partial, nonintegrated self- and object representations when early ego defenses predominate also contributes to creating fantastic transference developments. Therefore, the earlier the points of fixation or regression of the psychopathology, the greater is the gap between actual childhood experiences, the intrapsychic elaboration of such experiences, the structuring of these intrapsychic elaborations, and the nature of transference developments.

Although in all patients the predominant transference paradigm may be conceived as a "personal myth" that condenses conflicts from various stages of development, when there is a predominance of total object-relations and intersystemic conflicts in the transference, the genetic link between the transference and the antecedent childhood experiences is more direct, more readily available, and lends itself to earlier reconstructions than in cases of severe psychopathology or when severe regression occurs in the transference. In these latter cases, the road from present transference developments to the genetic or intrapsychic history of organization of the material is more indirect, and, paradoxically, early childhood experiences can be reconstructed only in advanced stages of the treatment; hence, the danger of equating primitive transferences with "early" object relations in a mechanical, direct way, and the misleading temptation to "reconstruct" the earliest intrapsychic development on the basis of primitive transference manifestations.

It is important to differentiate patients who have not reached object constancy, where the syndrome of identity diffusion and the chronic predominance of primitive defense mechanisms indicates the presence of borderline personality organization, from patients with stable ego identity and, therefore, the preconditions of object constancy, total object relations, and the capacity for maintaining reality testing in the transference even under conditions of severe regression. In these latter cases, when primitive transferences are activated in advanced stages of the treatment, an interpretive stance and technical neutrality can be maintained, while utilizing the understanding that object relations theory provides as one important viewpoint for the resolution through interpretation of primitive transferences.

In many neurotic patients and in patients with nonborderline character pathology, regressions to primitive transferences do occur in the analysis. Because of the intense affective developments, the temporary weakening of reality testing, the projective tendencies, and the chaotic interactions that develop at such points, the analyst is sometimes tempted to move away from a technically neutral and strictly interpretive attitude. Such moves away from an analytic attitude are often rationalized with the assumption that the patient has reached a stage of "ego deficit" or "fragility of the self" or "maturational arrest." In fact, what occurs at such points of regression is that the patient has regressed from some stage of his infantile (yet integrated) self relating to an infantile (yet integrated) parental object to a stage that predates object constancy. Now, both the self- and object representations activated in the transference are partial and reflect dissociated or split-off aspects of a warded-off, integrated object relation which the patient experiences as intolerable because of the intense ambivalence or contradiction between love and hatred involved. By the same token, the analysis of intrapsychic conflict in terms of defense and impulse is no longer facilitated by the organizing features of intersystemic conflict, but, rather, contradictory ego states— or ego-id states—constitute the polarities of the conflict, where both sides include primitive impulse derivatives imbedded in a primitive unit of internalized object relation. Under these circumstances, defense and content can rapidly be interchanged in shifting equilibria of such activated part-object relations, and contradictory impulses are conscious and mutually dissociated or split off rather than uncon-scious—that is, repressed. Here the nature of consciousness and unconsciousness no longer coincides with what is on the surface and what is deep, what is defense and what is content.

The analysis, at such stages, of the nature of the immediate predominant object relation in the transference and the predominant defensive operations connected with its dissociation from other, contradictory, object relations helps the analyst to clarify the predominant meaning of the transference, the defensive aspects of the object relation activated, its motivation in protecting the patient against a contradictory or opposite object relation, and the implicit conflict between primitive ego structures. In metapsycholog-ical terms, while the topographic approach to interpretation (the ordering of the material from surface to depth) no longer holds, the economic, dynamic, and structural aspects of interpretation as spelled out by Fenichel (1941) are still fully relevant. If, at this point, the analyst first interprets the part-object relation activated and its affect state, and later, its defensive function against other, contradictory, parallel or previously conscious affect states linked to other part-object relations, dramatic change and new understanding may be gained while the patient's reality testing returns to normal. This interpretative approach, however, requires that the analyst first ascertain whether the patient is still able to maintain some degree of self-observation and reality testing in the transference. Otherwise, it is crucially important to start out by clarifying the reality aspects of the psychoanalytic situation, then to focus upon the patient's "interpretation" of the analyst's interpretative comments, and, if this is not sufficient to restore the patient's analytic work, the analyst may have to apply the general approach recommended for cases in which there is a regression in the communicative function (see below).

The more the transference developments present the characteristics of activation of part-object relations, predominance of primitive defensive operations, and condensation of preoedipal and oedipal conflicts, the more it is indicated to interpret the transference in an "as if" that is, nongenetic mode. For example, I interpreted a patient's chronic frustrations with me at a certain advanced stage of her treatment as a search for a warm and giving, endlessly patient, and understanding father with strong maternal features, "as if" she were reliving a time in which she would have wished to have a father with breasts and a penis from which milk would flow endlessly. This interpretation stemmed from many dreams, masturbatory fantasies, and complex interactions in the transference, and I did not "place it historically" because of the reasons mentioned before. Such an "as if" qualification to genetic reconstructions permits a more natural sorting out of the initially condensed, mixed, compressed material stemming from various stages of development, and a gradual crystallization, on the basis of this same repetitive primitive transference pattern, of a sequence of early and later stages of development as issues within the same transference constellation.

For example, a patient's urgent demands that I listen to her with unwavering attention, accept her ongoing sharp criticism of me without arguing with her, and not say anything unless specifically asked seemed to reflect at one point an effort to control me sadistically and yet to feel reassured that I continued to love her, to be close to me and yet avoid my overwhelming her with my thoughts—all of which seemed to relate to a derivative constellation of the rapprochement crisis. However, this same transference disposition seemed to reflect, at a later stage of her treatment, a suspicion that all that was coming from me was bad, like poisoned food she should not ingest, while she still felt that I was the only source of potential satisfaction, of any kind of good; so she pleaded with me to give her good and not poisoned food. I interpreted all this as relating to a still earlier period of oral dependence, projection of aggression, and consequent fears of being poisoned by a malevolent, though desperately needed, feeding mother. I must point out that the actual reconstruction of developments from the patient's second to fifth year of life followed much later, so that the sequence of my interpretive comments reflected a layering—or the internal structure—of her "personal myth" and not yet a hypothesis regarding the actual sequence of developments that had taken place in her past.

It is important to differentiate actual regression to modes of functioning that predate object constancy from patients' fantasies about such regression. Patients may, for example, have fantasies about "merger" with the analyst which may have many meanings and does not indicate, by itself, that a regression to a symbiotic or an early stage of differentiation of self has taken place. Such "merger" fantasies may express regressively wishes for total dependence; or efforts to escape from guilt feelings by blurring the responsibility of, respectively, patient and analyst; or, quite frequently, regressive forms of expression of sexual impulses. Actual regression to subphases of separation individuation or even symbiosis occurs rarely in the analyses of well-selected patients, requires a long time to develop, and, above all, is reflected in significant regressive changes in the total therapeutic interaction, in the patient's nonverbal as well as verbal behavior, and in a regressive increase in his responses to the total psychoanalytic setting—more of this later. Psychoanalytic fashions may artificially increase a "language of regression," partially induced by inappropriate introduction of the analyst's theories into the interpretive comments.

Regression in the Communicative Process

Patients with well-integrated tripartite intrapsychic structure, a stable and solid ego identity, and the related integration of self- and of object representations are usually able, by means of verbal communication, to communicate to the analyst their internal world, their subjective experience in the broadest sense. Naturally, under the effect of repression and other defense mechanisms, such communication is restricted in certain areas. However, by means of ordinary empathic listening and transitory identification with the patient, the analyst is able to construct, in his own mind, a picture of the patient's experience, of the patient's personality and his interactions with significant others. In addition, of course, the analyst utilizes his direct observations of the patient's nonverbal communications, his attitudes and attire, all the behavioral elements that provide a key counterpart to the verbal communication and the subjective world it opens. It might seem trivial to repeat this well-known aspect of the psychoanalytic process were it not that the patient's very awareness and communication of his subjective world may become blurred, distorted, and mostly inoperative at points of severe regression when part-object relations predominate in the transference.

Under these conditions, the normally subdued influence of the psychoanalytic setting comes into the foreground of the analytic process, and the patient's communication of his subjectivity is replaced by severe distortions in the interactions with the psychoanalyst. I am not referring here to the ordinary acting out of a specific, clearly circumscribed transference reaction in the psychoanalytic situation, but to the more subtle, often uncanny combination of strange or unusual modes of behavior and relationships to the analyst that impress themselves strongly though confusingly upon the analyst's mind, and make it very difficult for him to maintain empathy with the content of the patient's verbal communications. Here, in short, communication occurs by means of the transformation of the patient's relation to the psychoanalytic setting and his expression of the uncanny in the interpersonal field, rather than by means of the ordinary predominance of shared subjectivity.

True regression to stages of development that predate object constancy—in contrast to fantasies about such regressive states or experiences—usually involve this formal regression in the transference, which permits the analyst to differentiate these two kinds of situations. Some symptoms of this regression in the communicative process include the gradual development of ineffectiveness of the analyst's interpretation, the analyst's feeling that his words no longer counted, a new use of language on the patient's part which would seem geared more to induce or block actions in the analyst than to provide him with information. Also, at this point, dramatic acting out and the communication to the analyst of a general sense of urgency may occur. In addition, the patient may appear more and more oriented to the immediate environment of the analytic situation, the analyst's room and its furniture, the duration of the hour, the analyst's availability and absences, the tone of the analyst's communication, rather than the content of what he is saying. Long periods of silence from the patient that induce unusual fantasy formations in the analyst, or a sense of paralysis of understanding in the analyst may also develop. The patient's incapacity to listen or interact by means of verbal communication may coincide with a total loss of what appeared previously as good capacity for introspection or insight. The patient may experience no emotions (thus reflecting, for example, severe splitting or fragmentation of affect, or a subjective sense of total artificiality or emptiness), or intense, overwhelming affects, or a chronic sense of confusion. In some cases there is a predominance of somatization or hypochondriacal tendencies at this point.

Under these circumstances, the analyst's sense of confusion or paralysis may appear to be a severe countertransference development, but, if explored over a period of time by means of the analyst's introspection, may emerge as a condensation of the analyst's countertransference potential with a stimulation in him of affects reflecting the patient's primitive object relations. The analyst's efforts to maintain emotional contact with his patient at times of regression fosters a special receptivity in the analyst that lends itself to or fosters the development in him or her of such an emotional response (Kernberg, 1975). Of particular importance here is the projection onto the analyst of split-off aspects of the patient's self, so that, in rapidly alternating reversals of the reciprocal enactment of self- and object representations in the transference, the analyst represents the patient's part-self-representation interacting with the part-object representation enacted by the patient himself and vice versa in cyclical fashion. In short, the rapid "cycling" of self- and object representations and the fantastic, unrealistic qualities of these representations and the respective interactions activated in the transference reveal the primitive nature of these part-object relations. Here, the analyst's effort to empathize with the patient's central subjective experience needs to be broadened to include empathy with the aspect of the currently dominant object relation the patient is projecting onto the analyst. In other words, the analyst's empathy has to incorporate the partial aspect of the self as well as the partial aspect of the object representation involved in this interaction, and empathy with mutually contradictory aspects of the patient's intrapsychic life that he himself cannot tolerate or, therefore, integrate.

This is a stressful situation for the psychoanalyst. He may be tempted to respond to the patient's incapacity to verbally communicate his subjectivity by a redoubled effort to interpret the material verbally, thus unwillingly shifting into what might be called an authoritarian use of interpretation as a defense against the difficulty in tolerating such vaguely experienced contradictory material in himself. Or else the analyst may be tempted to abandon the patient emotionally by the beforementioned thought that the patient presents ego defects that no longer have conflictual implications and require modifications of technique.

In contrast, the analyst's full exploration of his own emotional reactions, sorting out objective reactions to the patient's reality and transference from what might be his countertransference dispositions, may permit him to formulate to himself first, and to the patient later, how the patient is perceiving him and/or attempting to "redesign" him. The immediate meaning of the patient's relation to the analyst under such conditions has to be constructed out of the total emotional situation that now exists in the analysis. At such points, past and present are condensed so fully into one transference situation that it can be temporarily analyzed only in terms of the immediate relation, the "here and now." There are extreme circumstances in which even the stress on reality may have to be temporarily suspended, or at least left open. If the patient, for example, seems too involved in a severe paranoid distortion, perceiving the analyst as a dangerous, hostile, sadistic enemy who, however, he desperately needs, the analyst needs to acknowledge that this is the current unshakable vision that the patient has of him, that this conflict between need and suspicion is what the patient is struggling with, and that both patient and analyst have to tolerate the coincidence of very different ways of looking at the reality of this interaction.

Here, two major technical tools may prove very helpful. One is the analyst's effort to integrate cognitively the confusing and contradictory manifestations of the patient's immediate behavior, including his use of language, the nature of the acting out, the contradictory behavioral manifestations in the hours, and the emotional reactions induced in the analyst. This is a cognitive function, which temporarily makes the analyst an auxiliary ego to the patient within the preservation of a technically neutral position.

A second helpful attitude is what Winnicott (1958, 1965) has called the "holding" function of the analyst, namely, his ongoing emotional availability to the patient at points of severe regression, which includes at least three aspects: (1) the analyst's respecting the patient's autonomy, his not "impinging" on the patient at such points of vulnerability where the patient's "true self" may emerge; (2) the analyst's "survival" in the face of the patient's aggression, his "ruthlessness" before integration of good and bad self- and object representations has been achieved; and (3) the analyst's empathic availability for the provision of an emotionally supportive environment at points of significant regression.

The analysis of regressive transference developments, particulary when severely paranoid transferences emerge, is always stressful, difficult, and uncertain regarding its outcome. While suggesting that the application of an object relations focus as described improves the prognosis for a psychoanalytic approach and facilitates the maintenance of a technically neutral attitude, this cautious optimism should not be interpreted as an assurance of success in all cases.

There is a tendency among some analysts working with severely regressed patients to adopt an exclusively intellectual or cognitive stance. Others tend to abandon their efforts at intellectual understanding and stress the purely affective "holding." I think the analyst needs to maintain a balanced empathy toward the patient, an empathy that combines the maintenance of authentic concern with persisting efforts to cognitively understand him, even if verbal communication has to be temporarily adjusted to the limited degree to which the patient can understand and incorporate the analyst's contributions. As mentioned before, the analyst's empathic attitude also needs to incorporate empathy with what the patient cannot tolerate in himself—with the dissociated aspects of self- and object representations. This transcends ordinary empathy with the central subjective experience of another person, and brings us to our next point, the role of empathy.

Empathy and Regression in the Transference

The approach to regression in the transference from the organizing standpoint of the vicissitudes of internalized object relations may lead to a misunderstanding of the importance of the analyst's empathic presence for patients with severe regression or severe psychopathology (including the narcissistic personalities and the borderline conditions). This misunderstanding is that, the more severe the patient's ego distortion, the more it becomes necessary to replace a position of technical neutrality (which would permit interpretation of the transference) with the analyst's availability as an empathic, warm human being who permits the patient to internalize him in this function and thus to compensate for an arrested or incomplete early mother/infant dyad.

It seems to me that this quite prevalent misconception

stems from a misunderstanding of Loewald's (1960) and Winnicott's (1958, 1965) contributions. Loewald has focused on the therapeutic effects of the patient's internalizing a benign or positive dyadic interaction in the psychoanalytic situation, an interaction that reflects the relation between a mature, understanding, integrating person and an immature, uncertain, dependent one. This internalization strengthens the primal basis for all transferences stemming from a good mother/infant relation, consolidates the self, and permits identification processes to develop that strengthen ego functions.

It needs to be stressed, however, that such interaction and internalization processes imply a relatively normal early development, the achievement of object constancy, and have been described as an important yet unobstrusive mechanism of action of psychoanalysis, which constitutes a nonspecific effect, in contrast to the specific effects of interpretations. Within a different context, Winnicott's description of the analyst's "holding" function under certain conditions of severe regression in the transference referred to patients in whom, presumably, severely regressive conflicts expressed in intensely ambivalent transferences had been analyzed extensively before this particular regression occurred.

In other words, the analyst's empathy and intuition permit growth to occur in patients with good ego strength (or well-integrated tripartite intrapsychic structure) in the course of a standard psychoanalytic situation, and are also helpful at certain points of severe regression with patients in whom sufficient working through of regressive transferences has occurred.

The misinterpretation and overgeneralization of these findings imply that, for patients in regression, it is the therapist's empathic presence—rather than his interpretation—that is really helpful; that it is the patient's identification with this mothering function—rather than his coming to terms with his intrapsychic conflicts—that is important.

On the contrary, an empathic and concerned attitude on the part of the analyst is a necessary precondition in all cases of psychoanalysis. And, as mentioned before, at levels of severe regression, the analyst has to be empathic not only with the patient's central subjective experience at any particular point, but also with what the patient cannot tolerate in himself and has to dissociate or project. Empathy is a prerequisite for interpretive work, not its replacement.

In this connection, the dissociated or repressed material that patients defend themselves against may be expressed, clinically speaking, in the following ways: (1) it may be repressed, and only indirect manifestations of it are present in the content of the patient's free associations or in the transference; (2) it may be dissociated in mutually contradictory ego states that are alternatively conscious; (3) it may be expressed in acting out; and (4) it may be reflected solely in the nature of the interactional processes in the analysis, in the creation of an "uncanny" emotional atmosphere which does not, in a strict sense, belong to the patient's subjective experience and has to be diagnosed by the analyst's empathic awareness of the total emotional situation in the analytic hours. This requires a special "analytic empathy" that transcends ordinary mothering functions and has to be part of the analyst's capacity to diagnose all these various manifestations of unconscious intrapsychic conflicts in the analytic situation. The following will illustrate what has been said so far.

Clinical Example

The patient, a business man in his middle thirties, had consulted because of sexual inhibition, lack of interest in sexual relations with his wife, passivity, and procrastination in his work. He was diagnosed as an obsessive personality with some infantile features and referred to psychoanalysis. In the first year of treatment, submission to, fear of, and unconscious rebellion against authority by means of passive resistance were predominant features; in the transference was a fear that the analyst would criticize the patient for sexual fantasies and wishes toward women other than his wife and a pseudocompliance together with a deeper rejection of the analyst's comments as an imposition from what appeared to be an oedipal authority. I must stress that at no time did the patient appear to have borderline features or a narcissistic character structure; to the contrary, he impressed me in the analysis as presenting a rather well-consolidated tripartite structure and ego functioning.

In the second year of analysis it became clearer that severe repressive barriers interfered with his memories of any aspect of his childhood—a bare few were available from before age eight. He had a sense of chronic, almost total distance from both parents. He stressed that he had hardly mourned his mother's death, which had occurred several months before he started analysis, and experienced his father as cold, critical, and nagging.

The repeated interpretation of the patient's surface submission to me and his deeper underlying rejections of my interpretations did not lead to further awareness, but to the development of a new symptom: he fell asleep in the session every time I tried to focus on the transference. This symptom expanded to such an extent that even my indirect comments that the patient suspected might relate to the transference immediately induced sleep, first for a few seconds, then, gradually, over longer stretches of the session until he was sleeping during some one-fourth to one-third of his sessions. In the middle of these developments, it gradually became clearer that he now experienced me as cold, distant, and nagging, but also shy and withdrawn: all characteristics he had experienced in his father.

Two distinct developments then began to emerge: there were sessions in which the patient paid lip service to free association and self-observation, but fell asleep easily and repeatedly without any apparent feelings of anxiety or guilt; and there were other sessions during which he seemed very anxious, guilt-ridden because of his sleeping and yet extremely limited in his capacity to free associate; he seemed unable to tolerate in himself the expression of any thought or feeling he considered inappropriate, such as sexual impulses toward other women than his wife or angry thoughts about me. In this seemingly neurotic man, the relatively extreme loss of the ordinary capacity for reasoning and self-observation in both these mental states was startling.

At the same time, while complaining that analysis was not helping him, he not only came punctually, but also checked on whether I was giving him his allotted time. This was a permanent feature of both the sleepy and the guilt-ridden sessions, so that he might be fast asleep toward the end of the session, wake up following a comment of mine indicating that time was up, and, still half asleep, look at his watch as he rose from the couch before leaving. It also became clearer that in both his mental states there was a subtle but permanent oppositionalism to me, a hidden rejection of everything I was saying, linked to chronic suspiciousness about me.

Toward the end of the third year, the patient began to develop rage attacks in his home, treating his children tyrannically, feeling very regretful afterward, and eventually linking these attacks of rage with the sessions he slept in. My interpretations, which had centered around oedipal conflicts in the first year of his analysis and had focused on the analysis of his behavior in the sessions in terms of the same, predominantly oedipal, conflicts during the second year, now shifted to the analysis of the common features of the two apparently contradictory mental states: his desperate need to receive something from me without ever being able to achieve it, his fear and suspicion of me as cold and indifferent, but also exploitive and dishonest (my intention to rob him of his time, and the displacement of rage against me onto his own children because of this perception of me).

I interpreted this total situation "as if" he saw me as a cold, indifferent person from whom he wanted very much to receive love and support, but whom, at the same time, he had to control and suspect because I wanted only to extract money and time from him. I left it open what transference object that might be and the patient spontaneously said that all this had nothing to do with either of his parents, because he had never expected anything from his father, and his mother was always very giving (although she also required that everybody behave very properly, was disgusted by messiness and disorder, and was afraid that the neighbors spied on them in order to have something to talk about!). I then told the patient that in the sessions he slept in he was treating me as if I were his father and, in the sessions he tried desperately to be a good boy in, as if I were a harsh mother demanding perfection; I added that he felt there was nothing to hope from me as he had felt disappointment from both his parents. I also said that the rage attacks toward his children—he consistently had denied any emotion of anger toward me—was a displacement of rage against me representing both his parents.

The patient then experienced me more clearly as an authority who was trying to trick him: I was pretending to be warm and interested so that he would be forced to talk about his unacceptable sexual impulses and his rage, that is, all his badness, only so I could despise and punish him further by rejecting him, and he was not letting himself be tricked. These understandings were gained in brief intervals of communications during sessions in which he felt very guilty about his sleeping, at not giving thought to what I was saying, at forgetting me completely between the hours, and at depreciating me and my treatment. Now his sleeping during the hours increased even further, and so did his monotonous statements that the treatment was getting nowhere and that all this made no sense at all.

Simultaneously, however, the patient began to talk about his older and younger brother—how much he hated and depreciated the former, who was violent, derogatory, and totally insensitive psychologically. In contrast, his younger brother was friendly, patient, obedient, had always been loving and respectful toward their parents—strikingly different from the patient's own indifferent abandonment of them. I now interpreted the patient's alternate ego states in the hours as his identification with now his older and now his younger brother. I said he was trying to avoid the terrible conflict between feeling that if he were spontaneous and open he would be like his horrible older brother, and I would therefore hate and depreciate him; or, if he were like his young brother, he would have to renounce any change toward independence and would have to be a good boy eternally, who experienced no sexual urges or rage. I also added that he must have experienced a lack of emotional support from his mother to feel that his impulses were so unacceptable. I later connected this with his submission and rebellion toward his father: he did not dare express rebellion toward his father because all emotional expression was forbidden by the combined action of both parents. The fear of father's punishment had combined with mother's rejection of his sexual curiosity to induce total repression of his oedipal urges, and his solution was to remain withdrawn and passively resistant at home. I also reminded him that at age seventeen he had rather abruptly left home and all memories of his past, just as he was leaving me every session without giving me any further thought, or abandoning me in the sessions themselves by means of sleep.

The patient now began to experience me as a very patient, tolerant, understanding mother, and at the same time developed feelings of guilt because of his lack of feelings around the death of his own mother. For the first time, he cried in the session, and expressed gratitude because of what he experienced as my patience with him. He now began to understand that the incapacity to integrate his identifications with both his brothers was reflected in a combination of his sense of badness and the fear of rejection and attack from both parents. His emotional attitude toward himself in the hours changed, and he became able again to meaningfully observe and communicate what was going on in him, for the first time developing curiosity about himself and his internal life. I later interpreted his caring for himself as an identification with his caring mother and with me representing her, an identification he had earlier been unable to achieve because of his unconscious guilt toward her.

Gradually, his transference shifted again into a predominantly oedipal level, and toward examining the sexual inhibition with his wife. It now turned out that, at one level, his wife was like a superficially good mother who really replaced his own internal, bad, and guilt-provoking mother, toward whom he had to be a well-behaved little boy lest she severely attack and depreciate him (if, for example, he was sexually freer with her). At a different level, he felt that his marriage, with all its problems, was such an improvement over the marriage of his parents that he could not tolerate this triumph over his own father.

I have tried to illustrate how, in an ordinary neurotic transference, primitive dissociation or splitting in the transference (the contradictory ego states), regressive shifts from verbal to nonverbal communication, and temporary weakening of reality testing in connection with the activation of primitive defensive operations (splitting, projection, denial) were resolved analytically in a case that, at a certain point, might have been considered nonanalyzable.

To conclude: Object relations theory permits us to sharpen our understanding and technical handling of the various types of psychopathology and degrees of regression in the transference. A cohesive, holistic theory of technique, it seems to me, is far preferable to attempting to develop *ad hoc* theories of technique for various psychopathological conditions. Such *ad hoc* formulations contain within them the potential for disregarding contradictory implications in terms of psychoanalytic theory and technique and our understanding of normal and pathological development.

Summary

Whereas, traditionally, object relations theory—a refinement of structural theory that links structure more closely with genetic and dynamic aspects of mental functioning—has been applied mostly to the understanding and treatment of patients with severe regression in the transference, it also has application for technique in the standard psychoanalytic situation. This paper has focused on (1) the object relations approach to the nature of conflicts to be interpreted in the transference; (2) the varying relationships between transference, genetic history, and early development, revealed by an object relations focus; (3) the technique used under conditions of regression in the communicative process in the transference; and (4) the relation of empathy and regression in the transference. Two clinical cases are presented to illustrate the points made.

REFERENCES

Balint, M. (1965), Instincts and object relations. Part I. In: *Primary Love and Psychoanalytic Technique*. New York: Liveright, pp. 3-147.
——— (1968), *The Basic Fault: Therapeutic Aspects of Regression*. London: Tavistock Publications.
Beres, D. & Arlow, J. A. (1974), Fantasy and identification in empathy. *Psychoanal. Quart.*, 43:26-50.
Bion, W. R. (1967), *Second Thoughts: Selected Papers on Psycho-Analysis*. London: Heinemann.
Blum, H. P. (1977), The prototype of preoedipal reconstruction. *This Journal*, 25:757-785.
Erikson, E. (1956), The problem of ego identity. *This Journal*, 4:56-121.

_____ (1959), *Identity and the Life Cycle. Psychol. Issues*, Monogr. 1. New York: International Universities Press.

_____ (1963), *Childhood and Society*, 2nd ed. New York: Norton.

Fairbairn, W. (1952), *An Object Relations Theory of the Personality.* New York: Basic Books.

_____ (1963), Synopsis of an object relations theory of the personality. *Internat. J. Psycho-Anal.*, 44:224-225.

Fenichel, O. (1941), *Problems of Psychoanalytic Technique.* New York: The Psychoanalytic Quarterly, Inc.

Glover, E. (1955), *The Technique of Psycho-Analysis.* New York: International Universities Press.

Jacobson, E. (1964), *The Self and the Object World.* New York: International Universities Press.

_____ (1971), *Depression.* New York: International Universities Press.

Kernberg, O. (1975), *Borderline Conditions and Pathological Narcissism.* New York: Aronson.

_____ (1976a), *Object-Relations Theory and Clinical Psychoanalysis.* New York: Aronson.

_____ (1976b), Technical considerations in the treatment of borderline personality organization. *This Journal*, 24:795-829.

Klein, M. (1940), Mourning and its relation to manic-depressive states. In: *Contributions to Psycho-Analysis, 1921-1945.* London: Hogarth Press, 1948, pp. 311-338.

_____ (1945), The Oedipus complex in the light of early anxieties. In: *Contributions to Psycho-Analysis, 1921-1945.* London: Hogarth Press, 1948, pp. 339-390.

_____ (1946), Notes on some schizoid mechanisms. In: *Developments in Psychoanalysis*, ed. J. Riviere, M. Klein, P. Heimann, & S. Issacs. London: Hogarth Press, 1952, pp. 292-320.

_____ (1957), *Envy and Gratitude.* New York: Basic Books.

Lichtenstein, H. (1977), *The Dilemma of Human Identity.* New York: Aronson.

Loewald, H. W. (1960), On the therapeutic action of psychoanalysis. *Internat. J. Psycho-Anal.*, 41:16-33.

_____ (1978), Instinct theory, object relations, and psychic-structure formation. *This Journal*, 26:493-506.

Mahler, M. & Furer, M. (1968), *On Human Symbiosis and the Vicissitudes of Individuation*, vol. 1: Infantile Psychosis. New York: International Universities Press.

_____ Pine, F., & Bergman, A. (1975), *The Psychological Birth of the Human Infant.* New York: Basic Books.

Racker, H. (1968), *Transference and Countertransference.* New York: International Universities Press.

Sullivan, H. S. (1953), *The Interpersonal Theory of Psychiatry.* New York: Norton.

Winnicott, D. W. (1958), *Collected Papers: Through Paediatrics to Psychoanalysis.* New York: Basic Books.

_____ (1965), *The Maturational Process and the Facilitating Environment.* New York: International Universities Press.

21 Bloomingdale Road
White Plains, New York 10605

THE TECHNICAL SIGNIFICANCE AND APPLICATION OF MAHLER'S SEPARATION-INDIVIDUATION THEORY

SELMA KRAMER, M.D.

T HE SIGNIFICANCE AND APPLICATION of separation-individuation theory should be considered in the light of its place in the history of psychoanalytic developmental psychology. The use of the two main sources of developmental concepts—reconstruction from psychoanalysis of adults and direct observations of infants and young children—was exemplified by Freud, as Blum (1977) so elegantly described. Freud's reconstructions in his self-analysis and from the analyses of patients, as well as his formulations derived from observations of his grandchildren are, as Blum says, "the prototype of preoedipal reconstruction."

Abraham's (1924) outline of stages of object love, also from the analysis of adults, corresponds significantly to modern formulations of infantile development (Parens and Saul, 1971, p. 62n). And Wilhelm Reich's work on character (1933-1934) also added to knowledge of preoedipal development and its vicissitudes. The structural theory, Hartmann's

Training and Supervising Analyst, Adult and Child, Philadelphia Psychoanalytic Institute; Professor of Child Psychiatry, Medical College of Pennsylvania.

Presented at the Panel on "The Technical Consequences of Object Relations Theory" at the Fall Meeting of the American Psychoanalytic Association, New York, December 17, 1978.

I wish to express my thanks to Margaret Mahler, M.D., and Henri Parens, M.D., for their careful reading and most helpful suggestions.

241

perspectives on adaptation (1939), on the genetic approach
(Hartmann and Kris, 1945), and on autonomous ego
functions (1939, 1952), and Anna Freud's delineation of the
mechanisms of defense (1936) opened psychoanalysis to ego
psychology. Interest in psychic-structure formation led to
seminal papers on development by Hartmann, Kris, and
Loewenstein (1946) and to Jacobson's work on the self and
the object world (1964). Greenacre (1958, 1960), Loewald
(1960), Lewin (1946), and Isakower (1938) described
derivatives from infant and child developmental phases that
appeared in the analyses of their adult patients. Anna Freud
(1965) wrote on normal and pathological development in
children, using the concept of developmental lines. Investigations into early psychic development as it applies to
understanding and treatment of severe pathology in the adult
led to significant contributions by Kernberg (1975, 1976) and
Kohut (1971, 1977).

The most ambitious undertaking has been the longitudinal psychoanalytic observational studies of earliest development, parallel studies of psychotic and normal children, by
Mahler. Studies by Spitz culminating in his description of
the first year of life (1965) and of personality organizers also
stand as examples of observational studies. No one person
alone is responsible for the present interest in psychoanalytic
developmental psychology. There are many other contributors to development besides those I have already mentioned
(e.g., J. Benjamin, S. Brody, E. H. Erikson).

It is well known that Mahler's symbiosis-separation-
individuation theory, which derives from clinical practice as
well as observation, is much more than an object relations
theory. Her theory adds to that of the ego and its functions,
and to the theory of drives; it deals with basic moods,
addresses the vicissitudes of infantile omnipotence as well as
of depressiveness and, in much detail, describes the complex
and vital structuring of object and self from the undifferen-

tiated child-mother symbiosis to the attainment of object-and self constancy. (See also Jacobson, 1954.)

Her work, which is a study of intrapsychic processes, of structure formation, is an intrinsic part of classical psychoanalytic theory, following upon and in the context of the contributions of Freud, Hartmann, Kris, and other great contributors to psychoanalytic theory. There is little doubt that in the last few decades, advances in psychoanalytic developmental psychology made the most significant contribution to psychoanalysis as a "general psychology" (cf. Freud and Hartmann). It is less universally accepted that the ever widening knowledge of early preverbal and para-verbal communications of infants has added a substantial dimension to psychoanalytic technique of children, adolescents, and adults alike. Not all analysts are at ease with developmental concepts and their application to clinical psychoanalysis (Abrams, 1978). In this paper, I shall endeavor to explore some theoretical concepts and to demonstrate with clinical material ways in which developmental knowledge and Mahler's work on separation individuation in particular has influenced the clinical practice of psychoanalysis.

Understanding by the Analyst of Preverbal and Primary-Process Material

I would like at the start to emphasize how much more than purely verbal intercommunication exists between patient and analyst—something to which much lip service has been given in recent papers but is seldom spelled out—that it is the task of the analyst to understand this nonverbal communication and to use it, just as he notes and uses, when appropriate, the patient's verbal production. Such nonverbal communication includes changes of affect and mood; bodily states such as rigidity or fidgeting; anal or genital sensations; flushing, headaches, transient pain, spasm, or limpness; feeling "light" or "heavy"; dizziness; itchiness; the desire to urinate or defecate, to suck, to smoke, to keep the eyes open or closed; to struggle against remaining on the couch or in the office or against leaving the analytic session.

In applying her findings to analytic technique, Mahler stresses the importance of body language and screen memories and especially of screen sensations (Anthony, 1961) in eliciting preverbal (not yet internalized) conflicts that later become structure-forming, internal—at first pre-oedipal, thence oedipal—conflicts. She (1971) refers to "coenesthetic empathy" as a most important attribute of the analyst "essential for the clinical efficiency of psychoanalysis." Loewald (1970) speaks similarly of empathy as an important analytic tool, especially in the analyst's attempts to gain insight into the psychic *substructures* (my italics) and into the genesis of ego and superego defects. He comments (1979) on the "new luster" which such an attitude may give to the Oedipus complex.

I feel that "coenesthetic empathy" and the use of one's countertransference in analysis of primitive material do not stand alone, but, together with the analyst's alertness to repetitive themes that emerge in the transference, provide the laboratory par excellence for each analyst's study of psychoanalysis, as he "processes" his empathy in the context of his thoughts, feelings, and attitudes. Empathy can be used safely and securely only if one knows where the patient is and where he is going.

Freud's momentous disclosures of infantile sexuality, the stages of psychosexual development, and the role of the Oedipus complex, although they were initially met with skepticism and even rejection on the part of some of his contemporaries, have had a profound and lasting influence on the clinical practice of psychoanalysis and of psychiatry, as well as upon the average person's familiarity with child development. A seldom mentioned clinical gift from Freud to the practitioner, seldom mentioned because we take it for granted, is the comfort with which we can understand, accept, and anticipate material in our patient's productions from every psychosexual developmental stage, without the surprise or discomfort that could make us ill at ease or interfere with our basic neutrality.

The frame of reference offered us by developmental concepts has resulted in the fact that residues of preverbal (mostly projected) and preoedipal conflicts are not only less burdensome and easier to cope with, but are used to enrich the analysis by the analyst who understands and even anticipates such regressive behavior.

I venture to say that in analysis of neurotic patients as well as of more disturbed patients, the appearance of preverbal and preoedipal conflicts may give rise to sufficiently serious blind spots or countertransference reactions in analysts lacking such a frame of reference as to make successful analysis impossible. This is so particularly when rapprochement subphase conflicts emerge, with dramatic displays of ambivalence and ambitendency; with imperative efforts by the patient to seek and also to ward off extreme closeness with his analyst; with his attempts to prove his own and his analyst's omnipotence, only to follow this by having to angrily disprove that the analyst could be of any help to such a worthless creature.

We can now understand and interpret the aforementioned material quite differently and more explicitly, with the consequence that the analyst experiences less emotional strain, and more is achieved in the analysis. Freud and Abraham discovered that preoedipal and preverbal influences not only left a permanent cast on character, but that these influences could be reconstructed in adult psychoanalysis (Blum, 1977). Expanding our knowledge of developmental processes, Mahler integrated libido theory and separation-individuation theory as she emphasized the drive pressures added to the child's other developmental tasks. In the rapprochement subphase child, for example, she noted the coexistence with self and object-related rapprochement subphase conflicts, of anal-phase sensations and conflicts as well as early oedipal conflicts. This is an example of advance in psychoanalytic theory for which Freud so yearned.

The Broadening of Our Technique in Treatment of Neurotic Patients Utilizing the Transference Neurosis

I suggest that we can extend the scope of the transference neurosis to include the transference of *neurotic* conflicts involving not only the postoedipal superego, but also superego precursors arising in the rapprochement subphase. For where there has been a less than optimal mother-child relationship or serious preoedipal conflicts with resultant failure of libido to modulate aggression sufficiently, *precursors* of a too-harsh superego may also exercise · a profound influence upon the formation of the postoedipal superego, with resultant masochism and depressiveness which appear in the transference neurosis of the neurotic patient.

Another element of the transference neurosis with roots in unresolved rapprochement subphase conflicts is the patient's magical expectations of omnipotence of his analyst (see Greenacre, 1966).

The transference neurosis has been typically expressed in terms of oedipal conflicts and from the approach of the structural theory. Now we include the preoedipal coloring of the transference neurosis, and are aware of how each developmental phase influences later phases.

I refer to the 1973 Paris panel shared by Lebovici (1973), Ritvo (1974), Loewald (1974), and Mahler (1975) during which the panelists agreed that the "shape" of the Oedipus complex and the resultant infantile neurosis do not arise anew. Instead, the characterological and neurotic precursors, the psychic structure forming in the preoedipal child, not only create the *Anlage* upon which the Oedipus "settles" but determine the fashion in which the sexual drives interact with the state of self- and object differentiation and with self- and object relationship reached by the child. I agree with Shapiro who said (Panel, 1977), "The Oedipus complex is as much a result of the ego as of the drives, and its form as much an amalgam of experience in and with the world and inner maturational structure as any other psychic structure" (p. 209).

Clinical Examples

Case #1

I had the unique experience of supervising two analysts on the same adult case. The first, unreceptive to a theory of early development, opposed to my suggestion that one must take cognizance of preoedipal influences, uncomfortable with any disclosure of countertransference, and unable to learn from me in supervision, could not engage the patient in analysis. The second analyst, in contrast, a much more intuitive young man, more comfortable with his countertransference, able to tolerate and to understand his patient's immature and regressive needs, was able to use separation-individuation theory as a framework for the analysis of the patient's preoedipal conflicts. After and parallel to the dyadic transference manifestations, he was able to analyze the Oedipus complex, and was able to work through with the patient the re-emergence of dyadic transference during the termination phase of the analysis.

The patient was a depressed, hostile young woman of 24 in danger of being dropped from social work school because of her antagonistic attitude toward her supervisors from whom they felt she would not learn. She came to analysis under duress at the strong suggestion of her advisor and of a psychiatrist whom she had consulted for depression.

She was a resentful patient who felt blackmailed into treatment. However, when plans for analysis were completed she expressed relief and the hope that she would feel less depressed. These were the last kindly words she uttered to this first analyst, for she thereafter expressed mostly anger and scorn. Keeping the analyst at a distance, she attempted to conduct what I called a "Do-it-myself analysis." She dutifully came on time and, knowing what she was supposed to do, she "free associated." Speaking in a mechanical fashion with little affect, she reported the days' events with monotony and anger. Soon, she reported dreams which she immediately "interpreted" by herself. While she fumed that she was not being helped, it was my impression that she defended against any hint of understanding by her analyst, as if she needed to maintain considerable distance from him in order to avoid intrusion. In trying to help the analyst get a "handle" on this difficult analysis, I suggested that the monotonous reporting might be a re-enactment in the transference of early experiences. This made no sense to him, for he saw the configuration only as a resistance to "getting into the *real* (oedipal) analysis."

The analyst could not be empathic to and could not understand the patient's pain and frustration as she warded him off. He could perceive and therefore interpret her depression only as a reaction to oedipal disappointment, and her career problems as expressing her feelings of genital inadequacy. This intelligent young woman had, indeed, disclosed such concepts in her dutiful but monotonous "free associations," but while the words were oedipal and genital, I felt that "the music was not."

Just before her analyst's first vacation (she had been in analysis about seven months), she reported and immediately "analyzed" a short dream as follows:

"I was dancing alone. It was a strange thing to do. Soon I was picked up by someone bigger. I seldom recognize people in my dreams. At first it was nice, then it was sort of too tight, sort of bad. I know I'm supposed to associate. Well, I gained weight and my clothes are too tight. And I don't enjoy dancing. I can't relax. So much for the dream." The patient resumed her monotonous, cliché-filled verbal productions. My own supervisory "countertransference reaction" to the patient's material aroused concern about the regressive despair and loneliness that came through, and also about the latent meaning of the patient's being "picked up."

Before her analyst's vacation she denied having any reaction, yet, while he was away, she had a near-disastrous affair. The analyst interpreted this to mean that she was acting out what she thought his sexual activity might be on vacation. He could not see her angry, desperate search for a man who represented the only thing she deserved, a man of utter depravity. Nor could the analyst acknowledge her blame, when I suggested that her behavior had said, "See what trouble I get into when you leave. I needed you to watch over me, and you weren't here." After the analyst's second vacation the patient left treatment. Some modicum of a potential therapeutic alliance must have formed, for she soon entered analysis with the second analyst who, quite coincidentally, also conferred with me.

Because of her disappointment in and anger toward the first analyst, the early phase of this analysis was even stormier than the previous one, but the analyst's knowledge, his empathy, his use of his countertransference, and his ability to interpret on the level at which the patient was functioning were all very different.

To the "do-it-myself" attempt at dream interpretation, the analyst commented that she seemed afraid he might intrude on her, and later, in a similar situation, he added that she seemed afraid that by associating to the dream *in the office* she might lose her independence. Yet, he felt that in part she wanted to share. Almost for the first time, the patient had a free association that was meaningful. She said that she could not imagine why she thought of this right now, but she had had a learning problem all through school. She could not learn by any system the teachers taught, and she developed idiosyncratic ways of doing complicated procedures. She

hated to recite in class because of a fear of the teachers'
ridicule for her "private system."

The analyst's response was light but empathic as he
said, "So you have to invent the wheel all by yourself."
Slowly he focused on the patient's need to maintain autonomy
at any cost, including her need to reassure herself that he
would not know too much about her or make her do things
his way. The patient responded by recalling the past (and the
current) intrusiveness of her mother. She described her
mother's most frequently used expressions: "Tell me, tell
me," and "This is what you are to do." "Tell me, Tell me,"
caused the patient to feel trapped, "as if all of what is mine,
no, I mean all of what is *me*, is taken away."

"Tell me, tell me" had existed as far back as the patient
could remember, sometimes replaced by "Show me, show
me," which was said with the same urgency.

The disclosure suggested a meaning of the patient's need
to report to her analyst the boring and unusable details of the
day's events. ("I took the subway today. It was raining out.
The drug store was open today when I passed. Yesterday it
was not, so I couldn't get the toothpaste I wanted.") She was
outwardly complying to the mother analyst, and, although at
the same time she resisted her mother's "Tell me, tell me,"
she told enough, at times, to evoke the analyst's interest.
Then she stopped talking. After the disclosure of her learning
problem, she again retreated into angry silences and brought
more "do-it-myself dreams" into the analysis. The analyst
felt that the patient's picture was similar to an ambivalent
rapprochement subphase child who had to attract and yet
elude the swooping and shadowing mother (Mahler et al.,
1975). The "do-it-myself" dreams soon (the second year of
this analysis) became a sign to both patient and analyst that
the patient wanted to reassure herself of her autonomy but
also wanted the analyst to "move in." The analyst measured
his comments most carefully, fully mindful of the degree to
which they might be regarded as intrusions by the patient.

He addressed himself to her ambivalence, but mostly to her sense that sharing her thoughts and feelings caused her to feel little sense of gain or relief in not being alone, but mainly a desolate feeling of loss.

The patient recalled her very early anger when her parents exchanged knowing glances over her head and then told her *what* she was feeling. This was soon followed by "Tell me, tell me," for when she was still very young she tried to elude her mother's intrusive need to know what she was doing and especially what she thought or felt. Her mother accused her of being sullen, sulky, and silent.

Mahler et al. (1975) describe the rapprochement subphase toddler's "warding off" pattern directed against "impingement upon his recently achieved autonomy," adding that, "autonomy is defended by the 'No,' as well as by increased aggression and negativism of the anal phase" (pp. 77-78). They describe the ideal "gentle push toward independence" (of the toddler by his mother) which "may even be a sine qua non of normal (healthy) individuation" (p. 79). They also portray mothers such as this patient's whose own symbiotic-parasitic needs make *them* shadowers of the child.

The analyst continued to sense the patient's need to evoke the hated and wanted intrusiveness in the transference, followed by resistive withdrawal, and, especially during the first two years of analysis, technique had to be monitored most carefully. The very wording as well as the content of a confrontation, an interpretation, or a reconstruction were handled with great awareness of her problems about intrusiveness. Much like the mother of a rapprochement subphase child, the analyst had to be available but had to be careful not to "shadow," to be aware of the patient's conflict between the wish to manage by herself and the wish to partake in the mother's omnipotence. The analyst knew that his absences would evoke either the patient's angry withdrawal or a wooing of him by "flirting with danger." He understood that "where the mother was either dissatisfied with her child, terribly anxious about him, or aloof, normal rapprochement patterns become greatly exaggerated. In the two contrasting behaviors of approach and distancing, this ambivalence conflict had been acted out in either extreme shadowing of mother or darting away from her (in the late practicing and in the early rapprochement subphase), or else it had caused excessive wooing of mother, alternating with extreme negativism" (Mahler et al., 1975, pp. 96-97).

The analyst's continued effort to be available but unobtrusive eventually permitted the patient to form a good therapeutic alliance and a transference neurosis. The patient recognized and welcomed the therapeutic alliance when she recalled the earlier dancing dream and said that now she did not have to dance alone.

Case 2

I should like to focus on the influence of working through in analysis of separation-individuation transference phenomenology in a patient who showed evidence of more and deeper pathology than is encountered in the "normal neurotic" patient.

The patient, a 29-year-old homosexual woman, came to treatment because of work inhibition, severe recurrent depressions, and problems in relating to her lovers. She was born in Europe to very young teenage parents who had to marry because of the pregnancy. From reconstruction, and later verified by her mother's diary, it was apparent that the 15-year-old mother was depressed and angry at her well-endowed infant for whom she could not modulate tension. The transference material suggested that the young parents showed little regard for the needs of the infant, but that the infant received attention from many relatives, her grandparents in particular, and an elderly uncle who rocked her. I feel that this gratification of symbiotic-libidinal needs probably saved my patient from more serious pathology but problems in object relations resulted because, among other reasons, there was not one main libidinal object.

Material that emerged in treatment, and the diary, suggested that the early practicing subphase, although not especially joyous, aroused some pride in the parents. In the practicing subphase proper, the father left their country to establish himself in the United States, leaving the patient and her once more depressed mother to remain in a relative's home where the child's explorations were markedly curtailed. Now the depressed mother turned to her daughter for comfort, clinging to her. This too great closeness, too great an encroachment on the child's separation and individuation, continued into her pre- and postoedipal life. The father was not available to help the child separate from her overly binding mother. When they joined him in this country, his daughter, just past four years in age, considered him an ogre. At first he seemed to compete for her mother's attention, and she could not vie with her mother for *his* attention at this critical gender-formation period. The father, in a hurry to pursue a new career, soon encouraged his wife and daughter to keep each other company, and gradually actively assigned to my patient the responsibility of providing emotional support to her depressive mother.

Physical separation from the mother did not take place until the patient went to a college far from home. Mutual emotional separateness was not effected. Mother and daughter were depressed, lonely. The patient soon entered her first homosexual relationship. Her many homosexual partners were older women from whom she sought mothering, although initially in the office and to the world she presented herself as a "Dyke." When depressed she wished to be rocked, as we discovered she had been by the uncle in infancy. Then she fantasied herself as little "Raggedy Anne." When in close contact with a mothering object, she fantasied herself as "Raggedy Andy," a soft, spineless, cuddly and not yet phallic male. In a successful business career much like her father's, she fantasied herself as phallic and indestructible—"The Six Million Dollar Man."

The anamnesis and reconstruction in the analysis of early preoedipal experiences showed that the libidinal involvement of other family members, and the patient's excellent endowment, protected her against the most noxious effects of her early traumata. She did not achieve libidinal object constancy and repeatedly had to seek a homosexual partner when fear of abandonment and loneliness overwhelmed her. But she also could not remain attached to these objects because dread of loss of self gave rise to overwhelming anxiety.

I shall briefly report on the treatment, focusing especially on the analysis of the transference, through which it has been possible to facilitate the resolution of conflicts from early preoedipal stages as well as of negative oedipal and oedipal conflicts. I wish to make it clear that there was not an orderly sequential process in the analysis, i.e., the material did not follow orderly stages of development. At first, needs for negative oedipal gratification coexisted with needs for earlier gratification. Dyadic and triadic transference coexisted.

The formation of a therapeutic alliance took a long time, manifestly because my patient could not trust me, a "straight" woman. She was certain that I could not understand her, and that I would disdain her for being gay. Separations were very painful and caused her to get depressed. She fantasied that they meant disapproval, which sent her self-esteem plummeting.

After a time, evidence of existing and stabilizing basic trust progressively emerged. The patient, on entering or leaving the office, searched my face and during the sessions listened to my voice for cues. She felt that she perceived a lilt in my voice and fantasied a happy look in my eyes when I was about to make an important remark. I considered this a significant and welcome positive transference manifestation. She felt a sense of acceptance and empathy.

Early in treatment when she could not trust that I would be reliable, it became clear to me that the patient had a coterie of friends with whom she discussed her affects, dreams, fantasies, etc. I pointed out that in doing this, she was showing her need for so many others; I added that much, however, was lost to treatment. She cried and shouted, "But you're not here for two days each week!" It was at this time that the patient revealed in a "by the way" her insatiable need to be rocked by her homosexual partner, and fantasies that I could rock her and she could even get inside me.

Soon she dreamed about being very tiny, a mouse or flea on the shoulder of the Jolly Green Giant. But the little animal was plucked off and discarded. The mood in the dream, pleasant at first, changed to one of sadness and depression, the way she felt on weekends. She associated to an old favorite song, "I've got you under my skin," but she sang it as, "You've got me under your skin." To the mood change, she associated her feeling that I would object to her as a patient if I knew how close she wanted to get—not sexually— just close.

Further associations to the dream were of pleasant kinesthetic sensations of comforting·rocking movement. But she found herself angry at me for I didn't give her what she wanted, i.e., to feel better. If I would not do this every time, I should not begrudge her the comfort she got from her friends.

I interpreted this dream, not in terms of some of its sexual content which later surfaced, but in terms of her feeling that she had experienced as a child and wished for now in the transference: comforting by those who were not in a main (parent-child) relationship because the main relationship was not enough.

After a period during which the patient was less conflicted, she began to travel for her business. She became very uneasy, reminding me of a rapprochement child, and on some occasions phoned from across the country with desperation and anger. "What made you think I could do this?" or, "You should have told me to stay home." On her return she was relieved, yet blamed me, and said that if not for her appointment with me, she could have gone off in a new homosexual liaison. She then dreamed of a tea party. She, her mother, Raggedy Ann, Raggedy Andy, and Elizabeth Taylor sat around a nursery table pretending to have tea. There were sounds in the background that interested her. Someone said, "Sit down and pay attention." It was a little like Alice in Wonderland. Her associations were to the many tea parties she and her lonely mother had with her dolls. To Elizabeth Taylor she associated her attraction to beautiful older women who were bitches, as in *Who's Afraid of Virginia Woolf?* In that play, Taylor couldn't have children and her marriage was bad, as is everyone's heterosexual marriage. The patient associated to her parents' violent battles and her wish to get away. The background sounds seemed to be of children playing. "Sit down and pay attention" recalled both parents' admonitions, mother's that she should stay home with her, and her father instructing her to take care of mother.

I pointed out the difficulty that she and mother had about separations; that she liked to play with mother and the dolls, yet part of her wanted to go off. I connected this with recent transference material. The patient said, "You and I sit around here and play with my Raggedy Ann and Raggedy Andy selves. And *you* can go off if you want to, but you don't let me." She railed in an impassioned rage that I directed her life. Then she returned to the fact that she did not stay away from treatment to go off with the new homosexual partner. She admitted that she had been relieved for she had been afraid of the woman she called "Super-Dyke."

Dreams of negative Oedipus emerged soon. The background to a dream was a poem entitled "Mother Love."

Also, the patient wanted to return to graduate school to study law and business. She had fantasies of being rich and powerful and was not sure I would approve. (She was proud that I, a woman, earned a good living and furious that she had to pay my fee.)

The dream was as follows: she was dressed in yellow pajamas. They were baggy and not attractive. She had a dildo stuck in her in such a way that it made a 30-degree L. as on a Greek vase. It was pleasant to have the dildo. It was done to her by her. She was a girl, but "there it was."

Associations: her father used to parade around in floppy PJ's with the fly open. He thought he was hot stuff. She didn't think so, but sometimes mother did. If she (the patient) were hot stuff, she'd have something to stuff into her female lover. I would think better of her; I would not go away or ignore her. I commented that she must have felt when she was very young that mother would love her more if she had a penis and that when so close to mother, she fantasied taking father's role in sex. I cautiously extended this into the transference, for, although she could accept transference interpretations of her dependency, interpretations of her sexual feelings toward me caused great anxiety, shame, and guilt. Although the patient was furious with the implications of penis envy, she was less tense and hostile. There were many dreams and much transference material indicating that she would be loved and admired by mother and me if she were a male. At the same time, she derided men and openly and successfully competed with them in business.

Soon thereafter she had a dream of running, shouting over her shoulder, dragging Raggedy Anne. She associated to an earlier dream of making love to a new female partner. She had awakened in a panic. Other associations were to the fact that she always had toy guns as a child. And father had taught her how to shoot a real gun to protect her mother while he was away. She revealed teenage masturbatory fantasies of being a young man saving mother. Regression followed. She felt orally insatiable and felt orally teased and deprived, but later dreams reminded her of secret oral pleasures which angered her father.

Afterward, the analyst was less the rejecter, more the comforter. Also, the patient was able to comfort herself as she studied modern dance, and rhythmic exercises, living out a combination of rocking, bodily comforting, and gratification, as well as practicing subphase activity awakened by the transference experience. She began to feel freer in making business trips, after which she would show me souvenirs of her trip, with shades of the affect shown as the practicing subphase and then rapprochement subphase child shares things with mother.

Rapprochement-like crises were soon seen in the transference, ambivalence heightened, and she again became angry with me. As heretofore, quiescent genital-oedipal feeling emerged, again she felt that a "straight" woman could not help her. She hoped and feared that I might be tempted by her to be gay. She hated my husband and fantasied him to be tyrannical and abusive, and she recalled primal-scene exposure.

Exaggerations and ambivalence emerged in the transference. She was certain that I would be angry with her for having friends, for enjoying the wheeling and dealing of business, for having homosexual affairs. The crisis gradually diminished; the patient became more productive and creative in her work; the quality of her friendships improved, and life was better. Later the patient confessed with chagrin that a change had occurred in her sexual dreams and fantasies—her sexual partner was male and was not abusive or murderous. The patient became softer, more feminine as beginning positive oedipal material emerged.

In a dream she made love to a man, then she tried to wrap tiny baby mice in pieces of soft flannel. Associations led to her awareness that she'd like children. She also associated to her fear of rats, a fear that caused chagrin because it was "so typically female." Also, rats gnaw, are vicious, and carry rabies. The desired fetus was a dangerous, clawing, dirty, gnawing thing, her own anger at her mother projected on her fantasied fetus.

Oedipal, triadic material gradually became more consistent. About a year later the patient reported that if she submitted a bid, she was certain that an older woman from a competing company would receive the order, and was angry at the thought of having to capitulate. She associated to a question she had pondered in childhood, "Did her father have enough love for both her and her mother?" She connected this question with her fear of competing with older women in business, fearing she would lose mother's love if she did all right with father. She now recalled childhood masturbation fantasies about her father, but denied having been coy or seductive with him; she remembered his reading poetry to her as well as teaching her masculine things and thinking he looked like Errol Flynn. But she couldn't compete with any woman for any man.

This denial soon gave way as she fantasied again about my husband. Suppose she met him in business and something happened (sexually). Since she would not know he was married to me, it would not be her fault. She imagined my rage and then reminded me that it was inevitable that she would have had fantasies about her father, for he was only seventeen when she was born. She called him a "handsome bastard" with some warmth and added that she was no longer furious at men.

Further analysis resulted in increased separateness, especially from mother, and decreasing anger at father. She reported that she had better relationships with both parents, having established with mother that they are separate; she and father were friends at last.

The patient now had to take a business trip and knew she would miss me but would get along. There might be men on the trip. She was getting along better with them all the time. She wore skirts now for all encounters with men, and they liked it.

She knows from their responses to her that she must be sending "vibes" to them. Her positive oedipal feelings revived her fear of her father's sadism. Her anger at father eventually centered on the fact that if he loved her at all, and he may have, he did not respond sufficiently to her seductiveness, nor did he make her more important than her mother.

Throughout her analysis, while there were adumbrations of earlier phases of development, there was a powerful developmental thrust which aided the analytic process and encouraged the process of what traditionally is considered "working through." I wish to state that I in no way feel that the early stage material appearing in the analysis duplicated in an exact way, what actually occurred in the early preoedipal years (see also Blum, 1978).

Summary

Greater knowledge and integration of developmental concepts and of the frame of reference of separation-individuation, add to the analyst's richer insights and to his more complete interpretations and reconstructions.

Freud recognized the complexity of preoedipal development and the importance of the object and of object relations. Contemporary contributions have enabled us to proceed beyond the preoedipal conceptualizations of and since Freud, to better understand ego- and drive regression and evidence of fixations or ego distortions which may appear parallel to "normal neurotic" findings.

I question whether we encounter different patients today and suggest that we understand our patients better, thus making our analytic assessments and practices so different from 50 years ago. Separation-individuation theory encompasses and organizes findings from many sources, research and clinical, and permits us to perceive and process material in a multifaceted way. It must affect the timing and content of interpretations and reconstruction, and has a profound influence upon the understanding of psychopathology as well as normal development.

REFERENCES

Abraham, K. (1924), A short study of the development of the libido. In: *Selected Papers*. New York: Basic Books, 1953, pp. 418-501.

Abrams, S. (1978), The teaching and learning of psychoanalytic developmental psychology. *This Journal*, 26:387-406.

Anthony, E. J. (1961), A study of screen sensations. *The Psychoanalytic Study of the Child*, 16:211-246. New York: International Universities Press.

Blum, H. P. (1977), The prototype of preoedipal reconstruction. *This Journal*, 25:757-786.

—— (1978), Reconstruction in a case of postpartum depression. *The Psychoanalytic Study of the Child*, 33:335-363. New Haven: Yale University Press.

Freud, A. (1936), *The Ego and the Mechanisms of Defense. Writings*, 2. New York, International Universities Press, 1966.

—— (1965), *Normality and Pathology in Childhood. Writings*, 6. New York: International Universities Press.

Greenacre, P. (1958), Early physical determinants in the development of the sense of identity. In: *Emotional Growth*. New York: International Universities Press, 1971, pp. 113-127.

—— (1960), Considerations regarding the parent-infant relationship. In: *Emotional Growth*. New York: International Universities Press, 1971, pp. 199-224.

—— (1966), Problems of overidealization of the analyst and of analysis. In: *Emotional Growth*. New York: International Universities Press, 1971, pp. 743-761.

Hartmann, H. (1939), *Ego Psychology and the Problem of Adaptation*. New York: International Universities Press, 1958.

—— (1952), The mutual influences in the development of the ego and id. In: *Essays on Ego Psychology*. New York: International Universities Press, 1964, pp. 155-181.

—— & Kris, E. (1945), The genetic approach in psychoanalysis. *The Psychoanalytic Study of the Child*, 1:11-30. New York: International Universities Press.

—— —— & Loewenstein, R. M. (1946), Comments on the formation of psychic structure. *The Psychoanalytic Study of the Child*, 2:11-38. New York: International Universities Press.

Isakower, O. (1938), A contribution to the psychopathology of phenomena associated with falling asleep. *Internat. J. Psycho-Anal.*, 19:331-345.

Jacobson, E. (1954), The self and the object world. *The Psychoanalytic Study of the Child*, 9:75-127. New York: International Universities Press.

———— (1964), *The Self and the Object World*. New York: International Universities Press.

Kernberg, O. F. (1975), *Borderline Conditions and Pathological Narcissism*. New York: Aronson.

———— (1976), *Object Relations Theory and Clinical Psychoanalysis*. New York: Aronson.

Kohut, H. (1971), *The Analysis of the Self*. New York: International Universities Press.

———— (1977), *The Restoration of the Self*. New York: International Universities Press.

Lebovici, S. (1973), The current status of the infantile neurosis. Presented at a Panel, Association for Child Analysis, Paris, July.

Lewin, B. D. (1946), Sleep, the mouth and the dream screen. In: *Selected Writings*. New York: The Psychoanalytic Quarterly, Inc., 1973, pp. 87-100.

Loewald, H. (1960), On the therapeutic action of psycho-analysis. *Internat. J. Psycho-Anal.*, 41:16-33.

———— (1970), Psychoanalytic theory and the psychoanalytic process. *The Psychoanalytic Study of the Child*, 25:45-68. New York: International Universities Press.

———— (1974), Current status of the concept of infantile neurosis. *The Psychoanalytic Study of the Child*, 29:183-188. New Haven: Yale University Press.

———— (1979), The waning of the Oedipus complex. *This Journal*, in press.

Mahler, M. S. (1971), A study of the separation-individuation process and its possible application to borderline phenomena in the psychoanalytic situation. *The Psychoanalytic Study of the Child*, 26:403-424. New York: Quadrangle Books.

———— (1975), On the current status of the infantile neurosis. *This Journal*, 23:327-333.

———— Pine, F., & Bergman, A. (1975), *The Psychological Birth of the Human Infant*. New York: Basic Books.

Panel (1977), Varieties of Oedipal Distortions in Severe Character Pathologies, W. Robbins, reporter. *This Journal*, 25:201-218.

Parens, H. & Saul, L. J. (1971), *Dependence in Man*. New York: International Universities Press.

Reich, W. (1933-1934), *Character Analysis*. New York: Touchstone Books, 1974.

Ritvo, S. (1974), The current status of the infantile neurosis. *The Psychoanalytic Study of the Child*, 29:159-181. New Haven: Yale University Press.

Spitz, R. A. (1965), *The First Year of Life*. New York: International Universities Press.

3902 Netherfield Road
Philadelphia, Penna. 19129

THE ANALYSIS OF THE TRANSFERENCE

MERTON M. GILL, M.D.

T HE ANALYSIS OF THE TRANSFERENCE is generally acknowledged to be the central feature of analytic technique. Freud regarded transference and resistance as facts of observations, not as conceptual inventions. He wrote: ". . . the theory of psychoanalysis is an attempt to account for two striking and unexpected facts of observation which emerge whenever an attempt is made to trace the symptoms of a neurotic back to their sources in his past life: the facts of transference and of resistance . . . anyone who takes up other sides of the problem while avoiding these two hypotheses will hardly escape a charge of misappropriation of property by attempted impersonation, if he persists in calling himself a psychoanalyst" (1914a, p. 16). Rapaport (1967) argued, in his posthumously published paper on the methodology of psychoanalysis, that transference and resistance inevitably follow from the fact that the analytic situation is interpersonal.

Despite this general agreement on the centrality of transference and resistance in technique, it is my impression, from my experience as a student and practitioner, from talking to students and colleagues, and from reading the literature, that the analysis of the transference is not pursued as systematically and comprehensively as I think it could be and should be. The relative privacy in which psychoanalysts

This is a revised and expanded version of a paper read to the Chicago Psychoanalytic Society on May 23, 1978. It is a partial summary of a forthcoming monograph. Its preparation was supported in part by Research Scientist Award, N.I.M.H. Grant #19436. Drs. Samuel D. Lipton, Irwin Hoffman, and Ilse Judas have helped me develop and clarify the ideas expressed in this paper.

263

work makes it impossible for me to state this view as anything more than my impression. On the assumption that even if I am wrong it will be useful to review issues in the analysis of the transference and to state a number of reasons that an important aspect of the analysis of the transference, namely, resistance to the awareness of the transference, is especially often slighted in analytic practice, I am in this paper going to spell out these issues and reasons.

I must first distinguish clearly between two types of interpretation of the transference. The one is an interpretation of resistance to the awareness of transference. The other is an interpretation of resistance to the resolution of transference. The distinction has been best spelled out in our literature by Greenson (1967) and Stone (1967). The first kind of resistance may be called defense transference. Although that term is mainly employed to refer to a phase of analysis characterized by a general resistance to the transference of wishes, it can also be used for a more isolated instance of transference of defense. The second kind of resistance is usually called transference resistance. With some oversimplification, one might say that in resistance to the awareness of transference, the transference is what is resisted, whereas in resistance to the resolution of transference, the transference is what does the resisting.

Another more descriptive way of stating this distinction between resistance to the awareness of transference and resistance to the resolution of transference is between implicit or indirect references to the transference and explicit or direct references to the transference. The interpretation of resistance to awareness of the transference is intended to make the implicit transference explicit, while the interpretation of resistance to the resolution of transference is intended to make the patient realize that the already explicit transference does indeed include a determinant from the past.

It is also important to distinguish between the general

concept of an interpretation of resistance to the resolution of transference and a particular variety of such an interpretation, namely, a genetic transference interpretation—that is, an interpretation of how an attitude in the present is an inappropriate carry-over from the past. While there is a tendency among analysts to deal with explicit references to the transference primarily by a genetic transference interpretation, there are other ways of working toward a resolution of the transference. This paper will argue that not only is not enough emphasis being given to interpretation of the transference in the here and now, that is, to the interpretation of implicit manifestations of the transference, but also that interpretations intended to resolve the transference as manifested in explicit references to the transference should be primarily in the here and now, rather than genetic transference interpretations.

A patient's statement that he feels the analyst is harsh, for example, is, at least to begin with, likely best dealt with not by interpreting that this is a displacement from the patient's feeling that his father was harsh but by an elucidation of some other aspect of this here-and-now attitude, such as what has gone on in the analytic situation that seems to the patient to justify his feeling or what was the anxiety that made it so difficult for him to express his feelings. How the patient experiences the actual situation is an example of the role of the actual situation in a manifestation of transference, which will be one of my major points.

Of course, both interpretations of the transference in the here and now and genetic transference interpretations are valid and constitute a sequence. We presume that a resistance to the transference ultimately rests on the displacement onto the analyst of attitudes from the past.

Transference interpretations in the here and now and genetic transference interpretations are of course exemplified in Freud's writings and are in the repertoire of every analyst, but they are not distinguished sharply enough.

Because Freud's case histories focus much more on the yield of analysis than on the details of the process, they are readily but perhaps incorrectly construed as emphasizing work outside the transference much more than work with the transference, and, even within the transference, emphasizing genetic transference interpretations much more than work with the transference in the here and now (see Muslin and Gill, 1978). The example of Freud's case reports may have played a role in what I consider a common maldistribution of emphasis in these two respects—not enough on the transference and, within the transference, not enough on the here and now.

Before I turn to the issues in the analysis of the transference, I will only mention what is a primary reason for a failure to deal adequately with the transference. It is that work with the transference is that aspect of analysis which involves both analyst and patient in the most affect-laden and potentially disturbing interactions. Both participants in the analytic situation are motivated to avoid these interactions. Flight away from the transference and to the past can be a relief to both patient and analyst.

I divide my discussion into five parts: (1) the principle that the transference should be encouraged to expand as much as possible within the analytic situation because the analytic work is best done within the transference; (2) the interpretation of disguised allusions to the transference as a main technique for encouraging the expansion of the transference within the analytic situation; (3) the principle that all transference has a connection with something in the present actual analytic situation; (4) how the connection between transference and the actual analytic situation is used in interpreting resistance to the awareness of transference; and (5) the resolution of transference within the here and now and the role of genetic transference interpretation.

*The Principle of Encouraging the Transference to Expand
within the Analytic Situation*

The importance of transference interpretations will surely
be agreed to by all analysts, the greater effectiveness of
transference interpretations than interpretations outside the
transference will be agreed to by many, but what of the
relative roles of interpretation of the transference and interpretation outside the transference?

Freud can be read either as saying that the analysis of
the transference is auxiliary to the analysis of the neurosis or
that the analysis of the transference is equivalent to the
analysis of the neurosis. The first position is stated in his
saying (1913, p. 144) that the disturbance of the transference
has to be overcome by the analysis of transference resistance
in order to get on with the work of analyzing the neurosis. It
is also implied in his reiteration that the ultimate task of
analysis is to remember the past, to fill in the gaps in
memory. The second position is stated in his saying that the
victory must be won on the field of the transference (1912,
p. 108) and that the mastery of the transference neurosis
"coincides with getting rid of the illness which was originally
brought to the treatment" (1917, p. 444). In this second
view, he says that after the resistances are overcome,
memories appear relatively without difficulty (1914b, p. 155).

These two different positions also find expression in the
two very different ways in which Freud speaks of the
transference. In "Dynamics of Transference," he refers to the
transference, on the one hand, as *"the most powerful resistance
to the treatment"* (1912, p. 101) but, on the other hand, as
doing us "the inestimable service of making the patient's . . .
impulses immediate and manifest. For when all is said and
done, it is impossible to destroy anyone *in absentia* or *in
effigie*" (1912, p. 108).

I believe it can be demonstrated that his principal
emphasis falls on the second position. He wrote once, in

summary: "Thus our therapeutic work falls into two phases. In the first, all the libido is forced from the symptoms into the transference and concentrated there; in the second, the struggle is waged around this new object and the libido is liberated from it" (1917, p. 455).

The detailed demonstration that he advocated that the transference should be encouraged to expand as much as possible within the analytic situation lies in clarifying that resistance is primarily expressed by repetition, that repetition takes place both within and outside the analytic situation, but that the analyst seeks to deal with it primarily within the analytic situation, that repetition can be not only in the motor sphere (acting) but also in the psychical sphere, and that the psychical sphere is not confined to remembering but includes the present, too.

Freud's emphasis that the purpose of resistance is to prevent remembering can obscure his point that resistance shows itself primarily by repetition, whether inside or outside the analytic situation: "The greater the resistance, the more extensively will acting out (repetition) replace remembering" (1914b, p. 151). Similarly in "The Dynamics of Transference" Freud said that the main reason that the transference is so well suited to serve the resistance is that the unconscious impulses "do not want to be remembered . . . but endeavour to reproduce themselves . . . " (1912, p. 108). The transference is a resistance primarily insofar as it is a repetition.

The point can be restated in terms of the relation between transference and resistance. The resistance expresses itself in repetition, that is, in transference both inside and outside the analytic situation. To deal with the transference, therefore, is equivalent to dealing with the resistance. Freud emphasized transference within the analytic situation so strongly that it has come to mean only repetition within the analytic situation, even though, conceptually speaking, repetition outside the analytic situation is transference too, and Freud once used the term that way: "We soon perceive that the transference is itself only a piece of repetition, and that the repetition is a transference of the forgotten past not only on to the doctor but also on to all the other aspects of the current situation. We . . . find . . . the compulsion to repeat, which now replaces the impulsion to remember, not only in his personal attitude to his doctor but also in every other activity and relationship which may occupy his life at the time . . . " (1914b, p. 151).

It is important to realize that the expansion of the repetition inside the analytic situation, whether or not in a reciprocal relationship to repetition outside the analytic situation, is the avenue to control the repetition: "The main instrument . . . for curbing the patient's compulsion to repeat and for turning it into a motive for remembering lies in the handling of the transference. We render the compulsion harmless, and indeed useful, by giving it the right to assert itself in a definite field" (1914b, p. 154).

Kanzer has discussed this issue well in his paper on "The Motor Sphere of the Transference" (1966). He writes of a "double-pronged stick-and-carrot" technique by which the transference is fostered within the analytic situation and discouraged outside the analytic situation. The "stick" is the principle of abstinence as exemplified in the admonition against making important decisions during treatment, and the "carrot" is the opportunity afforded the transference to expand within the treatment "in almost complete freedom" as in a "playground" (Freud, 1914b, p. 154). As Freud put it: "Provided only that the patient shows compliance enough to respect the necessary conditions of the analysis, we regularly succeed in giving all the symptoms of the illness a new transference meaning and in replacing his ordinary neurosis by a 'transference neurosis' of which he can be cured by the therapeutic work" (1914b, p. 154).

The reason it is desirable for the transference to be expressed within the treatment is that there, it "is at every point accessible to our intervention" (1914b, p. 154). In a later statement he made the same point this way: "We have followed this new edition [the transference-neurosis] of the old disorder from its start, we have observed its origin and growth, and we are especially well able to find our way about in it since, as its object, we are situated at its very center" (1917, p. 444). It is not that the transference is forced into the treatment, but that it is spontaneously but implicitly present and is encouraged to expand there and become explicit.

Freud emphasized *acting* in the transference so strongly that one can overlook that repetition in the transference does not necessarily mean it is *enacted*. Repetition need not go as far as motor behavior. It can also be expressed in attitudes, feelings, and intentions, and, indeed, the repetition often does take such form rather than motor action. Such repetition is in the psychical rather than the motor · sphere. The importance of making this clear is that Freud can be mistakenly read to mean that repetition in the psychical sphere can only mean remembering the past, as when he writes that the analyst "is prepared for a perpetual struggle with his patient to keep in the psychical sphere all the impulses which the patient would like to direct into the motor sphere; and he celebrates it as a triumph for the treatment if he can bring it about that something the patient wishes to discharge in action is disposed of through the work of remembering" (1914b, p. 153).

It is true that the analyst's effort is to convert acting in the motor sphere into awareness in the psychical sphere, but transference may be in the psychical sphere to begin with, albeit disguised. The psychical sphere includes awareness in the transference as well as remembering.

One of the objections one hears, from both analysts and patients, to a heavy emphasis on interpretation of associations about the patient's real life primarily in terms of the transference is that it means the analyst is disregarding the importance of what goes on in the patient's real life. The criticism is not justified. To emphasize the transference meaning is not to deny or belittle other meanings, but to focus on the one of several meanings of the content that is the most important for the analytic process, for the reasons I have just summarized.

Another way in which interpretations of resistance to the transference can be, or at least appear to the patient to be, a belittling of the importance of the patient's outside life is to make the interpretation as though the outside behavior is primarily an acting out of the transference. The patient may undertake *some* actions in the outside world as an expression of and resistance to the transference, that is, acting out. But the interpretation of associations about actions in the outside world as having implications for the transference need mean only that the choice of outside action to figure in the associations is codetermined by the need to express a transference indirectly. It is because of the resistance to awareness of the transference that the transference has to be disguised. When the disguise is unmasked by interpretation, it becomes clear that, despite the inevitable differences between the outside situations and the transference situation, the content is the same for the purpose of the analytic work. Therefore the analysis of the transference and the analysis of the neurosis coincide.

I stress this point particularly because some critics of earlier versions of this paper argued that I was advocating the analysis of the transference for its own sake rather than in the effort to overcome the neurosis. As I cited above, Freud wrote that the mastering of the transference neurosis "coincides with getting rid of the illness which was originally brought to the treatment" (1917, p. 444).

How the Transference Is Encouraged to Expand within the Analytic Situation

The analytic situation itself fosters the development of

attitudes with primary determinants in the past, i.e., transferences. The analyst's reserve provides the patient with few and equivocal cues. The purpose of the analytic situation fosters the development of strong emotional responses, and the very fact that the patient has a neurosis means, as Freud said, that " . . . it is a perfectly normal and intelligible thing that the libidinal cathexis [we would now add negative feelings] of someone who is partly unsatisfied, a cathexis which is held ready in anticipation, should be directed as well to the figure of the doctor" (1912, p. 100.).

While the analytic setup itself fosters the expansion of the transference within the analytic situation, the interpretation of resistance to the awareness of transference will further this expansion.

There are important resistances on the part of both patient and analyst to awareness of the transference. On the patient's part, this is because of the difficulty in recognizing erotic and hostile impulses toward the very person to whom they have to be disclosed. On the analyst's part, this is because the patient is likely to attribute the very attitudes to him which are most likely to cause him discomfort. The attitudes the patient believes the analyst has toward him are often the ones the patient is least likely to voice, in a general sense because of a feeling that it is impertinent for him to concern himself with the analyst's feelings, and in a more specific sense because the attitudes the patient ascribes to the analyst are often attitudes the patient feels the analyst will not like and be uncomfortable about having ascribed to him. It is for this reason that the analyst must be especially alert to the attitudes the patient believes he has, not only to the attitudes the patient does have toward him. If the analyst is able to see himself as a participant in an interaction, as I shall discuss below, he will become much more attuned to this important area of transference, which might otherwise escape him.

The investigation of the attitudes ascribed to the analyst

makes easier the subsequent investigation of the intrinsic factors in the patient that played a role in such ascription. For example, the exposure of the fact that the patient ascribes sexual interest in him to the analyst, and genetically to the parent, makes easier the subsequent exploration of the patient's sexual wish toward the analyst, and genetically the parent.

The resistances to the awareness of these attitudes is responsible for their appearing in various disguises in the patient's manifest associations and for the analyst's reluctance to unmask the disguise. The most commonly recognized disguise is by displacement, but identification is an equally important one. In displacement, the patient's attitudes are narrated as being toward a third party. In identification, the patient attributes to himself attitudes he believes the analyst has toward him.

To encourage the expansion of the transference within the analytic situation, the disguises in which the transference appears have to be interpreted. In the case of displacement the interpretation will be of allusions to the transference in associations not manifestly about the transference. This is a kind of interpretation every analyst often makes. In the case of identification, the analyst interprets the attitude the patient ascribes to himself as an identification with an attitude he attributes to the analyst. Lipton (1977b) has recently described this form of disguised allusion to the transference with illuminating illustrations.

Many analysts believe that transference manifestations are infrequent and sporadic at the beginning of an analysis and that the patient's associations are not dominated by the transference unless a transference neurosis has developed. Other analysts believe that the patient's associations have transference meanings from the beginning and throughout. That is my opinion, and I think those who believe otherwise are failing to recognize the pervasiveness of indirect allusions to the transference—that is, what I am calling the resistance to the awareness of the transference.

In his autobiography, Freud wrote: "The patient remains under the influence of the analytic situation even though he is not directing his mental activities on to a particular subject. We shall be justified in assuming that nothing will occur to him that has not some reference to that situation" (1925, pp. 40-41). Since associations are obviously often not directly about the analytic situation, the interpretation of Freud's remark rests on what he meant by the "analytic situation."

I believe Freud's meaning can be clarified by reference to a statement he made in "The Interpretation of Dreams." He said that when the patient is told to say whatever comes into his mind, his associations become directed by the "purposive ideas inherent in the treatment" and that there are two such inherent purposive themes, one relating to the illness and the other—concerning which, Freud said, the patient has "no suspicion"—relating to the analyst (1900, pp. 531-532). If the patient has "no suspicion" of the theme relating to the analyst, the clear implication is that the theme appears only in disguise in the patient's associations. My interpretation is that Freud's remark not only specifies the themes inherent in the patient's associations, but also means that the associations are simultaneously directed by these two purposive ideas, not sometimes by one and sometimes by the other.

One important reason that the early and continuing presence of the transference is not always recognized is that it is considered to be absent in the patient who is talking freely and apparently without resistance. As Muslin and I pointed out in a paper on the early interpretation of transference (Gill and Muslin, 1976), resistance to the transference is probably present from the beginning, even if the patient is talking apparently freely. The patient may well be talking about issues not manifestly about the transference which are nevertheless also allusions to the transference. But the analyst has to be alert to the pervasiveness of such allusions to discern them.

The analyst should proceed on the working assumption, then, that the patient's associations have transference implications pervasively. This assumption is not to be confused with denial or neglect of the current aspects of the analytic situation. It is theoretically always possible to give precedence to a transference interpretation if one can only discern it through its disguise by resistance. This is not to dispute the desirability of learning as much as one can about the patient, if only to be in a position to make more correct interpretations of the transference. One therefore does not interfere with an apparently free flow of associations, especially early, unless the transference threatens the analytic situation to the point where its interpretation is mandatory rather than optional.

With the recognition that even the apparently freely associating patient may also be showing resistance to awareness of the transference, the formulation that one should not interfere as long as useful information is being gathered should replace Freud's dictum that the transference should not be interpreted until it becomes a resistance (1913, p. 139).

Connection of All Transference Manifestations with Something in the Actual Analytic Situation

As a prelude to a further discussion of the interpretive technique for expansion of the transference within the analytic situation, I will argue that every transference has some connection to some aspect of the current analytic situation. Of course all the determinants of a transference are current in the sense that the past can exert an influence only insofar as it exists in the present. What I am distinguishing is the current reality of the analytic situation, that is, what actually goes on between patient and analyst in the present, from how the patient is currently constituted as a result of his past.

All analysts would doubtless agree that there are both current and transferential determinants of the analytic situation, and probably no analyst would argue that a transference idea can be expressed without contamination, as it were, that is, without any connection to anything current in the patient-analyst relationship. Nevertheless, I believe the implications of this fact for technique are often neglected in practice. I will deal with them as my next point. Here I want only to argue for the connection.

Several authors (e.g., Kohut, 1959, Loewald, 1960) have pointed out that Freud's early use of the term transference in "The Interpretation of Dreams," in a connection not immediately recognizable as related to the present-day use of the term, reveals the fallacy of considering that transference can be expressed free of any connection to the present. That early use was to refer to the fact that an unconscious idea cannot be expressed as such, but only as it becomes connected to a preconscious or conscious content. In the phenomenon with which Freud was then concerned, the dream, transference took place from an unconscious wish to a day residue. In "The Interpretation of Dreams" Freud used the term transference both for the general rule that an unconscious content is expressible only as it becomes transferred to a preconscious or conscious content and for the specific application of this rule to a transference to the analyst. Just as the day residue is the point of attachment of the dream wish, so must there be an analytic-situation residue, though Freud did not use that term, as the point of attachment of the transference.

Analysts have always limited their behavior, both in variety and intensity, to increase the extent to which the patient's behavior is determined by his idiosyncratic interpretation of the analyst's behavior. In fact, analysts unfortunately sometimes limit their behavior so much, as compared with Freud's practice, that they even conceptualize the entire relationship with the patient a matter of technique, with no nontechnical personal relation, as Lipton (1977a) has pointed out.

But no matter how far the analyst attempts to carry this limitation of his behavior, the very existence of the analytic situation provides the patient with innumerable cues which inevitably become his rationale for his transference responses. In other words, the current situation cannot be made to disappear—that is, the analytic situation is real. It is easy to forget this truism in one's zeal to diminish the role of the current situation in determining the patient's responses. One can try to keep past and present determinants relatively perceptible from one another, but one cannot obtain either in "pure culture." As Freud wrote: "I insist on this procedure [the couch], however, for its purpose and result are to prevent the transference from mingling with the patient's associations imperceptibly, to isolate the transference and to allow it to come forward in due course sharply defined as a resistance" (1913, p. 134). Even "isolate" is too strong a word in the light of the inevitable intertwining of the transference with the current situation.

If the analyst remains under the illusion that the current cues he provides to the patient can be reduced to the vanishing point, he may be led into a silent withdrawal, which is not too distant from the caricature of an analyst as someone who does indeed refuse to have any personal relationship with the patient. What happens then is that silence has become a technique rather than merely an indication that the analyst is listening. The patient's responses under such conditions can be mistaken for uncontaminated transference when they are in fact transference adaptations to the actuality of the silence.

The recognition that all transference must have some relation to the actual analytic situation, from which it takes its point of departure, as it were, has a crucial implication for the technique of interpreting resistance to the awareness of transference, to which I turn now.

The Role of the Actual Situation in Interpreting Resistance to the Awareness of Transference

If the analyst becomes persuaded of the centrality of transference and the importance of encouraging the transference to expand within the analytic situation, he has to find the presenting and plausible interpretations of resistance to the awareness of transference he should make. Here, his most reliable guide is the cues offered by what is actually going on in the analytic situation: on the one hand, the events of the situation, such as change in time of session, or an interpretation made by the analyst, and, on the other hand, how the patient is experiencing the situation as reflected in explicit remarks about it, however fleeting these may be. This is the primary yield for technique of the recognition that any transference must have a link to the actuality of the analytic situation, as I argued above. The cue points to the nature of the transference, just as the day residue for a dream may be a quick pointer to the latent dream thoughts. Attention to the current stimulus for a transference elaboration will keep the analyst from making mechanical transference interpretations, in which he interprets that there are allusions to the transference in associations not manifestly about the transference, but without offering any plausible basis for the interpretation. Attention to the current stimulus also offers some degree of protection against the analyst's inevitable tendency to project his own views onto the patient, either because of countertransference or because of a preconceived theoretical bias about the content and hierarchical relationships in psychodynamics.

The analyst may be very surprised at what in his behavior the patient finds important or unimportant, for the patient's responses will be idiosyncratically determined by the transference. The patient's response may seem to be something the patient as well as the analyst consider trivial, because, as in displacement to a trivial aspect of the day residue of a dream, displacement can better serve resistance when it is to something trivial. Because it is connected to conflict-laden material, the stimulus to the transference may be difficult to find. It may be quickly disavowed, so that its presence in awareness is only transitory. With the discovery of the disavowal, the patient may also gain insight into how it repeats a disavowal earlier in his life. In his search for the present stimuli which the patient is responding to transferentially, the analyst must therefore remain alert to both fleeting and apparently trivial manifest references to himself as well as to the events of the analytic situation.

If the analyst interprets the patient's attitudes in a spirit of seeing their possible plausibility in the light of what information the patient does have, rather than in the spirit of either affirming or denying the patient's views, the way is open for their further expression and elucidation. The analyst will be respecting the patient's effort to be plausible and realistic, rather than seeing him as manufacturing his transference attitudes out of whole cloth.

I believe it is so important to make a transference interpretation plausible to the patient in terms of a current stimulus that, if the analyst is persuaded that the manifest content has an important implication for the transference but he is unable to see a current stimulus for the attitude, he should explicitly say so if he decides to make the transference interpretation anyway. The patient himself may then be able to say what the current stimulus is.

It is sometimes argued that the analyst's attention to his own behavior as a precipitant for the transference will increase the patient's resistance to recognizing the transference. I believe, on the contrary, that, because of the inevitable interrelationship of the current and transferential determinants, it is only through interpretation that they *can* be disentangled.

It is also argued that one must wait until the transference has reached optimal intensity before it can be advantageously interpreted. It is true that too hasty an interpretation of the transference can serve a defensive function for the analyst and deny him the information he needs to make a more appropriate transference interpretation. But it is also true that delay in interpreting runs the risks of allowing an unmanageable transference to develop. It is also true that deliberate delay can be a manipulation in the service of abreaction rather than analysis and, like silence, can lead to a response to the actual situation which is mistaken for uncontaminated transference. Obviously important issues of timing are involved. I believe an important clue to when a transference interpretation is apt and which one to make lies in whether the interpretation can be made plausibly in terms of the determinant I am stressing, namely, something in the current analytic situation.

A critic of an earlier version of this paper understood me to be saying that all that the analyst need do is to interpret the allusion to the transference, but that I did not see that interpretation of why the transference had to be expressed by allusion rather than directly is also necessary. Of course I agree, and meant to imply this as well as other aspects of the transference attitude in saying that when the analyst approaches the transference in the spirit of seeing how it appears plausibly realistic to the patient, it paves the way toward its further elucidation and expression.

The Relative Roles of Resolution of the Transference within the Analytic Situation and by Genetic Transference Interpretation

Freud's emphasis on remembering as the goal of the analytic work implies that remembering is the principal avenue to the resolution of the transference. But his delineation of the successive steps in the development of analytic technique (1920, p. 18) makes clear that he saw this development as a change from an effort to reach memories directly to the utilization of the transference as the necessary intermediary to reaching the memories.

In contrast to remembering as the way the transference is resolved, Freud also described resistance as being primarily overcome in the transference, with remembering following relatively easily thereafter: "From the repetitive reactions which are exhibited in the transference we are led along the familiar paths to the awakening of the memories, which appear without difficulty, as it were, after the resistance has been overcome" (1914b, pp. 154-155); and "This revision of the process of repression can be accomplished only in part in connection with the memory traces of the process which led to repression. The *decisive* part of the work is achieved by creating in the patient's relation to the doctor—in the 'transference'—new editions of the old conflicts. . . . Thus the transference becomes the battlefield on which all the mutually struggling forces should meet one another" (1917, p. 454; emphasis added). This is indeed the primary insight Strachey (1934) clarified in his seminal paper on the therapeutic action of psychoanalysis.

There are two main ways in which resolution of the transference can take place through work with the transference in the here and now. The first lies in the clarification of what are the cues in the current situation which are the patient's point of departure for a transference elaboration. The exposure of the current point of departure at once raises the question of whether it is adequate to the conclusion drawn from it. The relating of the transference to a current stimulus is, after all, part of the patient's effort to make the transference attitude plausibly determined by the present. The reserve and ambiguity of the analyst's behavior is what increases the ranges of apparently plausible conclusions the patient may draw. If an examination of the basis for the conclusion makes clear that the actual situation to which the patient responds is subject to other meanings than the one the patient has reached, he will more readily consider his pre-existing bias, that is, his transference.

Another critic of an earlier version of this paper suggested that, in speaking of the current relationship and the relation between the patient's conclusions and the information on which they seem plausibly based, I am implying some absolute conception of what is real in the analytic situation, of which the analyst is the final arbiter. That is not the case. My writing that what the patient must come to see is that the information he has is subject to other possible interpretations implies the very contrary to an absolute conception of reality. In fact, analyst and patient engage in a dialogue in a spirit of attempting to arrive at a consensus about reality, not about some fictitious absolute reality.

The second way in which resolution of the transference can take place within the work with the transference in the here and now is that in the very interpretation of the transference the patient has a new experience. He is being treated differently from how he expected to be. Analysts seem reluctant to emphasize this new experience, as though it endangers the role of insight and argues for interpersonal influence as the significant factor in change. Strachey's emphasis on the new experience in the mutative transference interpretation has unfortunately been overshadowed by his views on introjection, which have been mistaken to advocate manipulating the transference. Strachey meant introjection of the more benign superego of the analyst only as a temporary step on the road toward insight. Not only is the new experience not to be confused with the interpersonal influence of a transference gratification, but the new experience occurs together with insight into both the patient's biased expectation and the new experience. As Strachey points out, what is unique about the transference interpretation is that insight and the new experience take place in relation to the very person who was expected to behave differently, and it is this which gives the work in the transference its immediacy and effectiveness. While Freud did stress the affective immediacy of the transference, he did not make the new experience explicit.

It is important to recognize that transference interpretation is not a matter of experience, in contrast to insight, but a joining of the two together. Both are needed to bring about and maintain the desired changes in the patient. It is also important to recognize that no new techniques of intervention are required to provide the new experience. It is an inevitable accompaniment of interpretation of the transference in the here and now. It is often overlooked that, although Strachey said that only transference interpretations were mutative, he also said with approval that most interpretations are outside the transference.

In a further explication of Strachey's paper and entirely consistent with Strachey's position, Rosenfeld (1972) has pointed out that clarification of material outside the transference is often necessary to know what is the appropriate transference interpretation, and that both genetic transference interpretations and extratransference interpretations play an important role in working through. Strachey said relatively little about working through, but surely nothing against the need for it, and he explicitly recognized a role for recovery of the past in the resolution of the transference.

My own position is to emphasize the role of the analysis of the transference in the here and now, both in interpreting resistance to the awareness of transference and in working toward its resolution by relating it to the actuality of the situation. I agree that extratransference and genetic transference interpretations and, of course, working through are important too. The matter is one of emphasis. I believe interpretation of resistance to awareness of the transference should figure in the majority of sessions, and that if this is done by relating the transference to the actual analytic situation, the very same interpretation is a beginning of work to the resolution of the transference. To justify this view more persuasively would require detailed case material.

It may be considered that I am siding with the Kleinians who, many analysts feel, are in error in giving the analysis of the transference too great if not even an exclusive role in the analytic process. It is true that Kleinians emphasize the analysis of the transference more, in their writings at least, than do the general run of analysts. Indeed, Anna Freud's (1968) complaint that the concept of transference has become overexpanded seems to be directed against the Kleinians. One of the reasons the Kleinians consider themselves the true followers of Freud in technique is precisely because of the emphasis they put on the analysis of the transference. Hanna Segal (1967, pp. 173-174), for example, writes as follows: "To say that all communications are seen as communications about the patient's phantasy as well as current external life is equivalent to saying that all communications contain something relevant to the transference situation. In Kleinian technique, the interpretation of the transference is often more central than in the classical technique."

Despite their disclaimers to the contrary, my reading of Kleinian case material leads me to agree with what I believe is the general view that Kleinian transference interpretations often deal with so-called deep and genetic material without adequate connection to the current features of the present analytic situation and thus differ sharply from the kind of transference interpretation I am advocating.

The insistence on exclusive attention to any particular aspect of the analytic process, like the analysis of the transference in the here and now, can become a fetish. I do not say that other kinds of interpretation should not be made, but I feel the emphasis on transference interpretations within the analytic situation needs to be increased or at the very least reaffirmed, and that we need more clarification and specification of just when other kinds of interpretations are in order.

Of course it is sometimes tactless to make a transference interpretation. Surely two reasons which would be included in a specification of the reasons for not making a particular transference interpretation, even if one seems apparent to the analyst, would be preoccupation with an important extra-transference event and an inadequate degree of rapport, to use Freud's term, to sustain the sense of criticism, humiliation, or other painful feeling the particular interpretation might engender, even though the analyst had no intention of evoking such a response. The issue may well be, however, not of whether or not an interpretation of resistance to the transference should be made, but whether the therapist can find that transference interpretation which in the light of the total situation, both transferential and current, the patient is able to hear and benefit from primarily as the analyst intends it.

Transference interpretations, like extratransference interpretations, indeed like any behavior on the analyst's part, can have an effect on the transference, which in turn needs to be examined if the result of an analysis is to depend as little as possible on unanalyzed transference. The result of any analysis depends on the analysis of the transference, persisting effects of unanalyzed transference, and the new experience which I have emphasized as the unique merit of transference interpretation in the here and now. It is especially important to remember this lest one's zeal to ferret out the transference itself become an unrecognized and objectionable actual behavior on the analyst's part, with its own repercussions on the transference.

The emphasis I am placing on the analysis of resistance to the transference could easily be misunderstood as implying that it is always easy to recognize the transference as disguised by resistance or that analysis would proceed

without a hitch if only such interpretations were made. I
mean to imply neither, but rather that the analytic process
will have the best chance of success if correct interpretation
of resistance to the transference and work with the
transference in the here and now are the core of the analytic
work.

I close with a statement of a conviction designed to set
this paper into a broader perspective of psychoanalytic theory
and research. The points I have made are not new. They are
present in varying degrees of clarity and emphasis throughout
our literature. But like so many other aspects of psychoanalytic theory and practice, they fade in and out of prominence
and are rediscovered again and again, possibly occasionally
with some modest conceptual advance, but often with a
newness attributable only to ignorance of past contributions.
There are doubtless many reasons for this phenomenon. But
not the least, in my opinion, is the almost total absence of
systematic and controlled research in the psychoanalytic
situation. I mean such research in contrast to the customary
clinical research. I believe that only with such systematic and
controlled research will analytic findings become solid and
secure knowledge instead of being subject to erosion again
and again by waves of fashion and what Ernst Lewy (1941)
long ago called the "return of the repression" to designate
the retreat by psychoanalysts from insights they had once
reached.

Summary

Let me summarize. I distinguish between two major different
relationships between transference and resistance. One is
resistance to awareness of the transference and the other is
resistance to resolution of the transference.

I argue that the bulk of the analytic work should take
place in the transference in the here and now. I detailed
Freud's view that the transference should be encouraged to

expand within the analytic situation. I suggested that the main technique for doing so, in addition to the analytic setup itself, is the interpretation of resistance to the awareness of transference by searching for the allusions to the transference in the associations not manifestly about the transference; that in making such interpretations one is guided by the connection to the actual analytic situation which every transference includes; that the major work in resolving the transference takes place in the here and now, both by way of examining the relation between the transference and the actuality of the analytic situation from which it takes its point of departure and the new experience which the analysis of the transference inevitably includes; and that, while genetic transference interpretations play a role in resolving the transference, genetic material is likely to appear spontaneously and with relative ease after the resistances have been overcome in the transference in the here and now. Working through remains important, and it, too, takes place primarily in the transference in the here and now.

REFERENCES

Freud, A. (1968), Acting out. *Writings*, 7:94-109. New York: International Universities Press, 1971.

Freud, S. (1900), The interpretation of dreams. *Standard Edition*, 5.

———— (1912), The dynamics of transference. *Standard Edition*, 12:99-108.

———— (1913), On beginning the treatment (Further recommendations in the technique of psychoanalysis, I). *Standard Edition*, 12:123-144.

———— (1914a), On the history of the psycho-analytic movement. *Standard Edition*, 14:7-66.

———— (1914b), Remembering, repeating, and working through (Further recommendations on the technique of psycho-analysis, II). *Standard Edition*, 12: 147-156.

———— (1917), Introductory lectures on psycho-analysis. *Standard Edition*, 16.

———— (1920), Beyond the pleasure principle. *Standard Edition*, 18:7-64.

———— (1925), An autobiographical study. *Standard Edition*, 20:7-74, London: Hogarth Press, 1959.

Gill, M. & Muslin, H. (1976), Early interpretation of transference. *This Journal*, 24:779-794.

Greenson, R. (1967), *The Technique and Practice of Psychoanalysis*. New York: International Universities Press.

Kanzer, M. (1966), The motor sphere of the transference. *Psychoanal. Quart.*, 35: 522-539.

Kohut, H. (1959), Introspection, empathy, and psychoanalysis. In: *The Search for the Self.* New York: International Universities Press, 1978, pp. 205-232.

Lewy, E. (1941), The return of the repression. *Bull. Menninger Clinic*, 5:47-55.

Lipton, S. (1977a), The advantages of Freud's technique as shown by his analysis of the Rat Man. *Internat. J. Psycho-Anal.*, 58:255-274.

———— (1977b), Clinical observations on resistance to the transference. *Internat. J. Psycho-Anal.*, 58:463-472.

Loewald, H. (1960), On the therapeutic action of psychoanalysis. *Internat. J. Psycho-Anal.*, 41:16-33.

Muslin, H. & Gill, M. (1978), Transference in the Dora case. *This Journal*, 26:311-328.

Rapaport, D. (1967), The scientific methodology of psychoanalysis. In: *Collected Papers*, ed. M. M. Gill. New York: Basic Books, 1967, pp. 165-220.

Rosenfeld, H. (1972), A critical appreciation of James Strachey's paper on the nature of the therapeutic action of psychoanalysis. *Internat. J. Psycho-Anal.*, 53:455-462.

Segal, H. (1967), Melanie Klein's technique. In: *Psychoanalytic Techniques*, ed. B. Wolman. New York: Basic Books, pp. 168-190.

Stone, L. (1967), The psychoanalytic situation and transference. *This Journal*, 15: 3-57.

Strachey, J. (1934), The nature of the therapeutic action of psychoanalysis. Reprinted in: *Internat. J. Psycho-Anal.* (1969) 50:275-292.

The Abraham Lincoln School of Medicine
University of Illinois at the Medical Center
P.O. Box 6998
Chicago, Illinois 60680

TRUTH FROM GENETIC ILLUSION: THE TRANSFERENCE AND THE FATE OF THE INFANTILE NEUROSIS

JOSEPH T. COLTRERA, M.D.

> ... But I am the opposite of a stage magician. He gives you illusion that has the appearance of truth. I give you truth in the pleasant disguise of illusion.
> —Tennessee Williams,
> *The Glass Menagerie*

FROM ITS BEGINNING, PSYCHOANALYSIS has thought of itself as a genetic psychology, regarding each behavior as part of a historical sequence determined by epigenetic laws and cumulative experience (Freud, 1905). To put a finer epistemological edge on the preceding, each behavior has been thought of as part of a genetic series and, through its antecedents, part of the temporal sequence that brought about the present form of the personality and its psychic organization (Rapaport and Gill, 1959). In this sense, the infantile, the adult, and the transference neuroses may be considered to be joined referents within a genetic series. Even more pertinent to the greater methodological question before this panel[1] is the adductive relationship assumed to exist between the infantile and transference neuroses.

[1] "On the Infantile Neurosis in Child and Adult Analysis." A Panel sponsored jointly by the American Psychoanalytic Association and the Association for Child Psychoanalysis. Held at the Annual Meeting of the American Psychoanalytic Association, May, 1977, in Quebec City.

The above "complemental series" does not constitute an "infinite regress" (Hartmann and Kris, 1945)—a genetic fallacy of its own—but must be considered as leading back to a historical situation in which a particular phase-adaptive solution of a drive demand was first achieved, or a particular apparatus was first put to a certain kind of use.

In a more restricted declension of the above, we are met to discuss whether the transference neurosis is the genetic "royal road" to the recovery and eventual working through of a putatively causative infantile neurosis, with the subsumed questions of what is being reconstructed and which infantile neurosis is the focus of this analytic work. Beyond the question of whether the infantile neurosis is a reliquary of an older time in id psychology is the larger question of whether genetic interpretation and reconstruction have a viable role in the theory and practices of modern ego psychology. Is its contained belief in the model of hysteria and its reduction of all defense to repression a faith for a time now long past? What is really being put in question in any discussion of the role of the infantile neurosis in the working through of a transference neurosis is the operational intactness of the working definition of interpretation—held since 1900—as a *timed*, joined dynamic and genetic explanation given to the patient which ends in a dynamic insight (Hartmann and Kris, 1945; Coltrera and Ross, 1967).

Although Freud always distinguished between interpretation and reconstruction, for the purpose of this discussion, I shall consider both genetic interpretation and reconstruction to be subsumed within the genetic function of interpretation. " 'Interpretation' [Freud said] applies to something one does to some single element of the material, such as an association or a parapraxis. But it is a 'construction' when one lays before the subject of the analysis a piece of his early history that he has forgotten" (1937, p. 261).

The distinction reflects Freud's sense of the causal and discursive nature of genetic explanation, a technical legacy that has tended to restrict reconstructions of the infantile neurosis to the more discursively[2] recoverable events of the phallic-oedipal period, and to exclude its preoedipal determinants, which are most apt to be expressed within the nondiscursive modes of transference acts. I am inclined to follow Kris's (1956) more operational definition in the matter, wherein reconstruction is regarded as a historical interpretation that establishes a causal connection between past and present, and that not only stimulates memory to recognition but leads to further regressive recall by the patient in the transference.

In their strict sense, genetic interpretation and reconstruction may be said to be concerned with genetically significant, usually childhood, intrapsychic events. While this was strictly true in the reconstructions of the infantile neurosis of Little Hans and the Wolf Man, it was not so in the cases of the Rat Man or the eighteen-year-old Katharina—the girl Freud met on vacation—whose reconstructions concerned more recent events. As the Kris Study Group (Fine, et al., 1971) pointed out, Freud's (1909) saying of the Rat Man, "He must have known," was implicitly an interpretation of psychically significant *recent* events. This continuous and seemingly ambiguous shifting between an earlier past and a more recent past in the focus of genetic interpretation existed in Freud's mind right up to his last paper on reconstruction in 1937 and must be looked upon as an early and critical declension of the genetic view to include not only the past's determinancy in the present, but an appreciation of how the present can influence the recollection of that past. Freud wrote on screen memories in 1899, and

---

[2]Susan Langer (1942) developed certain distinctions between discursive and nondiscursive forms. Statements (e.g., historical, mathematical, psychoanalytic reconstructions) are discursive when they are capable of being refuted by other statements. Art forms (e.g., music, painting) are nondiscursive; one cannot refute one piece of music with another, or a painting with another painting. Freud (1891, 1904, 1922, 1940) was presciently aware of this rhetorical distinction, always referring to psychoanalysis as "the art of interpretation."

déjà vu phenomenon in 1914; both representing a clinical appreciation that the recollection of the past is an existential event in a resistive present.

And here lies the great methodological paradox intrinsic to the genetic working through of the transference neurosis, namely, that we adduce dynamic meanings about a significant displaced past in the present. The paradox is summarized in a cogent observation of Kurt Lewin (1937) that only forces and conditions that are *here-and-now* present can exert an effect in the here and now, so that the past recovered by the patient in the ongoing work of the analysis must necessarily be the past as he views it in the present. Rapaport (1959) has already made the point that this represents not so much a rejection of the validity of genetic interpretation and reconstruction on Lewin's part as it does a pertinent methodological note of caution about their orders of probability.

This methodological paradox has lent itself to a specific technical excess in modern analysis, wherein a phenomenological reduction of transference to its ongoing acts and modes has ended with equating working through with the continuing work done with patterns of wish and defense as they appear in a current situation (Greenacre, 1956; A. Freud, 1968, 1969). Greenacre (1956) believes that, apart from virtually restricting interpretation to dynamic explanation, this has led to ignoring the genetic persistence and determinacy of id drives, and a consequent neglect of the operational role of id resistance in persisting transference resistances. The exclusion of genetic transference ends, as it must, in a descriptive analysis of current defenses and ongoing transference conflicts.

This technical position, with its reduction of interpretation to dynamic explanation, to the virtual exclusion of its genetic function, must be considered a historical artifact of the so-called "rise of the transference" (A. Freud, 1968), and the impetus given that historical tendency by the advent of a structural theory, the widening of instinct theory to include aggression, and by longitudinal development studies. Interestingly enough, all recent commentators on the infantile neurosis also cite these same discoveries as historical pressures that must be accommodated in a developmental reconsideration of that concept.

Ferenczi and Rank (1924) were the first to advance this thesis, saying that the ongoing modes of the transference subsumed its antecedents within the conditions of displacement and that there was no valid need to genetically recover and work through a prior causative infantile neurosis. Similarly, Schafer (1973, 1975), in rejecting the place of energic and structural considerations in the concept of transference, seems to be arguing for a transference of "act psychology" restricted by its own terms to a phenomenological description of ongoing transference events.

To work through the transference neurosis solely in dynamic terms to the exclusion of its genetic antecedents seems to be returning transference analysis to its cathartic beginnings. The consistency and accuracy of genetic interpretation and reconstruction are integral to an effective working-through process, pre-eminently in the service of the synthetic and integrative ego work on which that process depends. In this context, Kris (1956) has emphasized how effective genetic interpretation and reconstruction lend psychological certitude to the patient's recognition of the pertinency of his genetic past, leading in consequence to further regressive recall in the transference situation. Almost as important, to my mind, is the critical role genetic reconstruction plays in maintaining an effective therapeutic alliance, arousing further introspective curiosity and fostering the patient's critical identification with the analyzing function of the analyst. This must be thought of as a resonating relationship, in that the presence of an effective therapeutic alliance is in turn critical for the "timing" of an effective genetic interpretation, the operational measure of a transference "readiness" on the part of the patient to use the genetic insight in the work of further significant regressive recall. The consensus of the Kris Study Group (Fine, et al., 1971) was that the effective "timing" of a genetic reconstruction depended upon both the analysis being well focused and the intensity and clearness of the transference neurosis, with these taken to be an indication that the data are preconsciously available to the patient and the ongoing work of the analysis.

Also, I consider a good working genetic reconstruction of determining early events in the patient's life—of childhood, latency, and adolescence—to be a critical criterion for a good termination. While some commentators conceive of termination criteria in terms of a consistent lifting of a childhood amnesia, I think this definition tends to parochialize the criteria to an early topographic model of the infantile neurosis.

It has been shown that a valid and effective working through of a transference neurosis depends upon a necessarily joined dynamic and genetic interpretation. The question then remains of why the genetic working through of the transference neurosis, with its implicit genetic assumption of a causative infantile neurosis, may be more honored in the breach than in the observances of present-day psychoanalytic practice. Although the great metapsychologists of modern ego psychology all begin from developmental premises, there has too often been avoidance of developmental principles and genetic interpretation in the everyday work of clinical adult analysis.

In the question before us, methodological problems reduce themselves in great part to the historically dependent relationships that exist between the nature of psychoanalytic explanation, the continued restriction of the infantile neurosis to the phallic-oedipal period, and the "rise of the transference" to technical dominance in the psychoanalytic idea.

Explanations in psychoanalysis turn on the original distinction made by Dilthey (1910) between sciences that explain causally—*erklärende Wissenschaften*—and those that understand—*verstehende Wissenschaften*—(Parsons, 1949; Bibring, 1954; Rycroft, 1958; Ricoeur, 1970; Coltrera, 1979a; Coltrera and Ross, 1967). Dilthey speaks of causal explanations in the physical sciences and of interpretation in the social sciences. Accordingly, Bibring (1954) and Rycroft (1958) make the point that Freud doesn't really explain causally, but uses interpretation to facilitate understanding. Psychoanalytic explanations are motivational and historical, being in the order of *if* . . . *then*, whereas the causal explanations of a physical science, being in the order of *this* . . . *because*, are ahistorical, and necessarily outside of genetic considerations. But this does not place psychoanalytic explanations outside science any more than it did Darwin's explanations demonstrating how the purposiveness of behavior of adaption could be accounted for by the mechanics of survival.

Genetic reconstructions taken as discursive and causal explanations are at best hypothetical fictive devices of reconstruction useful for the approximations of ongoing tentative hypotheses, whereas genetic interpretations properly made are heuristic explanations given to the patient to facilitate an *approximate* understanding of his determinate genetic past. If "timed" correctly, they will end in a self-reflective recognition that, in turn, will lead to a further regressive recall.

Where Freud always held fast to the sense of genetic reconstruction as a causal explanation, retaining to the end a belief in the central importance of reconstruction and memory recovery, Kris (1956) tended to emphasize the *approximate* nature of a reconstruction meant to facilitate futher understanding through transference recall, always pointing out that the genetic interpretation aimed at the anticathexis and not the original causative event. In this view, genetic reconstruction of childhood events must involve some processes and feelings that did not necessarily exist when the forgotten event took place. Loewenstein (1951) quotes Hartmann as saying that analysis sometimes establishes something new, as a connection which facilitates further recollection and regressive recall. The work of genetic interpretation and reconstruction, in this sense, is meant to facilitate an understanding of what the patient's significant past was like in terms of its displacement to a transference present. We do not work through the infantile neurosis as the *deus ex machina* of the transference neurosis, but rather its adaptive resonances within a regressive hierarchy of transference wishes and the defenses against those wishes, including their characterological variants. The extended, causal, genetic explanations given to the Rat Man (Freud, 1909, pp. 182, 205) in the reconstructions of his recent genetic past as well as his infantile neurosis must have contributed in great part to the "transference cure" achieved in this severely obsessive-compulsive patient. Ironically, the several alternate reconstructions of his infantile neurosis given to the Wolf Man (Freud, 1918, pp. 50-60) failed to effect a comparable "cure" in that interminable case, turning Freud, in methodological despair, to a critical notion of the role played by id resistance in the process of working through (Freud, 1914).

The so-called "rise of the transference" (A. Freud, 1968) in the psychoanalytic idea can be said to begin with the great empirical truth of the cathartic period, that explanations do not "cure," and with Freud's increasingly less than sanguine attitude about the therapeutic relevance of abreactive remembrance and his growing awareness that interpretation was a longitudinal process in psychoanalytic time imposed by resistance (Coltrera, 1979a; Coltrera and Ross, 1967). As early as 1892 (1893-1895, pp. 135-181), he seemed to be aware of the obvious disparate orders of explanation used respectively by the analyst and his patient. He apprehended early on the methodological paradox that flaws all interpretation, namely, that where the analyst discursively reconstructs, the patient more nondiscursively recovers. In the regressive recalls of the transference the several methodological problems resident to genetic inter- pretation, which have contributed in no small part to its relative neglect in present-day psychoanalysis, devolve on the commonplace experience that discursive and causal genetic explanations are more germane to the reconstruc- tions made by the analyst to himself than they are for the more nondiscursive modes by which the patient comes to insightful understanding and psychological certitude about his genetic past in the regressive self-states of transference recall. An argument may now be made for a stylistic analysis of the modes of transference, in addition to the more usual analysis of its contents, in which the associative contexts of the psychoanalytic hour can now be considered as a joined rhetoric of the ideational, affective, and sensorimotor events of the hour. In this model, even the nominally discursive verbal associations have important form elements, where the spoken associations of the hour can now be parsed like plain-chant for its cadences, tonalities, and silences.

Quite often, the first indication of an impending acting out in patients prone to such behavior, really the measure of the increased adaptive needs and cognitive regressions associated with a critical object loss or traumatic separation, will be expressed through the formal modes of the transference rather than its more discursive contents. Among these clinical formal signs I would cite the following: an increased sensorimotor activity on the couch, in dreams, and in the cadences of the associations; lapses in language, inclusive of malapropisms and reported misspellings, with an observed rise in nonverbal behaviors; an increase in *vivid* transference recoveries and recollections, as well as a rise in intense screen memories and the telling of dramatic fantasies; and an associated reduction in the reflective work of the analysis.

The "tact" and "timing" of an interpretation is the most arcane of our arts. For the most part, "timing" is a function of the autonomous cognitive gifts of the individual analyst as they serve analytic style—the autonomous organizational disposition of his ego as a responding system—insofar as that cognitive style significantly determines how the psychological evidences, by which an interpretation "explains," are gathered, codified, and conceptualized from the conjoined rhetoric of the ideational, affective, and sensorimotor associative events of the hour (Coltrera, 1979a). What is additional, and perhaps more critical for that analytic style, are the analyst's empathic gifts, which determine how "close in" to the transference he can work and how sensitive he is to the ongoing sea-changes of the transference. They reflect, in my mind, the quality of the analyst's own animate dialogue experience, not only as to the structural presence of reciprocity, but also as to whether that reciprocity adaptively subsumes in its function prior preverbal empathic experiences with the mother. This last recalls an earlier time when the nuances of act and response represented the semiverbal conversations of early object-relating. We must learn to parse transference acts and modes as acted speech, whose narcissistic regressions may recover not only the the semiverbal inceptions of adaptive epigenesis, but the very origins of basic trust on which the therapeutic alliance fairly devolves. If it is true that psychoanalytic technique in any time is the function of that time's model of neurosis, then it becomes clear how the older technical strategies of an id psychology skewed the gathering and codification of psychoanalytic evidence heavily in favor of an infantile neurosis restricted to the prototypic conflicts of the phallic-oedipal period. For where the libidinal events of the phallic-oedipal period may be recovered from the contents of the free associations, fantasies, and dreams, their aggressive referents are more likely to be elaborated according to a sensorimotor rhetoric expressed through transference acting-out or acting-in behaviors. Certainly the more preverbal early developmental events that most investigators cite as early genetic determinants of a later infantile neurosis are almost invariably expressed through the nondiscursive modes of the transference neurosis. Current critiques of the infantile neurosis (Greenacre, 1956; A. Freud, 1970; Mahler, 1975; Panel, 1954) note the critical lack, until recently, of a longitudinal developmental point of view in the concept, with the stress on the critical role early object relations and the development of narcissism play in determining the strength and form of the later oedipal conflict and its phase-adaptive resolution. To cite but one critical example, it may be said that the development of the ego—its "ego strength"—at the onset of the phallic-oedipal phase will largely determine the degree and amount of neutralized aggression available for the structuralization of the superego as a system at the close of that phase. This developmental contingency must therefore be considered a crucial determinant of the aggressivization of the superego's functions—its "sadistic" nature—and the quality and degree of superego anxiety thereafter. Addressing himself to the heretofore restricted developmental conception of the infantile neurosis and taking a longitudinal developmental view in the matter, Hartmann (Panel, 1954) would have us think of every new phase of maturation as creating new potential for conflict situations and new ways to deal with them. The new aspect of the subsequent phase would then be the changed dominance of certain instinctual drives and certain ego functions, including the phase-specific capacities to deal with conflict situations and, in the same measure, reverse old conflict situations.

Jacobson (1953, 1964, 1971), Greenacre (1956; Panel, 1954), and Mahler (1963, 1966, 1975) in another context have all noted how this developmental restriction has contributed to a continuing tendency to underestimate the role of ego and superego precursors in intrapsychic conflict.

And indeed, we have to look no further than our everyday practice for the truth of this last observation, being fairly inundated with patients whose initial complaints are referable to the causative role played by preoedipal events in their psychopathology, complaining as they do of separation anxiety and a range of self-esteem pathologies.

The question of preoedipal determinancy on the course of the infantile neurosis and its adult reprises has represented an implicitly joined historical and methodological problem for both psychoanalytic theory and practice almost from the beginning. On the one hand, in the technical convictions of some, the seeming increase in narcissistic complaints has become an occasion as much for excluding as for widening the application of psychoanalysis, where developmental contingencies are cited to permit preoedipal narcissistic conflicts to replace later oedipal ones as the organizing conflicts of psychosexual stage epigenesis and, by implication, their adult reprises as well. To offer preoedipal conflict as a fair developmental exchange for a later and more classical oedipal one in narcissistic disorders faults the very biological premises that join preoedipal and oedipal events in a developmental dialectic wherein each is the holistic condition of the other. For where there can be little doubt that severe preoedipal trauma distorts the shape and force of the organizing oedipal conflict and its resolution in the phallic-oedipal phase, it does not displace it in the developmental continuum of psychosexual epigenesis. Nor can we accept the associated burgeoning metapsychological conceit that the narcissistic disorder represents a neurosis for a modern predicament, with its contingent claim that preoedipal conflicts are the singular substance of such neurosis. To inferentially treat oedipal conflict as if it was a psychohistorical artifact of an older time in id psychology and the preoedipal conflict its successor for a newer time has ended in a technical bias which has contributed in no small part to the notorious propensity for interminable analyses in the treatment of narcissistic characters.

It may be further said that where the holistic nature of the developmental point of view insists that preoedipal statements have no final meaning apart from oedipal ones, the obverse is also true. Anna Freud (1970) ends with a significant diminishing of the role of preoedipal determinancy in infantile neurosis as well as in the broader question of the narcissistic disorders in the adult. She seems to be casting out these last into some extrapsychoanalytic netherworld of developmental problems, narcissistic defects, and deficiency disorders. Yet, they still continue to present themselves in an ever widening application of psychoanalysis, with an ever-lessening ability to effect a classical transference neurosis.

Indeed, looking at the severe narcissistic problems of the Wolf Man—more than likely a borderline personality (Blum, 1974)—one gets the impression that the problem of a "widening application of psychoanalysis" has been with us at least from the time of the early case histories. So it would seem that Freud was at least presciently aware of the profound effect of preoedipal events on the later resolution of oedipal conflicts long before any formal developmental interest in psychoanalysis. The analysis of the Wolf Man may be said to have turned on a preoedipal reconstruction with its remarkably detailed primal scene, first experienced in the middle of his second year, itself to be later crucially reprised in the oedipal nightmare of his fourth year (Freud, 1918; Blum, 1974).

Indeed, as Blum (1977) points out, a concern for preoedipal reconstruction has existed in psychoanalysis almost from its very beginnings, both as a technical tool and a contribution to theory. A measure of historical paradox becomes added to the question before us of why the infantile neurosis has been almost exclusively restricted to the phallic-oedipal period. Citing his self-analysis, Freud (1887-1902, pp. 218-221) wrote Wilhelm Fliess of his growing awareness of certain important preoedipal influences in his own life, going on to describe in particular his reconstructions of early memories of Julius Freud, the one-eyed doctor, and the Czech maid. Blum (1977) draws special attention to the overlooked preoedipal reconstruction Freud made from his own separation-individuation phase—between eighteen and 24 months—about his year-older nephew and his ill-fated, year-younger brother, who died at six months of age. The birth and death of this brother roughly bracketed Freud's own rapprochement subphase of his separation-individuation period, and Blum noted the uncanny concordance of Freud's first reconstruction with contemporary formulations. One must assume that this specific rapprochement trauma—in Mahler's (1963, 1972) sense—had to contribute to Freud's sensitivity to preoedipal influences, especially to object loss and his reparative defenses against such loss. The reprise of this special preoedipal sensitization to object loss most certainly bore significantly on that curious and repetitive drama of love gained and then lost that roiled and shaped Freud's creative years, his famed fierce commitments to and then stormy breaks with so many of the early great and seminal psychoanalytic figures—Breuer, Fliess, Jung, Adler, Rank.

It may be said, therefore, that Freud had an empirical appreciation of the role of early preoedipal events in later oedipal conflict from his own self-analysis and from that of the Wolf Man. However, the absence of developmental knowledge denied him the theoretical frame of reference necesary for the consolidation of these observations into a meaningful empirical statement. This last would have to wait until 1926 and the statement of a second theory of anxiety, with its new focus upon the preoedipal relation of the mother and child in the developmental reconsideration of anxiety as a genetic series. For sundry historical reasons Freud did not participate in the burgeoning of the metapsychological points of views of a just-emerging ego psychology after 1926, with its increased interest in preoedipal determinants and direct child observations.

It fell to a new generation of analysts to now lay stress on the primacy of this early child-mother developmental pair and the critical role of early object relations in determining the shape of all later transference reactions (Winnicott, 1958; Greenacre, 1958, 1963; Spitz, 1963; A. Freud, 1965). In this connection, observations of mother-child developmental pairs have shown developmental conflicts to be phase-specific, yet individually variable as well, from the second year onward. Preoedipal memories and reconstructions can be considered as screen memories, to be continually rectified consistent with analytic data and knowledge.

Since 1950, nearly all developmental thinking in ego psychology has emphasized the critical importance of the narcissistic modes established in this early symbiotic child-mother relation. Among these commentators, Mahler (1966, 1972, 1975), Jacobson (1953, 1964, 1971), and Anna Freud (1965, 1968, 1970) have laid special stress on the importance of the second year for the establishment of the child's sensoriaffective set to his needed object-world, and which will be carried forward into his characterological expectations of the world and the affective resources of his self-esteem mechanisms. The affective breadth and narcissistic resilience of an effective working transference may be said to be the developmental function in significant part of this original sensoriaffective set of the child to his immediate needed object-world. It would not stretch the assumption too far to say it is probably the develomental wellspring of the analyst's own narcissistic countertransference.

Anna Freud (1970) also believes the quality of this early relationship determines on one hand, the balance between narcissism and object relatedness and, on the other hand, such personal characteristics as optimism or pessimism, courage and cowardice, and outgoing or withdrawn attitudes to others. She declares it to be decisive for or against the occurrence of depression; for and against the choice of phobic mechanisms. The neutrality of the analyst revives for some narcissistic characters the meager "average expectable environment" that fate originally dealt them, so that the first transference frustrations must be parsed carefully in such patients lest they be experienced as devastating narcissistic injuries. Is the patient rebuffed, angry, silent, and what is the quality of the silence? These become critical questions for the viability of the therapeutic alliance in these difficult analyses.

Certainly, many of Mahler's (1963, 1966, 1972, 1975) observations on the process of separation and individuation in the child, especially with respect to the child's narcissistic vulnerability in the process of separation-individuation, particularly in the "rapprochement subphase," are especially pertinent in working through some special resistances seen in patients who had either climacteric, phobic, or severely narcissistic mothers during these critical developmental times. These patients are enormously sensitive to variations in their sense of transference distance—the critical object-distance experience between themselves and the analyst—and, like the child in rapprochement crisis, are greatly adept in evoking the active presence of the analyst. There is a genetic legacy of mutual preverbal empathy once shared with these narcissistic mothers during the invariably extended "rapprochement period" that, in the beginning of their analyses, often becomes a particular problem with basic trust, evinced as a cautious and wary commitment to the therapeutic alliance. Later on it may become a special resistance of the working-through process, wherein a silence of what can only be described as an empathic communion ends in a seeming nondiscursive achievement of insight. The patient experiences that something significant has happened, but cannot reflectively analyze what it was.

One becomes ever more impressed that the transference neurosis is very much developmentally determined, its character and focus changing throughout the life cycle according to phase-specific developmental and conflict resolutions and their subsequent internalizations. A growing body of literature on serial analyses done in the same patient when first a child, then as an adolescent, and into adulthood—at times with the same analyst (Adatto, 1971)— attest to the transmutation of the transference neurosis throughout a genetic series, different in its character and form during different developmental times.

Since the "failed" case of Dora (Freud, 1905), the question of analyzability has effectively turned on a clinical decision made by the analyst that the patient is capable of effecting dynamic changes in a genetic frame of reference, able to work through a psychically determinant, persisting, and recoverable infantile neurosis in a restricted transference situation (Freud, 1905, 1912a, 1913, 1914, 1915-1917). With the advent of ego psychology and its attendant concerns for psychic structure and ego integrity, analyzability has become further defined according to the presence or absence of certain structuralized developmental events. In this model, a working neurotic transference is possible if the following structural and developmental criteria are present: a cathectic differentiation of the self from its object world; a structuralized reciprocity; an ego ability to displace from the past to the present; a resistance to regression on the part of the reflective functions of the ego; a structured signal affect; and, an identity which will retain its autonomous integrity during transference regression (Coltrera, 1979a). The transference neurosis in this longitudinal developmental model may now be thought of, in Greenacre's (1959) sense, as a shifting texture of disparate genetic levels of recall, an ambiguous presentation of many neurotic transference manifestations rather than a synthetic reduction in form.

Anna Freud (1968, 1969), in particular, has placed special emphasis on the role of the "rise of transference" in the historic shift undergone by psychoanalytic technique, a shift from a reconstruction of a meaningful past through free association and dream interpretation to a recovery of that determinant past in a continuance of regressive recall within the transference. Among the historical forces acting on this change to an experiential recovery through transference acts and modes, she cites in particular the shift of interest from the id to the ego, and the widening of the instinct theory to include aggression. Also, after 1926, there was a shift of emphasis from the causative role of the phallic-oedipal phase in neurosis to one emphasizing preoedipal events, especially those of the oral period and its central mother-child pair.

The historical drift to experiential recovery in the self-states of the transference, as well as an increased interest in psychic functioning and a new technical stress on exploring the psychic surface, all contributed to the legitimization of the interventions of confrontation and clarification in modern psychoanalysis. Reflecting the greater methodological concerns of ego psychology, distinctions must now be made between those interventions which themselves end in a dynamic insight, and those which are the facilitating conditions of such insight. Confrontation and clarification do not end in a dynamic insight as such, but make that insight possible by reinforcing certain ego functions and raising the states of self-awareness on which the reflective work of the analysis devolves.

A good portion of the awkward accommodation made by the notion of an infantile neurosis within the methodological conditions of a modern conception of the transference neurosis is a historical artifact of how Freud himself stood apart from the transmutive "rise of the transference" his own ideas had initiated. He did not revise the concept of transference neurosis in conjunction with the formulation of structural theory. The principles of technique as we essentially know them today date to about 1913; really to five papers (1912a, 1912b, 1913, 1914, 1915) which were arranged in an ascending gyre around the idea of a working transference neurosis (Coltrera and Ross, 1967; Coltrera, 1979a). Yet Freud could write in that same time—in the same year he wrote of his problems with the resistances of the Wolf Man: "The aim of these different techniques has, of course, remained the same. Descriptively speaking, it is to fill in gaps in memory" (1914, pp. 147-148). He was soon being confronted on all sides by a rush to restate the transference neurosis according to a new ego rhetoric of structure, character, development, and adaptation. Holding fast to a simpler metapsychological faith, he never again mentioned the transference neurosis after 1920, using in its stead an older and more generalized sense of the transference. In that year, discussing the critical reconstruction in the case of a homosexual girl, Freud described two phases in an analysis thus: "In the first, the physician . . . unfolds [to the patient] the reconstruction of the genesis of his disorder as deduced by the material brought up in the analysis. In the second phase, the patient . . . recollects what he can of the apparently repressed memories, and tries to repeat the rest as if he were in some way living it over again" (p. 152). Unwavering to the last, he would again write (1937) that the analyst's task "is to make out what has been forgotten from the traces which it has left behind or, more correctly, to *construct* it" (pp. 258-259).

To the last, then, Freud believed it should be a reconstruction of an infantile neurosis placed firmly in the phallic-oedipal period and its prototypical conflicts, whose libidinal derivatives were discursively recoverable from the associations, dreams, and fantasies reported in the hour. As such, he never seemed to be part of the historical drift to an experiential recovery of aggressive derivatives and early genetic events in the more nondiscursive modes of transference acts and transference self-states.

Removed as he was in time from longitudinal developmental studies, which did not begin until his last years, Freud made several basic assumptions about the infantile neurosis and its subsequent conflictual revival in the adult that have left a legacy of technical and methodological problems. To begin with, Freud assumed that every adult neurosis was preceded by an infantile one and that the infantile neurosis was the basic psychopathology of childhood. But, as many have observed, not every infantile neurosis is followed by a neurotic illness in the adult, and not every disorder of childhood is an infantile neurosis (Panel, 1954; A. Freud, 1970; Mahler, 1975). Several important conclusions can be drawn from this, among them the pertinent observation that the infantile neurosis is more frequent, more "normal," than its adult counterpart. Looked at from a developmental point of view, the infantile neurosis represents a positive sign of personality growth, a progression from primitive to more sophisticated reaction patterns (A. Freud, 1970). In a similar vein, Hartmann (Panel, 1954) argues for the infantile neurosis as a phase-adequate neurotic reaction of childhood, and that what may appear to be "pathological" in a cross section of development may, in a longitudinal view of development, represent the best possible solution of a given childhood conflict. He quotes to that end an acute clinical observation made by Helene Deutsch, to the effect that in certain situations the fact that a depression develops is less damaging than if one does not. Looking at the infantile neurosis as a phase-adequate developmental response whose absence may portend graver psychopathology in later life than its expectable presence grants a significant insight in the case of those patients who suffered critical object loss early in life—e.g., a loss of one or both parents—and who could not, or were not permitted, to mourn through that loss when it occurred, and in whom a delayed mourning later on in adult life assumes the form of an intractable, and often suicidal, depression (Coltrera, 1979b). Occasionally, that delayed mourning will occur in the working through of the transference neurosis, with a consequent initiation of a severe period of negative transference, dominated by deep regressions and a profound, and frequently suicidal, depression.

Lastly, many infantile neuroses seem to be spontaneously "cured" at the point where the developmental storms of childhood are relieved by the onset of latency (Greenacre, 1956, 1957; A. Freud, 1970). If this is so, it would argue for a longitudinal developmental extension of the infantile neurosis to include postoedipal as well as preoedipal determinants. Can we validly exclude the postoedipal developmental condition of the usual resolution of the infantile neurosis in any developmental reconsideration?

I have argued that the relative decline of genetic interpretation and reconstruction in modern analysis is a combined function of both historical and methodological problems, built into an enduring and developmentally restricted model of the infantile neurosis. This has descended more or less intact into our own time in ego psychology, a model parochialized to the phallic-oedipal period and its contained prototypic conflict. However, mounting empirical evidences derived from both direct developmental observations and child analysis, as well as the more indirect evidences inferred from the genetic reconstruction of adult analysis, all argue for a developmental reconsideration of the concept of infantile neurosis to include preoedipal determinants. For approximately the same methodological reasons, I cannot see how latency events can be excluded from such reconsideration, insofar as that postoedipal period is the ordinary developmental condition of its resolution. Further, and now arguing from the holistic nature of behavior and the methodological principle of demarcation (Popper, 1934; Coltrera, 1965), which says conflict cannot be defined operationally apart from a working concept of what is not conflict, I would also ask that the concept of infantile neurosis be reconsidered according to all the metapsychological points of view in accord with Hartmann's (1939) notion of psychoanalysis as a general psychology.

In exploring some of the technical problems associated with the *approximate* reconstruction of these early developmental events, I realize that more questions have probably been begged than have been answered. Perhaps this is the way it must be; for in one measure, the vitality and continuing viability of an empirical idea like psychoanalysis derives as much from the questions it poses itself, as from the answers it fashions.

Summary

I have attempted to show that the relative decline of genetic interpretation and reconstruction in modern analysis is a result of historical and methodological problems built into an enduring and developmentally restricted model of the infantile neurosis which has descended more or less intact into our time, a model still parochialized to the phallic-oedipal period and its prototypic oedipal conflict. Mounting direct evidences from both longitudinal developmental studies and child analyses, as well as from the more indirect evidences inferred from the genetic reconstructions of adult analyses, all argue for a developmental reconsideration of infantile neurosis to include preoedipal determinants. I have also asked that we include a measure of postoedipal determinancy as well in any such reconsideration, insofar as latency is the developmental condition for the usual resolution of the infantile neurosis. It must be emphasized that to argue for preoedipal determinancy is to say that problems with early object relatedness and early narcissistic pathology deform the oedipal conflict and its phase-adequate resolution. It does not suggest that narcissistic conflict can replace an oedipal one as the organizing conflict of the infantile neurosis during the phallic-oedipal period.

The continuing parochialization of the infantile neurosis to the phallic-oedipal period has been perpetuated in great part by a technical legacy which has tended to restrict reconstructions of the infantile neurosis to the more discursively recoverable libidinal events of that period, and to exclude its preoedipal and aggressive determinants which are more apt to be expressed through the nondiscursive modes of the transference through its acts and self states.

REFERENCES

Adatto, C. P. (1971), Developmental aspects of the transference neurosis. In: *Currents in Psychoanalysis*, ed. I. M. Marcus. New York: International Universities Press, pp. 337-360.

Bibring, E. (1954), Psychoanalysis and the dynamic psychotherapies. *This Journal*, 2:754-770.

Blum, H. (1971), On the conception and development of the transference neurosis. *This Journal*, 19:41-53.

_____ (1974), The borderline childhood of the Wolf Man. *This Journal*, 22:721-742.

_____ (1977), The prototype of preoedipal reconstruction. *This Journal*, 25:757-786.

Coltrera, J. T. (1965), On the creation of beauty and thought: The unique as vicissitude. *This Journal*, 13:634-703.

_____ (1979a), On the nature of interpretation: Metaphysics as practice. (In preparation)

_____ (1979b), Lives, events and other players: Directions in psychobiography. (In preparation)

_____ & Ross, N. (1967), Freud's psychoanalytic technique from the beginning to 1923. In: *Psychoanalytic Techniques*, ed. B. Wolman. New York: Basic Books, pp. 13-50.

Dilthey, W. (1910), *Pattern and Meaning in History*. New York: Torch Books, 1962.

Ferenczi, S. & Rank, O. (1924), *The Development of Psychoanalysis*. New York & Washington: Nervous and Mental Disease Pub. Co., 1925.

Fine, B. D., Joseph, E. D., & Waldhorn, H. F., eds. (1971), *Recollection and Reconstruction. Reconstruction in Psychoanalysis. Kris Study Group Monograph*, IV. New York: International Universities Press.

Freud, A. (1965), *Normality and Pathology in Childhood: Assessments of Development. Writings*, 6. New York: International Universities Press.

_____ (1968), Acting out. *Writings*, 7:94-109. New York: International Universities Press, 1971.

_____ (1969), Difficulties in the path of psychoanalysis: A confrontation of past with present viewpoints. *Writings*, 7:124-156. New York: International Universities Press, 1971.

_____ (1970), The infantile neurosis: Genetic and dynamic considerations. *Writings*, 7:189-203. New York: International Universities Press, 1971.

Freud, S. (1887-1902), *The Origins of Psychoanalysis*. New York: Basic Books, 1954.

_____ (1891), *On Aphasia*. New York: International Universities Press, 1953.

_____ (1893-1895), Studies on hysteria. *Standard Edition*, 2.

_____ (1895), Project for a scientific psychology. In: *The Origin of Psychoanalysis:*

Letters to Wilhelm Fliess, Drafts and Notes (1887-1902). New York: Basic Books, 1954.

_____ (1899), Screen memories. *Standard Edition*, 3:301-322.

_____ (1900), The interpretation of dreams. *Standard Edition*, 4 & 5.

_____ (1904), Freud's psycho-analytic procedure. *Standard Edition*, 7:249-256.

_____ (1905), Fragment of an analysis of a case of hysteria. *Standard Edition*, 7:7-124.

_____ (1909), Notes upon a case of obsessional neurosis. *Standard Edition*, 10:153-320.

_____ (1912a), The dynamics of transference. *Standard Edition*, 12:97-108.

_____ (1912b), Recommendations to physicians practising psycho-analysis. *Standard Edition*, 12:109-120.

_____ (1913), On beginning the treatment. *Standard Edition*, 12:121-144.

_____ (1914), Recollecting, repeating, and working through. *Standard Edition*, 12:145-156.

_____ (1915), Instincts and their vicissitudes. *Standard Edition*, 14:117-140.

_____ (1915-1917), Papers on metapsychology. *Standard Edition*, 14:105-260.

_____ (1918), From the history of an infantile neurosis. *Standard Edition*, 17:7-122.

_____ (1920), The psychogenesis of a case of homosexuality in a woman. *Standard Edition*, 18:147-172.

_____ (1922), Psycho-analysis. *Standard Edition*, 10:235-254.

_____ (1925), An autobiographical study. *Standard Edition*, 20:7-74.

_____ (1926), Inhibitions, symptoms and anxiety. *Standard Edition*, 20:77-175.

_____ (1927), The future of an illusion. *Standard Edition*, 21:3-56.

_____ (1937), Constructions in analysis. *Standard Edition*, 23:257-269.

_____ (1940), An outline of psycho-analysis. *Standard Edition*, 23:144-208.

Greenacre, P. (1956), Re-evaluation of the process of working through. In: *Emotional Growth.* New York: International Universities Press, 1971, pp. 641-650.

_____ (1957), The childhood of the artist: Libidinal phase development and giftedness. In: *Emotional Growth.* New York: International Universities Press, 1971, pp. 479-504.

_____ (1958), The family romance of the artist. In: *Emotional Growth.* New York: International Universities Press, 1971, pp. 505-532.

_____ (1959), Certain technical problems in the transference relationship. In: *Emotional Growth.* New York: International Universities Press, 1971, pp. 651-669.

_____ (1963), Problems of acting out in the transference relationship. In: *Emotional Growth.* New York: International Universities Press, 1971, pp. 695-712.

Hartmann, H. (1939), *Ego Psychology and the Problem of Adaptation.* New York: International Universities Press, 1958.

_____ & Kris, E. (1945), The genetic approach in psychoanalysis. *The Psychoanalytic Study of the Child*, 1:11-30. New York: International Universities Press.

Jacobson, E. (1953), Contributions to the metapsychology of cyclothymic depression. In: *Affective Disorders*, ed. P. Greenacre. New York: International Universities Press, pp. 49-83.

———— (1964), *The Self and the Object World*. New York: International Universities Press.

———— (1971), *Depression*. New York: International Universities Press.

Kris, E. (1956), The recovery of childhood memories in psychoanalysis. *The Psychoanalytic Study of the Child*, 11:54-88. New York: International Universities Press.

Langer, S. (1942), *Philosophy in a New Key*. Cambridge: Harvard University Press.

Loewald, H. (1971), The transference neurosis: Comments on the concept and the phenomenon. *This Journal*, 19:54-66.

Loewenstein, R. (1951), The problem of interpretation. *Psychoanal. Quart.*, 20:1-14.

Lewin, K. (1937), Psychoanalysis and topological psychology. *Bull. Menninger Clinic*, 1:202-211.

Mahler, M. (1963), Thoughts about development and individuation. *The Psychoanalytic Study of the Child*, 18:307-324. New York: International Universities Press.

———— (1966), Notes on the development of basic moods: The depressive affect. In: *Psychoanalysis: A General Psychology. Essays in Honor of Heinz Hartmann*, ed. R. M. Loewenstein, L. M. Newman, M. Schur, & A. J. Solnit. New York: International Universities Press, pp. 152-168.

———— (1972), On the first three subphases of the separation—individuation process. *Internat. J. Psycho-Anal.*, 53:333-338.

———— (1975), On the current status of the infantile neurosis. *This Journal*, 23:327-333.

Panel (1954), Problems of infantile neuroses. *The Psychoanalytic Study of the Child*, 9:16-71. New York: International Universities Press.

Parsons, T. (1949), *The Structure of Social Action*. Glencoe: Free Press.

Popper, K. (1934), *The Logic of Scientific Discovery*. New York: Basic Books, 1959.

Rapaport, D. (1959), *The Structure of Psychoanalytic Theory: A Systematizing Attempt. Psychological Issues*, Monogr. 6. New York: International Universities Press.

———— & Gill, M. (1959), The points of view and assumptions of metapsychology. *Internat. J. Psycho-Anal.*, 40:153-162.

Ricoeur, P. (1970), *Freud and Philosophy: An Essay in Interpretation*. New Haven: Yale University Press.

Rycroft, C. (1958), An enquiry into the function of word in the psychoanalytic situation. *Internat. J. Psycho-Anal.*, 39:408-415.

Schafer, R. (1973), Action: Its place in psychoanalytic interpretation and theory. *The Annual of Psychoanalysis*, 1:159-196. New York: Quadrangle.

———— (1975), Psychoanalysis without psychodynamics. *Internat. J. Psycho-Anal.*, 56:41-55.

Spitz, R. A. (1963), Life and the dialogue. In: *Counterpoint: Libidinal Object and Subject*, ed. H. S. Gaskill. New York: International Universities Press, pp. 154-176.

Winnicott, D. W. (1958), *Collected Papers: Through Pediatrics to Psychoanalysis*. New York: Basic Books.

69 Willow Street
Brooklyn, New York 11202

SOME ADDITIONAL REMARKS ON PROBLEMS OF TRANSFERENCE

P. J. VAN DER LEEUW, M.D.

> As for transference it is altogether a
> curse ... nor have I overcome the
> countertransference.
> —Freud

THE FACT THAT IN OUR DAILY WORK we are increasingly being confronted with narcissistic problems in our patients must necessarily change our approach and result in a different clinical picture of the analysand and the analyst within the psychoanalytic situation. Narcissistic problems influence our technique, particularly our handling of the transference: indeed, they demand serious thought about the very concept of transference. This concept and those related to it, such as positive and negative transference, transference neurosis, and countertransference, as well as descriptions of the therapeutic process, were first introduced by Freud (Breuer and Freud, 1895; Freud, 1905, 1912a, 1912b, 1915) during the period when his thinking was based essentially on experiences with patients suffering from hysteria and obsessional neurosis, the so-called transference neuroses, which Freud distinguished from narcissistic neurosis. In other words, the investigation into sexuality and object relations and their clinical manifestations in the Oedipus complex were then of foremost importance. Such was the situation before Freud's repetition compulsion (1920), his dual theory of instincts (1920, 1923), his personality concept (the structural viewpoint, 1923), and preoedipal development

315

(1931) were made explicit in his work. After 1920 he but seldom discussed problems of transference, "Analysis Terminable and Interminable" (1937) being the exception to this rule.

In his description of the "narcissistic neuroses" (1911, 1914) Freud stressed their lack of transference and their inability to allow a sufficiently durable transference relationship between analyst and analysand to be created. He in fact indicated that in these disorders object relatedness is either nonexistent or hardly developed, a statement that has greatly influenced our thoughts on the concept of transference. In his studies on technique, Freud never explicitly described his experiences and technical procedures with narcissistic personalities, though there are hints of these experiences in his (1918) discussion of the Wolf Man's narcissism. The theory of psychoanalytic technique continued to develop from Freud's original formulations (Kanzer and Blum, 1967).

Today, we are mostly concerned with the mental condition of those of our patients who are unable to form a "relatively" mature object relation and who regard their analyst, not as a person in his own right, but rather as an extension of themselves. In other words, we are dealing here with "narcissistic neuroses," with narcissistic character pathology.

In my clinical work I make a deliberate effort to distinguish between aspects of object relatedness and the narcissistic tie in the relation between analysand and analyst. I have borrowed the term "narcissistic tie" from Lampl-de Groot (1975). I do not myself use Kohut's (1971) concept of narcissistic transference. This is a concept which confuses my thoughts and which seems to me self-contradictory. Transference in its classical sense implies an object relationship, even though one on an infantile level. We may attach too much importance to object relatedness in our clinical work with patients suffering from narcissistic disturbances. So often during treatment, conflicts come to the fore which derive from the separation-individuation phase (Mahler and Furer, 1968), the time when there is as yet no clear distinction between the "inner" and the "outer" world. The early need-satisfying and dyadic aspects of object relationships also play a large part in the analyses of these patients. The rupture of the symbiotic state; the loss of the narcissistic mother-child continuum (such as the feeling of oneness or fusion); the occurrence of unexpected and relatively sudden emotional changes from omnipotence to total helplessness; the patient's complete emotional empti- ness, his feeling of no relatedness, nothingness, accompanied by extreme anxiety, fear of annihilation, utter insecurity, and narcissistic rage—all those must be worked through during the analysis. Patients feel incapable of carrying any burden, they have no capacity for strength and no capacity for tolerating themselves and thus taking on responsibility for themselves. Any experience of "self" is lacking. There is longing, an immediate need for "rapport," for a tie, a bond; a need for what is at a later stage supplied by an object that is recognized as an external object, a recognition that is as yet not fully achieved, a differentiation of self and object that has not been fully completed, or a longing for reinstatement of symbiosis.

The crucial maturational process we aim for is the coming into existence of a stable ego-self continuum created "from within" that will finally enable the patient to carry a burden, to give full scope to ego development, and to establish object relatedness—object relations. It is of particular importance to make our patients aware of their innate primitive impulses to destroy and to murder when, during the analytic work, they are confronted with the loss of their omnipotence and feelings of being let down in response to their growing awareness of the separateness and independent existence of their objects. This also will mean a later inability to control and magically coerce the independent object. I attach high significance to "intensity," that is, the quantitative or economic point of view, when analyzing patients presenting narcissistic problems. I refer to the intensity of separation anxiety, narcissistic rage, symbiotic wishes, and annihilation anxiety.

It is my experience that these early separation-individuation conflicts come to the fore mainly toward the final phase of the analysis. It is only then that we realize their full intensity. My impression has been confirmed in cases where the termination of the treatment presented a grave problem, indeed, became a real stumbling block. I have become more cautious now regarding interpretations of the signs of object relatedness, of transference phenomena in the classical sense of the concept, during the final phase, as well as at the beginning phase. I have come to understand that they can serve as a defense against the underlying unresolved conflicts of the separation-individuation phase (Mahler, 1971). The contents as well as the defensive function of transference phenomena must be very carefully interpreted. Only when I have a clear insight into the relation between object relatedness and the narcissistic tie to the analyst can I decide how to direct my interpretation. As for termination, it seems to me to be of great importance not to impose upon the patient, not to burden him with a definite termination date. The patient should feel free to decide for himself. He needs, and he must be given, the opportunity to experiment, to test whether he is able and willing to be left alone, to function by himself. This does not mean that symbiotically clinging, orally dependent patients should not confront anxiety about termination.

Finally, I want to point out that in the treatment of early narcissistic disturbances, the working alliance (Greenson, 1965) is the major problem. What is the working alliance? What are its roots, its genesis? Which factors contribute to the phenomenon? From the literature on this subject we learn that the main factors responsible for a working alliance are: the existence of a split in the analysand's ego between an experiencing and observing part (Sterba, 1934); the analysand's capacity to identify with the analyst as an "analyzing instrument," as Isakower (1963) called it, and the quality of this identification; the "real" relation between analysand and analyst (Greenson and Wexler, 1969). We know that a relatively mature ego, a higher level of ego development must have been achieved and must be functioning adequately to assure some intact ego integration and object relationship.

The viewpoint, however, that the working alliance is primarily a narcissistic manifestation is to be almost nowhere found in the psychoanalytic literature. Lampl-de Groot (1975) has shown that the genetic roots of the working alliance lie in the very early mother-child bond, whereas transference is rooted genetically in the object-directed libidinal relationship. Lampl-de Groot has shown, like many other authors, that the working alliance is not transference, nor is it the same as the therapeutic alliance (Zetzel, 1956), and has to be differentiated from the latter. Why, then, is the working alliance the major problem when treating patients suffering from early narcissistic disturbances? Such patients demonstrate primitive transferences, but also serious impairment of the working alliance.

In order to create a working alliance the patient must have a capacity for work, working power, and energy. What do we actually mean by work? Among other things, a capacity for delay, for sacrifice, a tolerance of frustration, an ability to exert oneself, to be goal-directed, to sustain, to give something. This, however, can be achieved only when there is sufficient pleasure in functioning, which in turn depends partly upon the active operation of the mechanism of displacement. When Freud (Breuer and Freud, 1893-1895) first introduced the concept of transference, he linked it closely with displacement. Only later did object relatedness come to the fore and assume a dominant meaning, as in a particular parent or sibling transference.

Pleasure in functioning is to be differentiated from the experience of success; it is the pleasure related to the quality of the product, to achievement (I. Hendrick, 1943): feelings of triumph do not belong to it. In order to be able to work, one needs to have a feeling of safety. The analyst then functions as a protective barrier for his patient; not as an object, but as an instrument, a tool. Pleasure in functioning is closely related to the various developmental stages of such bodily functions as locomotion and bowel control. Further, the ability to verbalize is of utmost importance. Verbalization serves as an instrument, an aid, an organizer, a tool for the discharge of impulses, and for the modulation of affects and actions. The need to enact, induced by the inability to speak, is later replaced by the use of language, just as thought as trial action replaces literal action. Language promotes delay and helps to advance ego development and knowledge of inner and outer reality.

Analytic work can be done only when the imperative need—the urge to destroy—has been partially transformed into an activity aiming at uniting, joining, cooperating, preserving, being productive, and facing constructive change. The capacity to do analytic work depends partly upon such ability to transform destructive impulses and partly upon the ability to tolerate them without suffering too much anxiety. Tolerance of unpleasant affect is a necessary requisite for transformation and change. This also implies the transformation of automatic anxiety into signal anxiety. The ability to transform anxiety is also necessary in order to break down archaic fantasies and feelings of grandeur.

The notion of an outer world, the awareness of reality, is the starting point for the development of the sense of reality which insures a clear perception of the outer world. The basis for the idea of reality is formed at a very early stage, when reception alternates with perception. Only when one has experienced and accepted the loss of omnipotence and when its nonexistence has been recognized can a sense of reality and reality testing develop. A sense of reality essentially includes experiencing limitation and restriction. Differentiation of self and object, inside and outside, are also necessary. Fantasies and feelings of omnipotence must be mitigated. They belong to the notion of an inner world, as part of psychic reality, but this is not a matter for discussion here. The development of working power, pleasure in functioning, transformation of primitive destructive impulses, reality testing, and differentiation of the inner from the outer world belong to the same maturational early phases as those in which the working alliance is genetically rooted. Hence, the working alliance of patients presenting early narcissistic problems is of a precarious nature. We must, however, remember that concepts such as transference, narcissistic tie, and working alliance indicate the existence of processes that occur side by side and even intermingle (Lampl-de Groòt, 1975). If we keep this in mind, we are more capable of facing problems concerned with the transference neurosis in our daily clinical work as well as in our theoretical considerations. Patients with primary disturbances of narcissism and object relations may have difficulty in forming both the working alliance and transference neurosis (A. Freud, 1965). This suggests other clinical complications of the psychoanalytic process and additional theoretical considerations. In presenting my personal views here, I am not attempting to review the broad pertinent literature and e.g., the writings of Jacobson (1964), van der Waals (1965), Kernberg (1975), and many others.

As for our technique regarding the patient's narcissistic pathology, the analyst must pay particular attention to his own attitude, his own ability to follow the patient, especially in the nonverbal aspects of his communication and responses. To follow the patient means, among other things, to be mentally present, to be there, to be at the patient's disposal, to be available to him, and to respect his autonomy, to leave to him the decision to accept or reject. The analyst must avoid imposing upon him, he must keep the right distance and be concerned and willing to share.

I prefer the term sharing to alliance. Sharing indicates working together toward a common goal; by contrast, alliance indicates primarily an aspect of object relationship— the rapport or bond with an object. In these early phases, it is the other person as an instrument, a tool that dominates the situation and not object relatedness itself. It is the analyst's capacity to soothe, to create an optimal level of tension, an optimal state of pleasure, and also his ability to maintain the patient in a holding environment (Winnicott, 1965). It is important, however, not to confuse providing a holding function with abandoning the analytic attitude; the patient's regression must ultimately be interpreted. The holding function counteracts the patient's need to cling. The analyst's capacity to hold the patient is of the utmost importance when the urge to destroy, to murder, is uppermost in the patient's mind or when the patient is confronted with the danger of regressive loss of ego integration and regulation.

The analyst must never lose awareness of his own countertransference reactions. He must be aware of how his personality and behavior may influence the analysis. It is natural that his own therapeutic ambition and zeal play an important part, particularly as a reaction formation against his own innate destructive impulses and as a defense against his own feelings of powerlessness, helplessness, and anxiety. His self-analytic awareness also functions as a barrier against his own unsolved problems with his narcissistic and symbiotic needs. It is not the countertransference as such that is helpful, but the readiness to acknowledge it and the ability to overcome it (Heimann, 1950, 1960; Gitelson, 1952).

In conclusion, I would like to draw attention to some of our most difficult tasks in the treatment of patients suffering from early narcissistic disturbances.

We have to bring about a change in the functioning of their emotional life in such a way that the omnipotent and helpless narcissistic ultimatum of "all or nothing" turns into "neither all nor nothing." Realistic acceptance of limitations of oneself is bound up with the realistic recognition of the outer world: "There is something worthwhile, and I love what there is." A further change concerns the sense of time, so that the child (and patient) learns that there is continuity, reliance, and durability; the past is differentiated from the present and does not dominate the present through the repetition compulsion.

I agree fully with Kohut (1971) when he stresses the paramount importance of leaving the process of idealizing (e.g., mirror transference and the idealized parent images) undisturbed for a long time when treating narcissistic personality disorders. However difficult it might be for the analyst to endure this state of idealization for a prolonged period, it is necessary for the thorough analysis of the idealization. I would like to add, though, that the analyst has to administer an optimal dosage of disillusion (Winnicott, 1965). Disillusion and disappointment evoke narcissistic rage reactions in these patients (Kohut, 1972). Timing, tact, and wording are especially difficult in this respect, but confronting reality is important, and, here, the evoking of narcissistic rage cannot be avoided.

We are sometimes inclined to limit our attention to the aggressive aspect of object relatedness in our patients' material and to their self-directed aggression. Problems around parting with the products of the body receive too little consideration (Heimann, 1962). In neglecting these factors, we might hamper our patients' becoming aware of their bodies, on the one hand, and their bodies' products, on the other, as entities that can be separated from one another. We may disregard separation-individuation conflicts and feelings of omnipotence/helplessness. Devaluation of bodily products by the surroundings which then takes place, often enough a repetition and externalization of the patient's original childhood experience, stands in the way of a solution of these conflicts. The aforementioned has a certain bearing upon the part played by transitional objects (Winnicott, 1953) in the development of object relatedness and in preoedipal development. Urination, defecation, ejaculation, and childbirth have in common the fact that that part of one's own highly-valued self is being lost. The loss of body products or parts or alterations of the body image leads to disturbed narcissistic equilibrium. Destructive impulses are then once more mobilized, and narcissistic mortification must be worked through, i.e., narcissistic rage must be transformed to avoid serious personality problems. The mature assimilation of narcissistic mortifications and the transformation of narcissistic rage into modulated, tamed responses is a major task of analytic work with narcissistic disturbance.

Summary

I have dwelt on the nature of the analytic relationship with patients suffering from narcissistic character pathology. I prefer the term narcissistic tie to narcissistic transference. The narcissistic patient lacks the resources necessary to establish a working alliance, and the analyst's principal task is to bring the patient to the point where he is capable of a sense of reality, of tolerating frustration, of taming rage, and of true object relatedness. I have also pointed to the particular tasks these patients set for the analyst in terms of countertransference reactions.

REFERENCES

Breuer, J. & Freud, S. (1893-1895), Studies on hysteria. *Standard Edition*, 2.
Freud, A. (1965), *Normality and Pathology in Childhood. Writings*, 6. New York: International Universities Press.

Freud, S. (1905), Fragment of an analysis of a case of hysteria. *Standard Edition*, 7:3-122.

———— (1911), Psycho-analytic notes on an autobiographical account of a case of paranoia. *Standard Edition*, 12:3-82.

———— (1912a), The dynamics of transference. *Standard Edition*, 12:99-108.

———— (1912b), Recommendations to physicians practising psycho-analysis. *Standard Edition*, 12:110-120.

———— (1914), On narcissism. *Standard Edition*, 14:69-102.

———— (1915), Observations on transference-love. *Standard Edition*, 12:158-171.

———— (1918), From the history of an infantile neurosis. *Standard Edition*, 17:3-122.

———— (1920), Beyond the pleasure principle. *Standard Edition*, 18:3-64.

———— (1923), The ego and the id. *Standard Edition*, 19:3-66.

———— (1931), Female sexuality. *Standard Edition*, 21:223-243.

———— (1937), Analysis terminable and interminable. *Standard Edition*, 23:211-253.

Gitelson, M. (1952), The emotional position of the analyst in the psychoanalytic situation. In: *Psychoanalysis: Science and Profession*. New York: International Universities Press, 1973, pp. 173-200.

Greenson, R. R. (1965), The working alliance and the transference neurosis. In: *Explorations in Psychoanalysis*. New York: International Universities Press, 1978, pp. 199-224.

———— & Wexler, M. (1969), The nontransference relationship in the psychoanalytic situation. In: *Explorations in Psychoanalysis*. New York: International Universities Press, 1978, pp. 359-386.

Heimann, P. (1950), On counter-transference. *Internat. J. Psycho-Anal.*, 31:81-84.

———— (1960), Counter-transference. *Brit. J. Med. Psychol.*, 33:9-15.

———— (1962), Notes on the anal stage. *Internat. J. Psycho-Anal.*, 43:406-414.

Hendrick, I. (1943), Work and the pleasure principle. *Psychoanal. Quart.*, 12:311-329.

Isakower, O. (1963), Minutes of Faculty Meeting, New York Psychoanalytic Institute, November 20.

Jacobson, E. (1964), *The Self and the Object World*. New York: International Universities Press.

Kanzer, M. & Blum, H. (1967), Classical psychoanalysis since 1939. In: *Psychoanalytic Techniques*, ed. B. B. Wolman. New York: Basic Books, pp. 93-146.

Kernberg, O. (1975), *Borderline Conditions and Pathological Narcissism*. New York: Aronson.

Kohut, H. (1971), *The Analysis of Self*. New York: International Universities Press.

———— (1972), Thoughts on narcissism and narcissistic rage. In: *The Search for the Self*. New York: International Universities Press, 1978, pp. 615-658.

Lampl-de Groot, J. (1975), Vicissitudes of Narcissism and Problems of Civilization. *The Psychoanalytic Study of the Child*, 30, 663-682. New Haven: Yale University Press.

Mahler, M.S. (1971), A study of the separation-individuation process and its possible application to borderline phenomena in the psychoanalytic situation. *The Psychoanalytic Study of the Child*, 26:403-424. New York: Quadrangle Books.

_____ & Furer, M. (1968), *On Human Symbiosis and the Vicissitudes of Individuation*. New York: International Universities Press.

Sterba, R. F. (1934), The fate of the ego in analytic therapy. *Internat. J. Psycho-Anal.*, 15:117-126.

van der Waals, H. (1965), Problems of narcissism. *Bull. Menninger Clinic*, 29: 293-311.

Winnicott, D. W. (1953), Transitional objects and transitional phenomena. In: *Collected Papers*. New York: Basic Books, 1958, pp. 229-242.

_____ (1965), *The Maturational Processes and the Facilitating Environment*. New York: International Universities Press.

Zetzel, E. R. (1956), The concept of transference. In: *The Capacity for Emotional Growth*. New York: International Universities Press, 1970, pp. 168-181.

Rubensstraat 32
1077 MS
Amsterdam, the Netherlands

DEVELOPMENTS IN PSYCHOANALYTIC TECHNIQUE: A CRITICAL REVIEW OF RECENT PSYCHOANALYTIC BOOKS

Mark Kanzer, M.D.

PSYCHOANALYTIC TECHNIQUE INVOLVES principles and procedures that constantly require the analyst's review and self-supervision, activities as intermingled with and inherently related to the practice of therapy as is his self-analysis. The first survey of books on technique in this *Journal* was by Helen Tartakoff (1956), who commented wryly on the use of the term "psychoanalysis" in the titles of these books and reported that only one claimed it justly, the second edition of Edward Glover's *The Technique of Psychoanalysis* (1955), which brought up to date a classical contribution that had first appeared in 1928.

This later edition contained a questionnaire sent to English analysts in 1938, which, Glover surmised, would have shown little change in 1955. It revealed a great diversity of views and techniques, especially at a time when the teachings of Anna Freud and Melanie Klein were polarizing English analysis. It has often been the case that controversy has engendered new affirmative statements with respect to the

---

Charles Brenner: PSYCHOANALYTIC TECHNIQUE AND PSYCHIC CON-FLICT. New York: International Universities Press, 1976.

Ralph R. Greenson: THE TECHNIQUE AND PRACTICE OF PSYCHOANAL-YSIS. New York: International Universities Press, 1967.

Karl A. Menninger and Philip S. Holzman: THEORY OF PSYCHOANALYTIC TECHNIQUE. Second Edition. New York: Basic Books, 1973.

Joseph Sandler, Christopher Dare, and Alex Holder; THE PATIENT AND THE ANALYST. New York: International Universities Press. 1973.

327

Freudian position (as well as criticisms), and presumably the same may be said of Tartakoff's undertaking at a time when the revisions advocated by Franz Alexander and his group were troubling "classical analysts." (See the October, 1954 issue of this *Journal* for a particularly valuable debate by Alexander himself, E. Bibring, Gill, Greenacre, Rangell, and others, which has lost little of its pertinence today.)

There are thus diversities, consistencies, and advances to be noted in periodic self-searchings into analytic technique. The advances in Glover's second edition, as Tartakoff remarked, were especially in the fields of ego psychology and object relations. These advances have continued, as we glance even in a preliminary way at the four books we shall discuss, which prove to be as far-ranging in their conceptions and appeal to particular audiences as in their places of origin— Greenson's in Los Angeles; Menninger and Holzman's in Topeka and Chicago; Brenner's in New York; Sandler, Dare, and Holder's in London.

The titles do not vary greatly, and all the authors claim descent from Freud, who is usually reviewed in a careful historical context with more or less attention to his contemporaries and successors. Still, the irreverent questions arise: "Which Freud did you read?" and "Who that came after him?", and we agree with the position generally taken, that, in the end, analytic technique depends on the clinical experiences of the practitioner and on his personal analysis and individual training. The individuality of our authors emerges in very different ways and adds dimensions to the reading experience awaiting us.

Educational, historical, and chronological considerations alike suggest that we begin with the Menninger-Holzman book whose first edition appeared under the auspices of the senior author alone in 1958 and was based on his introductory seminars on technique to candidates in Topeka. Menninger rightly says of himself that it was "my good fortune to grow up with psychoanalysis in America." In 1920, he was a "young psychiatrist getting acquainted with such leaders as Adolf Meyer, Smith Ely Jelliffe, A. A. Brill, Adolph Stern, C. P. Oberndorf, William Alanson White, and many others." He was, however, not just another young psychiatrist as he found opportunities to become acquainted with these leaders, for he was already affiliated with the famous Menninger Clinic, and his recruitment to psychoanalysis facilitated its spread in America. He served as president of the American Psychoanalytic Association in 1942-1943 as did his brother William in 1947-1948.

In 1930, he began his didactic analysis with Franz Alexander, who had recently come to this country, and joined him two years later in founding the Chicago Psychoanalytic Institute. He did not follow his mentor along the paths of dissent when his teachings became controversial. During his apprenticeship, Menninger did not undertake the pilgrimage to Vienna that so many others did. Perhaps this circumstance and his mid-Western and institutional affiliations favored a native American strain, pragmatic and in the traditions of the pre-Freudian period. This is seen in such phrases as "the greatest good for the greatest number" (p. xii) as he gives the educational potentials of psychoanalysis more favorable weight than the therapeutic. It may also be found in a picture of Freud (whose foremost ambition throughout his scientific life was to further the understanding of the psychic apparatus) as a pragmatic practitioner who hit upon psychoanalysis as a "happy accident," a discovery "made by Freud in the course of several years of trial and error in trying to unravel the meaning of his patients' neurotic suffering" (p. 184). (Freud, as primal figure of the father for analysts, naturally offers a curious composite. Greenson, quoting Freud, is more impressed by his conquistador aspects [p. 8].)

The "happy accident" thesis unfortunately leads, as it must, to a dichotomy in relating analytic theory to analytic practice. (See, in contrast, the remarkably careful linkages that Freud (1887-1902) drew in his successive formulations of different schemata during the early days of psychoanalysis and also later!) For Freud is next supposed to have advanced such theories of mental functioning as "unconscious psychological processes, repression, projection, internalization and drive development—including psychosexual and psychoaggressive aspects and their interaction" as rationalizations for the technical procedures the analyst uses for they were "clearly not congruent" with these procedures (p. 183). We actually found this dichotomy remarkably useful ourselves in understanding the Menninger-Holzman work, which had otherwise puzzled us, and we shall soon return to their distinctions between actual clinical measures and the theories—usually quoted from other authorities—to account for them.

The 1958 edition of the book was very well received, and it was not until 1973 that Menninger, persuaded by Holzman, who had assisted in the preparation of the earlier work, proceeded to prepare a second edition with the latter as co-editor. It is difficult to establish what changes were made. The first person singular has been largely retained and only 33 of 207 references bear dates subsequent to 1958. Even these additions largely refer to footnotes, to discussions of topics of understandable interest to the authors (fees, termination), and to contributions by the very distinguished analysts who have served at Menninger's. A jarring note is occasionally struck, as in allusions to "our colleagues" Helmuth Kaiser (1934) and Wilhelm Reich (1933-1934).

The basic clinical continuity to which we have referred presumably derives from Menninger; the concepts of mental functioning are often of recent origin and stem, perhaps, from Holzman. It is the former to which we shall give most attention—as does the book. This begins with Menninger's famous "analytic contract," a pioneer among several alliances that were being put forward at the time, and took as model for the analytic relationship the businesslike procedure which its name suggests. The patient is introduced as the "sufferer," the "party of the first part" who "petitions" the analyst, "the party of the second part," for his services. If his petition is granted, the "preparatory instruction, which should be minimal" to deter intellectual resistances, requires that he enter the arrangement "with a certain blind faith"; (such details as diagnosis, selection, treatment of choice are not set forth since this is not a manual of procedure but merely a theory of treatment with little clinical material). The arrangement does not seem as businesslike for the patient as for the analyst, and the former, "if he has been well advised . . . should have reason to believe that he may advantageously enter into a contract with this fellow human being and expect professional integrity and professional competence" (pp. 37-38).

The potentials for difficulty mount as the meaning of the contract is borne home to the party of the first part. There are, of course, money matters to be arranged. It is assumed that minimal preparation includes, besides trust in the fellow human being, a general knowledge of the fees in a particular community. He will, of course, be expected to accept in his own interest a need to impose a financial sacrifice on himself so that he can benefit maximally from the treatment. It is difficult to foretell the length of the process, so that there is a "slight risk" of complications, such as the "unexpected illness of a wife, the loss of a job, and so forth" (p. 32). Ultimately, blind faith may no longer pay his bills, and the analyst will meditate as to whether he, too, should undertake any sacrifices for his fellow human being. Deterrent is the consideration that the analysis may be disturbed if he causes the patient to feel under obligations. Fortunately, as the authors assure the candidates, "chronic failure to pay the analyst's fee usually represents 'acting out'" (p. 32). Moreover, there is "the clear option of the patient to stop whenever he chooses" (p. 30).

Next follows the longest and most important chapter in

the book, that on "The Regression." There is no question but that regression, frustration, and the "principle of abstinence" play fundamental parts in the unfolding of every analysis. What is remarkable here is the pivotal place in the analytic process assigned to them. The requirement for the patient to maintain abstinence becomes "Freud's second 'fundamental rule' of psychoanalysis" (p. 55), and the maintenance of a state of "optimal tension" the foremost technical consideration of the analyst.

The principle of abstinence was first described by Freud in "Remembering, Repeating and Working Through" (1914) where, in conjunction with the recognition accorded the transference neurosis within the analytic situation, it was designed to curb acting out in the outer world. The resulting frustration would intensify the neurosis under the analyst's direct observation and clarify its origin. The principle of abstinence has also been invoked to curb excessive transference gratifications, sexual satisfaction of the patient by the analyst, and—more controversially—to deter instinctual activities outside the analytic situation.

The pivotal position assigned to abstinence by Menninger is unnecessary. Frustration and regression rarely need special measures for re-enforcement during analytic treatment. The patient's sufferings, the deprivations in the analytic situation, the sacrifices he must make to continue in therapy, the influence of the recumbent position that disposes to the revival of infantile functioning are usually adequate enough to maintain these conditions. Different analysts favor a variety of methods to inhibit acting out, but, as we shall see when we reach our discussion of Brenner, awareness and correct interpretations of the transference offer a preferable approach.

What is characteristic of the Menninger-Holzman use of the principle of abstinence to induce regression is its association with cultivated passivity on the part of the analyst. We begin by following the patient to his first analytic session, where for one hour "he pours out his thoughts, helter-skelter, into the ears of the physician." The latter makes no response except to indicate his close attention, e.g., ejaculations, such as "really" in the sense of mild astonishment, "a mild groan—when genuinely felt" to indicate sympathy, "a chuckle at an appropriate time in connection with an amusing episode" (p. 134).

We continue into the second session. "The patient returns, reclines, recites. Once more he gives, and gives, and gives. He tries his best to do as he thinks the analyst wants him to. He submits his 'free associations,' his memories, his reflections, his confidences, his intimate thoughts, his gravest fears. Again the analyst listens and is silent" (pp. 40-41). (We wondered why this was called "reciting," why "free associations" were put in quotes, why the analyst's silence was so necessary.) With "a minimum of participation by the listener except occasional indications of his attentive presence, the talker begins to develop expectations," begins to expect a "magic word," an "oracular pronouncement" (p. 43). (We ourselves suppose he might be looking for some signs of "sympathetic understanding.")

In time we came to an outline of seventeen stages of regression during which the analyst is all but completely silent, for a period that may last a hundred hours (presumably five months). The more silent the analyst, the more the patient regresses, and this is precisely the goal (pp. 57-58). At times, the latter rages at the analyst's "stupidity," at times, for reasons that are not made clear, he praises the goodness of the other in listening calmly and with understanding ("he asked a few questions"). Stage 17 is ultimately reached, and the patient is asking himself, "How *do* I get what I want? Is this the way I relate myself to other people? *What is the something I really want?*" (p. 58).

What is apparently expected now is a "reversal of regression." The party of the first part is pictured as saying, "When are you going to say something, Doctor? I have come here hour after hour now, for quite a while. I've paid my money, and I've spoken my piece. I have done what you told me to and what am I getting? I don't hear a word out of you. Isn't it about time that you woke up and said something?" (p. 60).

We were admiring this reversal, but found that we had missed our cue. Instead, the expectable reaction of the reader was given: "The young analyst, no matter how much he has prepared himself by reading, is certain to be startled when he first encounters this astonishing phenomenon—the frank 'admission' by the patient that he is not in treatment for the sake of getting better" (p. 60). After much pondering, we decided that the patient's error, and our own, was the expectation that, having paid his money to the analyst, the latter should do something. The message to be expected is that the analysand must learn to do things himself. He must understand that he has been whining and carrying on like a baby under the pressure of frustration. With this more appropriate way of looking at things, he now recognizes that "it is not the analyst who frustrates, but he, the patient, who frustrates himself. . . . He begins to feel that it is his own responsibility to take charge of his life, and not the analyst's function" (p. 59).

With this turnabout, the road to health is traversed rapidly. "The 'I' begins to grow up." He begins to realize that the analyst has been "a kind, friendly, incorruptible person who has stood by the patient, withstood his attacks and reactions and fulfilled the contract realistically" (p. 74). He has shown concern and "real" love for the patient (p. 160). The authors describe this as "objectivation" of the analyst, but we rather wonder how this objectivation had grown out of all this silence and frustration. We did find passages—after the seventeenth station of regression—to correct any one-sided notions we may have formed. "The patient does not feel frustrated all the time. There are waves of gratitude for being listened to and understood, surprised joy in the achievement of new insights and progress, relief from oppressive guilt feelings, dawning hope for new possibilities" (p. 61). No illustrations.

As a rule, gradual alternations are postulated as taking place during the analytic process, with cycles of regression and progression, frustration and satisfaction coinciding with the emergence of transferences and resistances that are interpreted by the analyst. These push back the limits of memory while preparing the way for advances through identification with the therapist as a new object (as indeed some of the theoretical expositions in the book, quoting from Greenacre, Loewald, Loewenstein, and others indicate). It is difficult to see how such postulates are to be made congruent with the overriding insistence on complete regression and the persistent silence of the analyst as necessary for recovery. The authors even suggest that, with regression launched, an automatic pathway may be followed that requires no analyst: "it is helpful to discuss the possibility of a psychoanalytic therapy proceeding from beginning to end without the analyst ever having said a word" (p. 129). Ultimately, however, it is decided that the presence of the analyst will "shorten the process, if it is possible" (p. 130).

The analyst's usual tools undergo redefinition and application under the guiding principles for the maintenance of optimal tension. Regression is sometimes simply equated with the transference neurosis. The interpretation, usually considered the primary tool of analytic therapy, is not so much aimed at the replacement of resistance by insight as to prevent frustration tension from becoming too painful. Then it must be "administered with parsimony—*the least necessary quantity of help should be given the patient*" (p. 136, italics ours). (We have underlined this doctrine, which is new to us.)

"To do otherwise," the authors continue, "tends to upset the desired optimum level of frustration tension by a swing in the opposite direction. It is, so to speak, too reassuring to the patient. It diminishes the internal incentive for him to plow forward" (p. 136). Along these lines, H. J. Schlesinger is quoted approvingly as describing how, "when the analyst finally 'gives' something to the patient" (an interpretation), it impinges "like a drought-breaking cloud-burst"—as much a danger as a "relief" (p. 53).

The latter danger was avoided, but the patient still was lost, in the only clinical vignette that comes to mind. A new patient who had started with some promise began to slow up and finally presented a dream remarkably similar in content to a semi-autobiographical incident described by Henry James in "The Jolly Corner" (1909): Toward the middle of life James's hero returns to the home of his childhood and searches through it for the ghost of what he might have been had he led the life that his destiny had seemed to hold for him—a successful American business man. He finally encounters this horrifying apparition, his own Double and—in the tradition of the meeting with the Double—falls into a deathlike trance. It is an acted-out self-analysis.

In the vignette, the dreamer wanders through a lonely if handsome house until finally in one room he encounters a loathsome mess in a corner, "something dreadful, disgusting, terrible." Naturally, the analyst was silent, and "a few days later the patient wrote that he was feeling better and believed that he would discontinue his analysis" (p. 104). The incident is presented to illustrate how the patient obstructs himself through his resistances. Perhaps it might have been more encouraging to the patient (and the candidates) to have shifted it to the chapter on interpretations.

No doubt we are inviting the same reproach that befell another critic who warned that "the patient may use regression as a direct defense against making progress in analysis . . . to block the analyst's endeavor to change him and bring him to a higher level of behavior." He was told sharply that "we do not think it is the analyst's proper task to 'endeavor to change' the analysand or 'to bring him' anywhere, be it higher or lower. This image presents a pouting patient hanging back against the pull of a leash held in the hands of an analyst" (pp. 45-46). We nevertheless do not think the authors' image entirely inappropriate to Freud's description of working through the resistances as "an arduous task for the subject of the analysis and a trial of patience for the analyst" (1914, p. 155).

We sought the key to the peculiar turn that Freudian analysis has taken in this volume. One lead comes from the authors themselves, when, at the end, they cite as the model of termination M. Balint's (1953) visualization of the rites in which the cry "The King is Dead" is followed by its counterpoint, "Long Live the King." Ancient totemistic solutions of the Oedipus complex combine with a rebirth fantasy as the patient sees light ahead of him at the end of a long therapeutic tunnel (p. 176). Certainly the regressive regimen ending in the renunciation of childish (oedipal?) ways and the grateful reconciliation with the silent analyst as new superego has elements of the fasts, the visions, the revelations by which the tribal initiate receives a new name and a place among the men of the clan.

We reflected on these perspectives as we learned of the model patient's expectable soliloquy as he neared the end: "I have my analyst's friendship, and I have his example. I have his point of view toward illness. What I *thought* I wanted from him (love) was in fact a childish fantasy, which I renounced. . . . I have gotten what I paid for. I can do for myself" (pp. 161-162).

Perhaps this is a termination with masochistic and idealized transferences as residua; perhaps an introjection of a mature new father figure. We could not help but think of a period of American mores in this connection—the traditions for inculcating rugged individualism, the sturdy character-building associated with relentless plowing ahead undeterred by interpretations, the adage that God (the party of the second part) helps those that help themselves. Neither the techniques of invisibility and silence nor the policy of the least helpfulness have ever lacked testimonials as to their efficacy. As a last note, a timely metaphor helped in following back a train of connections to Freud himself. "Psychoanalytic treatment is a little like removing an embedded fishhook that has to be pushed farther and the barb removed before the hook can be extracted. Freud hinted at this when he spoke of neurotic illness as expressing the suffering from reminiscences which can neither be fully repressed nor fully recalled. In psychoanalytic treatment they are, first, more completely recollected and then more fully repressed or more completely integrated" (p. 45).

This comment, like an interpretation, served to summon up our own reminiscences, which converged on the final page of the "Studies on Hysteria" (Breuer and Freud, 1893-1895) with its closing words; "I have described my treatments as psychotherapeutic operations; and I have brought out their analogy with the opening up of a cavity filled with pus, the scraping out of a carious region, etc. An analogy of this kind finds its justification not so much in the removal of what is pathological as in the establishment of conditions that are more likely to lead the course of the process in the direction of recovery" (p. 305). Now everything seemed to fit at last.

Very few, not including Freud, have attempted a full-scale textbook in a field so filled with differences over terms, procedures, aims, the recording of reliable data and results as is psychoanalysis. Ralph R. Greenson, undertaking to do so, has appreciated the difficulties and also commented on the reluctance of psychoanalysts to expose their methods of practice, since these depend on so many personal reactions within themselves. Greenson concedes that much subjectivity exists in the exercise of a "lonely profession. . . . [where] the analyst's own view of what he does is unreliable and apt to be distorted in some idealized direction" (p.4).

Such insight did not deter him from undertaking to write "a book which depicts the practice of classical psychoanalytic therapy" in the hope that it will "stimulate a full, open, and continuing discussion of psychoanalytic techniques" (p. 5). But what if the same book is devoted to a very personal viewpoint which challenges and offers alternatives to classical psychoanalysis? Is this inherently a "textbook" or rather the record of a particular experience, as various reviewers have opined (Waldhorn 1969; Zetzel, 1969; Kanzer, 1975)? In either case, this ambitious effort will next command our attention.

Greenson's general orientation does indeed continue the trend of modern psychoanalysis to develop in the direction of ego psychology and object relations. Therapy is seen as "aimed directly at the ego, since only the ego has direct access to the id, to the superego, and to the outside world. Our aim is to get the ego to renounce its pathological defenses or find more suitable ones" (p. 29). Metapsychologically, he adopts the six frameworks of Rapaport and Gill (1959)—the topographic, dynamic, economic, genetic, structural and adaptive. These prepare the way for the innovations he will make in this volume, delimiting a "real relationship" and a "working alliance" that are to be placed side by side with the more traditional transference as guides to the significance and management of events in the analytic setting.

To this significant project, Greenson brings energy, dedication, extensive clinical and teaching experience, as well as conscientious scholarship. Originally planned for two volumes—of which the second, after more than a decade, has not yet appeared—it contains only four chapters: 1. Basic Concepts; 2. Resistance; 3. Transference; 4. The Psychoanalytic Situation. The second volume was to have dealt with technical problems in chronological order. In many areas, the volume does offer traditional concepts that are well presented, often from an angle that is innovative and stimulating, even if we do not happen to agree with it. Topics are broken down into concrete subheadings—for example, under "Resistance" we find "The Patient is Silent," "The Patient is Bored," "The Posture of the Patient," etc.

Interpretations are preceded by confrontations and clarifications and followed by working through, which is defined as the activity of the ego that is interposed between insight and its effects. Reconstruction, however—and here we find the concretistic style more confusing than clarifying—is strung out, as indicated by eleven separate page references to it in the index (that invaluable guide to so much of the organization of a book and the author's mind).

We are nevertheless pleased when the passion for detail leads to a distinction between the analytic setting as the arrangements and rules which enclose the actual two-person interchanges (undervalued in one of our books by being called "the machinery") and the "analytic situation" in the sense that Freud (1940, p. 173) gave it as the "pact" between the participants that is consummated by the observation of the fundamental rule. The setting, which Green (1975) aptly called the "silent mute base" of the proceedings, is another compelling participant in the proceedings, and limits, controls, and determines the progress of the events that unfold within it.

Particularly abundant clinical illustrations are provided throughout. It is worth noting their impact on Waldhorn (1969), a none too friendly critic:

> Greenson offers an impressive array of detailed observations ... in a series of concise clinical vignettes, evidencing a consistent style of approach and intervention. In addition, a clear demonstration of the productive value of the confrontations and interpretations made in each clinical situation is regularly provided. No analyst will fail to be reminded of his own struggles with the counterparts of these various analytic crises in his own practice, and none will fail to envy Greenson his virtuoso perceptiveness and his brand of dramatic articulateness in dealing with each episode ... this rapid-fire sequence of brightly presented data will certainly stimulate a

sharpening of clinical vision and imagination [pp. 479-480].

As Greenson might say, "with such critics, who needs friends?" To which we may add that it is evident that his opinions have been tested in action and, whether or not they are "classical," a different slant can be most instructive.

It is not that either of the particular contributions of Greenson—and they *are* particular contributions—the "real relationship" between the patient and the analyst or the "working alliance," are entirely new to psychoanalysis. Greenson himself lists Freud's "effective transference" (1913) the "ego alliance" of Sterba (1934) (and why not the "analytic pact" of Freud, 1940?), and many more predecessors, to which can be added many since then, including the "treatment alliance" of Sandler et al. which we shall consider. All are part of the awareness of the analyst's need to ensconce himself in the position of the ego, with its boundaries turned inward (as required by traditional id-psychology endeavors to make the unconscious conscious) as well as outward through structural, genetic (maturational), and adaptive functions that mediate the interplay of the inner and outer worlds. It is in this wider perspective that object relations, condensing about the figure of the analyst, invite consideration of the latter's realistic as well as transference significance, as they enter into the need to accept his assistance (the working alliance) as well as to resist it (the transference neurosis).

Re-evaluation of the neutral and "mirror" concepts in terms of the two-front position of the analyst also has been furthered by child analysis and by the widened boundaries of treatment beyond the neuroses. There is no need to recapitulate these well-known trends and the conflicts, far from settled, to which they give rise. They help to explain, however, the quick receptivity with which Greenson's terms were met. The problems for many analysts lie more in his definitions and the technical consequences he draws than in the terms themselves.

Transference, according to Greenson and Wexler (1970), has a "very precise meaning" (p. 143), a conclusion to which one is not likely to come from the other volumes under consideration, or from the discussions of many other analysts either. This meaning, which was derived from Freud's 1912 paper on the subject, holds that it is "the experiencing of impulses, feelings, fantasies, attitudes, and defences with respect to a person in the present which do not appropriately fit that person but are a repetition of responses originating in regard to significant persons of early childhood, unconsciously displaced on to persons in the present" (Greenson and Wexler, 1969, p. 28). The inappropriateness and distortion of reality are especially underlined as points of departure for distinguishing a "reality relationship" which is "less rigid," "less distorted," more readily modifiable by internal and external reality.

Greenson and Wexler make these distinctions, scarcely "precise" either in clinical or metapsychological frameworks, criteria for contrasting them with "non-transference" and "real" relationships of the patient to the analyst, which are scarcely less ambiguous. To compound the perplexity, they concede that "all transference has real elements; all real object relations have transference components" (Greenson and Wexler, 1970, p. 144). Moreover, "real," as they define it can be used interchangeably or in combination to apply to the "realistic" (with external criteria) and the "genuine" (with inner criteria).

The "working alliance" is introduced into this shadowy realm of concepts as the real object relationship between the patient and his psychoanalyst, "the non-neurotic, rational, reasonable rapport which . . . enables him to work purposefully in the analytic situation despite his transference distortions" (1970, p. 144). (There is no discussion of Freud's descriptions of patients who, in the phase of positive transference, *seem* to be working purposefully only to swing in exactly the opposite direction when a vein of negative transference is hit.) In a statement that makes us wonder whether or not he is referring to psychoanalytic treatment, Greenson goes on to remark that it is only "when the analyst has perceived the patient as a whole human being and does not focus only on his neurosis, *and* has permitted himself to be perceived as a human being, not just an interpreting apparatus—only then do we have a living ongoing analysis" (1970, p. 144). The technical recommendation at this point is to "oscillate" between the "unwavering pursuit of insight" and suspension of this unwavering pursuit sufficiently long to show concern and compassion, perhaps by the tone of one's voice.

When we reach the section dealing with Brenner's work, we will find some direct and some indirect commentaries on this program. Perhaps it is more a matter of style and individuality than of substance, but in contrast to Greenson's thesis that the human element has to be added to "mechanistic" interpretations to make them effective, we have Greenacre's (1975) statement, which seems to have almost direct bearing on this conception: "Listening to his patient in an attentive and receptive attitude, the sensitive analyst has gradually familiarized himself with an increasing amount of the patient's life. He has lived with the patient, as it were. . . . Such an understanding is dependent on the interaction of the analyst's preconscious fusion of his own experiences with those of the analysand" (pp. 704-705). By means of this joint work throughout the analysis, a "new dimension to life has been added " (p. 701). (Further commentaries on this subject will be touched upon later in the review.)

Greenson himself draws on his own experiences, both through self-analysis and clinical work, to suggest that his more neutral colleagues have a need for isolation and concealment behind the couch that attests to their human limitations. Sometimes, no doubt. However, the opposite behavior may not necessarily indicate a freedom from limitations. It is nonetheless not to be questioned that the voice he raises against the use of neutrality for the pursuance of unnecessary aloofness and for distinctions between transference and countertransference as compared to realistic aspects of the patient-physician relationship during analytic treatment has found warm support and created stimulating debates.

In this connection, it may be noted that Greenson has at times used the term "working alliance" as interchangeable with Zetzel's "therapeutic alliance." She herself has correctly pointed to the differences: her own, directed primarily to the infantile element within the patient, encourages, regression, while Greenson, demanding respect for the mature aspect of the analysand's personality, counteracts regression (Greenson and Wexler, 1969). A more intermediate ground is to be recognized in Greenson's concern and compassion for the patient. This does not seem to us to draw upon a parental model as much as on a friendly one among equals (Kanzer, 1975)—a relationship that is assuredly not out of place in the totality of an analysis. Links between the two levels of sympathy seem to be provided by Fleming (1975) who sees in the working alliance a replica of a symbiotic relationship between mother and child. After all, there is a businesslike contract between these partners too!

According to Greenson, the analyst must help the patient's beleaguered ego distinguish between what is appropriate and distorted, correct and false, realistic and fantastic, in regard to his reactions to people, above all toward his psychoanalyst. If the analyst were to ignore a patient's realistic critical responses and treat them "merely" as free associations or as clinical data only to be analyzed, it might indicate to the patient either that the analyst was too upset to deal with his remarks forthrightly and humanly, or that his observations and judgments were "only" clinical material, that they had no intrinsic value, and hardly merited a response. Finally, he might think that his perceptions and judgments were faulty, sick or "only transference distortions" (Greenson and Wexler, 1970, p. 144).

Ultimately, Greenson, in his "respect" and "compassion" for the patient, which he sees as in conflict with the therapeutic techniques of the analyst, offers a new postulate: "To facilitate the full flowering and ultimate resolution of the patient's transference reactions, it is essential *in all* cases to recognize, acknowledge, clarify, differentiate and *even* nurture the nontransference or relatively transference-free reactions between patient and analyst. The technique of 'only analyzing' or 'only interpreting' transference phenomena may stifle the development and clarification of the transference neurosis and act as an obstacle to the actualization of the transference-free or 'real' reactions of the patient" (Greenson and Wexler, 1970, 143).

To this, Paula Heimann, as moderator of a plenary session, responded: "The authors' new contribution to psychoanalysis is stated boldly as a paradox: in order to facilitate the development, blossoming and resolution of the transference neurosis, the analyst must facilitate the development of a relationship which is 'real' and not based on transference. . . . In contrast to the transference neurosis, the 'real' non-transference relationship is not to be subjected to analysis . . . not to be interpreted away. It is to be encouraged and maintained. Taken literally, analysis then depends on and presupposes *not* analysing certain sectors of the patient-analyst relationship" (1970, p. 145). She added, "It is only the analytic relationship which is governed by the unique phenomenon of the fundamental rule" (p. 146). Greenson, answering a question as to what he meant by "caring" for a patient, declared that "to me, involvement means caring. . . . I think it is a matter of whether your heart as well as your mind is in what you are doing" (Greenson and Wexler, 1970, p. 150).

In the concluding chapter of his textbook, Greenson has an excellent assessment of "What psychoanalysis requires of the analyst." He clearly draws on his own experience and self-analysis. How could it be otherwise? New outlooks, for good or bad, have been associated with self-analysis from the very beginning. In reflecting on the circumstances that render it an "impossible profession," he raises the questions: "What motivations might impel a man to seek a career in a field where one of his major tasks is to comport himself as a relatively nonresponsive blank screen to the patient so that the patient can project and displace onto that screen the unresolved and warded-off imagos of the past?" (p. 399). The answer seems to stress the pathology of the analyst—a proclivity for isolation, a marked degree of stage fright when forced out from his hidden position behind the couch, a latent desire to bring pain to the patient in a passive aggressive manner. No doubt there is some truth in these observations, but the ability to be a good analyst is not necessarily a stigma of mental illness, nor is impatience with the technique of analysis necessarily a sign of greater health.

As David Beres puts it in his introduction to Charles Brenner's book *Psychoanalytic Technique and Psychic Conflict*, this is not a collection of rules and precepts. It approaches the problem of technique in terms of basic principles of methodology, the attitude of the analyst, and the relationship of theory and practice. The analyst must keep in mind the analytic task as a whole and seek to understand as fully as possible the nature and origin of each patient's conflicts.

Brenner expounds new approaches to technique based on the structural model of psychoanalysis and in the light of his own contributions to theories of affects and dreams. Beres feels that many ideas long taken for granted by analysts "require restatement, reappraisal, and the exercise of critical judgment that is based on a fresh view of the relevant critical data" (p. vi). Beres's promise of a lucid style and ample clinical data is duly fulfilled.

Brenner himself describes the volume as a collection of essays, "not an attempt to teach the practice of psychoanalysis in a thorough or systematic way." It is, rather, "a very personal contribution" that sticks to the subject of technique and omits what he believes to be "common knowledge." He further expresses doubts about the value of works on technique, insofar as their appeal is ultimately to the reader's own experience. These guidelines are, of course, quite differently conceived than a textbook, and in many respects complement Greenson's more general work. However, they do free the author to put forward his own ideas without the constant references to Freud and other authorities that we find in the other volumes under review here.

We must acknowledge, nevertheless, a certain uneasiness wandering about through such relatively uncharted fields, not entirely unfamiliar of course, but with too little help from those old stand-bys—reference lists, footnotes, appendices, and index. Good mental exercise, of course, and conducive to independent thinking (if it must be), but as we get our bearings, it seems to us that many of our usual conceptual landmarks are missing too. Hartmann, for example: the synthetic and organizing functions of the ego, the conflict-free areas, autonomy, the self-preservative and adaptive functions of the ego, etc.

External reality proved difficult to find, though we knew it must be around somewhere. The pleasure-unpleasure principles were prominent, but seemed unaccompanied by that harsh nursemaid *Ananke*, the reality principle. Neither the primary process nor the secondary process proved necessary companions on the journey. The maturational framework was also dispensable—early object relations and the preoedipal period, for example—while infantile neuroses were frequently invoked without recourse to Hartmann's admonitions against genetic fallacies.

There is no place for the concept of the self, or modern notions about narcissism, identity, the life cycle, which doubtless explains the absence of reference to authors in these fields. Moreover, as indications of the presence of a personal philosophy grew stronger and stronger, we came to suspect that the alleged intention of sticking to the subject of technique was filled with guile; even a new metapsychology was discreetly in evidence. When we found ourselves conjuring up the spirit of the author at times along the way and questioning and even arguing with him, we do not believe that this indicates our narcissism or even our contentiousness. It is, we feel, the intention of the author to provoke just such fireside debates between himself and his readers, and, if so, why not be properly stirred up as expected?

We report all this in a preliminary way, not in any sense critically but rather to help others get their orientation at an earlier stage than we did ourselves. We still are not altogether certain—after all, the negative may be difficult to locate—that there were presuppositions that should not have been taken for granted as far as we were concerned ("common knowledge," etc.), and who knows at what intervals our evenly-suspended attention may have failed to focus on this or that subtle point? We shall therefore borrow a leaf from the author and claim only that this is a highly personal review. For the rest, we recommend the book to the reader as a truly instructive, enjoyable, and sometimes perplexing excursion through vistas of current problems in psychoanalysis.

Brenner's basic positive tools are the following:

1. Analytic procedure is inevitably linked to analytic theory: "an application of psychoanalytic theories of mental functioning and development to the practical problem of attempting in a special way to alter that functioning in an individual case" (p. 2). The focus will be on "the part of the structural theory that has to do with psychic conflict."

2. Structural conflicts find the id ("the instinctual driving part of the mind") and the superego ("the moral part") schematically pitted against the ego ("the part that has to do with the outer world"). External reality is, of course, not a structure, and its conflicts with the ego, or total personality, are not mentioned even when dealing with psychotic symptoms, which are not to be analyzed differently from neurotic symptoms even when suicidal thoughts are present (pp. 12-13).

3. The "principle of multiple function" (Waelder 1930) provides the most fundamental model of conflict used in the book, accounting for compromise formations among the structures, which are "to some degree influenced by external reality" (p. 4). The final result brings together (id) wish, anxiety and guilt (the instigators of conflict), and defense in every case. While the relative importance of these components varies (we never really learn how or why), it becomes a major tenet that the analyst should scrutinize his material so as to include them all—never just one or two components of the conflict alone. This approach to conflict, the "proper analytic attitude," becomes the distinguishing element in Brenner's formulations, comparable to the "principle of optimal tension" for Menninger and the "working alliance" for Greenson.

A clash with Greenson's viewpoint quickly arises as Brenner decries the ready invocation of "normal" or "realistic behavior" to gloss over the actual complexities of the patient's conflicts. A full appraisal will neither "ignore reality" nor brand a reaction as neurotic (p. 26). (We cannot confirm a historical note that Freud abandoned distinctions between neurotic and realistic anxiety after 1926 (cf. Freud, 1933, pp. 62, 78, 81-82, 84-87, 93-95). Whether a hobby, a neurosis, a psychotic symptom, or a suicidal threat, each should receive "the consistent application of an understanding of psychic conflict" (p. 29).

This concept, called "a proper analytic attitude," is

quickly applied to examining the advocacy of other than neutral attitudes toward the patient. "For example, Fenichel (1941, p.74) was convinced of the value of behaving 'naturally' with one's patients, and recommended that the 'patient should always be able to rely upon the "human-ness"' of his analyst. True enough, but only within the limitations imposed by the analytic situation. Behaving naturally *as an analyst* is often a very different matter from behaving naturally as a friend, an adviser, a parent, or even as a good doctor" (p. 29).

Turning directly to Greenson, he argues that "even a 'simple practical' question about his analyst's schedule" calls not merely for a straightforward answer, but one that shows awareness of the subtleties that may lie behind the question, and should be brought into the open. "It is not possible, for example, to say to a patient, 'Let's put analysis aside for a moment. . .' and proceed to advise him about some practical matter in his life" (showing nonanalytic concern about the totality of his problems?). "Any such behavior must necessarily influence the transference" (p. 31) (and, for that matter, the "real relationship" and the working alliance, we would add, if the advice turns out poorly—or even if it turns out well. Is not the analyst's inherent sphere of competent "realistic" advice the demonstration of the unconscious components that enter into the patient's judgment?).

A chapter on "Conjecture and Interpretation" permits an important distinction to be made between the hypothesis-making of the analyst (which largely includes reconstruc-tions) and their submission to the patient in the form of interpretations. Brenner declares that the conjectural process has received little attention in the literature, and surveys the various mental processes by which they are arrived at—"Intuition, conscious reflection, unconscious motivated affec-tive reactions or fantasies"—and sees them all as potentially correct and useful, probably related to the analyst's own psychic conflicts and an aspect of the analyst's "professional style" (pp. 38-39). (A certain one-sidedness in the course of the analysis may nevertheless develop, we think!)

An interesting debate (in absentia) with Heinz Kohut (1959) on the matter of the empathic route to conjecture contributes to data with respect to Brenner's own approach to external reality, which has continued to puzzle us. Kohut "proposed to distinguish analysis from other natural sciences on the basis that in analysis introspection plays both an essential and a limiting role, something that is not true, he maintained, in other sciences. In fact, however, *empathy or introspection plays the same role in every science*" (italics ours).

Granted Brenner's contention that animistic thought precedes scientific thought in the natural sciences and has to be depersonalized, or even a concession that creative thinking by natural scientists draws on empathy and introspection (Kanzer, 1955); can it be said that the discovery of a new planet uses quite the same admixture of introspective and objective processes as the elucidation of a forgotten memory in a patient? Let us turn to the converse consideration Brenner raises, that empathy can lead the analyst astray in judging his patient, since the latter will display individual differences. "All analysts agree that it is himself that each patient must learn to know, not what he has in common with the rest of mankind" (p. 41). (One vote was not counted. Do not patient and analyst alike have to know both, and are not introspection and empathy more essential and limiting factors in determining these data also, compared, for example, to determining and validating the existence of a new planet?)

Among the means of confirming a conjecture, Brenner makes a particularly interesting study of its predictive aspects, which he apparently uses to a considerable extent in his own work. In a case that could be compared with Freud's "homosexual woman" for the advances in psychoanalysis since 1920 (Freud, 1920a), the patient "paused frequently, obviously waiting for her analyst to speak. The latter finally did intervene to say that she was trying to get him to order her to give up her girlfriend so that she could rebel, as she had so often tried to get her parents to take a position she could use as an excuse for rebelling against them" (p. 66). Having correctly predicted what the patient anticipated he would say, there was nothing else for her to do but go ahead with what she really wished to do—give up the girlfriend of her own volition—which in fact she proceeded to do (p. 65).

This vignette seems to us of further interest in that the crucial change came with a single interpretation, an intervention which Brenner (and also Sandler) tends to downgrade. Granted that the single interpretation achieved its effect only in a context of gradual insights that the girl was acquiring, the circumstances followed a classical model that is little cited in the group under review. The interpretation was offered at the moment of resistance to further association, with the patient pausing frequently, and the analyst then verbalizing for her what she was withholding. The result was a drastic change in the patient's balance between homosexuality and heterosexuality—a critical interplay between patient and analyst at this point, producing results well worth noting. It belongs, of course, to the general category of the "mutative interpretation" (Strachey, 1934).

This leads to another of our "puzzled" reactions. Brenner raises the pertinent question of "what it is that one hopes to accomplish by interpretation," and the main point seems to be "to increase the patient's knowledge of himself" (p. 49). This seems to be a remarkably intellectual reason, even though coupled with the observation that the chief *apparent* effect is likely to be emotional. Are these unrelated reactions, or has it not long since been clarified that acting out in the analytic situation *is* the way in which the past returns so recognizably that the analyst, with his interpretation, takes a part in permitting the patient to relive it differently (Freud, 1914, 1940)? This precisely fits the circumstances described with the homosexual girl—she expected the analyst to forbid her homosexuality, just as her parents had, and his refusal to play that role made her not only understand her motives better but—as one may surmise from the subsequent course—opened the way to her giving up her rage and proceeding to bring her positive feelings for the analyst to the surface. Would not this demand that she give up her homosexuality really convey the notion that he wanted her for himself? Her own choice was a confession that she wanted him (as we construe it).

We find similar problems arising in a valuable chapter on transference. More than insight is apparently required here: Brenner speaks of "managing" the transference. The "analytic attitude" is the key to the management. Coupled with this is the dictum that "*all* the problems that concern transference can be resolved into the single question of analyzability of transference wishes and fantasies" (p. 110). We do have to differ a bit from some of the historical retrospects that Brenner offers here, apparently to emphasize that earlier opinions of Freud are out of date. We do not think so, and will simply record our own differing impression:

1. Freud is said to have believed in *earlier* days (emphasis ours) that the analyst must use "positive transference as a lever to overcome (the patient's) resistance to accepting the analyst's reconstruction of the origin of the patient's infantile conflicts" (p. 110). We think the analyst did this himself with the homosexual girl, whose erotic positive transference is cited, though Brenner does not mention this factor in reporting the great changes that certainly followed. Nor did Freud's reliance on positive transference ever change (1940).

2. Other early formulations about transference that "are still, *on occasion* (emphasis ours), discussed and re-evaluated [include] the concept of transference neurosis" and the benign positive transference (p. 110). (To many, it is axiomatic that analysis involves the induction and resolution of the transference neurosis.)

Brenner stresses transference as a major factor in all

adult relationships and sees no difference between such phenomena outside of and in the transference setting. "It is the analytic attitude" that makes the difference (p. 112). (What of the regression and other circumstances in the analytic setting?) He takes issue with the precept that transference should be interpreted only when it has become a resistance and recommends interpretation if the transference is urgent at the beginning. Experiences of the patient gained through transference interpretation are convincing not only to himself but to the analyst as well.

The setting up of "alliances" in distinction from "transferences" expectably finds objection, although we do not get the impression that Brenner always does justice to the teachings about these matters. The working alliance, for example, is not a "consequence of transference resistance" (p. 119), but represents a divergent trend which ultimately depends on the real need for treatment. In the case of Freud's analytic pact, or, for that matter, wherever the fundamental rule is invoked (as by Brenner, of course), the alliance opposes resistances from the beginning (Kanzer, 1972). It is not clear on what he himself relies to gain the patient's cooperation. He defines as a "good analytic patient" one who complies with the rules, while failure to do so is a "symptom" (p. 121).

As we understand this, the "good patient" cooperates "as a matter of course, since he believes it to be in his own best interest to do it" (p. 120), and will give up his symptomatic deviation from the "ideal" when given an opportunity to bring an analytic attitude to bear upon it. (Sandler's discussion of the analysand's motivation will be pertinent here.) One question that arises in our own mind comes up in connection with a comparison between Brenner's "good patient" and the "fiction of a normal ego" postulated by Freud (1937, p. 239) as disposed to obey the fundamental rule. Since neither really needs analysis, it is to be assumed that their reasonable and amiable states will be reached only after the work of treatment is over, not at the beginning.

The contention that transferences within and outside the analytic setting are "the same" (related presumably to other equations we have noted) is carried over into several valuable clinical observations and a debatable formulation about "acting out." "A patient's report of his actions outside the analytic hour and his associations to them are an important source of information about the transference as well as an important confirmation of conjectures concerning it in every analysis" (p. 122). Actions are brought into the same mental field as dreams, fantasies, etc. for submission to the fundamental rule and psychic appraisal. Brenner is certainly correct in regarding much acting out as an indication of delay in interpreting the transference—i.e., calling for analysis rather than injudicious applications of the "principle of abstinence," taboos which may resemble the punitive and futile efforts of parents to control children whose problems they themselves create.

On the other hand, one can have difficulty with another of Brenner's "all the same" predilections—that since transferences are commonplace and so is acting out, there is no point giving a special categorization to such behavior by a patient in treatment. While transferences and acting out are indeed common to all people, reality-testing controls are less so for patients under treatment whose infantile neuroses are being stirred up and (a) either have not been lured into the safety of the analytic setting or (b) even assume greater "reality," thereby coming to life intensely in contacts with the analyst. It was precisely for this reason that Freud himself (1914) enjoined controls through the principle of abstinence to protect the patient, his associates, and the analysis.

A chapter on defense analysis brings out the view that there are defensive uses of the ego's functions but no special defense mechanisms. During analysis, it is the compromise formation that changes but not the defenses, which are never abolished. The changes in the compromise formations are "in the direction of mental health"—but we receive all too few geographic descriptions of the direction, except that it is so closely situated in the vicinity of the pathological "as to form what is essentially a coherent whole" (p. 194).

"Superego analysis" is taken up almost exclusively from the standpoints of punishment and remorse, and brings the author to widen the concept of conflict so that it may be instigated not only by anxiety but by any sufficiently intense unpleasure, such as depressive affects. The role of calamity in this respect is emphasized and used to modify traditional ideas about "penis envy" (p. 105). These chapters permit Brenner to take issue with such dicta as: defense should be analyzed before content, surface before depth (see also Brenner, 1969).

In the section on the analysis of dreams, he·declares that the reported content of a dream should not be taken at face value; (what, then, prompted the concept of secondary revision?). He has many illuminating things to say about the communicative function of the dream and the significance of forgetting dreams, including one or two fairly radical aphorisms: "Every dream a patient remembers during analysis is a communication to his analyst"; "every forgotten dream has as part of its latent content a wish not to tell something" (p. 143), etc. We can only agree that when we are sufficiently acquainted with a patient, we do not always need his associations to make an interpretation. In general, Brenner considers that there is no longer as great a need to place emphasis on dreams as in earlier days and that symptoms, fantasies, metaphors, jokes, etc., deserve equal or more attention.

We reach ultimate basic problems with the last chapter on the "Goals of Analysis." As specific an aim as the author can suggest is to continue until a patient's conflicts have been sufficiently altered as to promise maximum beneficial results. To the discouraged, he offers his own experience:

that the outcome of "a successful analysis can . . . be of immense practical importance in a patient's life. It can make the difference between crippling inhibition and successful functioning; between misery and happiness, or between life and death. . . . To realize its limitations is not to say that what it can do is of little value. On the contrary, it is of such great value that if there is a good chance of achieving it, it is well worth all the time, the effort, and the expense that analysis entails" (p. 175).

Beyond encouragement to the patient, there is also in these comments encouragement to his ally, the analyst, and with it, as we suggested, outlines of a metapsychology that apparently lies behind the puzzling outlooks we sometimes come upon in the course of our carefully adventurous Odyssey. This is the "holistic approach . . . based . . . on that part of psychoanalytic theory that concerns the relation between psychic conflict and conscious thought and behavior" and which "is valuable as part of the analyst's orientation to people in general and to patients in particular. . . . It is part of one's knowledge of how people are" (p. 197).

It is the holistic approach, one gathers, that is better served by compromise formations reflecting an equilibrium between all the forces in the personality than it is by an isolated concentration upon the ego. Undoubtedly, too, a continuum between inner and outer reality is more accurately descriptive of mental functioning than sharp boundaries between the "realities" of the outer and the inner world. In the course of pursuing this line of thought, Brenner comes upon that realization, so inherent to psychoanalytic practice, that, in the adult, "the child he once was still lives on within him"; and that "One often sees the child in action with special clarity in the transference. . ." (p. 197). "The adage that the child lives on in the man, or adult, can be useful as a guideline to the best solution of many technical problems in psychoanalysis" (p. 201). We feel we have been through this before with Menninger and Holzman, with Greenson, and with Freud, each in his own way.

In the Freudian tradition, too, is the acknowledgment that analysis itself may require supplementary methods or even replacement in the future—but that for Brenner himself, it has been a lifetime choice that he does not regret. It is here that we go beyond science to aspects of personal philosophy and perhaps even religion. Without such elements of "blind faith" in the practitioner, could he share and justify the "blind faith" of the patient that both have in common with the rest of mankind?

The Patient and the Analyst; the Basis of the Psychoanalytic Process by Joseph Sandler, Christopher Dare, and Alex Holder is in essence an elaborate glossary of clinical concepts and arose from the endeavors of the authors (hereafter "Sandler") to convey these "to intelligent postgraduate students of psychiatry, a difficulty which we had realized was due, in no small part, to a lack of clarity in the concepts themselves" (p. 7). We may now turn to it with profit, in view of the conflicting terms and concepts used by our previous authors.

The authors and other collaborators had put out a long series of preliminary studies attempting to remedy this state of affairs. Actually, these activities began with the establishment of an Index project at the Hampstead Child-Therapy Clinic in order to make the case material more available to research workers there (Sandler, 1960). Thus two aims—to clarify clinical concepts for analysts and to clarify them for workers in related fields—are attempted here.

As an example, in a widening circle of meanings, the concept of resistance arose in relation to difficulties in maintaining the stream of free associations, but came to include all forms of defense against the analytic process. Moreover, as Sandler brings out, "resistances" are familiar in their own fields to other workers as well, and there is benefit for all in comparative surveys with respect to this and other significant analytic concepts. The fact is, however, that in this book it is the first of these aims that has remained in the foreground while the second has been observed in a rather obligatory manner.

The study consists of an introduction and ten chapters that range in traditional fashion from "The Clinical Situation" and "The Treatment Alliance" (the overriding interest in this book), to "Interpretations, Other Interventions and Insight" and "Working Through." Concepts are thus presented in organized fashion, with an emphasis on placing them in an evolutionary context as well as in the light of the author's own commentaries.

For this purpose, the history of psychoanalysis is divided into four periods:

1. The *first phase*, until 1897, was dominated by the cathartic method devised by Breuer and Freud. It came to an end when Freud discovered that the "traumatic memories" of his patients, especially with respect to seduction, were largely fantasies. (His self-analysis played a major part in this reorientation.)

2. The *second phase* (1897-1923), brought the unconscious, and especially infantile sex wishes, into prominence. The notions of conflict between instincts and defenses, with compromise formations, repetitive and indirect expressions of these conflicts in efforts to obtain disguised satisfactions, and the therapeutic approach through interpretations followed. Experiences with "making the unconscious conscious" furthered a topographic concept of the mental apparatus as well as the development of the libido theory. The method of free association provided manifestations of these conflicts, to which the Oedipus complex provided the key. "Most of the clinical concepts which we consider in detail in this book, as we shall see, had their original elaborations in the second phase" (p. 15). Sandler underlines that instinctual drives should not be seen in isolation, that, from the beginning, they were attached to objects in the child's world.

3. The *third phase,* from the introduction of the structural model of the mental apparatus in 1923, until the death of Freud in 1939, marked the ascendance of ego psychology and assessments of ego functions in relation to the id (with its instinctual derivatives and unconscious activities dominated by the pleasure principle and the primary process) and to the superego (precipitate of the child's early conflicts and identifications with authority figures, who are represented in his conscience). The ego itself is self-preservative, seat of the secondary process, adapts to reality and is the problem-solver which creates the compromise formations that are essentially left unexplained in Brenner's model.

4. The *fourth phase* began with the death of Freud in 1939 and continues until the present. Actually, the last years of Freud's life saw a new epoch of ego psychology beginning with the works of Anna Freud (1936) and Heinz Hartmann (1939). The admixture of these latter phases is common in analysts' descriptions and metapsychological appraisals of their patients at the present time, "although heroic efforts have been made by certain psychoanalysts (e.g., Arlow and Brenner, 1964) to write current psychoanalytic theory entirely in terms of the concepts of the structural theory" (p. 20).

The chapter on "The Clinical Situation" which opens the survey of technical concepts, describes the "basic model of psychoanalysis" (Eissler, 1953). Much like Greenson and unlike Brenner, Sandler sees the transference as developing through distortion of the "real" characteristics of the analyst. He also agrees with Greenson in a general distinction between transference and a working alliance, but fashions his own "treatment alliance," which will occupy the same key position in the therapeutic scheme of forces. "Acting out" is defined in conformity with Freud's delineation as emergent transferences expressed in motor behavior displaced from the analytic setting.

Sandler proceeds, as has become increasingly common,

from a consideration of what psychoanalysis demands of the patient to a comparable consideration of what it demands of the analyst, his partner in the analytic setting. This includes the "self-scanning" of the countertransference. The analyst's interpretations are directed to providing insight—viz., "an understanding of links between his conscious and unconscious tendencies, and between the present and the past" (p. 24). Working through takes place between insight and effective change.

The general framework of the analytic situation is conducive to regression. In accordance with the over-all purposes of the book, Sandler refers to the many senses in which the term has been used and defines it as "the emergence of past, often infantile, trends where such trends are thought to represent the reappearance of modes of functioning which had been abandoned or modified" (p. 25). As he points out, this form of behavior may be observed outside the analytic situation and can be regarded, up to a point, as normal.

Regression both favors the analytic process by permitting the emergence of transferences and hinders it by weakening the capacity for self-observation required for the treatment alliance. Controlled regression may be regarded as in the service of progression. "It appears to be likely that different psychoanalysts vary in the degree to which they (consciously or unconsciously) encourage regressive trends in their patients" (p. 26).

Chapter 3, on "The Treatment Alliance," is the focal point for the object-relations orientation that is not too conspicuously present here but is more deliberately brought forward in Sandler's later work (Sandler and Sandler, 1978). After citing the well-known predecessors of the alliance concept, he proceeds to define his own concept. He rightly refers to Freud's writings that imply a two-person orientation in this area, but in reporting that "it was never designated by Freud as a distinctive concept" (p. 28), he overlooks the all-too-neglected "analytic pact" of 1940 (p. 173). To a certain extent, Sandler is correct in associating the alliance implications in Freud with the transference, though in fact the latter reported as far back as the "Studies on Hysteria" (Breuer and Freud, 1893-1895) that "we make the patient into a collaborator" (p. 282). Here, Freud was already evincing the deep respect for the patient's individuality and initiative that was implanted in his own personality and therapy (Kanzer, 1975). Moreover, the reliance on the patient's cooperation has been incorporated into the fundamental rule, which is the basis of the "analytic pact."

Richard Sterba (1934) did more than "imply," as Sandler (p. 29) says, the existence of an alliance. He spoke directly of an "ego alliance" and implemented the term by underlining its significance through use of the word "we" in inviting the patient to participate with him in the observing function—a course which would have to be regarded today as suggestive. (Similar implications adhere to the "analytic atmosphere" of Fenichel (1941) and Bibring (1954), which Sandler does not include in the precursors of the "treatment alliance").

In devising his own preferred concept of an alliance, he uses a broad canvas "based on the patient's conscious or unconscious wish to co-operate, and his readiness to accept the therapist's aid in overcoming internal difficulties. This is not the same as attending treatment simply on the basis of getting pleasure or some other form of gratification. In the treatment alliance there is an *acceptance* of the need to deal with internal problems, and to do analytic work in the face of internal or (particularly with children) external (e.g. family) resistance" (p. 30).

Sandler sees the treatment alliance as drawing on Erikson's "basic trust" (1950), e.g., on experiences with security in the earliest months of life, and explicitly cautions against reliance on the "wish for recovery" as a basis for judging the potential support of a patient. He regards many of the elements invoked in the alliances described by other authors as incorporated into his own.

He approaches Greenson in suggesting that analyzability is bound up with the capacity to form a treatment alliance, though adequate tests for this purpose are admittedly not more reliable as yet than use of a "trial period" (which, for many analysts, has fallen out of favor). The concept of a "capacity for treatment alliance" can also be extended outside the analytic setting, as in work with psychoses or in psychiatric and physical rehabilitation units.

Chapter 4 deals with that touchstone of analytic thinking and treatment, the transference. Sandler comments on "a strong tendency, within psychoanalysis, towards a widening of the transference concept" (p. 43). Among the influences in this direction have been the increasing recognition of its significance in the therapeutic process and the elaboration of the "transference neurosis" (Freud, 1914). Strachey's teachings about transference interpretations as "mutative" have also been influential, as were Kleinian tendencies to see references to early infantile relationships in all communications from the patient. On the other hand, Sandler thinks that Glover (1955), with his more classical leanings, has probably given us the most unrestricted definition: "an adequate conception of transference must reflect the *totality* of the individual's development . . . he displaces on to the analyst not merely affects and ideas but *all* he has ever learnt or forgotten throughout his mental development" (p. 43).

Sandler believes that Greenson finds in the transference "more than Freud had originally intended" (while Heimann [1970, p. 146] thought he found less). Greenson's characterization of the transference as repetitive would include normal traits of a personality, which is "quite different from a conception of the transference as the development, during the process of the psychoanalytic work, of feelings which were not apparent at the beginning of the treatment, but which emerged as a consequence of the conditions of treatment" (p. 44).

We seem to find ourselves once again in the midst of the usual impreciseness of definitions of transference, with Sandler, like Menninger and Holzman, having in mind the regressive background for the intensification of transference, Greenson failing to discriminate between normal and abnormal repetitions of infantile attitudes, and Brenner, as we recall, allying himself with Freud in stressing the ubiquity of transferences in everyday life. It seems to us that clearer distinctions between transference and transference neurosis would be helpful here. Waelder (1956) and Loewenstein (1969), mindful of all these divergences, wished to restrict the term transference to the analytic setting. This, Sandler regards as "unnecessary" (to say nothing of having to find new terms for transference outside the analytic setting).

We do have to take issue with what seems to us a misconception about Freud (p. 42), who said unmistakably enough (1940) that the patient delegates to the analyst powers of his superego that ultimately regress to those of the original parents, thus clarifying their influence on his childhood development. Sandler adds that of course the analyst refuses to accept this role—presumably a comment related to the fact that he is discussing, in the same paragraph, Alexander's ideas about role-playing. Whether we call it playing a role or not, there seems no other way of reading Freud's statement that the analyst as "[t]he new super-ego now has an opportunity for a sort of *after-education* of the neurotic; it can correct mistakes for which his parents were responsible in educating him. . . . In all his attempts at improving and educating the patient the analyst should respect his individuality" (1940, p. 175). We would be content to assume that Freud is speaking somewhat metaphorically of the uses of interpretation in filling in the gaps in the patient's knowledge of himself were it not for his addendum that "The amount of influence which he may legitimately allow himself will be determined by the amount of developmental inhibition present in the patient. Some neurotics have remained so infantile that in analysis too they can only be treated as children" (p. 175). Certainly there is a developmental, not merely conflictual, orientation reflected here.

Sandler, after surveying the wide range of meanings that transference has come to assume for different analysts, recommends that one should abandon the attempt to see in it a unidimensional phenomenon or a clear-cut distinction from nontransference. He suggests rather, that from the standpoint of a general psychology, transference is "a special clinical manifestation of the many different components of normal relationships." It "can be regarded as *a specific illusion* which develops in regard to the other person, one which, unbeknown to the subject, represents, in some of its features, a repetition of a relationship towards an important figure in the person's past" (p. 47).

Sandler also finds that, in addition to the illusory element, the transference may include unconscious and subtle attempts to manipulate or provoke situations which are a concealed repetition of earlier experiences (such as in the case that Brenner reported—an element, of course, that also enters into the "fate neuroses" described by Freud [1920b]). Sandler devotes a chapter to "Special Forms of Transference," including erotized types, transference psychoses, and delusional transferences. He concludes that, while repetition of the past appears to be common to all, "the form in which the past is reproduced may show substantial variation" (p. 58). In neurotic transferences, a degree of distancing from the illusion is possible; in erotized and psychotic forms, the "as if" quality recedes and the analyst is indeed the parent, not "like" him (p. 59). All these variants may be found in relationships outside the analytic setting.

Countertransference has also been a subject with a widening range of definitions (Chapter 6) and with increasing connotations of valuable rather than undesirable attitudes on the part of the analyst. (Could not a benign countertransference be distinguished from an erotized form?) Sandler (p. 66) cites Kernberg (1965), who, in a review of the subject, maintains that "the broadening of the term to include all emotional responses in the analyst is confusing and causes the term to lose all specific meaning." Nevertheless, to treat it merely as a symptom of the analyst's own problems may inhibit his freedom to understand the patient. The full use of the analyst's emotional responses is of particular importance in treating profound personality disorders.

Sandler concludes that "the most useful view of countertransference might be to take it as referring to the specific emotional responses aroused in the analyst by the specific qualities of his patient. This would exclude *general* features of the analyst's personality and internal psychological structure (which would colour or affect his work with all his patients). . ." (p. 68). He further distinguishes a "*professional attitude*" as of the greatest service to the analyst. (The study of Olinick and his co-workers (1973) on the analyst's "work ego" has an important bearing on these subjects.)

Chapter 7 on "Resistance" reviews the widening of this concept from the early days of analysis, when it referred to disturbances in the flow of associations, to later inclusion of all manifestations of opposition to the analytic process. Though regarded as a clinical phenomenon, it has become almost interchangeable with defense, a metapsychological concept. With the advent of the structural viewpoint, resistances became a clue to the organization and functioning of the mind (as we have seen happening to transference and countertransference). Wilhelm Reich's "character analysis" (1933-1934) was an early, if only partly successful, effort to advance in this direction.

Sandler reviews the categories of resistances drawn up on the basis of a structural approach to danger situations by Freud in 1926 and offers some extensions and modifications of his own, among them "resistances deriving from faulty procedures and inappropriate technical measures adopted by the psychoanalyst" (p. 80). (Should these not be called "defenses against danger?" Actually, each advance in analysis is likely to be attended by a re-evaluation of former "resistances" and the recognition of new ones.)

Varieties of negative therapeutic reactions and acting out are discussed. Again, the disposition to expand usages is noted, as well as resemblances to similar behavior outside the analytic setting. Interpretations, usually considered the most specific agency of analytic cure, came to the fore only as earlier efforts to uncover forgotten memories directly receded in interest. The analyst's interpretations of the material first took as their model the work on dreams and the probing for the latent beneath the manifest content. By the time the papers on technique were written, the divulgence of the interpretation became linked to the nature of the resistances and the effective means of removing them with the aid of the interpretation. The "single interpretation" was well characterized by Fenichel's admonition to lend an upward-striving impulse appropriate verbalization at the right moment (p. 107).

Sandler does not believe that the "single element" in the patient's material any longer receives emphasis as the subject of interpretation (p. 106n), though he does not explain why it should not (see Brenner's experience, reported earlier). Structural analysis, employing a more multidetermined approach, has helped advance interpretation not only as a science but also as an art (see also Loewald, 1975). Some concepts of interpretation are so broadly based that they include all the verbal and even nonverbal interventions of the analyst. Loewenstein (1951) sought to exclude instructions and explanations, Eissler (1953) to exclude commands, and Olinick (1954) to limit questions.

Sandler comments: "The degree of arbitrariness in many of these distinctions is striking. It is fairly generally assumed in the psychoanalytic literature that no interpretation can ever be complete, and perhaps the most practical use of the concept would be to include within it all comments and other verbal interventions which have the aim of immediately making the patient aware of some aspects of his psychological functioning of which he was not previously conscious. This would *include* much of what has been referred to as 'preparations for interpretation,' confrontations, clarifications, reconstructions, etc. It would *exclude* the normal and inevitable verbal social interchanges and instructions as to analytic procedure" (pp. 110-111). (Brenner's warnings against such sharp divisions seem to us applicable here.)

The mode of action of interpretations likewise finds diverse explanations. Therapeutic progress may still result from inexact, inaccurate, and incomplete interpretations (Glover, 1955). "Insight," so often assumed to be the prime result, has itself been something of a newcomer to the analytic vocabulary and is not to be found in the index of the Standard Edition (Richards, 1974)! Discussions of the intellectual and emotional aspects of insight are familiar. Sandler brings these problems into proposed perspective with the formula that "therapeutic change as the consequence of analysis depends, to a large degree, on the provision of a structured and organized conceptual and affective framework within which the patient can effectively place himself and his subjective experience of himself and others" (p. 119).

The concept and process of "working through" are intimately connected with the relationships between interpretation, insight, and the eventual changes that take place within the personality. Loewald's classical formulation of 1960 (p. 24) is quoted: "The analyst functions as a representative of a higher stage of organization and mediates this to the patient [through words], in so far as the analyst's understanding is attuned to what is, and the way in which it is, in need of organization."

Reconstruction, as a process of reliving the past through

shared experience with the analyst, has much to do with the restructuring and subsequent maturation of the personality. Sandler finds Kris's (1956) "new biography" concepts very pertinent. He quotes Kris's observation that "reconstruction of childhood events may well be, and I believe regularly is, concerned with some thought processes and feelings which did not necessarily 'exist' at the time the 'event' took place. . . . Through reconstructive interpretations they tend to become part of the selected set of experiences constituting the biographical picture which in favorable cases emerges in the course of analytic therapy" (p. 115).

Sandler has since placed his own concept of reconstruction on a more systematic basis (Sandler and Sandler, 1978), stressing the experiential side of mental phenomena. His concept departs from the idea of instinctual drives as sole motivators and deals with wishes and needs vis-á-vis the earliest objects and, hence, vis-á-vis the outer world. These wishes and needs contain representations of the self, of the objects, and the interactions between them. The Sandlers conceive of object relationships as wish fulfillments that actualize themselves in manifest form in the outer world. "The regulations of conscious and unconscious feelings is placed in the centre of the clinical stage. Interpretation of the feeling-state which is closest to the surface becomes a primary consideration in our technical approach, and we include, in our understanding of what may be happening to the patient, the notion that his feeling-states may be affected by stimuli which are not necessarily instinctual in origin. We are provided with a view of motivation, conflict, and possibly of psychopathology and symptoms, in which the control of feelings via the direct or indirect maintenance of specific role relationships is of crucial significance" (1978, p. 295).

The much-debated question whether classical analysis can deal with preoedipal stages of development receives a definitive answer from Harold Blum (1977) who demonstrates the far-reaching significance of Freud's early experience of a "sense of guilt" in the wake of the death of an infant brother when Freud was only nineteen months old. Blum concludes that psychoanalysis is reconstructive in more than one sense, "facilitating memory organization and new ego synthesis" (p. 783). He confirms his argument by pointing to numerous preoedipal reconstructions to be found in Freud's case histories, and in the interpretation of his dreams.

Ultimately, reviews of analytic technique and the theories on which they are based are also reconstructive. We can hardly expect that a single technique, a single theory, or even a single language will prevail. There can only be records, imperfectly kept, as testimony to long, drawn-out contacts between two persons that can be presented only imperfectly to a variety of witnesses, who form different impressions of them in their minds. The four books we have reviewed were like specimens dredged up from the deep, while the literature and hidden currents that were left behind were vast determining forces which, like the unconscious, could only be imperfectly registered by these hypercathected models.

Each of the four books bore signs of the practice of psychoanalysis as ultimately a lonely and highly individual profession. Each had a special focus and reflected in its own way the trends of the times. Conspicuously muted, however, are such vital influences as the role of child analysis, studies of object relations, and the tracing of lines of development from infancy to old age. New visions of narcissism and widening clinical and social applications of analysis that are hardly touched on here carry us beyond the notion that they represent alloys of pure gold with lesser metals and call rather for recognition as views of psychoanalysis in the light of wider experience. No doubt follow-up studies on technique will do them greater justice!

Perhaps these volumes, and those we have not reviewed, converge in a growing awareness of psychoanalytic therapy as a two-person process conditioned at each stage by the interactions of the personalities of both participants. These engage the structuring and functioning of their individualities as focused within the analytic setting. Three of our volumes place such alliances in the foreground; and the other, Brenner's, although oriented to conflict, nevertheless matches the "analytic attitude" of the physician with the compliance of the "good analytic patient." Moreover, in invoking the fundamental rule, Brenner inevitably accepts Freud's formulation of the "analytic pact."

Rigid concepts of neutrality as a façade to justify aloofness seem difficult to reconcile with the physicianly attitude that somehow must be integrated with the analyst's stance. Empathy, intuition, and tact provide avenues for affective sensitivity and rapport, as does the more constructive side of countertransferences. Increasingly, we find the analyst more boldly describing his own reactions to the patient and his self-analysis as part of the case report. Not merely neurosis and defense but health and creative solutions require constant weighing in relation to each other.

It is in the latter sense that we quote Greenacre's comment that "a thorough study of development throughout infancy and childhood, not merely in its metapsychological implications, would be most valuable as a fundamental part of our psychoanalytic training" (1975, p. 712). We would not stop with these earlier stages, however, but extend them into maturity and the progressive-regressive interplay between infantilism and adulthood. In the two-person relationship, it falls upon the analyst to represent the latter. It is not only that "he must possess some kind of superiority, so that in certain analytic situations he can act as a model for his patient and in others as a teacher" (Freud, 1937, p. 248). A third attribute, that of physician, is his own promised complement to the fundamental rule itself.

REFERENCES

Alexander, F. (1954), Some quantitative aspects of psychoanalytic technique. *This Journal*, 2:685-701.

Arlow, J. A. & Brenner, C. (1964), *Psychoanalytic Concepts and the Structural Theory*. New York: International Universities Press.

Balint, M. (1953), *Primary Love and Psychoanalytic Treatment*. New York: Liveright.

Bibring, E. (1954), Psychoanalysis and the dynamic psychotherapies. *This Journal*, 2:745-776.

Blum, H. P. (1977), The prototype of preoedipal reconstruction. *This Journal*, 25:757-786.

Brenner, C. (1968), Psychoanalysis and science. *This Journal*, 16:675-696.

_____ (1969), Some comments on technical problems in psychoanalysis. *This Journal*, 17:333-352.

Breuer, J. & Freud, S. (1893-1895), Studies on hysteria. *Standard Edition*, 2.

Eissler, K. R. (1953) The effect of the structure of the ego on psychoanalytic techniques. *This Journal*, 1:104-143.

Erikson, E. H. (1950) *Childhood and Society*. New York: Norton.

Fenichel, O. (1941), *Problems of Psychoanalytic Technique*. New York: The Psychoanalytic Quarterly, Inc.

Fleming, J. (1975), Some observations on object constancy in the psychoanalysis of adults. *This Journal*, 23:743-759.

Freud, A. (1936), *The Ego and the Mechanisms of Defense*. Writings, 2. New York: International Universities Press, 1966.

Freud, S. (1887-1902), *The Origins of Psychoanalysis*. New York: Basic Books, 1954.

_____ (1898), Screen memories. *Standard Edition* 3:301-322.

_____ (1912), The dynamics of transference. *Standard Edition*, 12:97-108.

_____ (1913), On beginning the treatment. *Standard Edition*, 12:121-144.

_____ (1914), Remembering, repeating and working through. *Standard Edition*, 12:145-156.

_____ (1920a), The psychogenesis of a case of homosexuality in a woman. *Standard Edition*, 18:145-172.

_____ (1920b), Beyond the pleasure principle. *Standard Edition*, 18:3-64.

_____ (1926), Inhibitions, symptoms and anxiety. *Standard Edition*, 20:77-175.

_____ (1933), New introductory lectures in psycho-analysis. *Standard Edition*, 22.

_____ (1937), Analysis terminable and interminable. *Standard Edition*, 23:216-253.

_____ (1940), An outline of psychoanalysis. *Standard Edition*, 23:141-207.

Gill, M. (1954), Psychoanalysis and exploratory psychotherapy. *This Journal*, 2:771-797.

Glover, E. (1955), *The Technique of Psychoanalysis*. New York: International Universities Press.

Green, A. (1975), The analyst, symbolization and absence in the analytic situation. *Internat. J. Psycho-Anal.* 56:1-22.

Greenacre, P. (1954), The role of transference. In: *Emotional Growth*. New York: International Universities Press, 1971, pp. 627-640.

_____ (1975), On reconstruction. *This Journal*, 23:693-712.

Greenson, R. R. (1965), The working alliance and the transference neurosis. In: *Explorations in Psychoanalysis*. New York: International Universities Press, 1978, pp. 199-224.

———— & Wexler, M. (1969), The non-transference relationship in the psychoanalytic situation. *Internat. J. Psycho-Anal.*, 50:27-39.
———— ———— (1970), Discussion of "The non-transference relationship in the psychoanalytic situation." *Internat. J. Psycho-Anal.*, 51:143-150.
Hartmann, H. (1939), *Ego Psychology and the Problem of Adaptation.* New York: International Universities Press, 1958.
Heimann, P. (1970), Discussion. The non-transference relationship in the psychoanalytic situation. *Internat. J. Psycho-Anal.*, 51:145-147.
James, H. (1909), The Jolly Corner. In: *The Short Stories of Henry James.* New York: Random House, 1945, pp. 603-644.
Kaiser, H. (1934), Probleme de technique. *Internat. Ztschr. Psychoanal.*, 20:490-522.
Kanzer, M. (1955), The reality-testing of the scientist. *Psychoanal. Rev.*, 42:412-418.
———— (1972), Superego aspects of free association and the fundamental rule. *This Journal*, 20:246-266.
———— (1975), The therapeutic and working alliances. *Internat. J. Psychoanal. Psychiat.* 4:48-76.
Kernberg, O. F. (1965), Notes on counterfransference. *This Journal*, 13:38-56.
Kohut, H. (1959), Introspection, empathy and psychoanalysis. In: *The Search for the Self.* New York: International Universities Press, 1978, pp. 205-232.
Kris, E. (1956), The recovery of childhood memories in psychoanalysis. In: *Selected Papers.* New Haven: Yale University Press, 1975, pp. 301-340.
Loewald, H. (1960), On the therapeutic action of psychoanalysis. *Internat. J. Psycho-Anal.*, 41:16-33.
———— (1975), Psychoanalysis as an art and the fantasy character of the psychoanalytic situation. *This Journal*, 23:277-299.
Loewenstein, R. (1951), The problem of interpretation. *Psychoanal. Quart..*, 20:1-14.
———— (1969), Developments in the theory of transference in the last fifty years. *Internat. J. Psycho-Anal.*, 50:585-588.
Olinick, S. L. (1954), Some considerations of the use of questioning as a psychoanalytic technique. *This Journal*, 2:57-66.
————, Poland, W., Grigg, K. & Granatir, W. (1973), The psychoanalytic work ego. *Internat. J. Psycho-Anal.*, 54:143-152.
Rangell, L. (1954), Similarities and differences between psychoanalysis and dynamic psychotherapy. *This Journal*, 2:734-744.
Rapaport, D. & Gill, M. (1959), The points of view and assumptions of meta-psychology. *Internat. J. Psycho-Anal.*, 40:153-162.
Reich, W. (1933-1934), *Character Analysis.* New York: Touchstone Books, 1974.
Richards, A. (1974), Indexes and bibliographies to the *Standard Edition. Standard Edition*, 24.
Sandler, J. (1960), On the concept of superego. *The Psychoanalytic Study of the Child*, 15:128-162. New York: International Universities Press.
———— & Sandler, A. M. (1978), On the development of object-relationships and affects. *Internat. J. Psycho-Anal.*, 59:285-296.
Spitz, R. (1956), Countertransference. *This Journal*, 4:256-265.
Sterba, R. (1934), The fate of the ego in analytic therapy. *Internat. J. Psycho-Anal.*, 15:117-126.
Strachey, J. (1934), The nature of the therapeutic action of psychoanalysis. Reprinted in: *Internat. J. Psycho-Anal.* (1969), 50:275-292.

Tartakoff, H. (1956), Recent books in psychoanalytic technique. *This Journal*, 4:318-343.

Waelder, R. (1930), The principle of multiple function. In: *Psychoanalysis: Observation, Theory, Application*. New York: International Universities Press, 1976, pp. 68-83.

————— (1956), Introduction to the discussion on problems of transference. In: *Psychoanalysis: Observation, Theory, Application*. New York: International Universities Press, 1976, pp. 240-243.

Waldhorn, H. (1969), Review of Greenson's *The Technique and Practice of Psychoanalysis*. *Psychoanal. Quart.*, 38:479-483.

Zetzel, E. R. (1969), Review of Greenson's *The Technique and Practice of Psychoanalysis*. *Internat. J. Psycho-Anal.*, 50:411-412.

120 East 36th Street
New York, New York 10016

THE EFFECT OF THE STRUCTURE OF THE EGO ON PSYCHO-ANALYTIC TECHNIQUE

K. R. EISSLER, M.D.

THE SUBJECT MATTER OF THIS PAPER is closely related to a problem which has occupied the minds of analysts for decades. It is within the scope of the question which Freud raised at the Berlin Psychoanalytic Convention (1922) when he asked: "What is the relationship between psychoanalytic technique and psychoanalytic theory?" Freud's question encompassed a vast area, only one portion of which pertains to the subject matter of this paper.

Freud's question of 1922 will interest us today particularly in conjunction with the structure of the ego. During the last two decades a certain sentiment has spread which might be formulated as follows: If our knowledge of the structure of the ego were complete, then a variety of techniques—ideally adapted to the requirements of the individual disturbance—could be perfected; thus we could assure definite mastery of the ego over those areas in which it had suffered defeat, that is to say, assure complete recovery. Like all sentiments, this one does not adequately reflect objective reality, but it is probably correct to say that greatly deepened, almost complete, insight into the structure of the ego would multiply the clinical effectiveness of psychoanalytic techniques. The pessimist's claim, however, must be conceded: Full knowledge of the structure of the ego would, no doubt, make the task of

changing that structure appear in its true and gigantic proportion, inducing us as a consequence to withdraw modestly
from such heroic attempts.

Before delving into the subject matter, I want to exclude
two variables which have great bearing on psychoanalytic
techniques. Such delimitation will facilitate a more precise
formulation of basic issues and avoid the bewilderment which
might arise in view of the great variety of problems involved.
Psychoanalytic techniques depend chiefly on three variables:
the patient's disorder and personality, the patient's present
life circumstances, and the psychoanalyst's personality. In the
following discussion the last two variables will be excluded. It
is assumed that the living conditions of the patient and the
personality of the analyst are both ideal; that is, entirely
favorable to the analytic process. Thus, in our assumption,
no disturbance of the psychoanalytic process originates either
from the patient's actual life circumstances or the analyst's
personality.

Failure to distinguish these variables has considerably
lowered the standards of discussions of psychoanalytic techniques.[1] Clinical reality, of course, is so highly varied and
provides so many unforeseen situations that it is impossible
to set up a standard technique which would meet all exigencies of practice. This is also true of other specialties. All
accepted rules of asepsis are thrown aside in some emergency
situations; nevertheless, when operating under optimal conditions, the surgeon follows these rules faithfully, and they are
still taught in approved medical schools, although the teacher
knows well the many situations in which there will be no
occasion for their application.

While the patient's particular life circumstances may
necessitate a certain technical measure, it is a grave mistake
to conclude that this measure has general validity because it

[1] Following Freud's concept of wild analysis (1910b) one may really talk of
wild discussions on psychoanalytic technique in this context.

has proved its usefulness under special conditions. To overlook the specificity of variables to which a technical measure is correlated means to discard sound scientific standards.

For the purpose of demonstrating the errors we may fall into when we do not distinguish between the variables of the technique, I wish to cite only one example. In discussing the principle of flexibility, Alexander and French (1946) quote Freud's technical advice that at certain points of the treatment phobic patients should be urged to expose themselves to the fear-arousing situation. Alexander uses this technical device as an additional argument in favor of his technique of giving his patients ample advice and encouragement. However, Freud's technical measure, as will be seen presently, does not at all lend itself to generalization if it is seen in its true proportion and context; that is to say, if it is correlated with that variable which forced its introduction.

Another general remark comes to mind. I mentioned earlier, as one variable of psychoanalytic technique, the psychoanalyst's personality. Freud reported some of the subjective factors which influenced the evolving of his technique. For example, in explaining his request that the patient take the supine position during analysis, Freud (1913) mentions his dislike of being stared at for several hours. And he goes on to add other reasons which make the supine position preferable.

When she discussed her deviation from classical psychoanalysis, analyzing in a face-to-face situation, Frieda Fromm-Reichmann (1950, p. 11) supported her argument by quoting Freud's idiosyncracy. Her argument is out of place. An analyst may be an exhibitionist and may therefore prefer a face-to-face technique. Whatever technique a therapist may devise can be used in the service of his pleasure principle. The value of a technical measure must rest on objective factors. If it coincides with the therapist's pleasure, all the better, but this coincidence is not a decisive factor in judging and evaluating the given technique.

Fromm-Reichmann calls the reader's attention to an-

other factor which deserves consideration when we speak of
Freud's aversion to being gazed at for eight hours. She claims
that the therapist of the time was "liable to share the embarrassment of his patient while listening to difficult communications" (1950, p. 11) and this made him prefer the patient's
supine position.[2] Fromm-Reichmann's reasoning, whether it
is correct or not, brings into the picture a cluster of factors
which I have deliberately deleted from my earlier enumeration
of variables, namely, the historical situation. There have been
attempts to correlate all kinds of historical factors with classical psychoanalysis: Victorianism and anti-Victorianism,
feudalism, Puritanism, etc. No individual can divorce himself
from the historical period in which he is living, any more than
he can put himself beyond time or space. Valuable as the
sociology of science is, it does not decide which scientific
finding is correct and which is not. The historical viewpoint
can be applied to any of the so-called modern psychoanalytic
innovations. Let us consider, for example, the technique of the
staggering of interviews which is now so often advised.

As is well known, Freud attributed to the constancy and
continuity of the technique—that is to say, to the technique of
daily interviews—great importance, whereas some contemporary psychoanalysts believe the frequency of interview
should be adapted to the therapeutic needs of the patient;
that is to say, he should be seen less often when it is desirable
to increase his emotional participation and more often to
assuage anxiety. The resulting technique accustoms the patient to see his analyst some times rarely and other times
frequently. A historical evaluation of this technique will show

---

[2] Fromm-Reichmann's reasoning in favor of face-to-face interviews cannot be
thoroughly discussed here; I will therefore limit myself to one statement. If the
author means to identify Freud with the above-quoted statement, as the context
suggests, she was mistaken. Freud reported that he had used the supine position
before he had discovered the sexual etiology of the neuroses, and, further, that he
had gained the full conviction regarding the correctness of the theory from his
interviews with neurasthenics whose sexual life he investigated in a face-to-face
position. (See Freud 1925, pp. 23-24.)

that the living pattern of many analysts, certainly of those who are nationally prominent, is quite different from that of Freud. They are prominent figures on the national scene, being called to Washington as government advisers, serving on numerous committees at all times of the year, lecturing at places hundreds or thousands of miles apart, participating in conventions—in short, they are kept busy in many extracurricular activities, so to speak. Can such analysts indulge in the luxury of daily interviews for ten months of the year without sinking into national oblivion? I have mentioned only the crudest historical reasons for the technique of staggered interviews; there are other, more subtle ones. A historical factor may well be a valid aspect of research. But we must remember that, although historical factors may be easily correlated with the techniques of a given period, the correctness or incorrectness of any technique is not decided by such correlation. Everything that is created by man must be deeply imbued by the historical climate at the time of its creation. In considering the creations of scientists we observe that at certain times and under certain circumstances the historical climate has led to a correct interpretation of reality; at other times it has led to an incorrect interpretation. Since it is idle to raise the historical argument in weighing the pros and cons of a scientific proposition, I have omitted the historical factor as one of the variables of psychoanalytic technique to be discussed here.

To return to the discussion of the effect of ego structure on technique: I will begin with a clinical example in which the psychoanalytic technique can be applied with the fewest complications. The basic model of the psychoanalytic technique can be discussed with relative ease in a case of hysteria. In such a case, we assume—and in this abstract context it is unimportant whether this assumption is clinically correct or not—that the hysteric patient has reached the phallic level and that his ego has all the potentialities for developing into an organization which can maintain an adequate relationship to reality. The task of therapy, at this point, is to give the patient that support which is necessary for the attainment of the genital level and to make possible the realization of those potentialities of the ego which have been held in abeyance chiefly because of traumatic experiences. Such a patient is informed of the basic rule and of his obligation to follow it. He adheres to it to the best of his ability, which is quite sufficient for the task of achieving recovery. The tool with which the analyst can accomplish this task is interpretation, and the goal of interpretation is to provide the patient with insight. Insight will remove the obstacles which have so far delayed the ego in attaining its full development. The problem here is only when and what to interpret, for in the ideal case the analyst's activity is limited to interpretation; no other tool becomes necessary.

In order to avoid misunderstandings, I want to stress that I do not discuss here the problem of what is therapeutically effective in the analysis of a neurosis. The therapeutically effective factors are, of course, of a far greater diversity than interpretation; among many others there is, for example, transference. It would, however, be a mistake to consider transference a tool of therapy, particularly in a case of hysteria. Transference in this instance is a source of energy which, if properly used, leads to recovery through the application of interpretation.

Another point should be clarified. There are other therapeutically effective factors which may look like tools, such as the denial of wish fulfillment, to which the patient must submit throughout the treatment, or, more generally, the psychoanalytic therapeutic attitude. I believe that these factors are secondary; that is to say, they are the necessary consequences when interpretation is the only tool of the analyst. Similarly, working through is a specific technique for using interpretation.

I have left out one tool which is indispensable for the basic model technique. It is doubtful if any person was ever analyzed without being asked questions by the analyst in the course of the psychoanalytic treatment. Indeed, I think that the question as a type of communication is a basic and therefore indispensable tool of analysis, and one essentially different from interpretation. Unfortunately this tool has been taken for granted. The principal investigations at the present time pertain to the proper use of questions in interviews and not in the psychoanalytic process itself (F. Deutsch, 1939, 1949). The psychology of "question" in terms of structural psychology has not yet been written. But though it offers a most challenging task, I shall not consider it further in this paper, but shall proceed to another neurosis, investigating the minimum tools necessary in the case of a phobia.

The technique required in a classical case of phobia is likely to be surprising at one point. The treatment begins and proceeds for a long time like that of a hysteria; that is to say, the analyst uses interpretation as the exclusive tool of therapy. However, in the treatment of some cases a point is reached when it becomes evident that interpretation does not suffice as a therapeutic tool and that pathogenic material is warded off despite the analysis of all those resistances which become clinically visible. In other words, despite maximum interpretation, the pathogenic area cannot be tapped. Even if all resistances are interpreted and every reconstruction obtainable from the material is conveyed to the patient, and even if the patient ideally adheres to the basic rule, the area constituting the core of the psychopathology will not become accessible to the analyst. At that moment a new technical tool becomes necessary. As is well known, this new tool is advice or command.

The analyst must impose on the patient a command: to expose himself to the dreaded situation despite his fear of it and regardless of any anxiety which might develop during that exposure. In extreme cases it may become necessary to threaten the discontinuance of treatment unless the patient takes on the burden of voluntarily suffering anxiety. Advising the patient to perform a certain action or even forcing him indirectly to do it is beyond the scope of interpretation and introduces a therapeutic tool which is of an entirely different type. In order to facilitate communication I introduce here the term *parameter of a technique*. I define the parameter of a technique as the deviation, both quantitative and qualitative, from the basic-model technique, that is to say, from a technique which requires interpretation as the exclusive tool. In the basic-model technique the parameter is, of course, zero throughout the whole treatment. We therefore would say that the parameter of the technique necessary for the treatment of a phobia is zero in the initial phases as well as in the concluding phases; but to the extent that interpretation is replaced by advice or command in the middle phase, there is a parameter which may, as in the instance cited here, be considerable, though temporary.

The justification of introducing a parameter into the treatment of phobia is based exclusively on clinical observation. Early experience demonstrated that the basic-model technique had led to a stalemate. It became clear to Freud that if phobias were to be treated at all by psychoanalysis, he had to deviate from the basic technical position, namely, not to impose advice or command on a patient after treatment has started. The parameter which he introduced was the minimum, without which no progress could be made. The great advantage of this parameter was that it needed to be used for only a short time, that once it had proved its usefulness it could be dispensed with, and the treatment could proceed with the basic-model technique. The parameter introduced into the psychoanalysis of phobia may serve as a model from which the ideal conditions which a parameter ought to fulfill can be deduced. We formulate tentatively the following general criteria of a parameter if it is to fulfill the conditions which are fundamental to psychoanalysis: (1) A parameter must be introduced only when it is proved that the basic-model technique does not suffice; (2) the parameter must never transgress the unavoidable minimum; (3) a parameter is to be used only when it finally leads to its self-elimination; that is to say, the final phase of the treatment must always proceed with a parameter of zero. These three conditions are ideally fulfilled by the parameter which has become part and parcel of the analytic treatment of phobic patients.

If we now turn to the next group of neuroses, the compulsive-obsessive ones, we encounter a still different situation. Here we can take the history of the Wolf Man as paradigmatic (1918).[3] As far as can be seen, for the greater part of the treatment Freud used the basic model technique. Toward the end—"not until trustworthy signs had led me to judge that the right moment had come" (1918, p. 11)—Freud introduced two parameters. One of them is well known: He appointed a fixed time for the conclusion of the treatment. The second, rarely mentioned, impresses me as even more consequential: "I promised the patient a complete recovery of his intestinal activity" (pp. 75-76). The patient must have experienced this as a definite surrender of the analytic reserve and as the analyst's admission and promise of omnipotence; hence the resurgence of the disease when the analyst became sick and proved himself to be not omnipotent (Brunswick, 1928, p. 442).

These two parameters are of a different order from that encountered in the treatment of phobias. They fulfill the first

[3] This patient has been diagnosed in various ways. Before his analysis some authorities claimed manic-depressive insanity (1918, p. 8). Freud's diagnosis was "a condition following upon an obsessional neurosis which has come to an end spontaneously, but has left a defect behind it after recovery" (1918, p. 8), but another passage suggests that Freud may have considered the patient an obsessional neurotic: "it [the patient's intestinal trouble] represented the small trait of hysteria which is regularly found at the root of an obsessional neurosis" (1918, p. 75). Freud later (1937, p. 218) referred to the paranoic character of some of the patient's symptoms. Yet the problems of technique which Freud discussed in the original paper pertained to those which are generally encountered in analyses of compulsive neuroses. I do not agree with Binswanger (1945), who considers the early history of the Wolf Man as typical of childhood schizophrenia.

demand we put on a parameter; they were introduced when it was proved that the basic-model technique would not bring about the patient's recovery. It is questionable whether they fulfill the second demand, of presenting the indispensable minimum deviation. Undoubtedly they do not fulfill the third requirement; they are not self-eliminating for two reasons: (1) Since the patient is to be dismissed at an appointed time, there is not time left for a concluding phase in which the basic-model technique will be the exclusive one. (2) The other parameter, the promise of omnipotence, extends vastly over the termination of the treatment and seems to have been, in the case of the Wolf Man, a precondition necessary for the patient's maintenance of mental health during the years following his analysis. This deviation is of interest for other reasons: It is possible that the introduction per se of some parameters has a lasting effect on the patient's transference, an effect which cannot be undone by interpretation. Deviations from the basic-model technique are occasionally light-heartedly suggested by some analysts under the assumption that the effect of any therapeutic measure can be "analyzed" later. As a general statement this is definitely wrong. Unfortunately, the boundaries have not yet been ascertained beyond which therapeutic measures create irreparable damage to the transference relationship. One must expect individual variations from one patient to another in this respect.[4]

Freud made a definitive statement with regard to this problem when he discussed the treatment of negative therapeutic reactions. After describing the parameter of the tech-

---

[4] Of the many examples which could be cited I arbitrarily select one. There are patients in whom the slightest deviation of the rule of conducting the treatment in the situation of frustration can have an extremely detrimental effect, and the fulfillment of a wish, trivial as the request for a cigarette, may endanger the further course of the treatment by establishing a fixed fantasy inaccessible to further analysis. Other patients, and I believe they are the majority, are less rigid. Whatever may, in them, be evoked in terms of transference formation by trivial wish fulfillments can easily be analyzed and does not become a stumbling block to further treatment.

nique which he would have to introduce if he were to effect clinical recovery in patients showing negative therapeutic reactions, he went on to state clearly and emphatically that this particular parameter is irreconcilable with psychoanalytic technique because it would convert transference into a relationship per se inaccessible to psychoanalytic interpretations.[5] Thus a fourth proposition must be introduced in order to delineate the conditions which a parameter must fulfill if the technique is to remain within the scope of psychoanalysis: The effect of the parameter on the transference relationship must never be such that it cannot be abolished by interpretation.

Returning to Freud's technique in the treatment of the Wolf Man, I want to re-emphasize what is generally known: That neither of the technical innovations in this case has become an integral part of analysis. We do not have a technique for this type of compulsive neurosis which is comparable in either adequacy or precision to the parameter of technique used in the treatment of phobias.

If we now approach the other two groups of disorders, the schizophrenias and delinquencies, the situation becomes infinitely more complicated. The technique of free association cannot be applied in either group. In the schizophrenias the patient would be incapable of cooperating; moreover, the technique might precipitate regressions. In the delinquencies the basic rule is inapplicable because of the patient's intentional and adamant refusal to follow it. In these two groups, not only is the basic rule inapplicable, but, simultaneously,

---

[5] See (1923, p. 50n). The content of this footnote is of formidable importance. Perusal of most books on psychoanalytic technique of recent date will show that Freud's spirit of intellectual honesty has largely been lost. Technical innovations are introduced in large number and are supported by the simple-minded justification that the innovator has noticed subsequent disappearance of symptoms. The question of "at what cost to and limitation of the ego" is no longer asked; instead, pride in the alleged superiority of the contemporary analysts' knowledge makes many authors believe that Freud's safeguards against the effect of the therapist's personality—in situations where a structural change, induced by the analytical process, ought to take place—have become superfluous.

the main tool of interpretation is thrown out of gear, and insight cannot be conveyed to these patients by verbal interpretation—at least not in the initial phase of treatment. Therefore, the parameters of the necessary techniques cannot be used to alter the basic-model technique at certain spots, nor can they be introduced as new devices in certain phases, as in the neuroses just mentioned: In the schizophrenias and the delinquencies the whole technique must be changed in all essential aspects.

Nevertheless, the four criteria just formulated, which a parameter must fulfill if a technique is to be accepted as psychoanalytic, are valid also for these two groups.[6]

It is impossible to demonstrate here the consequences which must follow when the basic-model technique is adapted to the necessities of such grave disorders as the schizophrenias always are and the delinquencies in almost all instances prove to be, but I do want to stress that, despite the claims to the contrary by a few analysts, I am convinced that it has not yet been proved that schizophrenic patients ever reach a state in which they can be treated in accordance with the basic-model technique. This is, to a certain extent, coincidental with a doubt that schizophrenic patients can be "cured" by psychoanalysis in that sense in which we commonly say neuroses can be cured. This statement is not to be construed as a denial of the effectiveness of psychoanalysis in the treatment of schizophrenic patients.

To return to the neuroses: We have taken the minimum requirements of a case of hysteria as our basic model and have compared them with the minimum requirements of other disorders. For historical reasons hysteria can be taken as the base line of the psychoanalytic therapy, since Freud demonstrated the basic technique and the basic concepts of

[6] The fourth condition, that the parameter must not give the transference a lasting direction, will be difficult to fulfill during the acute phases of the disease. If it has happened that a parameter has influenced the transference in a way which cannot be undone by interpretation, a change of analyst may become necessary.

psychoanalysis in conjunction with his clinical experiences with hysterias. However, there is also an intrinsic reason why psychoanalysis was evolved in the course of the treatment of hysterias. Tentatively I would say that the discovery of psychoanalysis would have been greatly impeded, delayed, or even made impossible if in the second half of the nineteenth century the prevailing neurosis had not been hysteria. Notwithstanding some inaccuracy, it can be said that the earliest psychoanalytic model of hysteria pertains to an ego which has suffered that minimum of injury without which no neurosis would develop at all. It is of interest to peruse the earliest publication by Breuer and Freud (1893) from this point of view.

In the paper of 1893, two different functions were assigned to the ego in the course of the development of hysteria: (a) Most hysterical symptoms were recognized as being consequences of traumata. Any experience which could elicit intensive painful affects could become a trauma, depending upon the sensitivity of the ego. This sensitivity was the only factor through which the ego contributed to the development of the disease, but nothing further was said about it. The psychic trauma had penetrated the patient like a foreign body and accomplished—well protected in its hideout—the whole variety of hysterical symptomatology. This early theory comes close to picturing the disease process as an event in which a part of reality has intruded into the psychic organism and pushed aside for a while the normal personality. Because of this interpretation of clinical observations, the structure of the ego did not need consideration. (b) That part of reality which remains isolated in the patient obtains its privileged function from the lack of affective abreaction, which would have been necessary in order to assimilate it. Two groups of factors were held responsible for the want of abreaction. First, the patient did not abreact because the nature of the trauma made it impossible or because the patient did not want to take notice of the trauma; that is to say, he did not want to abreact.

The second group of factors concerned the state of the ego at the time when the trauma occurred. The ego was either paralyzed by an inordinately strong affect or by a hypnoid state and therefore was incapable of contributing that amount of work which would have been necessary for rendering innocuous the poisonous effect of reality—if this kind of imagery is permitted.[7]

All these explanations had one point in common: They conjured away the bearing of the ego upon the disease process; the ego does not want to, or cannot, function, and thus an area is established in which the ego-alien puts forth roots and flourishes.[8] This disregard of the ego shows up also in the therapy, which was based on a maximum paralysis of the ego, induced by means of hypnosis.

We are not, in this paper, concerned with investigating the extent to which these conceptions correctly reflected clinical reality, but only with noting that in hysteria it was apparently possible to study the disease process quite apart from the rest of the personality. Consequently a technique was evolved which permitted concentration on the clinically most conspicuous part of the disease process and which succeeded in eliminating it, at least temporarily.[9]

A late statement of Freud's may now be brought into genetic connection with early theories. In "Analysis Terminable and Interminable," Freud reported that complete recovery could be achieved with relative ease in patients whose pathology was caused mainly by traumata (1937). Despite their symptomatology, the ego had not been noticeably modified in such patients. In view of this statement the following conclusion can be drawn: The basic-model technique, with-

[7] One receives the impression that these early theories might have been influenced by contemporary concepts of internal medicine regarding the origin of infectious disorders.

[8] To be sure, one of the authors must have seen beyond these conceptions, since at one point he speaks of "a hysterical individuality."

[9] Cf. for the foregoing A. Freud (1936, pp. 11-12.).

out emendations, can be applied to those patients whose neurotic symptomatology is borne by an ego not modified to any noteworthy degree. In other words, if the ego has preserved its integrity, it will make maximum use of the support it receives from the analyst in the form of interpretation. The exclusive technical problem in such instances is simply to find that interpretation which will provide the ego, in the respective phases of the treatment, with maximum support.[10]

For the type of phobia which I presented initially, this diagram must be slightly changed. Despite maximum assistance by means of interpretations, the ego cannot recover from the damage caused by the past. I believe that this fact has not made us marvel enough. It is still a riddle why a human being should refuse to make maximal use of the insight which is conveyed to him. It must be remembered that the insight offered him comprehends not only the history of his sickness but also all those resistances checking his recovery which manifest themselves during this treatment phase. Nonetheless, though recovery does not follow the offer of maximum insight, the process of recovery can be initiated after the patient has been forced to expose himself to the very danger he is so much afraid of. The patient behaves like someone who has in his grasp all the riches of the world, but who refuses to take them and must be forced by threat to do so.

Of course we know some of the reasons which make it necessary in such cases to deviate from the model technique and to demand of the patient that he expose himself to the feared situation. The prospect of anxiety is such a deterrent that it cannot be overcome unless the patient is threatened with the even greater pain of losing a beloved object. But this

---

[10] I will pursue this problem further in connection with Freud's concept of the hypothetically normal ego. The question of whether such a technique, based principally on interpretations, leads to intellectualization and lack of emotional participation on the patient's side will not be discussed here. Freud's papers on metapsychology and on the technique of psychoanalysis refute this argument. See also Alexander's (1925) incisive criticism of Ferenczi's and Rank's book *The Development of Psychoanalysis*.

does not explain why such an ego can give up a resistance and turn toward pathogenic, repressed material only when it is re-exposed to the pain of a dreaded anxiety. It is necessary to conclude that this ego had lost its capacity of adjustment to a larger extent than the ego of a hysteric patient. The ego organization in phobia must be significantly different from that of hysteria.

At this point it is wise to remember that the state of affairs alluded to above is not encountered in all patients suffering from phobias. Some of them recover without having recovery imposed upon them. Therefore it may be appropriate to say that it is not so much the particular combination of symptoms and defenses—that is to say, the structure of the symptom—which necessitates the specific technique but the ego organization in which the particular symptom is embedded. We must also remember that the pattern of the basic-model technique does not always suffice in the treatment of hysterias; sometimes a technique resembling that for phobias becomes necessary. A hysterical patient who consistently consults internists for the treatment of conversion symptoms or who uses physical means of therapy may have to be told that he must either abstain from such escapes or face a discontinuance of his psychoanalysis. In such instances we must assume that the ego has become modified to a larger extent than was to be expected from the classical description of the dynamics of hysteria. On the other hand, as Freud has shown in the history of the Rat Man (1909), it is possible to have a compulsive-obsessive neurosis which will subside on the mere application of the basic-model technique, and a comparison of the Rat Man's history with that of the Wolf Man will show that fairly similar symptoms may be combined with two entirely different ego organizations—one barely, the other severely, modified.

It may be worth while to demonstrate how little or how much a mechanism or a symptom as such may count, depending on the all-inclusive ego organization in which it occurs. In his essay on Leonardo da Vinci, Freud (1910a) investigated the circumstances which may have been responsible for the relative lack of artistic productivity which became increasingly noticeable in Leonardo's life. Science and scientific research gradually gained ground over artistic achievements. Freud thought that Leonardo's hesitation was caused by a lack of power to isolate the work of art by pulling it out of a broader context. Leonardo's want of capacity to isolate was correlated with a craving to express all of the associations linked with the artistic intention.

In contrast to this example of the lack of capacity to isolate, I want to cite a passage from a letter (21 November 1782) which Goethe wrote to a friend during a time when he was overburdened with administrative work as a Privy Councilor at the Court of Weimar: "I have totally separated (externally of course) my political and social life from my moral and poetic one and in this way I feel at my very best . . . . I leave separated the Privy Councilor and my other self without which the Privy Councilor can exist very well. Only in my innermost plans and purposes and endeavors do I remain mysteriously self-loyal and thus tie my social, political, moral, and poetic life again together into a hidden knot." Here isolation—and quantitatively a rather extensive isolation, cutting across Goethe's existence—functions as a truly life-saving device. I cannot go into the details of this period in the life of Goethe; suffice it to say that it was an extremely critical one, and that without some very felicitous circumstances he might have suffered injuries which could have endangered his future as an artist. Isolation was one of the mechanisms which enabled him to survive this period in a way which was of greatest benefit to him. I want to point out that the isolation of which Goethe speaks here is dangerous, and one which can be found in cases suffering from severe psychopathology; nevertheless, the mechanism which Goethe described cannot be classified clinically as part of a disease. Fortunately, Goethe made another remark which enlightens

us as to the reason why isolation did not lead to psychopathology. He mentioned briefly his loyalty to himself and the
hidden knot by dint of which the isolated activities were tied
again into a unit; that is to say, the powerful isolation was
counterpoised by an unusually strong capacity for synthesis.
This mysterious knot of which Goethe speaks is really the
subject matter of my exposition.

My third example is a patient whose whole personality
organization was interwoven with the effects of isolation, the
mechanism which dominated her life. For her, time had
separated into isolated moments, and her childhood recollections were remembered as disconnected flashes of an ego-alien
past. Likewise her various contemporary activities were isolated from each other, and probably body space, too, had
fallen apart into disconnected space units, as evidenced by her
difficulty in distinguishing right from left. Time and space
had become an aggregate. Isolation had achieved its maximum effect. As can be easily foreseen, a most severe psychopathology must flourish on such fertile ground. Interestingly
enough, the patient had no feeling of suffering about this part
of her psychopathology.

These three clinical examples show us three totally
different effects of the mechanism of isolation:[11] First, a deficit
in the capacity for isolation, leading to a deficit in artistic
creativity; second, a profusion preserving the continuity of
manifold functions; and third, an excessive growth decompos-
ing the ego into innumerable fragments.

In view of the relative independence of ego structure and
mechanism, the following conclusion can be drawn: The
behavior of the ego in the situation of the basic-model technique is specific. Here is the crucial point where it can be
determined whether or not the ego has suffered a modification. The symptoms or behavior deviations do not necessarily

[11] Of course, such variety of effects could be shown for any defense mechanism; it is not true of isolation only.

betray the true structure of the ego organization. This was brought conspicuously to my attention during the analysis of a patient who had spent one and a half years in voluntary commitment. At times this patient was believed to be schizophrenic because of the bewildering variety of bizarre behavior patterns. She made an astounding improvement under a technique which, with rather rare exceptions, followed the rules of classical analysis. Very much to my surprise, the many bizarre features melted away under the impact of a purely interpretative technique and a relatively unharmed ego strongly interested in and strongly attached to the world appeared from behind the maze of symptoms.

The rule that symptoms can only remotely be correlated with ego organization is true also for the allegedly symptom-free ego. I once had an opportunity to analyze a person who gave the impression, in the two initial interviews, of being relatively symptom-free and well adjusted, in accordance with his own claim of wanting treatment only for professional reasons. After several months the treatment was discontinued at the patient's request. It was my impression that the patient was not analyzable. His acting out, under the guise of conforming with the necessities of reality, firmly rooted mechanisms which compensated for an excessive castration fear and his tenuous object relationships, not unlike those often found in schizophrenics, both made me decide for a time that I would never again try the analysis of a "normal" person.

The problem which deserves keenest attention concerns the concept of ego modifications.[12] It must first be differentiated from an ego change. The ego, as are all parts of the personality, is constantly changing. Through new perceptions and by the acquisition of new knowledge and the formation of new memories it enriches itself; by the interplay of defense mechanisms it tries to discard part of these new acquisitions:

[12] Dr. Hartmann suggests in a personal communication "ego deformation" instead of "ego modification." The latter term follows Joan Riviere's translation of Freud's "Analysis Terminable and Interminable."

The ever changing constellations of reality and the unceasing rhythm of biological processes make it face an infinite variation of tasks. It is correct to say that while two cross-sections of the ego are never identical, it is nevertheless always the same. It shares this property with most organisms which can maintain their identity and constancy by means of constant and rapidly occurring changes. All of these changes—primarily changes of content—do not add up to modifications of the ego. However, some of these changes may in certain frames of reference be looked upon as modifications. In the state of sleep, for example, a profound—perhaps the greatest possible—reorganization of the ego occurs. If the state of sleep is considered as a preparation for the return to a temporarily relinquished state characterized by a series of constant indices, then it will be called an ego change. If, however, we are investigating thought processes—which appear greatly modified during sleep as compared with the thought processes of the state of wakefulness—or the laws of dream work or the shifts of cathexis which take place during sleep, then the sleeping ego will be classified as a highly modified one. Disregarding the rather special question of whether the biologically enforced fluctuations of ego states ought to be called changes or modifications, it can be said that if an ego is not normal it has been modified. But what is a normal ego? Freud answered this question in the course of devising a conceptual scale which permits the ranging of all possible ego modifications from a zero point (the hypothetically normal ego) to an absolute maximum (the psychotic ego). According to Freud's definition, a normal ego is one which "would guarantee unshakable loyalty to the work of analysis" (1937, p. 238), and since such an ego is a theoretical construction, he called it a hypothetically normal ego (*fiktives Normal-Ich*).

In my estimation, such an ego would be one which would react properly to the basic-model technique as outlined above. It would be an ego—and this I think is a crucial point—not characterized by specific defenses, attitudes, functions or by any other structural property, but characterized exclusively by a certain mode of behavior in the comprehensive situation of the analytic treatment situation.[13]

According to Freud's definition, the hypothetically normal ego is an ego which uncompromisingly assists in the psychoanalytic therapy. It surrenders, so to speak, to the voice of reason and unflinchingly makes maximum use of the help proffered during the treatment. This description of the hypothetically normal ego (though never encountered in clinical reality) introduces a new concept into psychoanalysis. The whole troublesome question of normal behavior is thus taken out of the context in which it has been discussed up to now. It is no longer a question of whether or not a person has adjusted to reality, whether or not he has integrated current value systems or has achieved mastery over his biological needs. The whole question of symptomatology has been brushed aside with one stroke, and all current static definitions of normality superseded by a new dynamic definition. Freud's separation of the concepts of "normality" and "health" and their re-definition were great steps forward and ought to facilitate communication. Here Freud laid the foundation of a metapsychology of the psychoanalytic technique in structural terms.[14] Thus a normal ego is one which, notwithstanding its symptoms, reacts to rational therapy with a dissolution of its symptoms.

It is necessary to follow up the implications of this concept. It implies that the normal ego also may suffer disease. The ego of the child, because of its weakness, cannot help building up defenses and in most instances cannot escape the formation of symptoms. Indeed, Freud's definition implies that under certain circumstances neurosis is a "normal"

---

[13] This definition presupposes optimal conditions in regard to the analyst's conduct of treatment as well as to the external conditions under which the treatment takes place.

[14] For a discussion of the concept of mental health from the point of view of ego pyschology see Hartmann (1939).

phenomenon. Once the seed of a psychopathological disorder has been planted in the child's personality, the later, adult, ego has no other choice under certain stresses but to fall back on the earlier adjustive process (Hartmann, 1939). The discovery that, in some of its most important aspects, the ego also is unconscious adds to the plausibility of this description. However, an ego which has thus been coerced into falling back on inappropriate solutions may have preserved its "normality" if it is still endowed with the capacity for capitalizing on proper help. If we may assume that psychoanalytic treatment is the most comprehensive psychological therapy because its goal is to provide the ego with all the knowledge and all the support it needs to regain its full competency, then psychoanalysis becomes the only procedure by which "normality" can be gauged.

In more general terms, the concept of the hypothetically normal ego presupposes that a childhood neurosis has developed as a result of the ego's infantile incapability of mastering the tasks put upon it by external as well as by internal reality. Yet, despite those neurotic solutions which were imposed upon the childhood ego, the development and the maturation of the ego organization were not essentially delayed or injured. Owing to the inheritance of childhood, the adult ego has not acquired its full freedom, but when it is brought into a situation in which it can obtain the assistance needed, it fights against this inheritance; and the ego's potentialities, which have been unharmed by past traumata, achieve full realization; in other words, one of the significant features of an ego essentially unharmed by traumata or constitutional factors or archaic fixations of libido is its responsiveness to rational, verbal communications which do not contain more than interpretations.[15]

I think this conception of the normal ego is in substantial

---

[15] See A. Freud (1945) for a brilliant clinical application of this theoretical problem.

agreement with a profound thought which Goethe expressed (probably in conjunction with an experience of impotence): "The disease only avers the healthy" (*Die Krankheit erst bewäh-ret den Gesunden*). Illness thus becomes the unavoidable accident of life; that is to say, it is a manifestation of life itself, and the ego's reaction to the sickness is the exclusive frame of reference of health.

At the other end of the scale is the ego of the psychotic, with whom the analytic compact is impossible (Freud, 1937). There is scarcely anything to say about this end of the scale aside from a historical remark: When Freud was sketching the maximal ego modification, he probably had in mind the acute hallucinatory confusion which so often had served him as the prototype of psychosis.[16] Indeed, during the acute phase of a psychosis, psychoanalysis in its usual form is of no therapeutic avail. At that stage the ego is at least temporarily "modified" in such a way as to make direct psychoanalytic interference impossible.[17] In the case of acute hallucinatory confusion, the ego derives all its wish fulfilments out of itself even in its state of wakefulness. Tension is removed by the hallucination of instinctual gratification. The ego falsifies reality in accordance with its own wishes and can thus dispense with reality. The analyst has lost every avenue of approach because the ego has become inaccessible. It is exclusively engaged in its subservience to the id. Since the normal ego is fictitious, it is evident that in clinical reality elements of the other extreme are always intermixed.[18]

As Freud said, "Every normal person, in fact, is only

[16] See Freud (1894, 1917). See also Freud (1924b) where he calls Meynert's amentia, the acute hallucinatory confusion, the most extreme and striking form of psychosis.

[17] This remark does not militate against psychotherapeutic measures of a different kind.

[18] I think that the clinical varieties of ego modification cannot be completely dissolved into varying mixtures of these two extremes, but require a third component whose extreme is the criminal. The analyst cannot establish with him any kind of alliance for which the hypothetically normal ego is ideally adapted.

normal on the average. His ego approximates to that of the psychotic in some part or other and to a greater or lesser extent; and the degree of its remoteness from one end of the series and of its proximity to the other will furnish us with a provisional measure of what we have so indefinitely termed an 'alteration of the ego'" (1937, p. 235).

This view of normality as cursorily outlined by Freud seems to coincide remarkably well with views advanced by modern biologists and physiologists. In describing the variety of meanings which the concept of normality has in biology, Ivy (1944) mentions the nonarbitrary statistical view which maintains "that a sharp distinction between 'normal' and 'abnormal' does not exist for a group or even an individual . . . . It recognizes that degrees of normality and abnormality exist. . . . It permits an absolute diagnosis of abnormality only when death occurs." Freud set up a series from the acute hallucinatory psychosis to the hypothetically normal ego and thereby established a point at one end of the scale of "absolute diagnosis of abnormality" from which various degrees of normality and abnormality lead to the hypothetically normal ego at the other end of the scale.

In an attempt to clarify the meanings which the concept of normality should have in physiology, Ivy makes a significant remark about physiological processes in disease. Defensive processes, he says, such as fever or leucocytosis are normal, although their effects may be abnormal. The defensive processes "are the usual physiological responses to insult. The process concerned is a statistically and physiologically normal response. The response, however, may produce abnormal effects in certain instances and hence is physiologically abnormal." Here, the problem of the "normal disease" is solved by differentiating process from response, the latter leading sometimes to abnormal effects. For example, the abnormal effect of a rise in body temperature is seen in its eventual disturbance of "other functions and margins of safety," when the fever reaches a certain height.

Likewise, according to Freud's conceptual frame of reference, psychogenic symptoms must be viewed as the logical and unavoidable consequences of the impact of external and internal reality on the childhood ego, still weak because still immature; thus symptoms may be the signs of the ego's basic health. The "physiologically normal response" would, then, become abnormal as soon as it led to an ego modification. Freud's concepts—(1) the hypothetically normal ego as defined by the response in the situation of the basic-model technique; (2) a scale leading by degrees to a state of absolute unresponsiveness to the analytic compact; and (3) the intervening variety of ego modifications to which a variety of techniques must be correlated—provide, in my estimation, a system which is ideally flexible and superbly adaptable to actual clinical work. Their heuristic value impresses me as an enormous, and—finally, but of greatest importance—these concepts ought to bring some rationale and order into psychoanalytical discussions of technique and thus end the contemporary arguments, most of which are based exclusively on utilitarian viewpoints. Points of expediency will always deflect the strict course which practice should take according to theory, but psychoanalysis will lose its standing as a science if problems of technique are discussed exclusively from the viewpoint of expediency.

I am aware that I follow a thought of Freud's, possibly too rigorously, by insisting that the baseline of psychoanalytic technique is one which uses a single technical tool, to wit, interpretation. In support of my contention, repeated clinical experience shows that there is a group of patients whose treatment does need scarcely more than interpretation to usher in the process of recovery and to lead the ego to the therapeutic goal. Clinical experience shows also that this group has an important structural factor in common—a relatively unmodified ego. Furthermore, it can be demonstrated that the introduction of an additional tool, one which will play a prominent part in the analytic technique, is necessitated by a structural defect in the ego. Therefore, we are warranted in classifying personality structures in accordance with the techniques required to deal adequately with their defects. This aspect justifies our assigning a special place to a purely interpretative technique.[19]

It is well known that the proper use of interpretation is difficult and complicated. But so central is this tool that any proposed variation or addition should be scrutinized with the greatest care. The introduction of parameters, even of such simple ones as are necessary in some cases of phobia, contains dangers which must not be overlooked. Each parameter increases the possibility that the therapeutic process may be falsified, inasmuch as it may offer the patient's ego the possibility of substituting obedience for a structural change.

The term obedience, not entirely an accurate one, is used here to designate all those improvements which a patient may show under the pressure of the therapy but which are not based on a dissolution of the corresponding conflicts. A patient often prefers to produce adjusted behavior instead of a structural change.[20]

Every introduction of a parameter incurs the danger that a resistance has been temporarily eliminated without having been properly analyzed. Therefore, after an obstacle has been removed by the use of a parameter, the meaning which this parameter has had for the patient and the reasons which necessitated the choice of the parameter must retrospectively be discussed; that is to say, interpretation must become again the exclusive tool to straighten out the ruffle which was caused by the use of a parameter.

At this point I must strongly emphasize that in my use

---

[19] This is not the place to discuss the epistemology of interpretation. For a comprehensive treatise on interpretation, see a paper by Bernfeld (1932) which regrettably is not available in English. See also Waelder (1939).

[20] This is one of the many reasons why in psychotherapy one so frequently has an opportunity of enjoying bristling clinical successes and why the proper psychoanalytic technique always works against a much heavier resistance than any other technique.

of the term interpretation I always presuppose the proper use of this technique. It would, of course, be foolish to suggest that just any kind of interpretation, or the mere act of interpreting, will do. Again, this paper is not the place for a discussion of what a proper interpretative technique is; it is mandatory, however, that a warning be raised against the quick introduction of parameters under the justification that interpretations have been of no avail. There is a great temptation to cover up, by the introduction of parameters, one's own inability to use properly the interpretative technique.

In view of the paramount importance which one must attribute to ego modification as an obstacle to psychoanalytic therapy and therefore to recovery, the question of the cause of ego modification must be raised. It is again Freud who gives us the answer by delineating the twofold effect which defense mechanisms may have on the ego. They may protect the ego or they may destroy the ego. "The mechanisms of defence serve the purpose of keeping off dangers. It cannot be disputed that they are successful in this; and it is doubtful whether the ego could do without them altogether during its development. But it is also certain that they may become dangers themselves. It sometimes turns out that the ego has paid too high a price for the services they render it" (1937, p. 237; see also A. Freud, 1936, p. 50). And Freud suggests that we consider these deleterious effects of the defenses upon the ego as ego modification.

I want to illustrate such an effect briefly with a clinical example. A three-year-old girl was awakened one morning by her mother, who carried a newborn baby, the girl's sister, in her arms, saying: "Look here, Mary, this is Marguerit. Isn't she sweet?" Showing all the signs of enjoyment, the little girl agreed that Marguerit was sweet. Twenty-eight years later, in her analysis, the girl described the incident, reporting that her mother had descended with incredible swiftness upon her and complaining that her mother had no reason to assume that Mary knew Marguerit was the name of a girl. She claimed she was given no choice but to show the same emotion as her mother and that to meet the situation "requested" by her mother, she had to rally an incredible amount of energy. At the time of her analysis the patient reported that after a day of responsible work, which she performed to the satisfaction of her superiors, she would return home in a state of complete exhaustion. However, she was not exhausted by the exigencies of her work, but because she must rally an incredible amount of energy to show the emotion requested by her environment. To say good morning to her co-workers, to "pitch in with the elevator man" when he made a trivial remark about the weather, absorbed her energy. She found it necessary to brace herself constantly when in the company of others in order to respond appropriately to the respective social realities. She really would have liked to sit in a rocking chair alone in her room and hold her head in her arms.

Here we see that the defense accomplished its goal ideally in the little child in terms of facilitating social behavior, and this patient's history may serve as an example that the relatively symptom-free child is often the most endangered one. The whole jealousy, the whole terrific anger about her mother's unfaithfulness and rejection were excluded from consciousness and were replaced by the socially required admiration of and love for the baby.[21] The little sister soon became the patient's favorite, and she cheerfully spent all her free time with the new companion, developing with surprising quickness strong maternal attitudes. None of her recollections indicated a disturbance of behavior or outward signs of ambivalence toward the baby. The ideal result of the defense, however, must be viewed simultaneously with the catastrophic effect it had on the ego organization. It seems that the defense devoured the ego like a cancerous growth devours the organisms harboring it.

---

[21] I delete from this description the severe anxiety this patient suffered as a child and delineate only the effect which the defense had on the child's external behavior.

A high degree of modification has occurred in the schizophrenic ego. The single defense mechanism and the individual patterns of defense mechanisms do not assist the ego, but are destructive; they burden the ego to such an extent that it is constantly on the verge of breaking off its relationship with reality. This appears to be a complete contradiction to what is usually described as the fundamental process in schizophrenia, that is to say, the ego's being made subservient to the id. No doubt, in most phases of the schizophrenic psychosis, wish fulfillments of the id play a great role, but the function of defense was not deleted from Freud's metapsychological diagram of psychosis.

> The fact that, in so many forms and cases of psychosis [writes Freud (1924a, p. 186)], the paramnesias, the delusions and the hallucinations that occur are of a most distressing character and are bound up with a generation of anxiety—this fact is without doubt a sign that the whole process of remodelling is carried through against forces which oppose it violently. We may construct the process on the model of a neurosis, with which we are more familiar. There we see that a reaction of anxiety sets in whenever the repressed instinct makes a thrust forward, and that the outcome of the conflict is only a compromise and does not provide complete satisfaction. Probably in a psychosis the rejected piece of reality constantly forces itself upon the mind, just as the repressed instinct does in a neurosis, and that is why in both cases the consequences too are the same.

Here, one of the defensive purposes is clearly described. The ego of the psychotic must defend itself constantly against the perception, recognition, and acknowledgment of objective reality. As the ego can postpone awakening by responding to the arousal stimulus by an arousal dream, so can the psychotic prevent the intrusion of objective reality by the maintenance of his own self-created reality. The arousal dream requires a minimum of cathexis, and the unmodified ego suffers the pain of having overruled reality when, upon awakening, it pays the price for having unduly indulged in the desire to sleep. The psychotic ego must garner a very large amount of energy in order to feed constantly its own reality, and the unceasing struggle against the pain which would be aroused by the perception of objective reality in turn results in pain.

In a thoughtful study, Katan (1950) clearly describes the defensive function of one of Schreber's hallucinations of little men descending upon his head and then perishing after a short period of existence. Schreber reached a stage in his psychosis where he could masturbate without erection and emission. ". . . the hallucination occurs instead of the excitement. . . . In the hallucination, sexual excitement does not occur at all, and instead of the idea of Schreber perishing, we find the idea of the other men losing their lives" (1950, p. 34). By hallucination, the ego anticipated danger and warded it off. The remarkable feature, however, is that a fantasy or daydream or a passing thought of the same (though usually less bizarre) content may occur in the neurotic for the same purpose and with the same effect of sparing himself anxiety or excitement. Indeed, one may even venture to say that an ego relatively free of symptoms may maintain its functional organization by a passing thought of such a kind. Yet, in Schreber, the defensive process leading to a hallucination imposed itself upon the total ego, absorbed all its functions, and took full possession of the visual apparatus. It is permissible to say that at that moment the ego could not do anything else but hallucinate or, in other words, that the defense process had spread itself out at the cost of the rest of the ego.

In the case of Schreber's hallucination, the content against which the defense was directed (passive homosexual wishes) was not different from those which one finds quite often in neurotics, if Katan's reconstruction is correct. Yet sometimes the contents which the schizophrenic tries to ward off are quite surprising. The schizophrenic patient I have mentioned before assured me for years that there was only hatred in her, that she would like to see the people killed with whom she had to deal and that she was incapable of feeling any interest in or longing for any human being. However, when she started to tell me the daydreams which filled her mind during the hour it took her to fall asleep—until then she had chiefly reported the feelings and fantasies which she had in the company of others—I was amazed to hear of a fantasy in which she took care of a crippled and mentally disturbed girl whom she knew. With great skill and tact she got me acquainted, in her fantasy, with the child and arranged for the child's treatment and cure. Aside from the narcissistic-erotic elements which undoubtedly are to be found in that day-dream, there was expressed a core of real warmth and affection. There was no doubt that this patient had kept repressed her social inclinations and that her elaborate fantasies of killing also served the purpose of denying her sociability.[22] This paradoxical constellation is not essentialy different from that which Freud described when he wrote: "I call to mind a case of chronic paranoia in which after each attack of jealousy a dream conveyed to the analyst a correct picture of the precipitating cause, free from any delusion. An interesting contrast was thus brought to light: While we are accustomed to discover from the dreams of neurotics' jealousies which are alien to their waking lives, in the psychotic case the delusion which dominated the patient day time was corrected by his dream" (1940, p. 202).

A few factors may be mentioned which are involved in the ego's being victimized by its defensive apparatus. I believe

---

[22] It is questionable whether my description of the patient's repressing her social tendencies is correct. One of her problems was to be different from her mother. Since her mother was social, the patient had to add to any expression of friendliness the feeling that this was pretense only. The feeling of hatred was the last anchor left to her for the purpose of making sure that she was not identical with her mother.

that all defense mechanisms are initially fed by energy which has not been neutralized, just as the child's early thought processes are closer to the primary process than to the secondary. In the course of development the defense mechanisms are subjected to a process which is comparable to the change from the primary to the secondary thought processes. The energy which they consume is delibidinized and freed of primary aggression. The schizophrenic ego does not achieve this.[23] Its defenses are driven by passion and destruction. The use of destructive energy seems to explain why the schizophrenic ego is primarily a masochistic or self-destructive one; the use of libidinal energies would explain why some schizophrenics in certain phases of their disorder can substitute defense processes for the whole sexual gratification.[24]

In the unmodified ego the whole apparatus of defense mechanisms functions vis-à-vis internal stimulation in the same way that the stimulus barrier functions to prevent overstimulation by external stimuli. In the schizophrenic the defensive apparatus does not posses the firmness necessary for this function. Therefore the ego is forced to respond in its totality without being able to channel adequately the internal or external demands, which threaten to engulf the whole ego. The world—the external as well as the internal one—always descends with incredible swiftness upon the schizophrenic.

The defense mechanisms, however, become particularly visible after the acute schizophrenic symptomatology has vanished and there emerges the organization of the ego which lies behind the picturesque schizophrenic symptomatology per se. Then one can observe the excessive demand which the schizophrenic puts upon the synthetic function (Nunberg, 1931). One can also see his inability to bear up under the impact of internal contradictions and his desperate fight for an ego purified of contradictory feelings; that is to say, for a

---

[23] I am continuing here Hartmann's (1950, pp. 132-133) suggestions regarding the energetics of defense mechanisms.

[24] Cf. Katan (1950).

purified pleasure ego—the only ego state known when we were completely one with ourselves, a state accessible to and desired by the adult chiefly in sleep. The fact that the defense mechanisms of the schizophrenic are still set in motion by, and use up, instinctual energy greatly reduces the seeming contradiction which I initially mentioned, the contradiction between the two metapsychological formulatons: (1) that in schizophrenia the ego loses territory to the id, (2) that the ego is devoured by its defenses. The vast majority of schizophrenic patients who are clinically observed are in a stage in which the defenses are still working, but independently of and unchecked by a comprehensive, over-all ego organization; yet, since these defense mechanisms work in close cooperation with the id owing to energic conditions, it is also correct to speak of the id's encroachment on the ego.

The hypothesis that in schizophrenia the defensive apparatus is kept in motion by energy which has not been desexualized or neutralized must not be confused with another psychoanalytic proposition, namely, that many defense mechanisms may lead to instinctual gratifications, despite their defensive function. The degree of gratification, of course, varies. We are accustomed to find this coincidence of gratification and defense in the neurotic symptom, but it is also true of some defense mechanisms.[25] This does not, however, mean that a defense mechanism—which, apart from its effect as a tool of warding off instincts, leads to a partial discharge of id energy—is itself cathected by id energy. I think that at this point one must distinguish with particular exactness between the accomplishment of a defense mechanism within the personality and the cathexis of the defense mechanism per se. Projection leads always to the transfer of a content from within the personality to without, but a comparison of the sporadic, neurotic projections in a hysteria and the stable,

[25] See Waelder (1930), Nunberg (1932), and others. The quantitative relationship between gratification and defense is probably quite different in symptom and defense mechanism.

rigid projections in a paranoid psychosis shows that the energic factors are quite different. The hypothesis that such differences are also based on the difference of the energies used by the mechanisms per se, facilitates, I think, the understanding of the ego modification encountered in schizophrenia.

Be this as it may, it is important to keep in mind Freud's statement thaththe defense mechanisms themselves present only one of the difficulties to be overcome in analysis. If the effect of these defense mechanisms has resulted in a modification of the ego, the analysis will face even greater difficulties, necessitating deviations from the basic-model technique.

Unfortunately we do not yet have an adequate conceptual frame of reference to describe these ego modifications, although we are constantly struggling with them in most patients who now come for analysis. Freud (1933) compared ego modifications with "dislocation or crippling,"[26] but the metapsychology of such ego modifications has scarcely been established.[27] Observing a patient, we watch the defense mechanisms and their interplay. We see single functions like judgment and perception and note their bearing upon each other. We observe some of the results such as the identifications and projections, but we are not able to perceive the ego organization which underlies them, the mysterious knot of which Goethe spoke and which makes a human being more than the aggregate of his defense mechanisms and functions. Indeed, it is most tantalizing to know of a problem, to observe its manifestation in clinical reality, but to be unable to evolve an adequate conceptual framework necessary for its solution.

---

[26] The German words are *Verrenkung* and *Einschränkung*. See also A. Freud (1936, p. 50): "Thus repression becomes the basis of compromise, formation and neurosis. The consequences of the other defensive methods are not less serious but, even when they assume an acute form, they remain more within the limits of the normal. They manifest themselves in innumerable transformations, distortions and deformities of the ego, which are in part the accompaniment of and in part substitutes for neurosis."

[27] See A. Freud (1936, pp. 93-105) for an attempt in that direction.

Since the ego modification presents itself most conspicuously in the schizophrenias, one is forced to return to this group of disorders when discussing the chances and limitations of psychoanalysis in grappling with this sector of psychopathology.[28]

Despite our great ignorance one statment can be made with certainty. The parameters necessary in the psychoanalysis of schizophrenia will be most extensive and numerous. The most remarkable difference, of course, concerns the essentially different technique of handling the transference.[29] In most neuroses the transference develops spontaneously, and the technical problem consists of converting transference into a helper of the analytic process by means of interpretation, while in some phases of the treatment of the schizophrenic transference must be produced by action, gesture, or words, and for long stretches the chief technical problem consists of manipulating the therapeutic situation in such a way as to effect, quantitatively and qualitatively, the proper accretion of transference.

In discussing parameters enforced by the ego modification which is prevalent in schizophrenia, a therapeutic task must be mentioned which holds no place, or only a very subordinate one, in the treatment of neurotic ego modifications. The schizophrenic must acquire a capacity which the neurotic possesses fully unless he is temporarily deprived of it under the onslaught of an acute, emotional upsurge. I refer to the capacity for putting a mental distance between oneself and the phenomena of the mind, whether these are correlated to external or internal stimulation. It is the privilege of man to possess the antithetical capabilities of feeling at one with his experiences and also of elevating himself above them. What may be now an experience which fills out completely

---

[28] See Freud (1917, 1933) for his remarks about psychoses in general and schizophrenia in particular as sources of insight into the structure of the ego.

[29] See Waelder (1925) for a comparison of the techniques in the treatment of neurosis and psychosis.

the borders of his consciousness may become at any moment a content of observation, judgment, or evaluation. The schizophrenic, however, has lost this capacity in respect to certain contents, although the function per se is not destroyed. But to one sector of his life at least he is bound so firmly that he is incapable of elevating himself beyond its sphere. This lack is one of the most significant indices of the profound modification which the ego of the schizophrenic has suffered.[30]

A schizophrenic once impressively said: "I could rather believe that you or the world around me do not exist than assume that the voices I hear are not real." The schizophrenic has lost the ability to differentiate between the possible and the real in certain sectors of reality.[31] This incapacity to lift himself out of the context of phenomena at one point at least must make the technique of treating schizophrenics essentially different from that of neurotics, if one extends the treatment to the treatment of the ego modification. It is strange to notice that this technical problem which is most typical of the treatment of schizophrenics is barely mentioned in the contemporary literature on the psychotherapy of schizophrenia.[32] The analyst meets in this instance a task of formidable extent which cannot be sufficiently discussed here. It can only be said that sometimes, when one succeeds in demonstrating to the schizophrenic that the symptom is a derivative of bodily sensations, one may reach a point where the schizophrenic can extend his faculty of objectivation also to this sector of his psychopathology.

In the following brief description, I have arbitrarily

[30] For a description and discussion of this problem, see the consequential thoughts about a typology of psychopathology as presented by Waelder (1934). See also Freud (1933, Lecture 31) and Sterba (1934).

[31] I take this formulation from Waelder (1934).

[32] Fromm-Reichmann (1950) seems to claim that there is essentially no difference between the technique of treatment of schizophrenics and neurotics, a point of view which in my opinion is tenable only if the field of therapeutic action is limited to the patient's interpersonal relationships with disregard of the patient's ego modification.

chosen two parameters which fairly regularly play a role in the treatment of schizophrenics: (1) goal construction, and (2) reduction of symptomatology.

(1) The goal toward which psychoanlaytic treatment strives is implicitly, though vaguely, represented in the neurotic's mind. The schizophrenic is deprived of such an integrated and elaborated goal. He must be provided with a diagram of the unmodified ego. Since the patient often does not know how such an ego does function, it is up to the analyst to provide the frame of reference, which often may be an entirely new one to the patient.[33]

Certainly the argument will be raised that such measures do not fall within the scope of psychoanalysis but belong to education or instruction or correction. Yet I wonder whether this parameter necessarily leads us outside psychoanalysis. Education is essentially a technique which tries to force the ego to assimilate the ego-alien or, in other words, to convert the ego-alien into the ego-syntonic.[34] The parameter which I am briefly mentioning here concerns the reconstruction of a viable ego. It concerns a goal which the patient once upon a time had aspired to though probably he had never reached it. Education always tries to implant values; this parameter is essentially divorced from any value system, although admittedly if it is not used wisely, it may become tainted by the tacit application of value systems.

Education always restricts the ego in some way, despite the accretion of content which it provides. This parameter, however, must never lead to a restrictive process within the ego. In other words, the reconstructive processes initiated by this parameter must lay the foundation for the later education of the ego. Therefore, I would rather say that this parameter is essentially outside of education.

(2) One of the most difficult tasks is to find and to

[33] Personal communication from Dr. Edith Jacobson.
[34] I am aware of the insufficiency of such a broad and vague statement, but to clarify it would necessitate the enumeration of its many exceptions.

demonstrate to the patient which function or which functions of the ego have been impaired and in what way. The dysfunctions which can be clinically seen on the surface are, of course, not the primary ones. The production of a delusion may occur owing to the injury of quite different functions of the ego. If the modification of the ego is to be undone, the specific function which is disturbed must be drawn into the treatment and brought to the patient's attention.[35]

This parameter partly overlaps one which may occur in the analysis of a neurotic. In the neurotic, however, the parameter will usually not transgress interpretation, whereas in the treatment of the schizophrenic it concerns a tool which is essentially beyond the scope of interpretation. The disturbed function must be isolated from interplay with others, and the patient must learn to study the way in which this particular function becomes altered under the impact of specific conditions. If a disturbed function is discussed while it is still riveted to others, interpretation will be far less successful than when the disturbed function has been presented to the patient in isolation. In one instance, distortions of reality which appeared like true delusions based on projection turned out to be supplements and confirmations of certain delusions which the patient had formed about herself. The complicated symptomatology could be reduced finally to a certain annoying bodily feeling on which the delusion of self was based. The distortions of reality were only a secondary formation produced by the patient's need (and her fear) of finding supported by external evidence that which she had asssumed beforehand to be true regarding a process belonging to internal reality.

I want to try to narrow down as much as possible the problem on which, in my opinion, the chief question of psychoanalytic theory as well as practice hinges today. It goes back to a point which Freud advanced for the first time in

---

[35] See also Waelder (1925).

1920 and which was taken up and continued by Alexander (1927, p. 5) seven years later, before being discussed once more by Freud (1937) in "Analysis Terminable and Interminable" when he spoke of the resistance against the uncovering of resistances. These secondary resistances become noticeable in the course of psychoanalytic treatment when the analyst tries to make the patient's consciousness focus on those resistances which ward off id impulses.[36] Then it becomes surprisingly evident that the modified ego is highly disinclined not only to become aware of id contents but also to become aware of some of those processes and contents which occur within its own boundaries.[37] Yet these secondary resistances are also active outside of the analytic situation, just as the primary resistances (directed against the id) are constantly active although they become palpable mainly in the psychoanalytic situation. What is the function of these secondary resistances? The primary ones protect the ego against the spread of the id, and one of the functions of the secondary resistances is to prevent the spread of the primary defenses.[38] They also would like to arrogate to themselves the maximum territory, as would the eternally insatiable id drives. Under normal conditions—that is to say, in an unmodified ego—they utilize neutralized energy and are fully occupied with their work against the id. In the modified ego, however, they turn also against the ego. In extreme instances the secondary defenses are swept away, and there is no barrier against the cancerous growth of which I have spoken figuratively before.

A clinical example may illustrate how the secondary resistances can make themselves noticeable in the treatment. A patient of superior intelligence, with unusually strong

[36] For the stratification of defenses, see Gero (1951).

[37] See Freud (1926, pp. 111-113). Helene Deutsch (1939) describes the narcissistic gratification which some patients derive from their defenses. This of course reduces the motivation to give up these defenses.

[38] See Rapaport (1951, p. 692) for the effect of delay in the formation of psychic structure.

pregenital fixations but well-preserved psychosexual genital activity, filled long stretches of his analysis with repetitive complaints about trivial matters regarding his wife. He did not show any understanding of the obvious fact that the discrepancy between the intensity of his complaints and the triviality of their content required a discussion and explanation. One day he reported, somewhat abruptly, that he enjoyed his wife's doing the very things he had always complained of and that he knew how secretly to manipulate situations in such a way as to make his wife act the way he had considered so obnoxious and which gave him occasion to be cold and unfriendly to her.

When the sadistic, aggressive nature of this impulse was explained, he acknowledged it and even volunteered that he had known this for a long time. He showed some understanding of the uncanny sadistic technique with which he maneuvered his wife into the situation of a helpless victim without giving her an opportunity of defending herself.

The sadistic impulse had been warded off by means of denial and substitution of the opposite, since the patient tried to prove to himself and to the analyst that he was not cruel, but that he deserved pity owing to his wife's deficiencies. I tried to show the patient that his incessant complaining had also served the purpose of assuaging his feelings of guilt. The more successful he was in gratifying his sadism in the camouflaged way he used so expertly, the more he had to present himself the next day as injured and unjustly treated by fate in being married to an allegedly unsatisfactory partner. This interpretation was not accepted by the patient. He could not understand it; he could not follow me; and he insisted upon the validity of his complaints, although he had just agreed that he himself secretly induced his wife to behave in the manner about which he habitually complained to me the following day.

Here we encounter the paradoxical situation in which a

patient accepts the interpretation of an id impulse and admits its existence but shows an excessive resistance against the interpretation of the corresponding defense mechanism. There are several reasons for the latter type of resistance. The patient's complaining was done with much emotion. The defense had become partly cathected with instinctual energy. Furthermore, in some instances it is questionable which is easier for the ego to give up, the gratification of an id impulse or the defense. I believe that this patient had come to a point when he would more readily forego the sadistic gratification and acquire mastery over this force than he would sacrifice the feeling of being unjustly treated by fate. Indeed, there is some wisdom in the paradox. As long as he holds to the defense which consists of his playing the role of the victim, there is hope that possibly in the future he can permit himself sadistic gratifications. Only after he has discarded this defense would his conscience no longer tolerate the camouflaged enjoyment of sadistic pleasures. In this instance the defense provided masochistic gratifications which rooted the mechanism with particular firmness in the ego. I have the impression that it is usually the masochism of the ego which makes the interpretation of defense mechanisms excessively difficult. The ego seems to feel particularly safe when the masochistic gratification is achieved in a process which genuinely wards off another drive.

In accordance with well-known features of the pathology of repression one can safely assume that the pathology of the secondary resistances will take one of two forms: It will be too strongly or too weakly cathected. Tentatively I would like to suggest that possibly the neurotic ego modification belongs to the former and the psychotic to the latter group. However, it is not probable that clinical reality would follow such neatly drawn lines. Be this as it may, in the patient just mentioned, the excessive growth of a defense mechanism can be observed, although the ego modification was not of the schizophrenic type. A less modified ego would have received the interpretation with some relief, and the resistance against the interpretation of the id impulse would have been much sharper.

The secondary defenses which do their main work subterreanly and which can be gauged predominantly by the study of their effect on the primary defenses probably form a part of a special organization within the ego and—depending on these secondary defenses—ego modification can, or cannot, be altered by psychoanalysis. There can be no doubt that the neurotic ego modification, such as that found in phobia, can be altered by psychoanalysis. In certain compulsive-obsessive neuroses of long standing, the possibility is questionable.

Although techniques have been devised to undo, at least temporarily, acute schizophrenic symptoms, it is highly debatable whether the modification which the schizophrenic ego so impressively shows can be altered by psychoanalysis. The psychotherapeutic techniques which are applied most commonly in the treatment of schizophrenics do not add substantially to our knowledge and understanding of schizophrenia, since most of them disregard the clinical fact that the problem of the therapy of schizophrenia is essentially the problem of undoing an ego modification. Many a psychotherapist takes on the schizophrenic to demonstrate his psychotherapeutic courage. He will not hesitate to apply any psychotherapeutic tool so long as it gives hope of forcing the schizophrenic out of his acute condition. In so far as such endeavors are heavily sprinkled with pseudo-analytic interpretations, one must call these techniques "wild" psychoanalysis. I think that the concept of a parameter and adherence to the four rules I mentioned may prevent us from falling into wild analysis, which is particularly tempting in the case of schizophrenia. In general, I think, one can say that the most promising source of knowledge of the structure of the ego will be found in an exact description and a justification—both in terms of metapsychology—of any deviation from the basic-model technique whenever such deviation becomes necessary.

REFERENCES

Alexander, F. (1925), Review of *The Development of Psychoanalysis* by S. Ferenczi & O. Rank. *Internat. Ztschr. f. Psychoanal.*, 11:113-125.

——— (1927), *The Psychoanalysis of the Total Personaltiy*. New York/Washington: Nervous and Mental Disease Publishing Co.

——— & French, T.M. (1946), *Psychoanalytic Therapy*. New York: Ronald Press.

Bernfeld, S. (1932), Der Begriff der "Deutung" in der Psychoanalyse. *Ztschr. f. angewandte Psychol.*, 42:448-497.

Binswanger, L. (1945), Zur Frage der Häufigkeit der Schizophrenie im Kindesalter. *Ztschr. f. Kinderpsychiat.*, 12:33-50.

Breuer, J. & Freud, S. (1893), Tl.e psychic mechanism of hysterical phenomena. *Standard Edition*, 2:1-17.

Brunswick, R. M. (1928), Supplement to Freud's "History of an Infantile Neurosis." *Internat. J. Psycho-Anal.*, 9:439-476.

Deutsch, F. (1939), The associative anamnesis. *Psychoanal. Quart.*, 8:354-381.

——— (1949), *Applied Psychoanalysis*. New York: Grune & Stratton.

Deutsch, H. (1939), A discussion of certain forms of resistance. In: *Neuroses and Character Types*. New York: International Universities Press, 1965, pp. 248-261.

Freud, A. (1936), *The Ego and the Mechanisms of Defense. Writings*, 2. New York: International Universities Press, 1966.

——— (1945), Indications for child analysis. *Writings*, 4:3-38. New York: International Universities Press, 1968.

Freud, S. (1894), The defence neuro-psychoses. *Standard Edition*, 3:43-61.

——— (1909), Notes upon a case of obsessional neurosis. *Standard Edition*, 10:153-249.

——— (1910a), Leonardo da Vinci. *Standard Edition*, 11:59-137.

——— (1910b), On "wild" analysis. *Standard Edition*, 11:220-227.

——— (1913), Further recommendations in the technique of psycho-analysis: On beginning the treatment. *Standard Edition*, 12:122-144.

——— (1916-1917), A general introduction to psycho-analysis. *Standard Edition*, 15,16.

——— (1917), A metapsychological supplement to the theory of dreams. *Standard Edition*, 14:219-235.

——— (1918), From the history of an infantile neurosis. *Standard Edition*, 17:3-122.

——— (1920), Beyond the pleasure principle. *Standard Edition*, 18:3-64.

——— (1923), The ego and the id. *Standard Edition*, 19:366.

——— (1924a), The loss of reality and neurosis and psychosis. *Standard Edition*, 19:183-187.

——— (1924b), Neurosis and psychosis. *Standard Edition*, 19:149-153.

——— (1925), An autobiographical study. *Standard Edition*, 20:3-74.

——— (1926), Inhibitions, symptoms and anxiety. *Standard Edition*, 20:77-174.

——— (1933), New introductory lectures on psycho-analysis. *Standard Edition*, 22:3-182.

———— (1937), Analysis terminable and interminable. *Standard Edition*, 23:211-253.

———— (1940), An outline of psycho-analysis. *Standard Edition*, 23:141-207.

Fromm-Reichmann, F. (1950), *Principles of Intensive Psychotherapy*. Chicago: University of Chicago Press.

Gero, G. (1951), The concept of defense. *Psychoanal. Quart.*, 20:565-578.

Hartmann, H. (1939), Psychoanalysis and the concept of health. In: *Essays on Ego Psychology*. New York: International Universities Press, 1964, pp. 1-18.

———— (1950), Comments on the psychoanalytic theory of the ego. In *Essays on Ego Psychology*. New York: International Universities Press, 1964, pp. 113-141.

Ivy, A. C. (1944), What is normal or normality? *Quart. Bull. Northwest. Univ. Med. School*, 18:22-32.

Katan, M. (1950), Schreber's hallucinations about the "little men." *Internat. J. Psycho-Anal.*, 31:32-35.

Nunberg, H. (1931), The synthetic function of the ego. *Internat. J. Psycho-Anal.*, 12:123-140.

———— (1932), *Principles of Psychoanalysis*. New York: International Universities Press, 1955.

Rapaport, D. (1951), Toward a theory of thinking. In: *Organization and Pathology of Thought*. New York: Columbia University Press, pp. 689-730.

Sterba, R. (1934), The fate of the ego in analytic therapy. *Internat. J. Psycho-Anal.*, 15:117-126.

Waelder, R. (1925), The psychoses: Their mechanisms and accessibility to influence. In: *Psychoanalysis: Observation, Theory, Application*. New York: International Universities Press, 1976, pp. 17-41.

———— (1930), On the principle of multiple function and overdetermination. In: *Psychoanalysis: Observation, Theory, Application*. New York: International Universities Press, 1976, pp. 68-83.

———— (1934), The problem of freedom in psychoanalysis and the problem of reality. In: *Psychoanalysis: Observation, Theory, Application*. New York: International Universities Press, 1976, pp. 101-120.

———— (1939), The criteria of interpretation. In: *Psychoanalysis: Observation, Theory, Application*. New York: International Universities Press, 1976, pp. 189-199.

CERTAIN TECHNICAL
PROBLEMS IN THE
TRANSFERENCE
RELATIONSHIP

PHYLLIS GREENACRE, M.D.

I N THE CONDUCT OF AN ANALYSIS, once treatment is established, the relationship of the analysand to the analyst is traditionally thought of as consisting of two main areas. The first is that of the verbal and other communication of the patient to the analyst, gradually revealing neurotic attitudes and behavior not only as these appear in current and past activity, but as they are reproduced, sometimes with additions, in the special attitudes and behavior toward the analyst himself. This is traditionally spoken of as the area of the transference neurosis. The other is the area of margin, frequently peripheral to this central area of communication; it consists of the relatively intact part of the ego which is depended upon to cooperate with the analyst in scrutinizing, understanding, and working over and through the communications of the first area. This has been spoken of as the area of the therapeutic alliance, and was clearly described by Richard Sterba in 1929. It is through the work in the therapeutic alliance that interpretation assumes dynamic therapeutic force. This paper will emphasize especially the changing relationships within and between these two areas of contact between patient and analyst. Some questions may be raised; and it is probable that not many will be answered.

The so-called transference neurosis varies markedly in

texture—the neurotic representations in the transference appearing (1) in direct behavior and attitudes experienced toward the analyst as though they were objectively determined; (2) in less massively projected and recognizable forms in the dreams and dream associations of the patient; and (3) in the frequent associative references connecting the analyst with events and people of the past and present. While the experienced analyst can usually detect according to what transference role or composite of roles the patient's relationship to him is being cast at any given time, the intensity, clarity, and availability of this for use with the patient is not as easily defined.

Fenichel (1941) described the handling of the interpretation of the transference as presenting "no special problem; everything that has been said of interpretation in general, holds true for analysis of the transference: the surface first of all, the defense before the instinct—the interpretation must be timely, not too deep and not too superficial; particularly necessary, preceding the interpretation is 'isolation' from the critical ego" (p. 73). This is certainly a fundamental basis for work, but sounds beguilingly uncomplicated and does not deal with the manifold accessory problems. It is clear enough that incompletely analyzed transference attitudes are expressed subsequently in continued direct or reversed form toward the analyst, or produce excessive pressures in other life relationships onto which they may be displaced postanalytically. Sometimes, indeed, the unanalyzed transference residuals seem to have amalgamated rather than dispersed neurotic attitudes.

Usually, except in certain cases of severe disturbances, the transference neurotic manifestations do not form a fabric of consistent pattern and thickness. Since they are in part historically and genetically determined, there is a constant panoramic procession of transference pictures merging into each other or momentarily separating out with special clarity, in a way which is frequently less constant than the symptoms and other manifestations of the neurosis itself.[1] The degree to which the transference attitudes are played out in current relationships (other than the analytic relationship) also varies considerably. For this reason, I have myself been a little questioning of the blanket term "transference neurosis," which may be misleading. I would prefer to speak of *active transference neurotic manifestations*. The need for a distance or isolation of the neurotic transference manifestations from the critical ego (site of the therapeutic alliance) has already been noted. But it is also true that one of the conditions facilitating analytic work is the flexibility within the psychic structure permitting regression during the analytic hour and free movement back and forth between the various regressively oriented experiences on the couch and a return to the seeing eye of the critical ego. Where this is possible without producing a sense of inner violence to the ego organization, i.e., where the ego organization is fairly firm but has a quality of inner plasticity, the analytic work is much facilitated.[2] Where the critical ego is overburdened with especially strong superego attitudes, however, the isolation may be only apparent and the superego form too ironclad a bridge to the central neurosis, vitiating or immobilizing the work of the therapeutic alliance. On the other hand, there are many instances in which, in spite of a fairly good working ego outside of the analysis, there is an overfluidity in the transference; and especially at certain critical times, the therapeutic alliance is lost sight of or can be maintained only with the greatest difficulty at exactly those times when it is most needed.

I am purposely avoiding categorizing situations according to diagnosis at this time. Further, the effort of this presentation is to focus on the interplay between these two parts of

[1] There is also a considerable variability of the margin of the ego's therapeutic alliance, not only from case to case or in different forms of neurotic disturbances, but in the same patient at different times.

[2] I would especially refer here to Glover's (1955) description of the manifestations of different aspects of the transference in different types of neurosis.

the transference relationship and to suggest, at least to myself, additional avenues of investigation, rather than to make any suggestions regarding standard technical procedures or desirable variations from them. Within this general frame of reference, then, I shall attempt to examine certain problems under two general headings: (1) the transference complications in handling questions of reality with the patient—not only in those cases in which there is some special difficulty of reality testing or of perception, but in other cases as well, where there are potential complications in the inevitable contact outside the analytic relationship between analyst and analysand; (2) certain conditions, already referred to, of too great fluidity between regressive neurotic manifestations and the critical ego, with a resultant tendency to temporary swamping or crowding out of the latter. I shall try to describe these situations and raise questions, answering them only incompletely if at all.

It would probably be generally agreed that in any psychoanalytic treatment, based as it is on the goal of producing change in the analysand through the agency of interpretation and the production of increasing insight, there must be a careful guarding of the autonomous attitude of the patient. Naturally, this also implies a prerequisite of at least such a degree of adequate functioning of the ego, even during the illness, that autonomy has not already been grossly sacrificed. For the furtherance of the preservation of autonomy, supportive measures, persuasion, direct encouragement, advice, and manipulation of the environment (such as interpretation and advice to the relatives) are consequently contraindicated. They are sometimes used as expedients under such exceptionally critical conditions as would be considered to endanger the life of the patient or the future of the analysis. Even in such situations there may be some risks of unsatisfactory sequelae, some of which may become immediately apparent and others remain hidden yet active for a considerable length of time or even impair the analytic result, and so approximate the very condition for which they have been invoked. The immediate result of such active support or intervention is to weaken the critical functioning of the patient's own ego. The practical impairment unfortunately sometimes spreads by rapid displacements to involve an increasing area, and undermines the therapeutic alliance rather than strengthens it—which is usually the result hoped for. The therapeutic alliance is thus insidiously diluted with ingredients of a narcissistic alliance. If the various elements of the recent crisis appear in the analysis quickly enough to be worked with fairly promptly, a favorable result may nonetheless ensue. But this does not always occur spontaneously, and pressures from the analyst to bring them to the surface are not always satisfactory or productive. In most instances, it will be some time before they are brought out again, and the risk of the situation having a distorting effect on the analysis in the meantime has occurred.

Some of the sequelae which may be recognized are: the production of an attitude of special gratitude (or its opposite), which interferes with the freedom of subsequent transference expressions; an increase in the appetite of the patient for such interventions, with an accompanying increase in the provocations to the analyst.

One instance of this is the granting to the patient of the right to telephone at any time that he is panicky. Under such circumstances there may grow up a kind of indulgence in subacute panic, with the sweetness of continued placation which then interferes with its analysis. A similar and sometimes more difficult situation may occur with the patient who achieves an even greater sense of contact on demand by writing full and frequent letters by which he further avoids full verbalization and also deposits material which belongs in the analysis—in his stuffed letters which serve as unreachable pockets. It may be a condensed form of acting out which cannot be quickly analyzed and makes serious inroads on the progress of the immediate analytic work. While it cannot always be analyzed quickly and sometimes must be tolerated until it can be understood, it should at least not be positively encouraged.

Finally, it is worth mentioning that interventions or the use of active accessory therapeutic measures outside of the restrictions of the usual analytic relationship may constitute an inadvertent and unrecognized playing into the transference and risk a rearousal of some old unrevealed traumatic experience, originating in fantasy or in the actual life of the patient's childhood, toward which he draws the analyst with subtle unconscious provocation and seductiveness, even in the production of his crisis. One thinks here of Fenichel's warning (1941) that not joining in the game is the principal task of handling the transference. Yet it is infinitely easy to be drawn into the game in seemingly neutral measures during near crises or pseudocrises, and the worst of it is that one may not discover until much later, and sometimes not at all, the full meaning of what has been thought of as neutral intervention. Many times what appear to an unwary person as critical situations in the patient's external life are at least partly due to un-understood transference demands, which may be increased in repeated or converted forms if met with active assuagement devoid of understanding. In this connection it can be emphasized that transference acting out, whether in a massive, clearly patterned form or in less clearly distinguishable outlines extending into the behavior in external life— that such transference acting out is given a special force and tends to become more fixed in spite of the specious appearance of relief through the discharge. The fixation is the greater, the more the acting out is discharged clearly in the transference, unless it is not only defined but is traced back to its nuclear source and seen in its various current manifestations. This increase in fixation is inevitable since the person of the analyst may assume even greater significance than that of reality relationships of past or present, and the experience in the transference, if uninterpreted, has then an extraordinary confirmatory effect on the neurosis itself.

Other special problems having to do with the attitude of the analyst toward the external reality of the patient may be considered under two headings: those derived from the analyst's need to help the patient to see and to define the outlines of the actual external reality elements in certain life situations which the patient's neurosis tends to present in a distorted form; and especially those arising from complicated situations where the analyst and analysand share certain external reality experiences, e.g., where they know some people in common and have occasional unplanned contacts outside of the analytic office. Obviously, the conditions of this latter group are obligatory in the analysis of analytic students.

It is an analytic platitude to observe that the patient may hold to his neurotic distortions with great conviction and that this can be changed only by analysis, which lessens the inner contributing pressures. Such distortions may appear in severely disturbed patients as transitory or quasi-permanent false perceptions (illusions or hallucinations). Again it is clear that correction by persuasion is either futile or is accomplished by the overwhelming of the neurotic pressures by the intensity of the patient's wish for approval or protection by the analyst, and again risks a narcissistic rather than a therapeutic alliance, with a transference alleviation rather than an analytic one. Illusions of considerable tenacity may occur during the analysis of not even very grossly disturbed neurotic patients and are probably basically due to individual variations between the intensity of the different sensory responses and the degree to which these could be communicated by speech in the patient's early childhood. What is true about the susceptibility to form visual misperceptions of objects or mishearing of spoken words is naturally even more true of the susceptibility to neurotic distortions of interpretations of other people's attitudes. Here I think we have quite definite technical dilemmas. On the one hand, it may be possible, and conceivably advisable, to confront a patient with a misperceived object and show him in a neutral way that he has misperceived. This may be necessary where the patient has clung to his distorted impression with such tenacity that it has seemed to preclude dealing further with the nature or reason for his distortion.

I recall once actually getting a hat to demonstrate to a patient who insisted erroneously that that particular hat was of a certain shape and color, and she had happened to see me wear it just a day or two earlier. In this instance the confrontation did shake her conviction of the rightness of her perceptions in a way beneficial in itself, and also sufficiently to permit her to examine the significance of her determined mistake. Parenthetically, the intensity of such an isolated illusion indicates that the distortion is referring in some way to an actual and important experience of the patient's childhood.

On the other hand, trying to help the patient to define reality as a frame of reference for examining exaggerations, false emphases, or additions of extraneous elements in situations involving interpretations of other peoples' attitudes presents many pitfalls. Freud (1912) emphasized that in questions involving a discrepancy between the patient's observation or memory and that of the analyst, the analyst's observation must be depended upon, since he is less likely to be emotionally involved than the patient. This seems as fundamentally sound a principle now as it was then, though it can never be regarded as *invariably* true, without implying an authoritative attitude in the analyst.

In situations outside the direct relationship between the analyst and analysand, the field becomes murkier and more difficult. While it is undoubtedly necessary under exceptional conditions to "nail down" the objective reality elements of a given specific situation of the patient's or to suggest certain probabilities for the patient's consideration, the analyst may have to resist a temptation to slip into a tendency to define external reality more and more, lest after a time he may find himself analyzing the patient's whole situation and the various people in it rather than focusing on the analysis of the patient and his attitudes toward various aspects of his situation. If the analyst continues to "define reality" to his patient, he gradually assumes a parental role in the transference reality rather than only in the patient's transference neurotic manifestation. Again this insidiously jeopardizes the patient's autonomy, compromises rather than develops the strengthening of the ego, and develops a reality situation in the transference more powerful than the original one. The patient will take up this game and, instead of focusing on himself and questioning his own attitudes, begin to deflect his concern and interpret the unconscious motivations of those around him. This is one of the easiest and most destructive bypaths away from a thorough analysis. Unless it is recognized by the analyst in time, it furnishes the patient with a set of tools, intended for his understanding of himself but misappropriated and used for resistance against such understanding. In any case, the analyst should know very clearly what he is about in any defining of reality with the patient; his assertion of the actual facts in a given situation should be securely founded and not represent simply a counteropinion or another person's interpretation. The analyst is obligated to be careful in any assertion of this kind, not only on the grounds of accuracy and aptness, but because the weight of his opinion in an active transference setting is such as to exaggerate the effect of these malapropos qualities of his statements.

Where analyst and analysand have mutual friends or acquaintances and certain experiences overlap outside the analytic relationship, there is especially likely to be a further complication in the transference relationship in deflections of certain attitudes from the analyst to others associated directly with him, and a concealed and rationalized acting out of them there. It may be that we pay too little attention to this phenomenon of the splitting of the transference relationship, even though it always occurs at some time in the course of the analysis, and may be one of the major defensive maneuverings in the analysis of analytic students.

I will attempt to bring out a further example of the possible implications of the reality contact between analyst and analysand, and question the significance of its handling. This is somewhat different from the other examples, since it is one of the conditions which is obligatorily present in every analysis, viz., the implications of the influence of the sex of the analyst in relation to the sex of the analysand. At present this subject is one of the most frequently spoken of topics in connection with finding an analyst or particularly a second analyst for a patient. It is my fortune to see a number of prospective analytic patients in initial consultative interviews. In quite a large number of instances these preanalytic patients ask, at the end of the interview if not during it, "Should I have a man or a woman analyst?" (There has been a distinct increase in the frequency of this query in the last decade.) Specific advice on the subject may have been offered by the first analyst or by some analyst friend or sometimes by some recently analyzed friend; or an analytically interested social worker may have cautioned that this is an important question which should be settled by the interview; or the patient may himself have gotten it out of the air, as it were. When the inquiry is put to me I always pay attention to it with as much consideration as such a preliminary interview affords, to determine on what this anxious inquiry is based. In many instances the anxiety does not really seem to belong to this question itself, but seems more to be part of the anxiety about beginning the analysis at all.

In 1936 Grete Bibring published a paper in which the significance of the sex of the analyst was dealt with in connection with certain aspects of what was then spoken of as transference resistance. The points which she made still seem valid, important, and worth reconsideration and restatement. She described the fact that sometimes when an analysis had become partly or almost completely stalemated and was interrupted because of this or for external reasons, it not infrequently went along better after its resumption with the original analyst or with a different analyst. This was to be attributed to the fact that the interruption served as a warning to the patient, convincing him of his need, which then increased his energetic coöperation. She emphasized very clearly that beyond this situation, there might exceptionally be certain others. She asserted that although the transference relationship is ordinarily not a reactive manifestation regulated by external reality, but is an active manifestation coming from the spontaneous, neurotic instinctual (and I would now add defensive) pressures from within the patient, there are certain instances in which the analyst may (through the possession of certain marked idiosyncratic traits of appearance or character) represent some important, even crucial part of the patient's past reality to a degree which may block the patient, since it is a continual reminder of that which was impossibly difficult for him in the past. Under these circumstances, the analysand may either withdraw into himself or act out so violently in the transference as to impede progress drastically, unconsciously trying to provoke the analyst to do exactly that which he has most suffered from in his childhood. It was further apparent that the stimulus of this partial revival of reality through its actual repetition in current reality focused in the transference relationship itself might be enhanced if the sex of the analyst coincided with the sex of the crucial person—usually a parent—of the past. Under these circumstances, then, it is clear that transfer to another analyst may undo the blocking and that a change in the sex of the analyst may simply be a background part of this. This is most likely to happen at the first stages of the analysis or at some crucial point involving a situation for which the analyst has a blind spot in regard to himself. Otherwise the chances are he will have detected the difficulty even before the patient reacts so forcibly and this "similarity" will be exploited for the benefit of the work. Bibring further warns, however—and this seems to me of the utmost importance—that the analysand may then attempt to keep the negative transference allocated to the first analyst and enjoy only the positive with the second.

This whole discussion of the reality effect of the sex of the analyst on the patient is a very useful one, since we have often tended to overlook the fact that the important factor is not the reality of the sex per se, but rather that it is the conveyor of the other less apparent partial reality. Unless these elements are disentangled in the handling of the transference of the subsequent analysis, the patient will continue to suffer the effects, one way or another, of the initial displacement. There is obviously another situation in which the reality sex of the analyst may exert a strong and sometimes drastic effect on the patient, viz., the situation of strong unrecognized homosexual tendencies with latent possibilities of panic. This is usually announced by the patient in some emphatic statement—often with a deceptively assured surface—that he or she "simply would not care to," or "could not possibly consider," or "has no confidence in" going to a man or to a woman, as the case may be. In such consultations, if a little discussion indicates that this is a definitely established attitude of the patient's, I myself always treat it with the utmost respect and compliance, since I recognize that such a patient really *would* find it difficult, if not impossible, to work with an analyst of the undesired sex. But I also know that in a number of these cases, a change in the analyst to one of the opposite sex may be desirable later.

It has seemed, however, that this question of the significance of the sex of the analyst has been clouded by the overly ready advice to a patient in a dragging or stalemated analysis that changing the sex of the analyst will have a beneficial effect on the analysis. Certainly, it may make the beginning of the next analysis easier. It has seemed, however, too often to be a terminal rationalization when the analysis has not gone well, and not sufficiently based on careful thought of where and how the stalemate has occurred. It is a recommendation which has sometimes delayed, I believe unnecessarily, the finding of a new analyst and has sometimes been ultimately disregarded due to the pressure of an inadequate market supply of analysts of the desired sex. I must add that I have seen few catastrophes from this disregard if the replacement was a thorough and careful therapist who handled the transference with discrimination and thoughtfulness. A timely consultation may help matters.

In recent years I have had the chance to know of a case in which an analysis never got off the ground, as it were, and dragged along for two years with some basic early work seemingly accomplished, and yet it could not really progress. It was discontinued then because the analyst, who was a very skillful and careful man, believed that the patient could not be analyzed. No recommendation was made by him to the patient to seek any further treatment. The patient did seek a consultation on his own initiative. During this it was revealed that not only did the analyst reproduce with striking fidelity certain of the qualities of the patient's older brother in an ever-stimulating way, much as in the case of Grete Bibring's patient, but furthermore, certain events had occurred in connection with the patient's first visits to the analyst's office, events about which the analyst did not and could not know, and which the patient in turn could not relate to the analyst, first, because their significance was such as to have a paralyzing effect on him, and second, because he was totally unaware of their significance. It happened to be a strange concatenation of several apparently incidental circumstances surrounding the first visits which thus stymied the analysis. The consultant sensed that these might be the source of the block and recommended a second analysis, which subsequently progressed satisfactorily.

Still another matter of concern about actual external reality components in the relationship between the analyst and the analysand consists in the everyday business of their relative postural positions. There is the assumption among many analysts that a neurotic patient must be analyzed prostrate and that a psychotic one must be treated sitting up. The firmness of this "rule" seems to me even greater among the younger than among the older analysts. It seems sometimes to be applied with a clichélike unquestioning attitude. I have heard more than one analyst say quite confidently something like the following: "Well, when he [the patient] began to talk that way, I just sat him up and I've kept him that way since!" Usually this has occurred when the patient showed paranoid or other passive aggressive dissociative attitudes. Sometimes the analyst has felt that having the patient sitting up was the index of transforming the procedure from a psychoanalytic one to a psychotherapeutic one; and that once the patient sat up, he might figuratively never lie down again. Psychoanalytic restriction was then dissipated, and the program was changed to an emphasis on day-by-day reality occurrences and relationships, supplemented by advice and generously supportive encouragement. Certainly, after a time it then becomes impossible to retrace the road back to an analytic relationship unless there is a change of therapists. It has seemed to me that the analyst who accepted this "rule" so uncritically was not generally much at home with psychotic patients and had a good deal of fear of them. He might prefer to keep his eyes directly on the patient, and, although such a belief is not factually supportable, he believed himself safer with the patient sitting up.

The origin of the use of the couch is familiar to all psychoanalytic students. The usefulness of the procedure has been justified through the decades, even though it has been much criticized. Certainly, the position of relaxation on the couch limits distraction, suggests sleep, and promotes thinking by free association. It has been asserted (Macalpine, 1950) that the recumbent position may create a feeling of dependence and helplessness in the patient. This must some-

times be true, though it is most likely to be so in some
specially susceptible patients. In others it places the patient
more definitely in the world of his own private life and
fantasies and diminishes the social obligation for conversa-
tion. The analyst, being out of sight, can then more readily
and naturally become the conveyor of an accessory function
to the patient than if he loomed up straight in the line of the
patient's vision, with his unique appearance and bearing
obligatorily and continuously brought to the patient's notice.
The analyst's position behind the patient favors the therapeutic alliance as well as the development of the transference-
neurotic manifestations.

Some analysts have the patient sit up when they wish to
talk to him "outside of the analysis"—to settle some factual
matter. It would then seem that sitting up means to the
patient, "You are fully conscious. You should speak in a factual
rational way. Do not confuse us with your fantasies now."
While this change of position quite often does mark such a
separation from the varyingly regressive movement of the
ususal analytic production, it by no means does so automatically or in a very consistent way. Everything that happens or
is spoken between analyst and analysand is really a part of
the analysis and may ultimately assert itself as such.

In my own experience with patients, the change from
recumbent to sitting posture has seemed to have many different meanings, first of all dependent in some measure on
whether the change is initiated by the analyst or by the
analysand. If I think a patient is saying in one way or another
that he would like to sit up, I may simply ask him if he would
prefer to sit up, but I leave the decision up to him. I do note,
however, the point at which he feels this need and what the
significance of it seems to be. The sitting up, in this particular
setting, is a limited acting out in the transference and a part
of the analysis rather than an escape from it. I have found
patients who wanted to sit up in order to watch me and check

their fantasies about me; others who wanted to sit up because they felt a desire to fight, and also had a fear of a retaliative attack from me; still others where the sitting up was a wish to assure themselves that they were alive; and again others where the rise to a sitting position was part of a body-phallus expression of an erection. There were some—quite a few— who had some temporary problem of identity and wished to sit up in order to orient themselves better in their surroundings and in space. I do not often work with schizophrenic patients, but I have had a few ambulant schizophrenic patients who generally preferred the recumbent position but would sit up if they felt a danger of losing contact. This may, in any case, depend on how much the person relies on vision for contact.

Please do not think that my patients bob up and down continuously during treatment. I have never had one who did this capriciously. Only very rarely indeed have I suggested to a patient that he sit up. But I always accept the suggestion at least as a possibility if it comes from the patient in whatever way it is communicated. Actually, all in all, the question does not often arise. When it does, I treat it like any other symptomatic transference act.

In connection with this question of couch or chair, it should be noted that the superficial sophistication of the public concerning analysis now includes knowledge of the couch, which appears in magazines, cartoons, in movies, plays, and TV productions. To lie on the couch for analysis now is socially sanctioned and no longer considered queer, as it was twenty or thirty years ago. Rather, if the analyst does not suggest the couch, the patient may readily become worried lest he is considered unanalyzable. This is a secondary development, but nonetheless sometimes exerts a powerful influence on the patient if the analyst suggests sitting up.

To return to a discussion of the situation, referred to earlier in this paper, in which there is too great a regressive fluidity during the hour so that the critical ego of the therapeutic alliance is crowded out—where the capacity to regress is not a sufficiently controlled one, to use Ernst Kris's term (1952)—we know that if this is generally true throughout the analysis, little can be accomplished. It means that much will be brought to the analysis but in an acting-out way, with such pressures that they figuratively elbow the analysis out while the patient seemingly earnestly seeks it. The few patients of this type whom I have had are people whose whole lives seem to have been a series of repetitive living out of basic fantasies so extensively as to engulf almost the total personality. If these patients can be analyzed at all, it is only after a long preliminary preparation and consistent patient work over an extended period of time. I might say, however, that I have found that certain unusually creatively talented people, in whom any adequate use of their talents has been blocked, may also react in this way. Although some analysts would place members of this group in the categories of schizoid, latent schizophrenic, essentially psychotic, or borderline patients, it is not from the angle of diagnosis that I am at the present interested, but from the angle of the transference— the shifts in relationship between the different parts of the transference, the movement within it, etc. It also seems dangerous to base a diagnosis on the behavior in the transference.

I want, however, especially to present illustrations from two cases which are closely related to this group. These two patients are both women whose lives have been dominated by the living out of massive neurotic patterns. It was not so much that they had obviously weak egos—both would have impressed people generally as being potentially very effective people, and it probably would have seemed puzzling why they had achieved little direction in their lives, although they were exceptionally bright and even talented. Both were crippled in their sexual interests, performance, and enjoyment. It was through a careful watching of the transference flux and movement within the different parts of the transference relationship that I came to understand certain important parts of the patients' development.

To speak more specifically of one of these patients: At certain times, often seemingly related to the menstrual period, she would behave in the most intensely provocative way toward me. This consisted in a kind of frenzied demand for reassurance. Focusing on some relatively unimportant and sometimes patently absurd issue, she would return again and again to this with obsessionally hairsplitting ramifications of her central question. Sometimes it would be a question of whether I thought she would ever be able to accomplish a certain thing—often trivial in itself—but somehow representing the question of whether or not she could ever get well. Sometimes the manifest pivot of her demands did not even have this much clarity of significance. At other times she would focus on the question of whether, on the basis of some minutia of behavior, I thought the current man friend was really interested in her or looked down on her. I cannot now go into all of the variations of my mistakes in attempting to deal with these infantile and gluttonous tantrums. She was not one of those patients who, if she succeeded in provoking me to some counter-response, was immediately calm and triumphant, and sometimes her frenzy would continue for more than one hour. Usually in any hour after the onset of the tornado, she would return in a kind of sultry, quiet, brooding state, determined not to let herself go, but it would not be long before she would again be involved in her exceedingly intricate doubts and questions—the whole thing usually ending by attrition rather than by a final satisfying fulminating explosion. This was superficially at least in contrast to the other patient who behaved in a somewhat similar way, but with less hairsplitting, more triumph if she succeeded in provoking me and more fear that I would discontinue the analysis. In both instances, although there was a great deal of neurotic shame in regard to other parts of the analytic revelations, there was no manifest shame or embarrassment over these extraordinary upheavals and, for a long time, no ability to discuss them afterward. It was as though, once they were over, the patient turned into a rather different person with no curiosity about and no contact with this storming child. It was obvious, too, that during the tantrum itself the critical ego was abolished.

It was true that in the first patient if the tantrum lasted more than an hour, sometimes at the beginning of the subsequent hour she would apparently be struggling to hold herself in check in a way that suggested that the self-critical faculty of the ego, probably largely invested in the superego, had been at work: but my presence was enough to restimulate the tantrum, and any sense of a therapeutic alliance was completely lost from the picture. At other times her margin of therapeutic alliance varied but was sufficiently present to permit slow but consistent work. It had become apparent to me that while she had shown a marked sensitivity in regard to possible homosexual implications in her positive feelings toward other women and especially toward me—and I had thought for a time that this was the essential nuclear tension involved—I had gradually become convinced that in a direct form this was only a contributing factor and that the tantrums had much of an acting-out quality of directly repeating some infantile situation and relationship. While she showed slightly comparable episodes of aggrieved feelings toward other people, with tendencies to get into obsessional whirls involving pressure for some discharge, there was never the same insistent demand for reassurance which was so central a part of her transference upheavals. It was only through watching this for a considerable period of time and allowing myself to drift into almost reveries of her life as it had been revealed to me that I was able to see the nucleus of these fits of acting-out in the transference.

What had gradually emerged and could be reconstructed had to do with a period especially during her third and fourth years. She was a bright and apparently very beautiful little girl, the fourth child and very much her father's favorite. He was a compulsive man, a civic leader, always interested in the welfare of the community and especially of his own small domestic group. The family possessed considerable wealth, which permitted this father to retire early from the profession to which he had been trained, spending much time at home engaging in his own obsessional ruminations and ritualistic training of his young children. My patient entered into a disturbed state, with much masturbatory activity during the infancy of a younger sister, who was born toward the end of the patient's second year, and of whom she seems to have been intensely jealous, especially of the mother's nursing and care of the young baby. The masturbatory activity was so great that the troubled father determined to cure the little girl by staying with her when she was put to bed either to nap or at night. He talked to her, admonished her not to touch herself in order to please him, and constantly reassured her that everything would be all right so long as she would cease masturbating. There developed between the father and child an intense attachment, something akin to a focal symbiotic relationship based on their mutual need to suppress masturbation. The suppression had been successful, but had carried with it a loss of awareness of the clitoris; and it had been followed during latency by an aggressive acting out of combined oedipal and sibling jealousy with a brother six years older than herself, the oldest of the children. This had been practically unchecked and had been accompanied by sleeping-beauty fantasies of marrying a Prince or a Duke. It had finally terminated by the brother's desertion of her when she was still in early puberty and he was entering college. The overt obsessional and compulsive neurosis had broken through very soon with the definite onset of the menses.

What concerned me most here was the re-enactment of these focused, symbiotically determined, masturbatory tantrums in which there was an intense unconscious pressure to draw me into the game, during which it was demanded that I should become frenzied with her and promise her incessantly that everything would turn out all right. The successful understanding of these episodes helped very much not only in the understanding of this particular case, but in evaluating certain less acute transference states in other patients who had temporary abrogations of any capacity for critical self-scrutiny and were, one way or another, trying to re-establish states of anxious parental concern which had given considerable gratification. In the second patient who was mentioned along with this one, there was a somewhat comparable history in that it was the father rather than the mother who had been so intensely distressed by the little one's masturbatory activities, to an extent that he was unable to stand her presence at such times and would demand that she be taken to her room and out of his sight. In her provocative tantrums with me, there was, then, not the demand for reassurance, such as the first patient had, but a real need to gain the upper hand through her provocation, after which she could sometimes be calmer, even though she repeatedly feared that I would terminate the analysis. In both patients, my transference role during the tantrums was predominantly that of the father.

This paper has not aimed to present anything new— unless possibly this last matter of the intrusion of a symbiotically based infantile experience, acted out in the transference in a way to intrude and completely upset the therapeutic tenor of the work, is a small contribution. Essentially, the intent has been to restate principles which were stated emphatically some years ago, but which may need re-emphasis in relation to newer concepts in analysis and in the setting of its wider scope, in which there appear some untoward tendencies to use psychotherapeutic methods rather than the stricter and, I believe, more effective analytic ones.

Especially would it seem worthwhile to pay consistent attention to the special forms, variations, and movements within the transference relationship itself. I suppose fundamentally my paper attempts to suggest caution in regard to the introduction of active procedures, since these may undermine the patient's sense of autonomy and risk establishing an actual relationship in the transference which may be more powerful than the corresponding one of the infantile neurosis, and have a confirmatory effect on the neurosis.

REFERENCES

Bibring, G. (1936), A contribution to the subject of transference resistance. *Internat. J. Psycho-Anal.*, 17:181-189.

Fenichel, O. (1941), *Problems of Psychoanalytic Technique*. New York: Psychoanalytic Quarterly, Inc.

Freud, S. (1912), Recommendations to physicians practising psycho-analysis. *Standard Edition*, 12:109-120.

Glover, E. (1955), *The Technique of Psychoanalysis*. New York: International Universities Press, pp. 119-120.

Kris, E. (1952), *Psychoanalytic Explorations in Art*. New York: International Universities Press.

Macalpine, I. (1950), The development of transference. *Psychoanal. Quart.*, 19:501-539.

Sterba, R. (1929), The dynamics of the dissolution of the transference-resistance. *Psychoanal. Quart.*, 9:363-379 (1940).

COUNTER-TRANSFERENCE: COMMENTS ON ITS VARYING ROLE IN THE ANALYTIC SITUATION

René A. Spitz, m.d.

T HE SUBJECT OF COUNTERTRANSFERENCE has been widely debated; the concept itself is still ill defined. Since Freud first coined the term,[1] despite frequent attempts at its definition both from the pragmatic and from the theoretical viewpoint, no final agreement has been reached on its formulation. We have made no effort to duplicate the excellent historical survey on countertransference by Orr (1954). Since Orr's review appeard, Benedek (1953, 1954) and Racker (1953) published further important papers on the subject. For the purposes of the present paper we will give a working definition covering the range of the phenomena of which we intend to speak. Furthermore, we will consider countertransference as something which takes place between two persons, the analyst and his patient.

We will define countertransference as one part of the analyst's relation to his patient; it is one of the determinants of the emotional climate of a given analytic relationship; it usually originates in the analyst; its manifestations are varied. The particular shape it takes is due to the way in which the

[1] To my knowledge the term "countertransference" was used for the first time by Freud in his letter to Ferenczi dated October 6, 1910 (Jones, 1955, p. 83).

given patient's personality, his behavior, and the manifestations of his transference act on and are responded to by the
given analyst's personality. The response will begin with a
dynamic process in the analyst's unconscious. This will trans-
late itself into derivatives, expressed in the attitude of the
analyst. When the patient becomes aware of the analyst's
attitude, changes in the nature of the patient's transference
take place. Thus a circular process between analyst and
patient is set in motion which determines the analytic climate.

The analyst's countertransference may be manifested
either in a sublimated form or in the form of id derivatives or
as a crude expression of a drive. The function of countertransference in the given analytic relationship will be determined
on one hand by the form in which it is manifested, on the
other by its content. In the further course of this paper we
will speak of some aspects of countertransference as well as of
its genetic origin, and we will attempt to investigate its
metapsychology.

The interpersonal aspects of this definition of countertransference coincide to a large extent with the one given by
Annie Reich (1951). We have for the moment omitted making
the distinction which she has clearly established between
countertransference proper, and the more general concept of
countertransference worked out by her and Fenichel (N.D.) in
their discussion on this topic, and which includes the analyst
using the analysis for acting-out purposes.

It follows from our definition of countertransference that
we believe that it is constantly present in analytic work and
that it is a normal phenomenon. As Adolph Stern (1924)
remarked, countertransference in the analyst is exactly the
same phenomenon as transference in the patient. Gitelson
(1952) expressed the same idea when he suggested abolishing
the term of countertransference and calling it instead "the
analyst's transference to the patient."

One of the most important single contributions on the
subject is Annie Reich's article (1951); it has influenced much

of my own thinking. She states, "Countertransference is a necessary prerequisite of analysis. If it does not exist, the necessary talent and interest is lacking." In this statement she indicates clearly the constructive function of countertransference. She explains that the psychological interest of the analyst is based on a very complicated countertransference which is desexualized and sublimated in character. In contrast to this she cites pathological examples in which the analyst's conflict persists in its original form and in which he uses the analytic situation for one of three purposes: (a) for the living out of the underlying impulses; (b) for defending against these impulses; (c) for proving that no damage has occurred in consequence of these impulses.

Racker (1953) and, in a recent paper, Lucia Tower (1956) have introduced the concept of "countertransference neurosis." Racker defines it as an independent entity, as the pathological part of countertransference and the expression of neurosis. He states that the countertransference neurosis, like any other neurosis, and also like the transference neurosis, is centered in the Oedipus complex.

In view of the recent conceptualization of this particular aspect of countertransference when it becomes pathological, it seems worth while to discuss it in some detail, particularly since the question has been raised whether the countertransference neurosis might not have its uses in treatment, just as the transference neurosis has.

In countertransference neurosis, as in any other neurosis, affect is released, except that in countertransference neurosis it is the analyst who releases his own affects, not the patient. We will now examine the conditions under which countertransference affects are released by the analyst, and the influence this has on the patient.

We attribute a goodly part of the therapeutic effectiveness of the analytic treatment to the release of affect by the patient and to his affective re-experience of repressed memories. This results in a modification of his personality. That is not necessarily the patient's intention; his intention, when he releases affects, is to modify the relationship between himself and the analyst. This may involve foisting on the analyst a role which is not justified by the reality situation. But the analyst refuses to change either the relationship or his own role in the relationship; instead of this, he attempts to understand the patient's affective behavior and to transmit this understanding to him.

One may then ask how analytic therapy can be benefited if the analyst releases affects as a consequence of a countertransference neurosis. If we pursue the analogy between the patient's releasing affects and the same process in the analyst, it would seem that such a release by the analyst is an attempt either to modify his relation to the patient or to modify the role he plays in this relation, or both. Eventually it would result in an effort of the analyst to modify the patient himself. As a therapeutic goal the latter might be acceptable. As a therapeutic method it is open to question. The method certainly is not in accordance with the principles of psychoanalysis and the goals of analytic training. The latter endeavors to replace in the analyst the need to release affects in the treatment situation by insight and understanding. This does not imply that affects should not arise in the analyst in response to his patient's productions, or that he should be in any way rigid, inflexible, or not subject to change. We will discuss further in what way the analyst's personality should be flexible and what use he should make of his affects.

Continuing our parallel between countertransference neurosis and any other neurosis, we are reminded that neurosis is characterized by its compelling nature—a fact also stressed by Racker (1953). This does not apply to compulsion neurosis only. Any neurotic finds himself under the inner constraint to act in terms of his neurosis rather than in terms of reality. He is under an inner constraint to act out his neurosis. He is under the constraint of the repetition compulsion. He is not a free agent.

This is exactly the opposite of what we expect of the analyst, whose activity in the treatment situation should be controlled only by his ego. An analyst acting under the compulsion of id impulses in the treatment situation has relinquished his therapeutic role. The degree of freedom available to the analyst is well formulated in the witticism of a Viennese comedian, who described the normal person as somebody who *may* do anything, but does not *have* to do it.

We would then say that in the analytic procedure countertransference neurosis in the analyst is not only not useful but highly undesirable. What we expect of the analyst is that he achieve a countertransference sufficiently *sublimated,* so that he can make use of it in identifications of brief duration with his patient. This process has been aptly described by Kris (1952) in regard to the artist. He called it a "regression in the service of the ego." That is exactly what we expect of the analyst.

In my recent discussion of transference (1956) I referred cursorily to its dynamics and to some of its economic aspects, while elaborating extensively its genetic aspect.

If we agree to consider countertransference as an analogue of transference in the patient, then it follows that its genetic history is the same as that of transference. In other terms, it is a new edition, a facsimile, of impulses and fantasies belonging to the past. The past to which they belong, as I have shown in the previously mentioned communication, is the earliest parent-child situation. In agreement with Greenacre (1954), Macalpine (1953), Lagache (1952), and others, I explained how the situation of the child's helplessness was re-created in the analytic setting and would inevitably result in the reproduction of fantasies originating in that situation.

Countertransference assigns a role to the analyst which is the obverse of that of the patient. The patient is helpless, while the analyst's role is to be helpful. The situational stimulus in the analytic setting which acts on the analyst is, therefore, the patient's helplessness. It evokes in the analyst fantasies derived from the ego ideal which he formed in identification with his parents.

We have postulated that the analytic setting places the patient into an anaclitic relationship. I may be permitted to suggest a distinctive term for the role of the analyst in this setting. *Anaclitic* means leaning onto; I recommend for the analyst's attitude the term *diatrophic*,[2] which means supporting.

The diatrophic attitude has its origin in a developmental stage of the infant which emerges toward the end of the anaclitic relationship. The diatrophic attitude is a facsimile of the fantasies which belong to the stage in which the young child forms his secondary identifications with the parental figures. I am referring here to those early make-believe games, to be seen in the first half of the second year, when the child feeds its Teddy-bear from a nursing bottle, copies the nurse in a nursery by distributing diapers to the other children, etc.

There is a basic countermovement in the unfolding and the fate of the anaclitic attitude on the one hand, of the diatrophic attitude on the other. The anaclitic relationship is based on an experience of which in the normal course of development the reality aspects recede progressively and are lost, leaving behind them only memories and wish fulfillment fantasies. With advancing age anaclitic relations are relegated more and more to the realm of fantasy or pathology.

The diatrophic relation begins with an identification fantasy, but with progressive development will end up in the reality situation of the subject becoming himself a parent.

In the analytic setting, in the ideal case, both anaclitic and diatrophic relations have to operate on the level of fantasies, conscious and unconscious, triggered by the conditions of the setting itself. Neither of them should be translated into action. The patient, in acting out, attempts to achieve reality fulfillment. The aim of the rule of abstinence is to

---

[2] From the Greek: $\delta\iota\alpha\text{-}\tau\rho\epsilon\phi\omega$ = to maintain, to support throughout.

frustrate this fulfillment. The analyst becomes able to impose this frustration on the patient only if he himself does not act out the diatrophic attitude. He has to understand the origin of his diatrophic fantasies sufficiently to be able to accept as a matter of course that *the rule of abstinence operates for himself as much as it does for the patient.* This is a point touched upon by Racker. I would say specifically that this unconditional acceptance of the rule of abstinence requires not only the working through of the analyst's oedipal and pregenital development, but also his becoming able to relinquish the archaic wish for magic omnipotence.

Acting out the diatrophic attitude, of course, is not the only pitfall of his own unconscious which the analyst faces. If we disregard the well-known and extensively discussed acting-out possibilities presented by unresolved problems of the analyst in connection with the partial drives of the pregenital phase and those connected with the conflicts of the oedipal phase, there still remains the temptation for him to succumb to an unconscious wish for an anaclitic relationship to his patient. Obviously the analytic setting does not make acting out the latter easy. But if acting out in a countertransference neurosis disregards reality, it does not preclude it either. Needless to say that to act out anaclitic wishes is as undesirable for the therapeutic process as the other forms of acting out; indeed, it is one of the more dangerous ones of these forms.

The early secondary identificatory fantasies which underly the diatrophic attitude have a very great adaptive value for individual development. They have mostly been studied in their significance for pathology, and little has been written about their importance in the formation of personality. They operate at first in the process which I have called the humanization of the infant. This begins with the acquisition of language and of the first elements of the "Do's and Don't's." Eventually these secondary identifications will serve the process of the socialization of the child. The formation and the subsequent liquidation of the Oedipus complex is but one of the stations on this road.

In the course of the child's development, the progressive elaboration of these identifications is ensured, on one hand, by the pleasure gain of drive satisfaction; on the other, these identifications are infinitely valuable to the child by providing him with ever-increasing mastery over the environment and with the concomitant narcissistic gratification. Throughout life successive and ever more intricate elaborations of the diatrophic attitude in identification with the parents establish a genetic sequence in its development. Various stages of these identifications will be used for the purpose of occasional regressions.

In the analyst, the diatrophic attitude offers two possibilities. If ego-controlled, his brief regression to the parent ideal can be made therapeutically effective for the patient. Such transitory identifications with the parent ideal enable the analyst to empathize with the infantile aspects of the patient's behavior and to re-interpret them in terms of infantile experience. On the other hand, this same regression, if not controlled by the ego, may give the therapist the opportunity to find a gratification of repressed drives. Identifications with the patient, with his parents, or with the vicissitudes of their relations which permit the surfacing of the analyst's repressed drives should be considered as acting out on his part.

I have stated that I do not consider acting out desirable on the part of the analyst. Such acting out can be an occasional one, provoked by transference manifestations of the patient. Alternatively, it can take place in the framework of a real countertransference neurosis, as a consequence of the neurotic personality of the analyst. In either case, it can only be an obstacle in what we call the analyst's understanding of the patient.

As we have stressed, a great deal of the analyst's insight results from brief temporary identification with the patient, that is, from ego-controlled regression on the part of the analyst. If the ego-controlled regression is replaced by acting out, then the analyst can no longer remain aware of the derivatives of his own unconscious and cannot make appropriate use ox them in therapy. When the analyst acts out in response to the patient's provocation, an interchange of acting out betweeen analyst and patient takes the place of an understanding of the patient's productions. Therefore, the analyst's acting out cannot lead to a therapeutic interpretation.

When acting out replaces interpretation, the results will sometimes be spectacular. Such results are comparable to the successes seen in cathartic therapy. The dynamics of the two are different; but the successes will be haphazard and transitory at best, and it is to be expected that the drawbacks of such methods will far outweigh their advantages.

Acting out, as stressed by Reich (1951) and Fenichel (N.D.), is but one of the manifestions of countertransference. It is the most obvious and easily recognized one. There is much less unanimity on what constitutes the other forms. I believe that many of our disagreements on countertransference are caused by misunderstandings provoked through the careless use of the term in our writings. We are prone to speak of countertransference, which is an unconscious process, when what we really mean are its conscious derivatives. It is only with these that we can deal on the conscious level; taking cognizance of these derivatives enables us to perform what Glover (1955) called "the analytical toilet."

One of the reasons why the analytic candidate undertakes a training analysis is to enable him to recognize the underlying unconscious motivation of these conscious derivatives in himself. When he performs this task, he becomes able to fulfill the diatrophic role of the analyst: like the parent ideal, he can tolerate aggression as well as the pressure of the patient's libidinal demands without retaliating in kind. He can permit the patient's initiatives to unfold into directions, however different from his own ideals, as long as they do not endanger the patient. Analysis has to be carried out in abstinence, said Freud; I may add, abstinence of the patient and abstinence of the analyst. For the analyst this does not apply to countertransference as such, but to its acting out, as well as to those others of its forms which are not syntonic with the requirement of free-floating neutral attention.

Countertransference is a necessary prerequisite of analysis. Its proper use involves three steps:

1. The analyst becomes aware in himself of the derivatives of his unconscious as they arise in response to the patient's unconscious.
2. From these derivatives he infers the underlying unconscious processes in himself.
3. He has now to possess sufficient freedom to perform a transitory identification with those processes in the patient which had provoked his own responses.

This, then, would be my concept of the metapsychology of what we call "understanding the patient."

REFERENCES

Benedek, T. (1953), Dynamics of the countertransference. *Bull. Menninger Clinc.*, 17:201-208.
———— (1954), Countertransference in the training analyst. *Bull. Menninger Clin.*, 18:12-16.
Fenichel, O. (N.D.), Theoretical implications of the didactic analysis. Privately printed. Topeka Institute for Psychoanalysis.
Freud, S. (1910), The future prospects of psycho-analytic therapy. *Standard Edition*, 11:140-151.
Gitelson, M. (1952), The emotional position of the analyst in the psychoanalytic situation. In: *Psychoanalysis: Science and Profession*. New York: International Universities Press, 1973, pp. 173-200.
Glover, E. (1955), *The Technique of Psycho-Analysis*. New York: International Universities Press.
Greenacre, P. (1954), The role of transference. In: *Emotional Growth*. New York: International Universities Press, 1971, pp. 627-640.
Jones, E. (1955), *The Life and Work of Sigmund Freud*, 2. New York: Basic Books.
Kris, E. (1952), The psychology of caricature. In: *Psychoanalytic Explorations in Art*. New York: International Universities Press, pp. 173-188.
Lagache, D. (1952), Le problème du transfert. *Rev. Franç. de Psychanal.*, 16:5-122.

Macalpine, I. (1953), The development of the transference. *Psychoanal. Quart.*, 19:501-519.

Orr, D. W. (1954), Transference and countertransference. *This Journal*, 2:621-670.

Racker, H. (1953), A contribution to the problem of counter-transference. *Internat. J. Psycho-Anal.*, 34:313-324.

Reich, A. (1951), On countertransference. In: *Psychoanalytic Contributions*. New York: International Universities Press, 1973, pp. 136-154.

Spitz, R. A. (1956), Transference: the analytical setting and its prototype. *Internat. J. Psycho-Anal.*, 37:380-385.

Stern, A. (1924), On the countertransference in psychoanalysis. *Psychoanal. Rev.*, 11:166-174.

Tower, L. E. (1956), Countertransference. *This Journal*, 4:224-255.

CONTRIBUTORS

Jacob A. Arlow
Past President, American Psychoanalytic Association; and Formerly, Editor-in-Chief, Psychoanalytic Quarterly.

Harold P. Blum
Editor, Journal of the American Psychoanalytic Association; and Clinical Professor of Psychiatry and Training Analyst, Department of Psychiatry, Psychoanalytic Institute, New York University Medical Center, New York.

Charles Brenner
Training and Supervising Analyst, New York Psychoanalytic Institute; and Clinical Professor of Psychiatry, State University of New York, Downstate Medical Center, Brooklyn, New York.

Joseph T. Coltrera
Clinical Associate Professor of Psychiatry, Psychoanalytic Institute, New York University Medical Center, New York

Homer C. Curtis
Clinical Professor of Psychiatry, Hahnemann Medical College; and Training and Supervising Analyst, Institute of the Philadelphia Association for Psychoanalysis, Philadelphia, Pennsylvania.

K. R. Eissler
Member of New York Psychoanalytic Society, American Psychoanalytic Association, and International Psycho-Analytical Association.

Anna Freud
Director, Hempstead Child Therapy Clinic, London.

Merton M. Gill
Professor of Psychiatry, Abraham Lincoln School of Medicine, University of Illinois; and Supervising Analyst, Chicago Institute for Psychoanalysis, Chicago, Illinois.

453

PHYLLIS GREENACRE
Honorary Vice-President, International Psycho-Analytical Association; and Professor Emeritus, Clinical Psychiatry, Cornell Medical College, New York.

EDWARD JOSEPH
President, International Psycho-Analytical Association; and Professor of Psychiatry, Mount Sinai School of Medicine, New York.

MARK KANZER
Professor Emeritus, Clinical Psychiatry, State University of New York, Downstate Medical Center, Brooklyn, New York.

HANSI KENNEDY
Co-Director, Hempstead Child Therapy Course and Clinic, London.

OTTO F. KERNBERG
Medical Director, The New York Hospital-Cornell Medical Center, Westchester Division; Professor of Psychiatry, Cornell University Medical College; and Training and Supervising Analyst, Columbia University Center for Psychoanalytic Training and Research, New York.

SELMA KRAMER
Training and Supervising Analyst, Adult and Child, Philadelphia Psychoanalytic Institute; and Professor of Child Psychiatry, Medical College of Pennsylvania, Philadelphia, Pennsylvania.

P. J. VAN DER LEEUW
President, International Psycho-Analytical Association 1965-1969; and Training and Supervising Analyst, Dutch Psychoanalytic Society.

PETER B. NEUBAUER
Director, Child Development Center, Jewish Board of Family and Childrens' Services; and Clinical Professor, Psychoanalytic Institute, New York University, New York.

LEO RANGELL
Clinical Professor of Psychiatry, University of California, Los Angeles; Clinical Professor of Psychiatry (Psychoanalysis), University of California, San Francisco; and Past President, American and International Psychoanalytic Associations.

Renè A. Spitz
Author of the First Year of Life; No and Yes: On the Genesis of Human Communication; *and* A Genetic Field Theory of Ego Formation.

Arthur F. Valenstein
Clinical Professor of Psychiatry, Faculty of Medicine, Harvard University, Boston, Massachusetts; and Past Vice-President, International Psycho-Analytical Association.

NAME INDEX

Abraham, K., 245, 261
Abrams, S., 243, 261
Adatto, C. P., 305, 311
Adler, A., 302
Alexander, F., 46, 67, 96, 98-99, 108, 112, 119, 134, 328-329, 364, 372, 377, 389, 417n
Alpert, A., 35, 40
Anthony, E. J., 244, 261
Arlow, J. A., 137, 156, 172, 190, 193-206, 212, 238, 360, 372

Balint, M., 208, 238, 337, 372
Baranger, M., 182, 190, 198, 205
Baranger, W., 182, 190, 198, 205
Benedek, T., 441, 450
Benjamin, J., 242
Beres, D., 202, 205n, 212, 238, 346-347
Bergman, A., 68, 239, 262
Bernfeld, S., 400, 417
Bibring, E., 43, 47, 67, 87n, 96, 108, 117-118, 135, 137, 156, 160, 165-166, 169-171, 184, 190, 295, 311, 328, 362, 372, 428-431, 440
Bibring, G. L., 123, 135
Binswanger, L., 383, 417
Bion, W. R., 97, 108, 209, 238
Bird, B., 44, 67, 85, 88, 108
Blum, H. P., 2, 27, 41-69, 95, 99, 108, 220, 238, 245, 260, 261, 301, 311, 316, 325, 369-370, 372
Brenner, C., 89, 95, 105, 108, 137-157, 172, 190, 194, 205, 327, 343, 346-356, 360, 367-368, 371, 372
Breuer, J., 62-63, 66, 67, 83, 108, 160, 190, 302, 315, 319, 324, 338, 359, 372, 387, 417
Brill, A. A., 329
Brody, S., 242
Brunswick, R. M., 383, 417
Bush, M., 10, 27

Coltrera, J. T., 289-313
Curtis, H. C., 159-192

Dare, C., 68, 327, 328, 358
Darwin, C., 295
Deutsch, F., 381, 417
Deutsch, H., 413n, 417
Dickes, R., 161-163, 190
Dilthey, W., 294-295, 311

Eissler, K., 46, 48, 67, 73, 79, 116, 119, 135, 172, 176, 190, 360, 367, 372, 375-418
Erikson, E. H., 87n, 93, 108, 168, 190, 209, 238, 242, 362, 372
Eysenck, H. J., 72

Fairbairn, W., 208-209, 239
Fenichel, O., 87n, 88-89, 94-95, 97-99, 101, 103, 106, 108, 123-124, 129, 135, 164, 190, 223, 239, 350, 362, 372, 420, 424, 440, 442, 449, 450
Ferenczi, S., 95-96, 98, 108, 123, 127, 135, 187, 190, 293, 311, 389, 417
Fine, B. D., 291, 294, 311
Finesinger, J., 52, 68
Fleming, J., 344, 372
Fliess, R., 182, 190, 202, 205
Fliess, W., 302
French, T., 46, 67, 96, 127, 129, 134, 165, 190, 377, 417
Freud, A., 3-7, 18, 27, 40, 47-48, 56-58, 60, 67, 81-82, 89, 108, 124-125, 135, 242, 261, 284, 287, 292, 296, 299, 301, 303-306, 308-309, 311, 321, 324, 327, 360, 372, 388, 396, 401, 408, 417
Freud, S., 27, 29, 31, 40, 47, 52, 67, 68, 79, 92, 94, 96-97, 101-102, 108, 135, 154, 163, 168, 174, 181, 185, 190, 191, 202, 205, 243, 266, 287,

457

SUBJECT INDEX

Abreaction, 43, 124, 280, 296, 387-388
Acting out, 13, 124, 149, 179-180, 212-218, 226, 229, 232, 249, 252, 268-271, 298-299, 393, 423, 433-435, 437-438, 442, 446-449
Action language, 82, 105
Adolescent, and insight, 21-25, 33, 58, 209, 243, 294, 305
Adult analysis, 35, 37-38, 40, 57, 95, 243, 309
Affect
    and cognition, 29-30, 32, 36, 39, 56, 96-99, 101, 107, 120, 132-133
    and drive, 36-37, 161-163, 208, 210-213
    and ego, 103
    and object relations, 220-221, 226-227, 232
    signal, 52-53
    and transference, 283, 297-299, 303, 443-444
    see also specific affects
Aggression, 229, 323, 432, 438, 449
    and defense, 23, 218-219, 251, 406
    and drive, 31, 107, 163, 246, 293, 299, 307, 406, 414
    and libido, 92, 128, 311, 449
    see also Drives; Libido; Rage
Ambivalence, 93, 163, 222, 245, 251, 258, 402
Anaclitic relation, 446-447
Anality, 25, 251
Analysand, 376-377, 419-440, 442, 445
Analyzability, 10, 44, 48, 56, 125-127, 145
Anxiety, 5, 82, 88, 92, 96, 106n, 141, 143, 169-170, 172, 174-175, 299, 302, 317, 349, 381, 390, 402n, 404, 428
    and defense, 92-93, 138, 167, 177, 186, 194, 322

and guilt, 50, 162, 234
phobic, 101
separation, 91, 168, 170, 300, 318, 439
signal, 56, 104-105, 169, 171, 320
see also Castration; Phobia
Avoidance behavior, 6

Body language, 244
Borderline personality, 48, 66, 73, 91-92, 94-95, 106n, 125, 127, 130-131, 134, 198, 435
    and object relations, 211, 218-219, 221, 230, 233
    and treatment, 159, 167, 171, 186

Castration anxiety, 17, 91, 210, 393
Character disorder, 3, 41, 186, 210-211, 221, 246
Child analysis, 3-6, 57, 95, 243, 310
    model of, 185, 187, 341
    role of insight in, 3-6, 9-27, 33, 35-40, 48
Childhood
    pathogenic conflicts and, 44, 242, 291, 294-296, 308-309, 371, 401, 402
    schizophrenia, 383
Child(ren)
    -mother relation, 142, 167, 172, 199, 243, 303, 306, 317, 319
    prelatency, 35
Clinical example of
    acting out, 213-218, 423-424
    adolescent analysis, 21-23
    child analysis, 14-17, 19-21
    countertransference, 179-180
    defense mechanisms in therapy, 401-402
    depression, 174-175

and transference, 137-156, 293, 298, 304, 319
see also Working alliance
Time, sense of, 38, 392
Topographic theory, 29, 32, 34, 222, 294
Training analysis, 449
Transference, 2-3, 6, 11, 17, 22, 25, 98, 102, 105n, 107, 116, 120, 160-166, 197, 220, 233, 244-245, 251-260, 315-324, 337, 353-355, 360-365
and defense, 86, 88-90, 95-96, 138, 149
gratification, 172, 180-181
and identification, 46-47, 138, 144, 164-165, 168, 172, 184-187, 198-199, 202, 210
and infantile neurosis, 289-311
and insight, 31, 34-35, 38, 43, 45, 48, 51, 53, 55, 57
and interpretation, 75, 77, 83-84, 86, 88-89, 93, 95, 122, 127, 138, 142-146, 150, 152, 160, 166-167, 174-175, 183, 186-188, 190, 212, 221-223, 226-229, 232-235, 261, 263-287, 290-292, 296, 298, 318, 322, 342-343, 350-352, 364, 367-370
mirror, 128, 199, 323
negative, 163, 430
and psychoanalytic technique, 263-287, 419-440
vs. reconstruction, 84-91, 220-221
and regression, 46, 86, 120, 166, 168-169, 184, 209, 211-213, 222-232, 238, 247, 291, 293-294, 296-298, 305-306, 322, 332-335, 361, 420-421, 434
and schizophrenia, 409-412
and therapeutic alliance, 166-173, 181-183, 187-190
and working alliance, 137-156, 173-180
Transference neurosis, 44, 46, 58, 84-

86, 91, 116, 122, 124, 211-212, 246, 252, 267, 269-270, 273, 289-294, 296, 299, 305-309, 315, 335, 341, 345, 353, 364, 419-420, 443, 445
and narcissistic neuroses, 126, 129
and therapeutic alliance, 138-139, 143-145, 155, 166, 169-170, 186, 188
Trauma, 380, 387-388
early, 128, 254, 297, 300, 424
and ego mastery, 47, 51, 58, 103-104
Treatment
of neuroses, 99, 380, 386, 396, 403-404, 407, 409-410, 412, 415, 424-427, 432-433, 435-440, 444
of phobia, 83, 381-383, 385, 390, 400, 416
and psychopathology, 94, 381, 392, 396, 409-410
of schizophrenia, 403-412
see also Psychoanalytic technique
Treatment alliance, 360-363; *see also* Therapeutic alliance; Working alliance

Ucs system, 197

Verbalization and analytic process, 13-15, 18, 25, 43, 47, 52, 67, 121, 243, 297, 320, 367, 386, 419, 423

Wild analysis, 376n, 416
Withdrawal, 199, 202, 236, 277, 429
Wolf Man, 291, 296, 301-302, 307, 316, 383-385, 390
Working alliance, 137-156, 159-190, 319, 321, 324, 341-342, 344, 360-361; *see also* Therapeutic alliance; Treatment alliance
Working through, 50, 76, 87, 116, 121-122, 124, 126, 169, 176-177, 187, 252-260, 283, 287, 292-294, 304, 308-309, 332